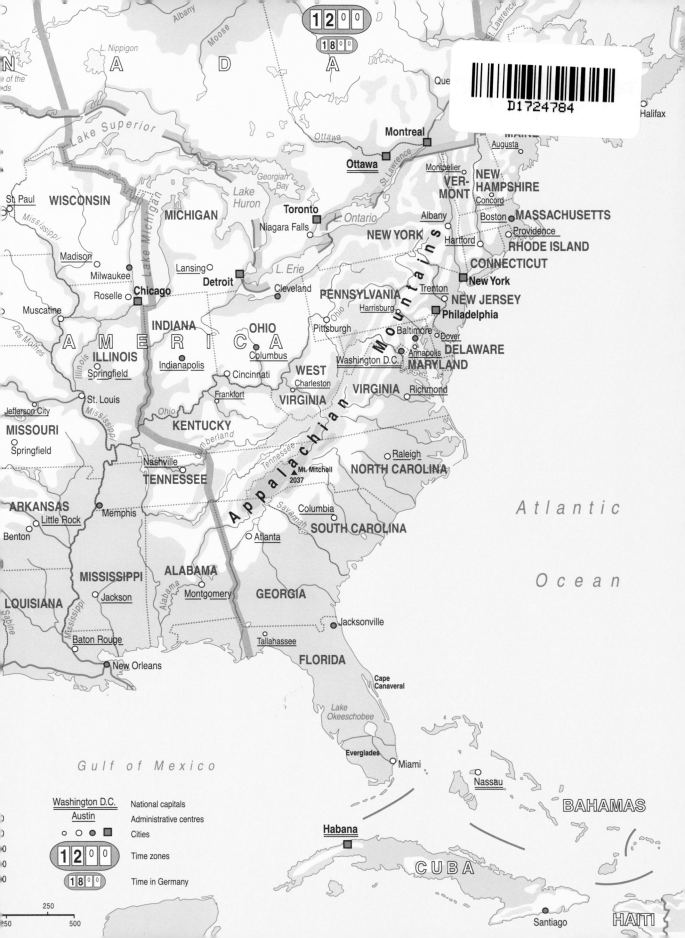

westermann

NOTTING HILL GATE

Textbook 8
Basis-Ausgabe

Erarbeitet von:
Nathan Giles (Thedinghausen), Penelope Pedder (Köln),
Maike Pegler (Sarstedt/Gödringen), Susanne Quandt (Bremen),
Dr. Stefanie Quinlan (Frankfurt am Main)

sowie Denise Arrandale (Neumünster), Michael Biermann (Hamburg),
Hannelore Debus (Mörfelden-Walldorf), Phil Mothershaw-Rogalla
(Volkmarsen-Külte), Dr. Ivo Steininger (Wetzlar)

Fachliche Beratung:
Dörte Gudjons (Hamburg), Martina Pods-Sievers (Ahrensburg),
Martin Weber (Wiesbaden)

Notting Hill Gate 8
Basis-Ausgabe
Textbook

Zusatzmaterialien zu Notting Hill Gate 8

Für Lehrkräfte:

- Textbook für Lehrkräfte 8 (ISBN 978-3-14-128291-7)
- Materialien für Lehrkräfte 8 (ISBN 978-3-14-128297-9)
- Lernerfolgskontrollen 8 (ISBN 978-3-14-128323-5)
- CD für Lehrkräfte 8 (ISBN 978-3-14-128311-2)
- DVD für Lehrkräfte 8 (ISBN 978-3-14-128317-4)
- Online-Diagnose zu Notting Hill Gate 8
  www.onlinediagnose.de

Für Schülerinnen und Schüler:

- Workbook 8 (inkl. Audios) (ISBN 978-3-14-128217-7)
- Workbook 8 mit interaktiven Übungen (inkl. Audios)
  (ISBN 978-3-14-145265-5)
- Interaktive Übungen 8 (WEB-14-128227)
- Arbeitsbuch Inklusion 8 (inkl. Audios)
  (ISBN 978-3-14-128233-7)
- Klassenarbeitstrainer 8 (ISBN 978-3-14-128249-8)
- Grammatiktrainer 8 (ISBN 978-3-14-128389-1)
- Wortschatztrainer 8 (ISBN 978-3-14-128243-6)

Das digitale Schulbuch und digitale Unterrichtsmaterialien für Schülerinnen und Schüler und für Lehrkräfte finden Sie in der BiBox – dem digitalen Unterrichtssystem passend zum Lehrwerk. Mehr Informationen über aktuelle Lizenzen finden Sie auf www.bibox.schule.

www.westermann.de/nhg

 DIGITAL+

Alle digitalen Ergänzungen zum Buch erkennen Sie an dem Symbol ▦ DIGITAL+. Dazu zählen Audiotracks, Videoclips, Arbeitsblätter zur Medienbildung, zusätzliche Übungen zu den Practise-Seiten und Zusatzmaterialien zum Buch. Gehen Sie auf www.westermann.de/webcode und geben Sie den Webcode WES-128207-001 ein. Sie können auch den QR-Code scannen.

© 2025 Westermann Bildungsmedien Verlag GmbH, Georg-Westermann-Allee 66, 38104 Braunschweig
www.westermann.de

Druck A[1] / Jahr 2025
Alle Drucke der Serie A sind im Unterricht parallel verwendbar.

Redaktion: Doris Bos sowie Lisa Fast und Dr. Katja Nandorf
Vokabelanhang: Doris Bos
Illustrationen: Mario Ellert, Bremen
Umschlaggestaltung: LIO Design GmbH, Braunschweig
Layout: LIO Design GmbH, Braunschweig
Druck und Bindung: Westermann Druck GmbH, Georg-Westermann-Allee 66, 38104 Braunschweig

ISBN 978-3-14-**128207**-8

So arbeitest du mit dem Buch

Im Buch findest du folgende Verweise:

1 audio — Hier gibt es einen Audiotrack, den du auch online abrufen kannst.

2 video — Hier gibt es einen Videoclip, den du auch online abrufen kannst.

3 workbook — Hier siehst du, auf welcher Seite im Workbook es weitere Übungen gibt.

4 wordbank — In den Wordbanks findest du Wörter nach Wortfeldern geordnet.

5 skill — Auf den Skills-Seiten findest du Tipps und Strategien fürs Lernen.

6 grammar — Zu dieser Aufgabe gibt es Erklärungen und Beispiele im Grammatik-Teil.

7 media worksheet — Dieser Hinweis kennzeichnet Aufgaben, in denen du Medienkompetenz aufbaust und trainierst. Zu diesen Aufgaben gibt es Arbeitsblätter, die du über den Webcode oder den QR-Code auf Seite 2 abrufen kannst.

DIGITAL+ practise more — Dieser Hinweis zeigt, dass es zusätzliches Material auf der Webseite gibt.

In den Units gibt es verschiedene Arten von Aufgaben:

8 CHOOSE YOUR LEVEL — Bei diesen Aufgaben gibt es drei unterschiedliche Schwierigkeitsgrade:
I leicht **II** mittel **III** schwierig

9 GET TOGETHER — Hier arbeitest du mit einem Partner oder einer Partnerin zusammen. Entscheidet, wer Partner A und wer Partner B ist und wählt jeweils einen Schwierigkeitsgrad. Geht dann zur entsprechenden Seite und bearbeitet die Aufgabe.

Partner A   Partner B
I   Go to page 130.   I   Go to page 139.
II Go to page 133.   II Go to page 142.
III Go to page 136.   III Go to page 145.

10 CHOOSE YOUR TASK — Hier gibt es drei Aufgaben, von denen du dir eine aussuchen kannst. Du kannst auch mit einem Partner oder einer Partnerin oder in einer Gruppe arbeiten.

TARGET TASK — In der Target Task wendest du an, was du gelernt hast. Du erarbeitest ein kleines Produkt, das du in der Klasse vorstellen und in deinem Portfolio aufbewahren kannst.

> **!** *In Notting Hill Gate 8 wird der Unterschied zwischen britischem und US-amerikanischem Englisch thematisiert. Die US-amerikanische Schreibweise findet sich dort, wo die Texte aus einem US-amerikanischen Kontext stammen, ansonsten folgt das Buch der britischen Rechtschreibung.*

Ein ausführliches Inhaltsverzeichnis befindet sich auf den Seiten 266 bis 271.

What do you know about the USA?

In this book you will learn a lot about the USA. What do you already know about the country? Try to answer the questions. The correct letters make a sentence.

1 In the USA there are ...
- **B** 5 states.
- **A** 25 states.
- **W** 50 states.

2 The capital of the USA is ...
- **E** Washington, D.C.
- **A** New York City.
- **P** Chicago.

3 The first president of the USA was ...
- **L** Arnold Schwarzenegger.
- **A** George Washington.
- **N** John F. Kennedy.

4 The USA has a population of ...
- **E** about 33 million people.
- **R** about 330 million people.
- **H** about 3.3 billion people.

5 The most important American film awards are called ...
- **J** the Adams.
- **T** the Leonardos.
- **E** the Oscars.

6 An important American holiday in November is ...
- **G** Thanksgiving.
- **B** Independence Day.
- **M** Pancake Day.

7 The Statue of Liberty is in ...
- **O** New York City.
- **U** Los Angeles.
- **E** San Diego.

8 The very first people who came to America were probably from ...
- **S** Antarctica.
- **I** Asia.
- **C** Australia.

9 Martin Luther King Jr. ...
- **W** was a US president.
- **N** fought for equal rights for African Americans.
- **R** was the first US-American to win an Olympic gold medal.

10 In New York City there are …
- **F** about 2.5 million people.
- **I** about 5.5 million people.
- **G** about 8.5 million people.

11 What is the official language of the USA?
- **I** English.
- **Q** Spanish.
- **T** There is no official language.

12 In the 1850s the first jeans in America were made by …
- **A** Billy Jean.
- **D** Johnny Blue.
- **O** Levi Strauss.

13 'Moccasins', 'anorak' and 'kayak' are words from …
- **T** indigenous languages.
- **L** Asian languages.
- **R** European languages.

14 The letter 'B' in 'NBA' stands for …
- **P** bowling.
- **O** baseball.
- **H** basketball.

15 Cheerleaders …
- **E** shout, dance and do stunts at games.
- **O** play American football at school.
- **N** run around the stadium.

16 The first hamburger in America was sold in …
- **V** 1495.
- **J** 1605.
- **U** 1885.

17 Hip-hop originated in …
- **D** Hawaii.
- **S** New York City.
- **Z** Hollywood.

18 The Super Bowl can be won in …
- **A** American football.
- **G** mini golf.
- **K** cooking.

Your sentence:

     10   14 15 16 17 18 .

Landscapes and cities in the USA

Match the photos to the places on the map. The correct letters make a word.
You can find help on the map in the front of your book.

L Golden Gate Bridge in San Francisco

C Desert in Arizona

M Statue of Liberty and skyline in New York City

E Alligator in Florida

W Surfing in Hawaii

E Dog sled ride in Alaska

O Farmland in Kansas

Your word:
(1)(2)(3)(4)(5)(6)(7)**!**

1. Look at the pictures. What are the people doing?
2. Where do you think the people are?
3. Where would you like to be? Why?

Welcome to the USA

Part A Impressions of the USA

· Du lernst einige Aspekte der Geschichte und Kultur der USA kennen.
· Du hörst dir einen Podcast über National-feiertage in den USA an.
· Du fertigst einen Steckbrief über einen Bundesstaat der USA an.

Part B New York City

· Du findest etwas über Sehenswürdigkeiten in New York heraus.
· Du liest darüber, was Menschen in New York über ihr Stadtviertel sagen.
· Du erstellst einen digitalen Reiseführer von New York.

Welcome to the USA

1a skill: talking with people p. 154

How much USA is there in your life?
Talk to a partner and make notes.

1b workbook p. 4/1

Share your ideas in class and make a word web.

You can say:

I think ... is from the USA.
I often / sometimes eat / listen to ...
I like American sports like ...

Spotlight on ...

2a

Look at the pictures and talk about them in class.

2b

Read the info texts.
What do you find most interesting?

... geography

The United States of America covers an area of 3.8 million square miles (9.83 million square kilometres) which is about 27.5 times bigger than Germany. The USA has six time zones from east to west. There is a wide variety of climate zones and landscapes, for example deserts, beaches, mountains, forests and tropical islands. There are big cities like New York and Philadelphia in the east and San Francisco and Los Angeles in the west, and long stretches of farmland in the states of Kansas and Oklahoma. In California there are sunny beaches, and in Alaska you can see mountain peaks covered with snow all year round.

... technology

US-American innovations are important all over the world. In 1913, for example, Henry Ford installed the first assembly line in his car factory in Michigan. This changed the whole industry because it reduced the time it took to build a car, and so cars became a lot cheaper.
In the 1960s, American innovation extended into space.
In 1969, Neil Armstrong became the first man to set foot on the moon. American companies have also made important innovations in the field of information technology (IT). Companies located in Silicon Valley, south of San Francisco, California, have played an important role in developing Internet technology and artificial intelligence.

... national parks

In 1872, the world's first national park in the state of Wyoming was established: Yellowstone. Politicians wanted to preserve and protect natural beauty and diverse ecosystems and provide public areas for people to have fun and relax. Today, there are 63 national parks and hundreds of state parks all over the USA, for example Grand Canyon National Park in Arizona or the Everglades in Florida, famous for its tropical wetlands and alligators.

... food

There is a lot more to US-American food than just hamburgers and hot dogs. You can find a lot of regional specialities like huckleberry pie from the state of Montana or Philly cheesesteak sandwich from Philadelphia, Pennsylvania. Immigrants from all over the world also influenced eating habits in the USA with the recipes they brought with them. In recent years, healthy eating and the use of fresh ingredients, less meat and lots of vegetables have become more and more popular.

... pop culture

American pop culture has influenced and inspired people all over the world. Many different music styles came from the US, especially in the last century. Country music, for example, came up in the 1920s, and Nashville, Tennessee, became one of its hotspots. Hip-hop also has its roots in the USA. It started in New York City in the 1970s. Hollywood is the birthplace of the American film industry, and American films, TV series and TV shows have also had a huge influence on youth culture.

2c CHOOSE YOUR LEVEL skill: reading p. 156, workbook p. 4/2

I   Take notes on two of the states mentioned in the texts. Then find the states on a map.
II Take notes on three of the states mentioned in the texts. Then find the states on a map.
III Take notes on four of the cities mentioned in the texts. Then find the cities on a map.

ACTIVATE PRACTISE DEVELOP PRACTISE APPLY

GRAMMAR HELP the simple past (R) p. 174-175

Das *simple past* kennst du bereits. Erinnerst du dich noch, wie es gebildet und verwendet wird? Sieh dir die Beispielsätze an. Woran erkennst du, dass hier das *simple past* benötigt wird?

In 1969, Neil Armstrong became the first man to set foot on the moon.
1969 wurde Neil Armstrong der erste Mensch, der einen Fuß auf den Mond setzte.
Many music styles originated in the US, especially in the last century.
Viele Musikstile nahmen in den Vereinigten Staaten ihren Anfang, vor allem im letzten Jahrhundert.
Hip-hop started in New York City in the 1970s. Hiphop fing in den 1970ern in New York City an.

Auf den Seiten 174-175 findest du weitere Erklärungen und Beispiele zum *simple past*, und auf den Seiten 263-265 gibt es eine Liste mit unregelmäßigen Verben.

A trip to Yellowstone National Park

3 grammar: simple past (R) p. 174, workbook p. 5/3, 4

Copy the text and fill in the gaps with the correct verb form. Remember: some verbs are irregular.

Hi everyone, greetings from Yellowstone! We ??? (arrive) here three days ago. On our first day, we ??? (drive) around a lot and ??? (see) some of the highlights of the park. The views ??? (be) really amazing. We ??? (have) a fantastic day yesterday, too. We ??? (walk) so much that our feet ??? (hurt) in the evening. We all ??? (sleep) really well last night because we ??? (be) so tired. And there is so much more to see – I ??? (not expect) the park to be so big! It's definitely an amazing place!

Innovations

4 grammar: simple past (R) p. 174, workbook p. 6/5

Unscramble the questions and write them in your exercise book. Then answer them.

1 first assembly line – Where did – install the – Ford – ?
2 the car industry – Why – the assembly line – change – did – ?
3 the first – moon – on the – Who – man – was – ?
4 country music – come up – When – did – ?
5 the 1970s – What – in – started – New York City – in – ?

How to pronounce the letters -*ed*

5 audio 1/1

Listen to the words and repeat them. Then copy the table and sort the words into three lists according to the sound at the end of the words.

installed · changed · reduced · influenced · extended · played · inspired · established · originated

/-t/	/-d/	/-ɪd/
reduced	installed	extended
...	...	...

DIGITAL+ practise more 1-2

ACTIVATE **PRACTISE** DEVELOP PRACTISE APPLY

Sightseeing in the USA

6a

Look at the three travel ads. Which destination do you find the most interesting? Why?

https://www.???????/????????   × –

**Welcome to Arizona,
the land of natural wonders!**
With breathtaking landscapes and endless adventures, Arizona is a must-see for nature lovers. Start your trip at the Grand Canyon, one of the most magnificent natural wonders in the world. For the ultimate thrill, step out onto the Skywalk, a glass bridge 70 feet over the canyon's edge.

→ Find out more in the video clip

Experience the ultimate adventure in Alaska!
Enjoy outdoor activities and stunning natural beauty in the north of the USA.
Visit the charming town of Skagway and step back in time to the gold rush era or take a dog sled ride!

→ Find out more in the video clip

Discover the magic of Pennsylvania!
Pennsylvania is perfect if you are interested in history and like charming small towns.
Visit the historic town of Gettysburg, and enjoy the delicious food in Lancaster. If you prefer bigger cities, you can learn about American history at Independence Hall in Philadelphia.

→ Find out more in the video clip

6b CHOOSE YOUR LEVEL 🎞️ 📺 video 1, 2, 3, skill: watching a video clip p. 158, media worksheet 8

I Watch the video clips. Choose two of the states and take notes on the sights there.
II Watch the video clips. Take notes on the sights that you can visit in the three states.
III Watch the video clips and take notes on what you can see and do in the three states.

6c workbook p. 6/6, 7

Collect the information from the video clips on the board.

ACTIVATE   PRACTISE   **DEVELOP**   PRACTISE   APPLY

Some glimpses of US-American history

7a

**Look at the pictures. What aspects of US-American history
do you expect to learn about in the texts? Then read the texts.**

You can say:

I expect to learn about …

I think the texts are about …

1 The first people on the American continent probably appeared about 20,000 years ago.

2 Around 1,000 AD, people from Scandinavia reached North America and lived there in small settlements in what is known as Canada today for about 100 years.

3 In 1492, Christopher Columbus landed in the Caribbean. Although there were already people living there, he claimed the land for Spain.
His "discovery" marks the beginning of the European colonization of the American continent.

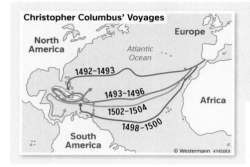

Christopher Columbus' Voyages

4 In the 17th century, people from Britain and other European countries began to settle on the east coast of what is the USA today. Many of them came to America for political or economic reasons and some wanted religious freedom. Among these groups were the British Pilgrim Fathers, who reached America in November 1620 on the ship *Mayflower*.

5 When the settlers from Europe arrived, there were hundreds of different Native American nations in North America who spoke different languages and had different ways of living. The European settlers took their land from them, often with violence, and they brought diseases with them that the Native Americans were not familiar with. Millions of them died in the following centuries.

6 By 1733, there were 13 British colonies on the east coast of North America. These colonies were governed by Great Britain and had to pay taxes to the British government. In 1775, the colonies began a war for their independence from Great Britain.
On 4 July, 1776, the United States of America was declared an independent nation. The American War of Independence lasted until 1783.

7 Until 1865, slavery was legal in the USA. Slaves from Africa were forced to work under horrible conditions in almost every field of work. Slavery only ended after the Civil War. It was fought from 1861 to 1865 between the more industrialized northern states, that were against slavery and wanted freedom for the slaves, and the agricultural southern states.

8 In the first half of the 20th century, the USA was involved in World War I (1914-1918) and World War II (1939-1945). In 1941, Germany declared war on the USA, and the USA entered the Second World War. In 1945, after years of fighting, the USA and its allies won the war. Since then, there has always been a US-American military presence in Europe.

9 The end of slavery in the 19th century did not lead to complete equal rights for black and white people, especially in the south of the USA. Until the mid-1960s, there was racial segregation in public places and institutions. In the 1950s and 1960s, the civil rights movement became more and more important. Martin Luther King Jr. was one of its leaders.

10 On 11 September 2001, terrorists hijacked four planes and flew two of them into the twin towers of the World Trade Center in New York. Around 3,000 people died in the attack, and the World Trade Center was completely destroyed. In 2006, rebuilding began. The One World Trade Center is now the main building of the new complex.

11 In 2009, Barack Obama, born in Honolulu, Hawaii, in 1961, became the first African American president of the United States. He served as the 44th president until 2017.

7b CHOOSE YOUR LEVEL skill: reading p. 156

I Write down these events in the correct chronological order.

[The end of slavery] [The first people on the American continent]
[The Pilgrim Fathers reach America]
[The colonies become independent] [Columbus lands in the Caribbean]

II Write headings for six or more of the texts.
III Make a timeline of the events mentioned in the texts.

7c workbook p. 7/8

Have you heard of other historical events in US-American history that you think are important? Talk about them in class in German.

LAND & LEUTE 1 🎬 video 4, 5, workbook p. 8/9

The Trail of Tears

Die Ankunft der Siedler aus Europa veränderte das Leben der schätzungsweise sieben Millionen indigenen Menschen im heutigen Kanada und den USA dramatisch. Die Siedler brachten nicht nur Krankheiten mit, die für viele *Native Americans* tödlich waren, sie stahlen auch ihr Land und vertrieben sie mit Gewalt oder brachten sie um. Die *Native Americans* wehrten sich, aber bis circa 1900 hatte sich ihre Zahl auf ungefähr 300 000 reduziert.

Im 19. Jahrhundert führte die US-Regierung das System der Reservate ein und zwang *Native Americans*, in bestimmten Gebieten auf oft schlechtem Land zu leben, das häufig sehr weit von ihrem ursprünglich bewohnten Land

Trail of Tears / Jerome Tiger 1961

entfernt war. Eines der schlimmsten Beispiele dieser Vorgehensweise fand zwischen 1830 und 1850 statt. Weiße Siedler wollten im Südosten der USA Baumwolle anbauen, und die Regierung zwang ungefähr 60 000 *Native Americans*, ihr dortiges Land zu verlassen und über den Mississippi über 1000 Meilen in den Westen zu laufen. Tausende von ihnen starben auf dem Weg, und der lange und schwierige Weg wurde *"Trail of Tears"* genannt.

Sprecht zu zweit. Was war euch neu?

National holidays

8a 🔊 audio 1/5, skill: listening p. 153

Listen to the podcast about four American holidays. Write down the names of the holidays in the order they are presented in the podcast.

| Independence Day | | Thanksgiving | | Martin Luther King Jr. Day | | Juneteenth |

8b skill: mediation p. 157, workbook p. 8/10

Listen again and take notes. What does each of the four holidays commemorate? Tell someone in German what you have learnt about the holidays.

American history and culture

9   CHOOSE YOUR TASK B: wordbank: descriptions p. 163, B+C: skill: searching the internet p. 159, presentations p. 160, B+C media worksheet 6

A **Make a collage about one event or person from American history and label it.**

B 🟫🟦 **Prepare a one-minute talk on an American sportsperson, actor or actress, musician, …**

C 🟫🟦 **Find out about the American flag and tell your class about it.**

The American Dream

10a

Read the quote. What is the "American Dream" according to James T. Adams?

*"The American dream, that dream
of a land in which life should be better
and richer and fuller for every man,
with opportunity for each."*

James T. Adams

James T. Adams
(1878 – 1949)
was an American
historian and
author.

10b CHOOSE YOUR LEVEL

I **What three topics from the box do you think are the most important for a "better and richer and fuller life"? Explain your choice in German.**

II **What do you think: what do you need to lead a "better and richer and fuller life"? Choose three of the topics from the box and rank them.**

III **What do you think: what do you need to lead a "better and richer and fuller life"? Choose three of the topics from the box. Give reasons for your choice.**

money · health · education · personal freedom · security · peace · tolerance · …

10c

Read this passage from a dictionary entry about the American Dream.
What are important aspects of the American Dream according to the dictionary entry?
Explain them in German.

The American Dream is a set of ideals such as democracy, rights, freedom and equality.
Freedom in this case means that everyone – regardless of his or her social class or origin –
can become rich and successful if he or she just works hard enough.

10d wordbank: expressing opinions p. 168, workbook p. 8/11, 12

Read this statement about the American Dream. Do you agree or disagree with it? Say why.

"Only in America can someone start
with nothing and achieve the American Dream.
That's the greatness of this country."

Rafael Cruz, born 1939

You can say:

I agree with the statement that …

I disagree with … I think …

In my opinion, the American Dream …

Mixed numbers

11   wordbank: numbers p. 171, workbook p. 9/13

Copy the sentences and fill in the correct words and numbers from the box. You can find help in 2a and 7a.

> 1776 · 44th · 13 · 2009 · first ·
> 20,000 · 27.5 · 4th · 9.83 million

1 The USA is about ??? times bigger than Germany.
2 It is about ??? square kilometres big.
3 The ??? people appeared on the American continent about ??? years ago.
4 Barack Obama became the ??? US president in ???.
5 In the year ???, the ??? British colonies declared themselves independent.
6 Independence Day is celebrated on ??? July.

You can write:

1. *The USA is about 27.5 times …*

Discover more

12   CHOOSE YOUR LEVEL   workbook p. 9/14

▌ Write about Florida. Fill in the gaps with words from the box.

1 The first people ??? Florida more than 12,000 years ago.
2 Today, about 20 million people ??? in Florida.
3 Florida ??? one of the most popular tourist destinations in the USA.
4 Another name for Florida ??? "sunshine state".

> is ·
> is ·
> live ·
> reached

▌▌ Write about Nevada. Fill in the gaps with words from the box.

1 The first people ??? to settle in Nevada at least 14,800 years ago.
2 Nevada ??? a US state in 1864.
3 Las Vegas ??? the most famous and the biggest city in Nevada.
4 Nevada ??? the driest state in the US and ??? large desert areas.
5 Nevada ??? also called the "Silver State".

> is ·
> is ·
> started ·
> became ·
> has ·
> is

▌▌▌ Write about Massachusetts. Choose the correct word from the brackets.

1 The first people ??? to what today is called Massachusetts about 12,000 years ago. (comes / came)
2 In 1620, settlers called the Pilgrim Fathers ???. (arrives / arrived)
3 Massachusetts ??? a US state in 1788. (become / became)
4 Today, Boston ??? the biggest city and the capital of Massachusetts. (is / was)
5 Boston ??? situated on the east coast of the USA. (is / were)
6 Massachusetts ??? known for its many different landscapes. (is / were)
7 It ??? sometimes called the "Baked Bean State". (is / were)

DIGITAL+ practise more 1-2

ACTIVATE   PRACTISE   DEVELOP   **PRACTISE**   APPLY

Presenting a state TARGET TASK

13   workbook p. 10/15, wordbank: around the world p. 162, numbers p. 171

Your task is to present one of the fifty states of the USA. Create a fact file.
Before you start, look at these steps:

STEP 1

Which states would you like to learn more about? Make a list in class.

STEP 2

Work in groups or with a partner. In class, decide which team is going to work on which state.

STEP 3

Do your research. Choose two of these categories:
- geography (area, population, capital, big cities/rivers/mountains)
- history (important events)
- economy (which industries, where most people work)
- tourist attractions (sights, events)
- famous people (actors or actresses, musicians, sportspersons, writers, politicians)
- ...

STEP 4

Which information do you want to include in your fact file?

STEP 5

Make a first draft. Decide on a suitable layout and add pictures.

STEP 6

Ask a partner for feedback. Edit your fact file if necessary.

STEP 7

Display your fact files in class.

Fact file – Iowa

Capital: Des Moines
Area: 145.743 km^2
Longest river:
Missouri River
Highest mountain:
Hawkeye Point
Population: about
3,000,000 people

First impressions

1a   video 6, media worksheet 8

Watch the video clip.
What is your first impression of New York City?

You can say:
My first impression is that New York is ...

1b   wordbank: around the world p. 162

Which words would you use to describe New York?

busy · noisy · fascinating · quiet · boring · lively · great · ...

1c   workbook p. 11/1

Can you imagine living in a big city like New York? Why? Why not?

You can say:
I can / can't imagine living in New York because it's very ... / too ...

Messages from New York

2a   audio 1/6, skill: reading p. 156

Listen to the tourists and read along. Who is where? Take notes.
Then find the places on the map of New York at the back of your book.

Ben: The show was awesome! I haven't seen anything like it before. The costumes, the music, the actors – just awesome! Now I know why Broadway is so famous for its theater productions. I'm definitely going to see another show while I'm here. It's been the best part of my trip to New York so far.

Suri: Hi everyone! Can you see me? I'm up here, INSIDE Lady Liberty's crown. I've wanted to do this since I was a kid. I've had to climb 162 steps to get up here, but it's worth it! The trip on the ferry was great as well – the view over the harbor and the skyline of New York was amazing, but I can see even better from up here inside the Statue of Liberty. Next stop is Ellis Island, the place where so many immigrants entered the United States in the late 19th and early 20th century.

Kim: This is so cool. I'm riding a bike across Brooklyn Bridge right over the East River. I always thought New York would be too dangerous for cycling, but there are now so many good bike lanes that I've decided to tour the city on a bike. This bike lane across the bridge is a great way to get from Manhattan to Brooklyn.

ACTIVATE   PRACTISE   DEVELOP   PRACTISE   APPLY

Andrea: It's lovely here in Central Park. It's so green and calm. I think it was a brilliant idea to build such a big park right in the middle of New York. There are even lakes, a zoo and museums inside the park. We've been on our feet all day long to see as much as possible, but I'm really happy that we've rented this boat and can relax a little. I don't think my feet have ever hurt as much as today.

Fabio: I'm at the 9/11 Memorial, at the site where the Twin Towers were hit by a terrorist attack in 2001. It's amazing what has been built here since then. I'm standing at the North Pool that was built in the footprint of the former North Tower, and there are new skyscrapers all around me. There's also a South Pool where the South Tower was. The atmosphere here is quite moving.

2b

Talk about the places in class. What do the tourists like about them?

2c CHOOSE YOUR LEVEL

I Read Ben and Suri's statements again and answer the questions.

1 What is Broadway famous for?
2 How many steps do you have to climb to get to the top of Lady Liberty?
3 How did Suri get to the Statue of Liberty?
4 Where does Suri want to go next?

II Read the first four statements again and answer the questions.

1 What has been the best part of Ben's trip to New York so far?
2 Since when has Suri wanted to visit the Statue of Liberty?
3 How does Kim tour New York?
4 What can you rent in Central Park?

III Read the statements again and answer the questions.

1 What does Ben say about the show that he has just seen on Broadway?
2 What do you learn about Ellis Island?
3 Which boroughs of New York does Brooklyn Bridge connect?
4 What does Andrea say about Central Park?
5 What can you see at the 9/11 Memorial?

2d workbook p.11/2

Which of the places would you like to visit? Say why.

| GRAMMAR HELP | the present perfect (R) p. 176-177 |

Das *present perfect* kennst du bereits. Erinnerst du dich noch, wie es gebildet wird und wann man es benutzt? Sieh dir die Beispielsätze an. Woran erkennst du, dass hier das *present perfect* benötigt wird?

It's been the best part of my trip to New York so far.
Es ist bisher der beste Teil meiner Reise nach New York gewesen.
I've wanted to do this since I was a kid.
Ich habe das machen wollen, seit ich ein Kind war.

Auf den Seiten 176-177 findest du weitere Erklärungen und Beispiele zum *present perfect*.

Visiting New York

3a grammar: present perfect (R) p. 176

Copy the sentences and fill in the gaps. Use the present perfect.

1 Many people ??? (visit) Broadway since the first show in 1866.
2 Suri ??? (climb) 162 steps, and now she has an amazing view over the harbour.
3 Kim ??? (decide) to tour the city on a bike.
4 Andrea's feet ??? (never hurt) like that before.

3b grammar: present perfect (R) p. 176, workbook p. 11/3

Complete the sentences. Use the present perfect or the simple past.

I ??? (**already** see) many cities in the US, but I ??? (**not** be) to New York **yet**. My friend ??? (go) there **last month**, and she ??? (enjoy) it a lot. She ??? (show) me some amazing pictures **yesterday**. She also ??? (recommend) a hotel and I ??? (**just** check) it out on the Internet.

Have you ever …?

4a grammar: present perfect (R) p. 177

Write down five or more questions for a partner.

Have you ever	travelled seen been visited …	by ferry? a musical? to New York? the USA? …

4b grammar: present perfect (R) p. 177, workbook p. 12/4

Work with a partner and ask and answer questions. When your partner says "Yes, I have.", react by asking follow-up questions.

You can answer:
Yes, I have.
No, I haven't.

You can ask follow-up questions:
What was it like?
What did you do there?

DIGITAL+ practise more 3-4

ACTIVATE **PRACTISE** DEVELOP PRACTISE APPLY

Brandon's vlog about New York

5a 🎬📺 video 7, skill: watching a video clip p.158 , media worksheet 8

Watch the video clip.
What is Brandon's favourite time of the year?
Why?

5b CHOOSE YOUR LEVEL 🎬📺 video 7, skill: watching a video clip p.158

▎ **Read the statements. Watch the video clip again and choose the right statements.**

1 Brandon is **a tourist in New York City** / from New York City.
2 The Empire State Building has **102 floors** / 176 floors.
3 You have a great view of **the whole city** / Central Park from the top.

▎▎ **Read the statements. Then watch the video clip again and choose the right information.**

1 This building is 1,776 feet high.
  A One World Trade Center   **B** Empire State Building

2 An old railroad has been turned into this park.
  A Central Park   **B** The High Line

3 In winter, they put up a huge Christmas tree here.
  A Chinatown   **B** Rockefeller Center

▎▎▎ **Read the statements. Then watch the video clip again and match them to the sights.**

1 From up there, you have a great view of the whole city.
2 It is often called the "Freedom Tower".
3 You've probably seen it in films or on TV.
4 It is also a great example of New York City's multicultural history.
5 In winter, a huge Christmas tree is put up in front of it.

| Central Park | Chinatown | Empire State Building | Rockefeller Center | One World Trade Center |

5c 🎬📺 skill: searching the internet p.159, media worksheet 6

Choose one of the sights from the video clip and find out more about it.
Work with a partner and tell each other what you found most interesting.

5d 📺 wordbank: (digital) communication p.167, workbook p.12/5,6

Imagine you are a tourist in New York.
Write a text message to a friend and
recommend one or more of the sights to
them.

You can write:
Hi …, I'm here at the …
It's amazing / great / …
You should come and see the …
…

Boroughs and people

6a 🔊 audio 1/7

Listen and read along. Which teenager lives in which borough: the Bronx, Manhattan, Brooklyn, Queens and Staten Island? Find the boroughs on the map at the back of your book.

My family is originally from Lebanon, but we've lived in Manhattan for eight years now. There are a lot of different neighborhoods in Manhattan. Our apartment is in the north, in the part called Harlem. You can see many of the typical New York brownstone houses here. Harlem is not a bad place to live. It is not as expensive as many other parts of the city. My dad has an old food truck, and we sell hot dogs at different places in Harlem. It's hard work and we don't make a lot of money. *(Bilal Hinawy, 16)*

Brooklyn is the best. I grew up around here. I go to high school in downtown Manhattan, but I'm glad to get back here in the evenings.
It's not as loud as Manhattan, the sidewalks are clean and there are lots of parks and beaches. Brooklyn also has cool little stores with clothes and shoes. To me, Brooklyn's special – I wouldn't want to live anywhere else.
(Marian Jones, 14)

I think there is no better place than Staten Island. It's not as loud and busy as Manhattan or Brooklyn, and there are lots of lakes and parks.
Some people think that living on Staten Island must be boring because it's so quiet. But it's near downtown Manhattan with all its great entertainment. There's a ferry so you can get there fast. And you don't have to pay for the ferry! *(Tami Webb, 18)*

I moved to Queens from the Caribbean. I've lived here for ten years, and I'm really proud of my borough. People from all over the world live here, so you can hear a lot of different languages and eat all kinds of food. People learn to get along with each other or just leave each other in peace. *(Paul Beliard, 17)*

I'm from the Bronx. It's a busy and culturally diverse place with lots of street art. Many people here are Hispanics. My family is from Puerto Rico, and at home we speak Spanish. Lots of people who work in Manhattan live in my borough. Many years ago, the Bronx had a high crime rate, but now it's a good place to be. Hip-hop started around here, and that's my favorite kind of music. We also have the best baseball team in the world – the Yankees. Whenever I have enough money, I go and watch a game.
(Joshua Rodriguez, 16)

ACTIVATE   PRACTISE   **DEVELOP**   PRACTISE   APPLY

6b
skill: reading p. 156

Do you think the teenagers are happy where they live? Find statements in the texts that show how they feel about their boroughs. Take notes.

You can write:

Bilal: Harlem not a bad place to live, typical …
Marian: Brooklyn the best, glad to …
…

6c
workbook p. 14/7, 8

Which borough would you like to live in? Give some reasons for your answer.

An open letter to NYC

7a
wordbank: around the world p. 162

Read this extract from the song "An open letter to NYC" by the Beastie Boys. What picture of New York comes to mind?

(...)

Brooklyn, Bronx, Queens and Staten
From the Battery to the top of Manhattan
Asian, Middle-Eastern and Latin
Black, White, New York you make it happen

Brownstones, water towers, trees, skyscrapers
Writers, prizefighters and Wall Street traders
We come together on the subway cars
Diversity unified, whoever you are, uh

(...)

Dear New York, I hope you're doin' well
I know a lot's happened, and you've been through hell
So, we give thanks for providin' a home
Through your gates at Ellis Island, we passed in droves

(...)

Dear New York, this is a love letter
To you and how you brought us together
We can't say enough about all you do
'Cause in the city we're ourselves and electric, too

(...)

I see you're still strong after all that's gone on
Lifelong we dedicate this song
Just a little somethin' to show some respect
To the city that blends and mends and tests, uh

Since 9/11, we're still livin'
And lovin', life we've been given
Ain't nothin' gonna take that away from us
We lookin' pretty and gritty 'cause in the city we trust

Dear New York, I know a lot has changed
Two towers down, but you're still in the game
Home to the many, rejectin' no one
Acceptin' peoples of all places, wherever they're from

(...)

7b
CHOOSE YOUR LEVEL skill: reading p. 156

⏐ **What places and landmarks are mentioned in the lyrics? Make a list.**
⏐⏐ **Find words and phrases in the lyrics that show how the speaker feels about New York.**
⏐⏐⏐ **In the song, the speaker addresses New York like a person. Find words and phrases in the lyrics that describe the city's character and copy them into your exercise book.**

7c
skill: writing p. 155, workbook p. 15/9, 10, media worksheet 11

Write a (love) letter to the place where you live or would like to live.

LAND & LEUTE 2 🎞 video 8

Kultur für jeden

New York hat eine lebendige Kulturszene. Es gibt Tausende von Theatern, Kunstgalerien und Museen, und man kann Musicals, Konzerte und viele andere kulturelle Ereignisse genießen. Du hast bestimmt schon mal vom Broadway gehört, auf dem viele Musicaltheater zu Hause sind. Die *Metropolitan Opera*, auch als *Met* bekannt, zeigt weltberühmte Aufführungen. Wenn man moderne Kunst der Weltklasse sehen will, kann man ins *MoMA* gehen, das Museum für Moderne Kunst in Manhattan. Es wurde 1929 eröffnet und ist eines der führenden Kunstmuseen der Welt.

Hiphop nahm seinen Anfang in der Bronx. DJ Kool Herc spielte 1973 auf einer Party auf eine neue und besondere Art Soul und Funkmusik, was heute als Geburt des Hiphop angesehen wird. Man kann das *Universal Hip-Hop Museum* besuchen, wo es Schallplatten, Musik-Equipment, Kleidung und Hiphop-Zeitschriften zu sehen gibt.

Finde heraus, was momentan auf dem Broadway gespielt wird. Welche Show würdest du dir gerne ansehen?

New York tips

8   skill: mediation p. 157, workbook p. 15/11

Help someone who does not speak English understand this flyer. Tell them in German about the opening times, fees and activities.

TIPS FOR THE CITY THAT NEVER SLEEPS

YANKEE STADIUM ○ BRONX   *Tour times vary – please book in advance on our website*

Take a tour of the Yankee Stadium and visit the exhibition to learn about the rich history of New York's baseball champions. Each tour is led by one of our tour guides.
- Standard Adult Tour Admission: $35
- Seniors aged 65 & above: $24
- Kids aged 14 & under: $24

The B, D and 4 trains stop at 161st Street / Yankee Stadium. Follow the signs within the station to Yankee Stadium.

MUSEUM OF MODERN ART ○ MANHATTAN   *Sat 10:30am – 7:00pm, Sun – Fri 10:30am – 5:30pm*

Enjoy one of the largest collections of modern art in the world, including works of architecture and design, drawings, paintings, sculptures, photographies, prints, films, and electronic media.
- Adults: $30
- Students: $17 (full-time with ID, including international students)

Please note: Due to renovations, the cafeteria on the 2nd floor will be closed from March.

CENTRAL PARK ○ MANHATTAN   *open 6am to 1am daily*

Enjoy a walk in one of the most famous parks of the world or book an official Central Park tour like *the Statues and Monuments Tour, the Bike Tour* or *the Playground Adventure*.
- Prices starting at $25.

Check our website for special offers.

At Grand Central Station

9 GET TOGETHER

Get together with a partner.
Buy and sell train tickets at
Grand Central Station.

Partner A	Partner B
‖ Go to page 130.	‖ Go to page 139.
‖ Go to page 133.	‖ Go to page 142.
‖ Go to page 136.	‖ Go to page 145.

Immigrant Heritage Week

10a

Look at the poster. What is celebrated
during Immigrant Heritage Week?

10b audio 1/10, skill: listening p. 153

Listen to the podcast episode. Which of
these events are mentioned by the hosts?

1 Coney Island walking tour
2 Mexican art exhibition
3 Stories from Home
4 Parade of Flags
5 Home-made

IMMIGRANT NEW YORK

Join us for a week of events to honor
New York's legacy as a **city of immigrants**
and **celebrate New York's cultural diversity!**

Discover how essential immigrants have
always been and still are to the city's life.

IMMIGRANT
HERITAGE
WEEK

10c workbook p. 16/12

Listen again and write down the statements with the correct information.

1 Coney Island is famous for its **forests / amusement parks**.
2 At the "Stories from Home" event, **memories / hot dogs** were shared.
3 At the "Parade of Flags", each flag represented a different **language / nationality** that can be
   found in Brooklyn.
4 At the "Home-made" event in Harlem, you could see **fireworks / live performances**.

New York, New York

11 CHOOSE YOUR TASK C: skill: searching the internet p. 159

A **Write an acrostic about New York.**
B **Write multiple-choice quiz questions about
   New York for your classmates.**
C   **Find out about the many nicknames New York has
   been given in its history. Tell your class about them.**

A   DIFFERENT NEIGHBOURHOODS
IN THE CITY THAT NEVER SLEEPS,
              AWESOME AND
                 YOUNG,
              OPEN AND
              FRIENDLY.
        MY KIND OF PLACE!

ACTIVATE   PRACTISE   **DEVELOP**   PRACTISE   APPLY

New York facts

12   grammar: passive (R) p. 178

Copy the statements and choose the correct passive forms from the brackets.

1 Many languages ??? (are spoken / have been spoken) in New York.
2 Many brownstone houses ??? (have been seen / can be seen) in Harlem.
3 The Empire State Building ??? (was built / is built) from 1930 till 1931.
4 A new exhibition at the museum ??? (will be opened / has been opened) in June next year.
5 The Immigrant Heritage Week ??? (has been celebrated / was celebrated) every year since 2004.

Curious tourist

13   **CHOOSE YOUR LEVEL** grammar: passive (R) p. 178, workbook p. 16/13

▌ Unscramble the questions and write them down.

1 opened – When was – the MoMA – ?
2 is celebrated – What – during – Immigrant Heritage Week – ?
3 every year since 2004 – celebrated – has been – What – ?
4 seen – What – at the – can be – Parade of Flags – ?

▌▌ Unscramble the questions and write them down.

1 built – When – the – was – Statue of Liberty – ?
2 New York – How many – are – spoken – in – languages – ?
3 every year since 2004 – celebrated – has been – What – ?
4 will – Christmas tree – When – be put up – this year's – ?

▌▌▌ Write questions in the passive.

1 How long ??? the café ????
2 Why ??? the Immigrant Heritage Week ??? each year?
3 When ??? the Empire State Building ????
4 When ??? we ??? again by the bus?
5 Where ??? many skyscrapers ??? since 2001?

will ... be picked up ·
have ... been built ·
will ... be closed ·
is ... celebrated ·
was ... completed

Spelling

14a   wordbank: American and British English p. 165

Sort the words into two lists: one for British spelling and one for American spelling.

center · centre · favourite · favorite · traveled · travelled · theatre · theater · harbour · harbor

14b   workbook p. 16/14

Are there similar words in German or another language that you speak? Tell the class.

DIGITAL+ practise more 5-6

ACTIVATE   PRACTISE   DEVELOP   **PRACTISE**   APPLY

A New York travel guide TARGET TASK

15 ▓▓ 🖥 workbook p. 16/15, wordbank: around the world p. 162, skill: writing p. 155, media worksheet 1, 6, 13

Your task is to create a page for a (digital) travel guide of New York.
Before you start, look at these steps:

STEP 1

In class, collect ideas for your guide. Think about:
· places
· sights
· activities
· neighbourhoods to visit
· …
Get together with a partner or in a small group. Decide who is going to work on which topic.

STEP 2

In your group, plan your page.
Make notes on what you already know and what you have to find out. Think about:
· What can you see and do there?
· What are the opening times?
· Where is it?
· How much are the entrance fees?

STEP 3

Do your research. You can also look for pictures.

STEP 4

Make a first draft. Then check and edit your texts.

STEP 7

Present your pages in class. Give each other feedback.

STEP 8

You can put all your pages together to create a (digital) travel guide.

> You can use phrases like:
>
> *Make sure you visit …*
> *… is a must-see because …*
> *… is the biggest / best / most exciting / …*
> *… is a perfect / beautiful place to relax / enjoy / see / …*
> *… is the ideal place to watch …*
> *At the … you can …*
> *The … is a famous sight.*
> *… is a very interesting place.*

Check out

1. Kannst du kurze Infotexte über die USA verstehen?	Workbook, p. 18
2. Kannst du einen Podcast über amerikanische Feiertage verstehen?	Workbook, p. 18
3. Kannst du die Aussagen von Zitaten verstehen?	Workbook, p. 19
4. Kannst du Informationen über Sehenswürdigkeiten in New York verstehen?	Workbook, p. 20
5. Kannst du jemandem sprachlich aushelfen, der touristische Informationen nicht versteht?	Workbook, p. 20
6. Kannst du mit passenden Redewendungen über Sehenswürdigkeiten schreiben?	Workbook, p. 21

What is the real story of Thanksgiving?

1 For a long time, history books told a story of "The First Thanksgiving" as shown in this picture painted by Jean Ferris in 1915. The story goes like this:

Jean Ferris: The First Thanksgiving, 1621. The scene is not historically accurate.

5 In 1620, the Pilgrim Fathers arrived in what is now the state of Massachusetts.
That winter was very cold and the Pilgrims did not know how to find food in their new country. Many died from hunger, the cold and disease.

10 The same area was home to Native Americans – the Wampanoag. In March 1621, two Wampanoag men called Samoset and Squanto decided to help the new settlers. They showed the Pilgrims how to hunt, catch fish, grow food and build houses.

15 In November 1621, the Pilgrims invited the Wampanoag to celebrate their first harvest with them. Many Wampanoag chiefs came with their families and brought food with them. They celebrated together for three days – and that was the first Thanksgiving.

But did it really happen like that? And what does the story leave out?

Although there is evidence that Chief Massasoit of the Wampanoag had a peaceful relationship
20 with the Pilgrims when they arrived, there is no evidence of a harvest celebration during the second Pilgrim winter in America. And the relationship between the settlers and the Native Americans in that area did not stay peaceful for long. In 1657, there was a massive conflict and about 5 per cent of the White population and 40 per cent of the Native American population in the region were killed.

25 It is difficult to find out what really happened, and there is not only one story of the first Thanksgiving dinner – as is often the case with historical events. But it is quite obvious that the first Thanksgiving did not take place as many people believed it did.

Look at the picture. What do you think: what is not accurate?
Collect ideas and talk about them with a partner.

> **NOTE:** In Canada people use the official term "First Nation" but in the USA there is still a debate about the best words to use when talking or writing about Native Americans.
>
> Anton Treuer, a member of the Ojibwe First Nation, explains in his book "Everything you wanted to know about Indians but were afraid to ask" that "there is no way to solve the terminology debates to everyone's satisfaction right now, (…)." Besides Indigenous and Native American, he himself uses the terms Native American and Indian, but it is highly controversial to use these terms as an outsider.

cold = *Kälte*; to hunt = *jagen*; harvest = *Ernte*; chief = *Herrscher/in (Fremdbezeichnung)*; evidence = *Beweis*; relationship = *Beziehung*; massive = *enorm, riesig*; per cent = *Prozent*; historical = *historisch*; obvious = *offensichtlich*; accurate = *genau, richtig*; debate = *Debatte*; Indian = *Indianer/in (generalisierende Fremdbezeichnung)*; satisfaction = *Zufriedenheit*; besides = *abgesehen von*; highly controversial = *stark umstritten*; outsider = *Außenseiter/in*

Fighting against racism

After the end of enslavement in 1865, Black people in the USA still suffered from racist discrimination.
Many Black Americans were very poor, and laws limited their freedom.

"Colored" referred to Black people during segregation. It is considered offensive today.

5 There was segregation – the practice of keeping Black and White people apart from each other and treating them differently – in many places. Cinemas, hotels, restaurants, buses and other places had separate entrances and seating areas for African Americans and Whites. There were separate
10 public schools for Black and White students.
In 1909, a group of Black and White people in New York City founded the National Association for the Advancement of Colored People (NAACP). They wanted to fight against racism. They organized marches, demonstrations and court cases.
15 One of the cases that they brought to court was in 1951 that of seven-year-old Linda Brown from Kansas. She was not allowed to go to a school which was just a few blocks away from her home because she was Black. Linda's father went to the Supreme Court, and in the end it was ruled that segregation in public schools was illegal.
Another important battle that the NAACP fought took place in Alabama in 1955. Rosa Parks, a
20 Black woman, was told to give up her bus seat to a White man. She refused and was arrested. So the NAACP started a bus boycott. For 381 days, Black people did not use the buses in Montgomery and the bus companies lost a lot of money. Finally, the Supreme Court decided that Montgomery could no longer have a segregated public transportation system.
On August 28, 1963, about 250,000 people, Black and White, led by Martin Luther King Jr., marched
25 to the Lincoln Memorial in Washington to protest peacefully against racism and segregation. This march is seen as a milestone for the civil rights movement.

Two years later, President Lyndon B. Johnson signed a law which promised equal rights for Black Americans in jobs, voting and the use of public
30 facilities.
But although open segregation is a thing of the past, there is still no complete equality. Racism continues to exist and statistically, Black Americans are poorer, less well educated and more often victims
35 of crime than White Americans.

Find out more about Linda Brown, Rosa Parks or Martin Luther King Jr. and the times they were living in. Share your findings in class.

racism = Rassismus; enslavement = Versklavung; to suffer from = erleiden; racist = rassistisch; discrimination = Diskriminierung; law = Gesetz; to limit = einschränken; to keep apart = getrennt halten; separate = getrennt; seating area = Sitzbereich; public school (AE) = staatliche Schule; to found = gründen; march = Marsch; court case = Gerichtsverfahren; Supreme Court = Oberstes Bundesgericht; to give up = aufgeben; seat = Sitzplatz; to refuse = sich weigern; to arrest = verhaften; segregated = getrennt; voting = Wählen; facility (AE) = Einrichtung

The father of hip-hop – DJ Kool Herc

1   On the evening of 11 August 1973, 15-year old Cindy Campbell organized a "back to school" party in the community room of her apartment house at 1520 Sedgwick Avenue in New York.

5   She sold tickets for her party and asked her brother Clive, known as DJ Kool Herc, to provide the music.

DJ Kool Herc

There were not many options for teenagers to party in safe surroundings in New York City at

10   that time, so her party was a huge success. Over 300 people showed up, and DJ Kool Herc became a local celebrity overnight.

His special innovation was what he called the Merry-Go-Round. People waited for the moments in a song when you can only hear the beat – the drum breaks – to hit the dance floor. In order

15   to enable them to move longer to the beat, DJ Kool Herc used two turntables and two identical records. So he made the drum breaks longer by switching between the records.

Party-goers developed a special dance style to these longer drum breaks. They became known as b-boys and b-girls, and the thing they were doing became b-boying and b-girling, or breaking, or breakdancing.

20   By the summer of 1973, DJ Kool Herc had been using and refining his break-beat style for about a year, but at his sister's party there was his biggest audience yet. It was the success of that party that began

25   a musical revolution, a full six years before the term "hip-hop" entered popular vocabulary.

Since then, hip-hop has been going strong. DJ Kool Herc is still performing and

30   producing music today.

Breakdancers on a street in New York in 1984

Explain in a few sentences what role DJ Kool Herc played in the history of hip-hop.

---

option = *Möglichkeit*; to party = *feiern*; surroundings *(pl)* = *Umgebung*; to show up = *erscheinen*; celebrity = *Berühmtheit*; overnight = *über Nacht*; Merry-Go-Round = *Karussell*; beat = *Takt*; to hit the dance floor = *auf die Tanzfläche gehen*; to enable = *ermöglichen*; turntable = *Plattenspieler*; to switch = *wechseln*; party-goer = *Partygänger/in*; to refine = *verbessern*; audience = *Publikum*; to enter = *Eingang finden in*; popular = *allgemein*; vocabulary = *Wortschatz*; to go strong *(informal)* = *erfolgreich sein*

1. What do you think: who are the people? Where are they?
2. What are the people doing?
3. What looks familiar to you? What looks different?

High school

Part A Welcome to high school!

- Du liest Einträge aus einem amerikanischen Highschool-Jahrbuch.
- Du erfährst etwas über das Schulleben in den USA.
- Du erstellst einen Eintrag für ein Jahrbuch.

Part B After-school activities

- Du findest etwas über Nachmittags-Aktivitäten an einer Highschool heraus.
- Du liest etwas über einen Nachmittag bei einem American Football-Spiel.
- Du machst ein Rollenspiel zu einem Interview.

School life in the USA

1

What do you know about school life in the USA? Think about films, songs, books etc. Talk about it in class.

You can say:

I think they have …

In the United States, schools are …

American schools have got …

A high school yearbook

2a

Look at these yearbook photos from a high school in Philadelphia and talk about them.

2b   skill: reading p. 156

Now read the yearbook entries. What do you find interesting or surprising?

Last year's highlights!

Student exchange program

Last year, we welcomed five new exchange students who had traveled to Philadelphia from different parts of the world. They all had a great time with their host families.

Welcoming new friends

1

Summer reading challenge

In June, the library club published a list of great books and organized a competition. There were prizes for readers who had read at least five books over the summer vacation. Eric Johnson from the 9th grade had finished the most books – twelve in total! Congratulations!

Good summer reads

2

Homecoming

In October, we celebrated homecoming week. Lots of students who had graduated from high school in June came back to visit us. This included last year's homecoming king and queen. They crowned the new king and queen. Once the cheerleaders had finished, there was a fantastic football game. What an awesome week!

The new homecoming queen Linda Chang and homecoming king Bradey Parekh

3

Marching band

Our marching band is always a great support for our football team, and it takes part in parades and competitions. One highlight last year was the Pennsylvania state championship last fall where our marching band came second. Thanks for some awesome moments!

Our marching band in full swing!

4

ACTIVATE PRACTISE DEVELOP PRACTISE APPLY

Cheerleading classes

The freshmen presented their new skills in a short demonstration at the school basketball tournament in November after they had practiced cheer basics and a dance in the weeks before.

Cheer for our team!

5

Swimming club

In January, the swimming team won the state championship. Our top athlete Katie Miller broke her personal record after she had trained hard. She won gold in the singles in an exciting final and later won bronze in the team event. Congratulations to all!

6

Swimming to the top

Fundraising

The Fundraiser Club has always been very creative and full of energy when it comes to finding ways to raise money. Last year, the members of the club provided a healthy lunch for all students once a week. They raised $9,200 to help graduates from our school with their college fees – what a success!

Great success for our fundraisers!

7

Prom night

What a night! A big thank you to the prom team for organizing a fantastic prom night to celebrate our senior students' graduation. Everyone looked great in their best suits and dresses! After the formal dinner had ended, the party continued with the traditional dance and the crowning of the prom king and queen.

A spectacular night!

8

2c CHOOSE YOUR LEVEL   skill: mediation p. 157

A friend has questions about the yearbook. Answer them in German.

▍ Choose three or more questions.
▍▍ Choose four or more questions.
▍▍▍ Choose five or more questions.

1 Was musste man machen, um einen Preis fürs Lesen zu bekommen?
2 Was ist Homecoming?
3 Was macht die Musikgruppe auf Bild 4?
4 Das sieht ja interessant aus, wofür trainieren die denn da auf Bild 5?
5 Wie erfolgreich war der Schwimmclub?
6 Was steht da mit 9200 Dollar?
7 Eine Frau mit Krönchen auf dem Kopf? Was war da der Anlass?

2d workbook p. 22/1, 2

What is similar and what is different to your school? Talk about it with a partner.

You can say:
At our school, there is / are …
There is no … / There are no …

ACTIVATE PRACTISE DEVELOP PRACTISE APPLY

GRAMMAR HELP the past perfect p.179

In den Beispielsätzen wird über Ereignisse berichtet, die in der Vergangenheit geschehen sind. Welches der beiden Ereignisse in einem Satz fand jeweils zuerst statt? Was fällt dir an den farbig markierten Formen auf?

Katie Miller broke her personal record <u>after</u> she had trained hard.
Katie Miller brach ihren persönlichen Rekord, <u>nachdem</u> sie hart trainiert hatte.

<u>After</u> the formal dinner had ended, the party continued with the traditional dance.
<u>Nachdem</u> das formale Abendessen geendet hatte, ging die Party mit dem traditionellen Tanz weiter.

Die Zeitform, die verwendet wird, um anzuzeigen, dass ein Ereignis in der Vergangenheit vor einem anderen Ereignis stattgefunden hat, heißt *past perfect*. Auf Seite 179 findest du weitere Erklärungen und Beispiele.

High school life last year

3   grammar: past perfect p.179, workbook p.22/3-5

Match the sentence parts and write down the sentences.
Underline the part of each sentence that tells you what happened first.

You can write:

1. *Before the exchange students arrived in the USA, <u>they had only talked to their host families online</u>.*

1	Before the exchange students arrived in the USA,	A	celebrated homecoming week in October.
2	Eric Johnson won the reading competition	B	Katie Miller won gold in the singles.
3	After the cheerleaders had trained dancing in the weeks before,	C	they presented their skills at the basketball tournament.
4	Lots of students who had graduated in June	D	because he had read twelve books over the summer holidays.
5	After she had trained hard,	E	they had only talked to their host families online.

Chain game: Suzie's dream

4   grammar: past perfect p.179, workbook p.24/6

Look at what Suzie did and write about a chain of events.

> 1 had come home
>
> 2 talked to mum / had talked to mum
>
> 3 did homework / had done homework
>
> 4 lay down / had lain down
>
> 5 fell asleep / had fallen asleep
>
> 6 dreamt of winning with cheerleading team

You can write:

*After Suzie **had come** home, she **talked** to her mum.*
*After she **had talked** to her mum, she …*

DIGITAL+ practise more 7

ACTIVATE   **PRACTISE**   DEVELOP   PRACTISE   APPLY

LAND & LEUTE 3  video 9

Highschools in den USA

Highschools sind in den USA oft unterschiedlich organisiert, aber meist müssen Schülerinnen und Schüler in den letzten vier Jahren vor dem Abschluss eine bestimmte Anzahl von Punkten oder Scheinen sammeln, um einen Abschluss zu bekommen. Manche Fächer wie Mathe und Englisch sind verpflichtend. Es gibt aber auch Wahlpflichtfächer, für die man Punkte oder Scheine bekommen kann, zum Beispiel Fremdsprachen, Kunst oder Hauswirtschaft.

Bei der Abschlussfeier, wenn die Schülerinnen und Schüler ihr Abschluss- zeugnis bekommen, tragen sie normalerweise beson- dere Kappen und Roben. Es gibt am Ende des Abschlussjahres meist eine formelle Tanzveranstaltung, „prom" genannt. Hierfür trägt man traditionelle Abendgarderobe.

Sieh dir den Videoclip an. Was ist anders als bei Schulsystemen, die du kennst?

Amy in Philadelphia

5a audio 1/14-16, workbook p.24/7a

Amy, 16, from Bath in England is going to spend one year in the USA.
Listen to the three scenes and find out: who are the people? Where are they in each scene?

5b CHOOSE YOUR LEVEL skill: listening p.153

I Listen again and choose the correct word.
1 The Bakers meet Amy at the **airport** / **station**.
2 They have a sign with her **age** / **name**.
3 Amy is happy because of the fantastic **burger** / **welcome sign**.
4 She goes to the **cafeteria** / **toilet** before they drive home.

II Listen again and choose the correct word.
1 The Bakers have brought **flowers** / **a welcome sign** with them for Amy.
2 Amy likes the **pumpkin pie** / **burger**.
3 Amy is a bit nervous about her first day **at school** / **at her host family's house**.
4 Jenna's school has no **dress code** / **café**.

III Listen again and complete the sentences.
1 Amy is a bit ??? about her first school day.
2 Jenna thinks Amy's accent sounds ???.
3 You do not have to wear a ??? at the school.
4 "French fries" is what Americans call ???.
5 Jenna's room is ??? ??? Amy's room.

5c wordbank: American and British English p.165

Listen again. What differences between American and British English do you notice?

5d workbook p.24/7b, 8

Imagine you are Amy. At the end of your first day in the USA, write a text message home and tell your family or friends about your first day.

Amy's first day at school

6a   skill: reading p. 156

Amy has promised her friends and family to blog about her experiences. Read about her first day at school. Who does she meet?

https://www.pic-on-air.co.uk/holidays   × −

1   *Philadelphia, 2 September*
Hi everyone,

Today was my first day at school. It took me some time to decide on an outfit, but I really liked wearing my own clothes to school. After breakfast (there are so many different kinds of cereal
5   here, I hope I can try them all before the year is over), we went to the school bus stop.

We were picked up by a yellow school bus that looked exactly like the ones you see in American films. They are for schoolchildren only. Almost everyone goes to school by bus,
10   or they drive their own car if they are over 16.

I was a bit nervous, but my host sister, Jenna, was with me. She thinks that it is really cool that I can cycle to school at home. Hardly anyone cycles to school over here – either the
15   journey is too long or the parents think it's too dangerous.

Jenna introduced me to some of her friends and they were all really friendly.

At school, I had to go to the school registrar's office first. The registrar gave me my ID card that I have to have with me all the time, my timetable (which is called a 'schedule' over here), all
20   the books I need and the combination number for my locker. Then I had to put all my books in my locker and go to homeroom. That's where they check attendance and give out important information first thing in the morning. It's a bit like registration at home. I was late and they were right in the middle of the Pledge of Allegiance when I opened the door.

American students begin their day by saying: "I pledge allegiance to the flag of the United States of America, and to the republic for which it stands, one nation under God, indivisible, with liberty and justice for all."

Well, anyway, when I walked into the classroom late everyone stared at me and I felt a bit uncomfortable. But my homeroom teacher Mr de Sousa was very nice. He introduced me to the students in my homeroom and asked a girl to help me find my classrooms.

My first lesson was maths (or math as it
is called here …). It's good that I like maths
because school days here are more or
less the same every day. So maths is first
period (as they say here) every day!
Apart from maths, I have science, gym
(we would say PE) – that's only on
Tuesdays and Thursdays – history, English
and my elective, robotics. The electives
are only on the schedule twice a week, too.

Schedule Student ID 130970 Name: Amy Milligan		Grade: 11		
	Mon–Fri	**Subject**	**Room**	**Teacher**
1	7:25 – 8:15	Homeroom, math	W276	de Sousa, Enrico
2	8:20 – 9:10	Science	W161	Birk, Wendy
3	9:15 – 10:05	Geography	W223	Mulvern, Jack
4	10:10 – 11:00	History	W262	Pearce, Sandra
5	11:05 – 11:55	English	W140	Alvarez, Ramos
6	11:55 – 12:45	Lunch; Study period	Cafeteria; Study hall	
7	12:50 – 1:40	Gym (Tue and Thur)	W220	Kracinski, Lea
8	1:45 – 2:35	Elective: robotics (Mon and Fri)	W105 (lab)	Monterres, Patsy

After every lesson I have to go to my locker in the
hallway outside my homeroom and get the books for
my next lesson. We're not allowed to carry big bags
around in the school building.

For lunch, Jenna met me at my locker and took me to
the school cafeteria, which was very busy. There is an
early lunch for freshmen and sophomores (students
in grade 9 and 10) and a late lunch for juniors and
seniors (students in grade 11 and 12).

Jenna and her friends invited me to sit outside with
them. The school has an outside lunch area where
you can eat when the weather is good. There's a wide
variety of food on the menu to choose from.

Jenna told me that the school's fundraiser club served
healthy meals to raise money last year.
They were so successful that the school now takes part
in a "farm to table" programme which means that they
serve organic food that is produced locally.

6b wordbank: American and British English p. 165

**Look at Amy's blog post again and find words that are different in British and American English.
Write them in a list. Do you know any more words in British and American English? Add them.**

6c CHOOSE YOUR LEVEL skill: reading p. 156, writing p. 155

I **Read Amy's blog post again. Find a caption for each picture.**
II **Read Amy's blog post again and write one or two sentences for each picture.**
III **What did Amy do on her first school day? Read her blog post again and take notes.**

6d wordbank: school life p. 164, workbook p. 25/9-11

What did you learn about school life in the USA? Make a list.

A video chat

Listen and read along. What is the difference between clubs and electives?

Amy is videochatting with her best friend Emma in Bath.

Emma: Hi Amy, great to see you. How are you? How was your first week at school?

Amy: I'm fine. I'm doing OK at school although I'm a bit behind in geography and American history. But I really like my elective.

Emma: What's an elective?

Amy: Electives are subjects that you can choose. They're not optional like clubs. You need electives like all your other subjects to collect credits. For your elective you can choose something you really like.

Emma: Ah, OK. So what's your elective?

Amy: Robotics. It's so good. They have a robot here that's like one of those used in car factories. Our teacher has already shown us how to program it to pick up a pen and draw a line on a piece of paper.
That was so amazing. But we can also build robots ourselves. In January, there's going to be a show of different science projects and we'll try to program a short cheerleading routine.

Emma: Wow, cool! You'll have to send me a video!

Amy: Of course I will.

Emma: So, what other electives do they have?

Amy: There are so many! There are different languages, business law, IT stuff like computer repairing and web programming, but also for example auto body repair.

Emma: Business law? That sounds like university.

Amy: Jenna, my host sister, is doing business law because she's thinking about doing law or business at university.

Emma: Can you do more than one elective? Or a different one next term?

Amy: I'm not sure. I'll have to talk to my school guidance counsellor about it.
There are no terms over here. We have two semesters per school year. I'd really like to try plumbing, women's studies and Chinese next semester. Or video game development, fashion design and literature?

Emma: You're so lucky! The only choice I had this year was between French and Spanish.

Ⅰ **Read the dialogue again. Which elective did Amy choose? Does she like it?**

Ⅱ **Read the dialogue again. Make a list of all the electives that Amy mentions.**

Ⅲ **Read the dialogue again. What do you learn about Amy's elective? Take notes.**

High school electives

8a

Read about the high school electives. Which one would you choose? Why?

---

https://www.oldname.co.uk/holidays   × —

Electives

all electives two semesters, 2 credit points, open to grades 10 to 12

× **PERSONAL FINANCE** × × × × × × × × × × ×
Students will learn how to manage their own finances.

× **MARKETING** × × × × × × × × × × × × × × ×
Students will learn about marketing plans and strategies that businesses use to market their products.

× **MOVIE PRODUCTION** × × × × × × × × × ×
Students will learn to write scripts and get to know how to produce a movie.

× **MAINTENANCE** × × × × × × × × × × × × × ×
Students will learn basic repair skills and how to use different tools on household machines.

× **CULINARY ART** × × × × × × × × × × × × × ×
This course will give students experience in the field of food preparation.

× **BASIC WOODWORKING** × × × × × × × × × ×
This course will show students the skills needed for wood processing, the design process and safety precautions.

8b

Which of these electives do you think is most useful? Which is least useful? Why?

You can say:

I think ... is most useful because ...

I think ... is least useful because ...

8c workbook p.27/14

What electives are there at your school? What electives would you like to have?

Different schools

9 skill: talking with people, p.154

Talk about what you know about schools in the UK and the USA. What is the same at your school? What is different? What would you like to have at your school, too?

School life

10 CHOOSE YOUR TASK wordbank: school life p.164

A **Design a poster for prom night.**

B **Write a radio commercial for a student exchange programme to the USA. Record it.**

C **Find out more about cheerleading or prom night. Do some research and give a short presentation.**

COME TO **PROM** *Night*

WHEN: 30 July
WHERE: in the auditorium
HOW MUCH: $50.00 – $80.00 per ticket
DRESS CODE: evening dress

ACTIVATE   PRACTISE   **DEVELOP**   PRACTISE   APPLY

British or American?

11 audio 1/20, wordbank: American and British English p. 165

Listen to the three mini dialogues. Say whether the first or the second speaker is American. Compare your results in class.

You can say:

Dialogue 1: I think the first / second speaker is ...

A German elective

12 skill: mediation p. 157

Read the description of an elective from a German school. Explain in English what it is about.

> **Technik im Haushalt**
>
> In diesem **Wahlpflichtkurs** untersuchen wir elektrische Haushaltsgeräte. Wir schauen uns zum Beispiel Mixer, Taschenlampen, elektrische Zahnbürsten und Toaster genauer an. Ihr könnt kaputte Gegenstände mitbringen, die wir dann versuchen zu reparieren. Außerdem finden wir heraus, wie die Geräte möglichst lange halten.
>
> Wir beschäftigen uns mit verschiedenen Möglichkeiten des Energiesparens im Haushalt, bestimmen den Energieverbrauch der Geräte und überlegen, wie möglichst wenig Strom verbraucht wird.

Words and phrases you might need: *household machines, to last as long as possible, to save energy, to find out how much energy the devices need, ...*

The yearbook club

13a audio 1/22

Listen to the meeting of the yearbook club. What do the students and the teacher talk about?

13b CHOOSE YOUR LEVEL skill: listening p. 153, workbook p. 27/15

Unscramble the sentences and write them down.

1 welcomes everyone – of the yearbook club. – The teacher – to the third meeting
2 to have all the clubs and – on the agenda is – The first point – sports teams covered.
3 some of – Catherine, Carlos and Li – cover – clubs. – the teams and
4 needs a choice of – pictures – from each club and team. – The yearbook club – texts and

Read the questions. Then listen again and take notes. Answer the questions.

1 What team is Catherine writing about?
2 What club is Carlos writing about?
3 What is Li writing about?
4 What does the teacher ask the club members to do?

1 What teams and clubs are Catherine, Carlos and Li writing about?
2 What does the teacher ask the club members to do?
3 How long should the texts be?
4 What problem does Michael mention?

DIGITAL+ practise more 7

ACTIVATE PRACTISE DEVELOP **PRACTISE** APPLY

A yearbook entry TARGET TASK

14 workbook p. 28/16, wordbank: school life p. 164, wordbank: American and British English p. 165, media worksheet 1, 6

Your task is to create one page for an American high school yearbook.
Before you start, look at these steps:

STEP 1

Work with a partner or in a small group.

STEP 2

Imagine you are American high school students. Choose a topic for your page.
You can think of:
· a typical American sport like baseball, football, lacrosse, …
· an elective like welding, business law, light and sound technology, …
· an event like prom night, homecoming, …
· …

STEP 3

Research your topic and take notes.
Make sure to write down the sources of your information.

STEP 4

Write a first draft. Add matching pictures.
Think of a good headline.

STEP 5

Ask classmates for feedback.
Edit your page if necessary.

STEP 6

Create the final version of your page.

STEP 7

Present your page in a gallery walk.
You can put all your pages together
and make a (digital) yearbook.

The **Fundraiser Club** came up with
a lot of fun ideas to raise money.
Everyone's favourite was
PAJAMA DAY
in June.

Your school clubs

1 skill: talking with people p.154, workbook p.29/1

What school clubs do you go to? What do you do there? What do you like about the clubs? Talk to each other in small groups.

You can say:
I go to the …
We usually …
I really like … because …

High school clubs

2a workbook p.29/2, 3

Read about some of the clubs that students at Amy and Jenna's school in Philadelphia can join. Which of them do you find interesting? Say why.

Clubs and activities

Mathletics club
Come and stretch your brain muscles! We take part in mathematics competitions for all levels. Classroom 4b, Wednesdays at 4pm.

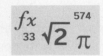

Baseball club
Are you our next best pitcher or catcher? Join the best baseball team in the state of Pennsylvania! Sports hall, Thursdays, 3-5pm.

Glee club
We love singing! If you love singing, too, you should join us in the music room on Tuesday afternoons from 4pm.

Model congress
A role-playing simulation of the United States congress is not only fun but also a place to debate the latest topics.
We meet Mondays, 3-5pm in room 201.

Theater group
Do you love acting and improvising? Then come and join our theater group. Meet us in the auditorium on Tuesdays, 4-5:30pm.

Debating society
Bring your best arguments and help us succeed in the Pennsylvania debate tournament. We meet Thursdays from 4pm in room 201.

Future Business Leaders of America
FBLA High School is a program that helps high school students prepare for careers in business.
Fridays, 3-5pm in room 405.

ACTIVATE PRACTISE DEVELOP PRACTISE APPLY

2b audio 1/24

**Listen to Amy and Jenna and read along.
What school clubs are they talking about?**

Jenna: Hi Amy, what are you up to?

Amy: Hey Jenna, I'm just looking at the after-school clubs.

Jenna: You'll have a lot of fun if you join a club. Don't you have clubs at your school in the UK?

Amy: Not exactly. We have a few clubs, but most of them are only lunchtime clubs. We can't choose from so many cool things like you can here. We also start school later and don't finish lessons until 3pm, so there's less time for after-school clubs. And we definitely have fewer sports clubs.

Jenna: What about younger kids? Are there any school clubs at elementary school?

Amy: When I was in primary school, I went to an after-school club at my school. My parents had to pay for it, and we did lots of different activities there, not just one.

Jenna: I don't think there are clubs you have to pay for around here. Anyway, let's find a good one for you at our school. Is there anything you're especially interested in?

Amy: Not really. It all sounds good. What do

you think of the mathletics club?

Jenna: I did that in my first year at high school, my freshman year. It was fun, but I'm just not good enough at math so I dropped out. If you're really good at math, I think you'll enjoy it.

Amy: I don't think I'm THAT good at maths. Which other clubs have you tried?

Jenna: A lot. Cheerleading, history club, chemistry club, drama, glee club and Future Business Leaders of America.

Amy: Wow! That *is* a lot. What exactly is a "glee club"?

Jenna: It's a singing group! You get together once a week to sing all kinds of songs. The club usually organizes a concert in the fall. If you're interested, we can go to the concert together.

Amy: That sounds good. I'm not great at singing, but I'd love to see the club perform.

2c

Look at the dialogue again. What does Amy say about the school clubs at her school in the UK?

2d CHOOSE YOUR LEVEL audio 1/25, skill: listening p. 153

I Listen to the rest of the dialogue. Which club is Jenna going to this year?

II Listen to the rest of the dialogue. Which clubs does Amy choose in the end?

III Listen to the rest of the dialogue. Which clubs do the girls choose?

2e workbook p. 30/4

**What is the same at your school?
What is different?
Are there any clubs you would like to have?**

You can say:

At Jenna's school there is / are ...

We also have ... / We don't have ...

I would love to have ... at our school.

GRAMMAR HELP   conditional clauses type 1 (R) p. 180

Bedingungssätze kennst du bereits. Sie drücken aus, was geschehen wird oder kann, wenn etwas anderes passiert. Sieh dir die Beispielsätze an: In welchem Teil wird die Bedingung genannt? In welchem Teil wird ausgedrückt, was passiert, wenn die Bedingung erfüllt ist?

If you're really good at maths, you'll enjoy the mathletics club. You will have a lot of fun if you join a club. If you love singing, you should join us.	Wenn du in Mathe wirklich gut bist, (dann) wird dir die Mathe-AG gefallen. Du wirst viel Spaß haben, wenn du in eine AG gehst. Wenn du gern singst, solltest du zu uns kommen.

Auf Seite 180 kannst du nachlesen, was bei dieser Art von Bedingungssätzen zu beachten ist.

Choosing a club

3   grammar: conditional 1 (R) p. 180, workbook p. 31/5

Match the sentence parts and write down the sentences.

1 If you love singing,
2 If you're interested in the work of the congress,
3 You'll enjoy the debating society
4 If you see yourself as a future leader,

A if you like competing in debate tournaments.
B the FBLA could be a good club for you.
C you should join the glee club.
D you can join the model congress.

What if …

4   grammar: conditional 1 (R) p. 180, workbook p. 31/6

David from London is thinking about spending a year in another country as an exchange student. Copy the sentences and fill in the gaps to make conditional sentences (type 1).

1 If I ??? (go) to Germany as an exchange student, I ??? (be able to) improve my German.
2 If I ??? (spend) a year in Australia, I ??? (not be able to) fly home for Christmas.
3 I ??? (not be) here for my best friend's birthday if I ??? (go) abroad.
4 If my friend ??? (have) a party for his birthday, I ??? (miss) it.
5 If I ??? (stay) at home, I ??? (not know) what it is like to go to school in another country.
6 If I ??? (go) to another country, my friends and family ??? (miss) me and I ??? (miss) them.

You can write:

1. If I go to …, I will be able to …

Different languages?

5a   workbook p. 31/7

Unscramble these American English words and write them down.

prgraom · lfal · viemo · mhat · csheudle

5b   wordbank: American and British English p. 165

Find the British English words for the American words and write them down.

 DIGITAL+ practise more 8

ACTIVATE   **PRACTISE**   DEVELOP   PRACTISE   APPLY

Plans for next Friday

6a

**Amy and her host family are talking about their plans for next Friday.
Look at the pictures. What do you think are they going to do?**

6b ▣ audio 1/27

Listen to Amy and her host family. What is a "tailgate party"?

6c CHOOSE YOUR LEVEL skill: listening p. 153, workbook p. 32/8

▌Listen again and match the sentence parts. Write the sentences down.

1 Her mum tells Jenna	A first performance with the marching band.
2 Ben is a little nervous about his	B tailgate party of the season.
3 Dad is looking forward to the first	C what there is for dinner.

▌▌Listen again and take notes. Then complete the sentences with the words from the box.

1 The family is having ??? for dinner.
2 Ben is going to ??? with the marching band at the football game next Friday.
3 Before the football game, there will be a ??? in the parking lot.
4 Jenna's dad is going to make ??? for the tailgate party.

> perform ·
> tailgate party ·
> chilli ·
> salad and baked
> potatoes

▌▌▌Listen again and take notes. Write about what each family member is going to do on Friday.

A high school football game

7a skill: writing p. 155, media worksheet 7, 10

Read what Amy wrote about the football game in her blog. Write down at least three words from the blog entry that you would hashtag.

× −

1   Wow, I have so much to tell you about the football game last Friday. It was brilliant – not only the game but the whole afternoon and evening.

Before the game, I had my very first tailgate party and I LOVED it! It's like an opening act for the
5   game and happens in the school's parking lot (that's a car park) around the cars. "Tailgate" is the American English word for car boot. They also call it "trunk". Sometimes these different words are a bit confusing …

10   My host family and I and a lot of other families drove up to the school and took out camping tables and chairs from our car boots. Everyone unpacked lots of tasty food and drinks to share, like popcorn and chips (or as we would say "crisps"). Some people even barbecued hot dogs and burgers. It smelt delicious! We brought a large pot of "the best chilli in the world", which I had helped my host dad prepare. The chilli was REALLY good.

15   Getting to know people and chatting to them in such a relaxed atmosphere was really nice. Everyone was so friendly, they all introduced themselves to me. I met some more of Jenna and Ben's friends, and I ate too many hot dogs …

Then we went to our seats in the stadium, which looks like a stadium for professional football and not like a school playing field at all. Jenna explained the rules to me, but I'm still not sure
20   if I understand everything correctly. But watching the players, the cheerleaders and the brilliant marching band was amazing anyway. The atmosphere in the stadium was electric. It was really exciting. Everyone seemed to be enjoying themselves so much. There is an incredible team spirit at the high school – most of the students and many of their families come out to watch, cheer for their team and have a good time.

25   My host brother, Ben, is a member of the marching band who played before the match and at half-time. They played their instruments while walking in patterns on the field – it all looked quite complicated. Ben had been a bit
30   nervous before, but everything went well, and he was really happy with himself afterwards.

The cheerleading was also really cool. I have never seen such high jumps and impressive flips before. There are both boys and girls in the team and they did a really good job in cheering the players on to do their best. They created a very special atmosphere.

     ACTIVATE   PRACTISE   **DEVELOP**   PRACTISE   APPLY

35 There was so much going on – it was almost like a carnival! I also liked the cheerleaders' chant. Everyone in the stadium knew it and shouted it really loudly. It goes like this:

Hey, Hey

Hey, Hey are you ready? *(double clap)*

Are you ready? *(double clap)*

40   To play *(clap)*

Say go team *(clap)*

Go team *(clap)*

Panthers all the way!

"The Panthers" is the name of the school team. They won the match, and the stadium went crazy!
45 I'm really looking forward to the next football game!

7b CHOOSE YOUR LEVEL   skill: reading p.156

▌ Read the blog entry again and answer the questions.

1 What are the two American English words for "car boot"?
2 What is the American English word for "crisps"?

3 Where did Amy's host family drive to?
4 What was in the pot that Amy's family brought?
5 What did Amy find really nice?

▌▌ Read the blog entry again and answer the questions.

1 Where does a tailgate party take place?
2 What two other words for the word "tailgate" are mentioned?
3 What did Amy and her host family take to the tailgate party?

4 What does the high school stadium look like?
5 Who comes to the stadium to watch the game?

▌▌▌ Read the blog entry again and answer the questions.

1 What do people take to a tailgate party?
2 What do people do at a tailgate party?
3 What does Amy say about the stadium?

4 What did the marching band do?
5 What did the cheerleaders do?
6 How did the game end?

7c

Find words and phrases in Amy's blog post that can be used to describe an atmosphere.

You can write:

brilliant, I loved it., such a relaxed …

7d wordbank: descriptions p.163, media worksheet 13, workbook p.32/9, 10

What other words or phrases to describe an atmosphere can you think of?
Add them to your list. Use them to write a short text about a school event at your school.

LAND & LEUTE 4 📺 video 10

Sport in den USA

Sport spielt in den USA eine wichtige Rolle, vor allem in der Schule. Es ist für viele amerikanische Schülerinnen und Schüler genauso wichtig, gut in Sport zu sein wie in Mathe, Naturwissenschaften oder Englisch. Manche Feiertage sind auch sportliche Höhepunkte. Am Neujahrstag und an *Thanksgiving* finden die Footballspiele der Colleges statt. Jedes Team hat seine eigenen Cheerleader, Sprechgesänge und Tänze, um die Zuschauerinnen und Zuschauer dazu zu animieren, ihr Team anzufeuern. Manche Sportereignisse sind sogar nationale Ereignisse, die im Fernsehen gezeigt und von Millionen von Menschen gesehen werden, zum Beispiel der *Super Bowl* (American Football) oder *Opening Day* (Baseball).

Sieh dir den Videoclip an. Was findet ihr über Baseball heraus? Sprecht darüber.

American football

8a 📺 video 11, skill: watching a video clip p. 158, media worksheet 8

Watch the video clip. What is the main aim in American football?

8b   workbook p. 33/11

Watch the video clip again and answer the questions.

1 When was the first football match?
2 How many players are on the field?
3 Why can a 60-minute game take up to 3 hours?
4 What is a full-contact sport?
5 What does NFL stand for?

Sports

9 CHOOSE YOUR TASK   C: media worksheet 6

A **Create a poster for a sports event.**
B **Search the Internet for cheerleading chants or write your own chant.**
C 📺 **Choose one sport that is popular in the USA. Do some research, make a fact file and tell your class about the sport.**

C
       Fact File: Baseball
Number of players: 9 in each team
Aim of the game: to score more runs (= points) around the 4 bases than the other team by hitting the ball as far as possible
Equipment: a baseball bat, gloves, a helmet and a ball
Famous players: "Babe" Ruth, Max Kepler, Mike Trout

Exchange challenges

10 GET TOGETHER

Get together with a partner.
Do a role play about an exchange student's problems.

Partner A
▎ Go to page 131.
▎▎ Go to page 134.
▎▎▎ Go to page 137.

Partner B
▎ Go to page 140.
▎▎ Go to page 143.
▎▎▎ Go to page 146.

A video call

11a   skill: mediation p. 157

Your school has invited some exchange students from the USA. Before they travel, you and your mother have a video call with your exchange partner, Aaron. Your mother cannot speak English very well. Help her and Aaron to understand each other.

Aaron: How will I get to your house?
Is there a bus from the airport?
(1) You: *Er fragt, wie …*

Your mother: Sag ihm, dass wir ihn mit dem Auto vom Flughafen abholen.
(2) You: *We'll …*

Aaron: That's very kind of you. I'm already looking forward to my trip.
(3) You: *Er sagt, dass …*

Your mother: Frag doch mal, was er gerne isst oder gar nicht mag. Und ob wir irgend-welche Allergien berücksichtigen müssen.
(4) You: *…*

Aaron: I'm not allergic to anything.
But I am a vegan so I don't eat any animal products. I like to eat toast and jam in the morning so I don't need any special milk. The only thing I really don't like, aside from animal products, is carrots.
(5) You: *…*

Your mother: Sag ihm, dass das gar kein Problem ist. Er kann auch gern mit zum Einkaufen kommen und sich ein paar Sachen aussuchen.
(6) You: *…*

Aaron: Oh great. Thank you very much.
(7) You: *…*

11b   workbook p. 34/12

What could you do to make your exchange student feel welcome?
Collect ideas and write a dos and don'ts list.

You can write:
dos: write a welcome sign, …
don'ts: cook what they don't like, …

Enjoy yourself!

12 grammar: reflexive pronouns p. 181, workbook p. 34/13

Choose the correct reflexive pronouns from the box and complete the sentences. There are more pronouns than you need.

1 After their performance, the cheerleaders were happy with ???.
2 I cut ??? when I was making the chilli.
3 Before the game, the coach told his team: "Enjoy ???!"
4 Ben was proud of ??? after his performance.
5 We really enjoyed ??? at the game.

> myself
> yourself
> himself, herself, itself
> ourselves
> yourselves
> themselves

Doing an interview

13a skill: talking with people p. 154, media worksheet 17

Here are seven tips on how to do an interview. Find a good order and write the tips down.

You can write:

1. E: Think about …

A Ask him or her to repeat their answer if you don't understand it.
B Thank your interview partner politely.
C Introduce yourself politely.
D Say goodbye.
E Think about an interview topic and prepare questions.
F Ask your questions.
G Give your partner enough time to answer your questions.

13b

Compare your results with a partner.

Preparing for an interview

14 CHOOSE YOUR LEVEL

▌ Unscramble the questions and write them down.
1 like – exchange experience – your – Did you – ?
2 meet – When did – host parents – you – your – ?
3 new school – did you – How – like – your – ?

▌▌ Match the sentence parts and write down the questions.
1 Did you
2 What did you enjoy most
3 Was there
4 What was
5 What could have been

A about your exchange experience?
B like your exchange experience?
C surprising about your exchange experience?
D better?
E anything you didn't like?

▌▌▌ Complete the questions with question words and write them down.
1 ??? did you contact when you started planning your exchange?
2 ??? did you start planning your exchange?
3 ??? did you like your exchange experience?
4 ??? exactly did you like or not like?
5 ??? could have been better?
6 ??? do you think of life in the United States?

DIGITAL+ practise more 9

ACTIVATE   PRACTISE   DEVELOP   **PRACTISE**   APPLY

Interviewing an exchange student TARGET TASK

15 workbook p. 35/14, skill: performing a scene p.161, media worksheet 2, 5, 17

Your task is to carry out a role play of an interview with an exchange student. Before you start, look at these steps:

STEP 1

Work with a partner. Imagine you get the chance to interview Amy or another exchange student about their experiences.

STEP 2

Collect questions and answers.
Think about:
· the host family
· new friends
· lessons at the new school
· electives and school clubs
· sports and activities
· …

> **TIP**
>
> Choose questions that make your interview partner talk, for example
> "What do you think …?",
> "How was …?",
> "When did you …?" or
> "Where did you …?

STEP 3

Plan your role play.
· Decide who is playing which role.
· Decide on the questions you are going to ask and in which order to ask them.
· Write cue cards if you need help.

STEP 4

Practise your role play.

STEP 5

Present your role play as an audio recording or a video clip or act it out in class.

Check out

1. Kannst du kurze Texte aus einem Jahrbuch verstehen?	Workbook, p. 36
2. Kannst du darüber sprechen, was du über den Schulalltag in den USA weißt?	Workbook, p. 37
3. Kannst du den Inhalt einer deutschen Kursbeschreibung auf Englisch wiedergeben?	Workbook, p. 38
4. Kannst du einem Gespräch über Schul-AGs wichtige Informationen entnehmen?	Workbook, p. 38
5. Kannst du einen kurzen Text über eine Schulveranstaltung schreiben?	Workbook, p. 39
6. Kennst du Unterschiede zwischen dem britischen und dem amerikanischen Englisch?	Workbook, p. 39

You should see me in a crown

1 *Liz Lighty, the main character in Leah Johnson's novel You should see me in a crown, had plans. She's going to win a scholarship*
5 *to Pennington, the college she's always wanted to go to, and leave her old life behind as quickly as possible. But then she gets the letter telling her that she*
10 *didn't get that scholarship. There might still be a chance for her to get another scholarship – the one her school gives out every year to prom king and queen.*

15 "I'm not running for prom queen." I fold the paper and shove it back into his hand. Now I am laughing. I seriously can't help it. "Are you kidding me?"

"I'm serious (…), big sis. (…) You need the
20 money, and they're giving money away. It seems like the perfect solution to me." Other schools have huge endowments for athletics or the arts, but Campbell County High School has one for prom.

25 (…) our rich alums (…) ensure that we have the biggest, most elaborate spectacle of a prom season in Indiana every year. And part of that spectacle happens to be the massive scholarships they give to the prom
30 king and queen, for what they like to call the "outstanding service and community engagement" the winners must display. (…)

"Look, this money could be enough to at least get you to Pennington, you know?
35 You win, and Granny and Grandad keep the house."

My stomach churns at the thought of one of my classmates getting that scholarship. All that money just for playing dress-up and
40 picking up trash on the playground. All that money going to another Campbell County rich kid with too much time on their hands and no fear of the spotlight. It isn't fair. None of it is fair.

45 I think about the speeches and the public events and how visible the prom court candidates are every year. (…) There's no way to hide when you run for prom queen; there's no way to fly under the radar when
50 you want that title. (…)

---

novel = *Roman*; **scholarship** = *Stipendium*; **to run** = *kandidieren*; **prom queen** *(AE)* = *Ballkönigin*; **I can't help it.** = *Ich kann nicht anders.*;
Are you kidding me? *(informal)* = *Ist das dein Ernst?*; **to be serious** = *es ernst meinen*; **sis** *(informal)* = *Schwester*; **endowments** *(pl)* = *Stiftungsgelder*; **alum** *(informal)* = *Absolvent/in*; **to ensure** = *garantieren*; **elaborate** = *raffiniert*; **outstanding** = *außergewöhnlich*; **to churn** = *sich heftig drehen*; **fear** = *Angst*; **none** = *nichts*; **speech** = *Rede*; **visible** = *sichtbar*; **candidate** = *Kandidat/in*; **to fly under the radar** = *unter dem Radar fliegen*

Everything about the idea is ridiculous, but I
can't stop thinking about it. (…)
"Ro, be realistic." I shake my head and
slip down to the floor. "I'm nobody's prom
55 queen."
"Pennington is important to you, right?"
He sits down next to me and bumps my
shoulder with his.
I nod, even though he already knows the
60 answer to that. (…)
"You got three days to get thirty signatures
and declare yourself a candidate. You've got
my vote, big sis. (…)"

The next day, when they meet at the store
65 *where Liz works in the afternoons, Liz*
tells her friends that she hasn't gotten the
scholarship to Pennington.

Their reactions are immediate.
Britt cracks her knuckles. "That's such
70 garbage! Nobody deserves that scholarship
more –"
Gabi shakes her head. "I'm going to take care
of this, I'll have my parents' lawyer call –"
Stone grabs the crystal pendant hanging
75 from her necklace. "I have palo santo in my
purse. We can cleanse your clarinet and –"
I wave my hands in front of me with a quiet
laugh. (…)
"Guys, it's cool. It's fine. Well, not fine. It's
80 pretty awful actually. But it'll be okay. I have
a plan."
Like a lightbulb, Gabi's face instantly shifts
from rage to recognition.

"We're going to make you prom queen," she
85 says simply, reading my mind.
"We're gonna what?" Britt narrows her eyes.
"My sentiment exactly," I mumble. (…)
In a concert band, you're arranged into
sections so that the instruments and
90 sounds in your ear are the most similar to
your own (…).

High school friend groups are something
like an ensemble in that way. My friends
are certified oddballs, the inkblots on an
95 otherwise pure white page, and it's why we
work together so well. Because as long as
they're my people, as long as they're the ones
on my left and my right, sometimes I can
forget that I don't fit in anywhere else in this
100 town. (…)

"Lizzie; I was born to be a fairy godmother;
it's my destiny." Gabi plops her highlighter
yellow (…) bag next to the register and pulls
her phone out of it. Her fingers fly across
105 the screen so quickly, I almost don't notice
she's speaking. "A couple slight changes, and
you'll be as good as new. Certifiably prom
queen ready." (…)

And just like that, I'm Campbell County High
110 School's newest prom queen contender.

What is Liz's first reaction to her brother's suggestion?
What do you think: how will the novel end? Why?

ridiculous = *albern;* signature = *Unterschrift;* vote = *Stimme;* gotten *(AE) = Partizip von get;* to crack = *knacken;* knuckle = *Knöchel;* garbage *(AE) = Müll, Abfall;* to deserve = *verdienen;* lawyer = *Rechtsanwalt/Rechtsanwältin;* purse *(AE) = Handtasche;* to cleanse = *reinigen;* clarinet = *Klarinette;* rage = *Wut;* recognition = *Anerkennung;* to read one's mind = *jemandes Gedanken lesen;* sentiment = *Ansicht, Meinung;* to mumble = *murmeln;* certified = *geprüft, garantiert;* oddball = *Verrückte/r;* inkblot = *Tintenklecks;* fairy godmother = *Märchenfee;* destiny = *Schicksal;* register *(AE) = Kasse;* slight = *gering;* certifiably = *nachweisbar;* contender = *Bewerber/in*

prom dress

I'm nearing the end of my fourth year
I feel like I've been lacking crying too many tears
Everyone seemed to say it was so great,
but did I miss out
Was it a huge mistake?

I can't help the fact I like to be alone
It might sound kinda sad, but that's just what I
seem to know
I tend to handle things usually by myself
And I can't ever seem to try and ask for help

I'm sitting here, crying in my prom dress
I'd be the prom queen, if crying was a contest
Make-up is running down, feelings are all around
How did I get here? I need to know

I guess I maybe had a couple expectations
I thought I'd get to them, but no, I didn't
I guess I thought that prom was gonna be fun
But now I'm sitting on the floor and
all I wanna do is run

I keep collections of masks upon my wall
To try and stop myself from revealing it all
Affecting others is the last thing I would do
I keep to myself, though I want to break through

I hold so many small regrets
And what-ifs down inside my head
Some confidence it couldn't hurt me
My demeanor is often misread

I'm sitting here, crying in my prom dress
I'd be the prom queen, if crying was a contest
Make-up is running down, feelings are all around
How did I get here? I need to know

I guess I maybe had a couple expectations
I thought I'd get to them, but no, I didn't
I guess I thought that prom was gonna be fun
But now I'm sitting on the floor and
all I wanna do is run

All I wanna do is run
All I wanna do is run
All I wanna do is run

I'm sitting here, crying in my prom dress
I'd be the prom queen, if crying was a contest
Make-up is running down, feelings are all
around
How did I get here? I need to know

I guess I maybe had a couple expectations
I thought I'd get to them, but no, I didn't
I guess I thought that prom was gonna be fun
But now I'm sitting on the floor and all I wanna
do is run

All I wanna do is run

Listen to the song by mxmtoon.
How does it make you feel?

to near = *sich nähern*; to lack = *nicht haben*; to miss out = *verpassen*; to tend to = *neigen zu*; to handle = *bewältigen*; by oneself = *allein*; crying = *Weinen*; contest = *Wettbewerb*; expectation = *Erwartung*; to get to = *hier: erfüllen*; mask = *Maske*; upon = *an*; to reveal = *enthüllen*; to affect = *Einfluss haben auf, schaden*; to keep to oneself = *ein/e Einzelgänger/in sein*; to break through = *durchbrechen*; regret = *Bedauern*; confidence = *Vertrauen, Zuversicht*; to hurt = *schaden*; demeanor *(AE)* = *Benehmen, Auftreten*; to misread = *falsch verstehen*

1. Describe the pictures. What situation do you think the people are in?
2. What do the pictures have in common?
3. Think of a caption for each picture.

My world today

Part A Relationships

· Du sprichst über Freundschaft und was gute Freundschaft ausmacht.
· Du hörst dir eine Podcast-Episode über Freundschaft an.
· Du schreibst einen Text für einen Freundschaftsbaum.

Part B Digital communication

· Du unterhältst dich über digitale Kommunikation.
· Du hörst dir eine Podcast-Episode über Cyberbullying an.
· Du sammelst Tipps für Online-Kommunikation.

Friends and friendship

1   workbook p. 40/1

What comes to mind when you think about the terms "friends" and "friendship"? Collect ideas in class and talk about them.

You can say:

"Friends" are … to me.
I think "friendship" means …
A friend should / shouldn't …
…

What is going on?

2a   wordbank: feelings p. 166

Look at the pictures and describe what you see. How do you think the teenagers are feeling?

depressed · happy · excited · angry · glad · upset · worried · unhappy · disappointed · …

2b

Choose one picture. What do you think happened before the picture was taken? What is going to happen next?

You can say:

I think the boy in picture 1 …
Maybe they are going to …
…

Friends

3a   skill: reading p. 156

Read what these teenagers say. Who says that their brothers are their best friends? Who says that their best friend has just moved to another city?

 Janet: I don't have one best friend. I have a group of friends and some other kids I talk to sometimes, but there is no one I would call my BFF. I always have someone I can talk to or do things with. I like it that way.

 Linh: I have two good friends, Ruby and Anne. They are both great! The problem is: Ruby and Anne can't stand each other. That can be quite difficult for me because we can never do things as a group. I wish they would get along with each other.

Arda: My friends are the guys I play games with online. I've tried to make some friends in real life, but there's no one who's interested in the same things. My online friends are all into the same stuff as I am. They just don't live near me. I will keep on trying to make some "offline friends", though.

Reese: Some people think it's strange, but my brothers are my best friends. We are very close in age: Matt is in 7th grade, and Andy is one year older than me. We spend almost all our free time together. Who needs other friends when you have the best brothers in the world?

Luis: Jake and Mason were my friends in 7th grade, but this year they only want to hang out with their other friends from the basketball team. I'm not good at basketball, and I don't really like those other guys. I told Jake and Mason that I was unhappy with the situation, but nothing has changed so far.

Lucia: I've been a little sad lately because my best friend Tom moved to another city two weeks ago. We used to do everything together. There are a few kids I hang out with, but it's just not the same without Tom. I didn't think it would be so hard! I talked to him yesterday, and he told me that most of his classmates seemed OK but that he hadn't made any new friends yet. He said that the first week had been really boring and that he missed me a lot.
I wonder if I'll ever be able to make a new best friend …

3b CHOOSE YOUR LEVEL workbook p.40/2

I Read the statements again. Who is unhappy with their situation? Why?

You can write:

Linh is not happy with the situation because …
She wants to … but …
…

II Read the statements again. Choose one of the unhappy teenagers and give them some advice.

You can write:

Dear …, I think you could …
Why don't you …?
…

III Read the statements again. Choose one of the other people who are mentioned in the statements and write a statement about the situation from their point of view.

You can write:

… was my best friend but now …
I'm not happy that … but …
…

GRAMMAR HELP reported speech 2 p. 182

Indirekte Rede *(reported speech)* verwendest du, wenn du wiedergeben möchtest, was jemand sagt bzw. gesagt hat. Wenn das Verb im einleitenden Satz in der Vergangenheit steht, gibt es Veränderungen im Satz. Was fällt dir auf? Was verändert sich?

Direkte Rede:
Arda: "I **will keep on** trying to make some offline friends." „Ich **werde** weiter **versuchen**, ein paar Freunde offline zu finden."
Tom: "Most of **my** classmates **seem** OK."
Tom: "**I haven't made** any new friends yet."
Tom: "The first week **was** really boring."

Indirekte Rede:
Arda said that **he would keep on** trying to make some offline friends. Arda sagte, dass **er** weiter **versuchen werde**, ein paar Freunde offline zu finden.
Tom told me that most of **his** classmates **seemed** OK.
Tom told me that **he hadn't made** any new friends yet.
Tom told me that the first week **had been** really boring.

Auf Seite 182 findest du weitere Beispiele und Erklärungen zur indirekten Rede.

What Tom said

4   grammar: reported speech 2 p. 182

Imagine you met Tom at a party and talked to him. The next day, you report to another friend what Tom told you.

1   Tom: "I have lots of hobbies."
2   Tom: "I like music and basketball."
3   Tom: "I haven't played basketball for two weeks."
4   Tom: "I'm also thinking of joining a band."
5   Tom: "My best friend Lucia and I were in a band."

You can write:
Tom told me that he had …
He said that he …
…

Reporting statements

5   grammar: reported speech 2 p. 182, workbook p. 41/3, 4

Write down what the people said. Underline the words that you had to change.

1   Janet: "I don't have one best friend."
2   Linh: "Ruby and Anne aren't talking to each other."
3   Arda: "My online friends are my best friends."
4   Reese: "My brothers are very important to me."
5   Luis: "I spoke to Jake and Mason yesterday."
6   Luis: "They want to meet me next weekend for a game of basketball."

You can write:
Janet said that <u>she</u> <u>didn't</u> have …
Linh said that …
Arda mentioned that …
Reese said that …
Luis mentioned that …
He added that …

 DIGITAL+ practise more 10-11

ACTIVATE   **PRACTISE**   DEVELOP   PRACTISE   APPLY

Penny's podcast

6a

How would you finish this sentence: "Friends are people who ...?" Share your ideas in class.

6b 🎧 audio 2/1

Listen to the podcast episode about friendship.
Which of your ideas from 6a can you hear in the podcast?

6c CHOOSE YOUR LEVEL skill: listening p. 153, workbook p. 42/5, 6

I Listen again and choose the right words. Copy the sentences into your exercise book.

1 Friends are people who are interested in your **thoughts / looks**.
2 Friends are people who you feel **shy / good** around and who are **polite / honest** with you.

II Listen again and complete the sentences with the words from the box.

1 Friends are people who are ??? in you.
2 Friends are people you feel ??? around.
3 Friends are people who are ??? with you.
4 Friends are people who accept that you aren't ???.
5 Friends could be people who you don't ???.

honest · perfect ·
expect · good ·
interested

III Listen again and complete the sentences with the words from the box.

1 Friends ask lots of ??? and are interested in your ???.
2 Friends always make you feel ??? to talk about ??? stuff, too.
3 Friends don't talk about you behind your ???.
4 Friends understand that you have ??? and ???.
5 Any new ??? you ??? might ??? a friend.

strengths · back ·
weaknesses · become ·
meet · difficult ·
safe · person ·
questions · answers

Your opinion

7a wordbank: expressing opinions p. 168

What are your thoughts on what makes a good friend? Make notes.

You can write:
· *being honest, loyal, fun, ...*
· *someone you can rely on*
· *...*

7b 🎬📱 media worksheet 15

Use your notes from 7a and write a short comment.

What makes a really good friend?
Some people say that ..., others think that ...
In my opinion, ...
To sum it up, ...

An interview

8a   skill: reading p. 156

Scan the interview with Professor Miller about friendship. How many readers have sent in questions? What do they ask?

1 *Professor Rosanne Miller is a child psychologist and friendship expert from Wisconsin. Jo, a reporter for a teen magazine, asked her to answer some readers' questions.*

5 **Jo:** First, we have an email from Ashley from Buffalo, New York. Her question is: "Why do some people have best friends, and others have just friends?"

Professor Miller: That's a very good question.
10 It's important to know that not everybody has a best friend. If you look at the research on the topic, only one out of four kids say that they have a best friend. So, although it's fantastic to have a best friend, it's actually
15 quite rare.

Jo: Could you give us an example of what you mean by that exactly?

Professor Miller: Sure. Even if you don't have that one person in your life, remember that
20 you may have all kinds of other friends. You may have a neighborhood friend, or a friend you see every week at swim practice. You may have several school friends. And all of those friendships are important. Focus on what you
25 have, not on what you think you're missing.

Jo: Great, thanks. So, next we have a question from Christopher from Denver, Colorado: "I had a friend for a long time, but then he started acting strangely. He said some mean stuff or ignored
30 me. I finally told him I didn't want to be friends anymore. Was that the right thing to do?"

Professor Miller: Now, that's difficult. Maybe other readers have had similar experiences. If you feel very hurt, or you feel like your friend is
35 not listening to you at all, then it might be right to end the friendship. It is essential, however, to stay fair.
Remember that this situation might be difficult for both of you.

40 **Jo:** Do you think it is common for teenagers to end friendships?

Professor Miller: Absolutely. If we look at the research again, we see that in 8th grade, for example, one out of four friendships
45 does not last until the end of the year. It can be difficult to get along with others, for anyone at any age.

Jo: That's quite sad, but it makes sense. Our next question picks up on what you have
50 just said. Sarah from Davis, California, asks: "What if a friend is being mean to you, but you still want them to be your friend?"

Professor Miller: In any friendship, you're going to experience difficult situations.
55 But let me remind you that no one is perfect. And we have to forgive our friends – and ourselves! – for not being perfect. If you do not get along with a friend, it is important that you talk about it. If you, or your friend,
60 are sorry about what happened, you have to tell each other. Sometimes it helps to spend a few days apart and think about what happened, and then talk to each other. Talking, being honest, acting responsibly and
65 being fair are important behaviors in staying friends.

ACTIVATE   PRACTISE   **DEVELOP**   PRACTISE   APPLY

8b CHOOSE YOUR LEVEL

❙ Read the interview and answer the questions.

1 Who is Rosanne Miller?
2 How many people ask questions and what are their names?
3 Who can be a friend?

❙❙ Read the interview and answer the questions.

1 What is Rosanne Miller's job?
2 How did Christopher's friend hurt him?
3 How should you behave when you end a friendship?
4 How many friendships do not last during 8th grade?

❙❙❙ Read the interview and answer the questions.

1 Why did Jo talk to Professor Miller?
2 If you look at the research on the topic, how many teenagers have a best friend?
3 How did Christopher's friend's behaviour change?
4 When should you think about ending a friendship?
5 According to studies, how many friendships end during the 8th grade?

8c

**Look at the readers' questions again and write down one or two statements from
Professor Miller's answers that you think sum up each answer best.
You can find help in the box.**

- Talking, being honest, acting responsibly and being fair are important.
- It's important to know that not everybody has a best friend.
- If you feel very hurt, and you feel like your friend is not listening to you, it might be right to end the friendship.
- Although it's fantastic to have a best friend, it's actually quite rare.
- We have to forgive our friends for not being perfect.

You can write:

*Ashley asks: "Why do some people have best
   friends, and others have just friends?"
   Professor Miller's answers are: "It is ..."
Christopher asks: "Was that ...?"
   Professor Miller's answer is: "If you ..."
Sarah ...*

8d wordbank: expressing opinions p. 168, workbook p. 43/7-9

**Professor Miller says that sometimes
it is better to end a friendship.
Do you agree with her?
Write a text and say why or why not.**

You can write:

*In my opinion, ...
I agree / don't agree with her. I think ...
I agree / disagree with what she says about ...
I think ...*

Six-word stories

9a

You can tell a very long, very interesting story in only six words.
Read the stories and collect ideas in class. Who could be talking? What could have happened?

1   Strangers, friends, best friends, lovers, strangers

2   Love her? Hate her? Said nothing …

3   Painfully he changed "is" to "was".

4   You. Me. Her? I don't know.

9b

Choose the six-word story you like best. What longer story might be hidden within it?
Write down your ideas.

9c   skill: writing p. 155, workbook p. 44 / 10

Write your own six-word story. First choose a topic, for example:
- the best birthday ever
- a bad day at school
- …

Think of words that make the reader imagine a story behind your words.

A video about friendship

10   video 12, skill: watching a video clip p. 158, mediation p. 157, workbook p. 44 / 11

Watch the video clip and take notes on the
most important information. Tell someone
who does not understand English the most
important information in German.

What makes a
good friendship?

Friendship

11   CHOOSE YOUR TASK   A+B: wordbank: feelings p. 166, B: media worksheet 11

A   **Create a picture or collage about what "friendship" means to you and label it.
You can also include sayings and quotes.**

B   **Write a letter or a text message to a friend and tell them why they are such a good friend.**

C   **Present a song or song lyrics about friendship to your class. Tell the class about the
message of the song and what you like or dislike about it.**

A poem

12a

Read the poem. What is your first reaction? What do you think about it?

On the Discomfort of Being in the Same Room as the Boy You Like

1 Everyone is looking at you looking at him.
Everyone can tell. He can tell. So you
spend most of your time not looking at him.
The wallpaper, the floor, there are cracks
5 in the ceiling. Someone has left a can of
iced tea in the corner, it is half empty,
I mean half full. There are four light bulbs
in the standing lamp, there is a fan. You
are counting things to keep from looking
10 at him. Five chairs, two laptops, someone's
umbrella, a hat. People are talking so you
look at their faces. This is a good trick. They
will think you are listening to them and not
thinking about him. Now he is talking. So
15 you look away. The cracks in the ceiling are

in the shape of a whale or maybe an elephant
with a fat trunk. If he ever falls in love with
you, you will lie on your backs in a field
somewhere and look up at the sky and he will
20 say, *Baby, look at that silly cloud, it is a whale!*
and you will say, *Baby, that is an elephant
with a fat trunk*, and you will argue for a bit,
but he will love you anyway.
He is asking a question now and no one has
25 answered it yet. So you lower your eyes from
the plaster and say, *the twenty first, I think*,
and he smiles and says, *oh, cool*, and you
smile back, and you cannot stop your smiling,
oh you cannot stop your smile.

Sarah Kay

discomfort = *Unbehagen*; **wallpaper** = *Tapete*; **crack** = *Riss*; **ceiling** = *Zimmerdecke*; **light bulb** = *Glühbirne*; **fan** = *Ventilator*;
to keep from looking at someone = *sich verkneifen, jemanden anzusehen*; **umbrella** = *Regenschirm*; **shape** = *Form, Gestalt*;
trunk = *Rüssel*; **to look up** = *hochschauen*; **to argue** = *sich streiten*; **plaster** = *Verputz*; **smile** = *Lächeln*

12b CHOOSE YOUR LEVEL skill: reading p. 156, wordbank: feelings p. 166

▌ **Read the poem again and answer the questions.**
1 What does the person in the poem do in order to *not* look at the boy?
2 What does the person think everyone can tell?

▌▌ **Read the poem again and answer the questions.**
1 What is the person in the poem trying *not* to do?
2 What do you think: how is the person feeling at the end of the poem?
3 How would you describe the person in the poem? Write down adjectives to describe him or her.

▌▌▌ **Read the poem again and answer the questions.**
1 What is the person in the poem doing to avoid looking at the boy?
2 What is the "trick" the person in the poem is talking about?
3 Why do you think the person cannot stop smiling at the end of the poem?
4 What is the person in the poem like? Describe him or her.

12c workbook p. 45 / 12

Imagine that the person in the poem and the boy talk to each other after school. Write their dialogue.

You can write:

*I felt … / I tried not to … / I was surprised that …
I'm happy school is over. I …*

ACTIVATE   PRACTISE   **DEVELOP**   PRACTISE   APPLY

He said, she said

13   CHOOSE YOUR LEVEL grammar: reported speech 2 p. 182

Ⅰ Write down what the people said. Choose the correct verb form. Copy the sentences into your exercise book.

1 Michael: "I like Fred." – Michael said that he **had liked / likes / liked** Fred.
2 Sue: "I met Dan on Tuesday." – Sue said that she **meets / met / had met** Dan on Tuesday.
3 Michael: "I have always known Fred." – Michael said that he **always knew / had always known / has always known** Fred.
4 Sue: "I will see Dan on Saturday." – Sue said that she **saw / will see / would see** Dan on Saturday.

Ⅱ Write down what the people said and fill in the verb in the correct tense.

1 Camila: "I like Taylor." – Camila said that she ??? Taylor.
2 Taylor: "I saw Camila yesterday." – Taylor said that he ??? ??? Camila the day before.
3 Taylor: "I will ask Camila on a date." – Taylor said that he ??? ask Camila on a date.
4 Camila: "I have always liked Taylor." – Camila said that she ??? always ??? Taylor.
5 Camila: "I am thinking about Taylor a lot." – Camila said that she ??? ??? about Taylor a lot.

Ⅲ Write down what the people said. Use the verb in the correct tense.

1 Lauren: "I can't sleep because I am so excited."
2 Gabriel: "I am going to the cinema with Lauren next weekend."
3 Lauren: "I have already bought the tickets."
4 Gabriel: "Maybe we will share some popcorn."
5 Lauren: "I spent all my pocket money on the tickets."
6 Gabriel: "I don't really like romantic comedies."

You can write:

Lauren said that she ...

Gabriel ...

...

Quotes on friendship

14a   🔊 audio 2/4

Listen to the quotes and pay particular attention to the way the underlined parts are connected when you speak. What do you notice? Talk about it in German.

1 Good <u>friends are</u> like stars. You <u>don't always</u> see them, but you know <u>they are always</u> there. *(Unknown)*

2 <u>There are</u> friends, <u>there is</u> family, and then <u>there are</u> friends that become family. *(Unknown)*

3 <u>Friends are</u> those rare people who ask how we <u>are and</u> then wait to hear <u>the answer</u>. *(Ed Cunningham)*

14b

Listen again and repeat the quotes.

14c   workbook p. 45/13

Which quote do you like best? Learn it by heart.

🖥 **DIGITAL+** practise more 10-11

ACTIVATE   PRACTISE   DEVELOP   **PRACTISE**   APPLY

A friendship tree TARGET TASK

15 workbook p. 46/14, wordbank: feelings p. 166, skill: writing p. 155, media worksheet 1, 9–16

Your task is to write one or more texts for a friendship tree.
Before you start, look at these steps:

STEP 1

Plan your tree. Decide in class:

- how to make the tree
- what materials to use
- how big it will be
- where to put it
- …

STEP 2

Decide what kind of text or texts you would like to write.
For example:

- collages with pictures and texts
- slogans or quotes
- song lyrics
- poems
- six-word stories
- stories
- …

STEP 3

Write a first version.
Work with a partner and give each other feedback.

STEP 4

Edit your text if necessary.
Write a final version.

STEP 5

Hang your texts on the friendship tree and talk about them.
You can also read out some of the texts in class.

"Many people will walk in and out of your life, but only true friends will leave footprints on your heart."
Eleanor Roosevelt

"Only a true friend would be that truly honest."
Donkey, Shrek

"It's not enough to be friendly. You have to be a friend."
R.J. Palacio

"You can count on me like one, two, three I'll be there."
Bruno Mars

Forever
help each otheR
lIsten to music together
watch moviEs
haNg out
play viDeo games

football friend
LIAN
video games
biking

Digital communication

1   workbook p.47/1

What kinds of digital communication channels do you use?
How often do you use digital communication in your everyday life?

You can say:

I like to share … on …
I prefer voice messages to text messages because …
I check our class group chat every day for …
…

Virtual connections

2a   skill: reading p.156

Work with a partner. Skim the texts. What are they about? Take notes.

Teens on their smartphone habits

I'm **Jayden** and I live in Chicago. I usually spend around three hours a day using my phone. I mostly message my friends, play games and listen to podcasts. I'm really glad there is so much technology nowadays because it means I can keep in touch with my friends that live further away. I also often watch videos without really paying attention – because it helps me relax.

I'm **Olivia** from Tulsa, Oklahoma. I spend very little time on my phone compared to most people I know. I find staring at a little screen all day just boring – I live my life more happily in the real world, not online! I use my phone to contact people. I like the fact that it's fast since they usually reply right away.

I'm **Liam** from Pittsburgh, Pennsylvania, and I'm a phone addict. I even sleep with my phone under my pillow! I probably send more than 200 messages a day, and I can text faster than anyone I know. I also look up everything on the Internet – I love the fact that today we can access information more easily and more quickly than ever before.

GLUED TO OUR SCREENS

According to a study, the majority of US-Americans spend at least <u>five hours on their smartphone each day</u>. That's almost as much time as they spend at school or work! Our cell phones are never far from reach, with the <u>average person sending 13 text messages per day</u>. In fact, 95% of text messages are read and responded to within three minutes of being received.

ACTIVATE   PRACTISE   DEVELOP   PRACTISE   APPLY

https://www.????/?????   × –

299 Comments

 Pete, 43 from Michigan

I am a parent to two teenagers, and I was shocked to learn this week that 59% of US teens have been bullied or harassed online. They are humiliated, or they receive nasty messages and even physical threats, or false rumors are spread about them. Apparently, most of this cyberbullying happens over social media. It has become a major problem. Why can't social media companies react more quickly once you show them proof, and ban bullies from their platforms or block their social media accounts? Why can't schools be stricter and expel students who bully others?

Communication in a digital age

In today's digital age, our communication habits are constantly developing. It seems that what was once not OK can become normal very quickly. A new survey has shown that many young adults are now ending relationships via text or social media – in fact, up to 30% of teenagers admit that they have broken up with their partner via text. Many say that it allows them to choose their words more carefully than in a face-to-face communication.

2b CHOOSE YOUR LEVEL skill: reading p. 156

▌ Read the texts and answer the questions.

1 How much time does Jayden spend using his phone?
2 What is he glad about?
3 What does Olivia think about spending a lot of time on the phone?
4 What does Liam call himself?

▌▌ Read the texts and answer the questions.

1 What does Jayden often do to relax?
2 What does Olivia like about her phone?
3 How many messages does Liam usually send per day?
4 How many messages does the average person send every day?
5 How many US teens have been bullied or harassed online?

▌▌▌ Read the texts and answer the questions.

1 What does Jayden mostly do with his phone?
2 What does Olivia use her phone for?
3 What does Liam love about the Internet?
4 How much time do the majority of US-Americans spend on their phone every day?
5 What was Pete shocked about?
6 How many teenagers admit that they have broken up with someone via text?

2c workbook p. 47/2, 3

When do you prefer face-to-face communication, when digital? Give reasons for your answer.

You can say:

I prefer ... when I ... because ...
I like ... better, but when I ..., I ...

ACTIVATE PRACTISE DEVELOP PRACTISE APPLY

GRAMMAR HELP   adverbs of manner (R) p. 183, comparison of adverbs p. 184

Mit Adverbien der Art und Weise *(adverbs of manner)* kannst du Tätigkeiten näher beschreiben. Adverbien werden in der Regel aus Adjektiven gebildet, indem man *-ly* hinzufügt (z. B. *quickly, easily*), allerdings gibt es auch unregelmäßige Formen (z. B. *fast*).

We can access information easily and quickly.	Wir können leicht und schnell an Informationen gelangen.
I can text fast.	Ich kann schnell texten.

Adverbien der Art und Weise können auch gesteigert werden. Was fällt dir bei den folgenden Beispielen auf?

We can access information today more easily and more quickly than ever before.	Wir können heutzutage leichter und schneller an Informationen gelangen als jemals zuvor.
I can text faster than anyone I know.	Ich kann schneller texten als jeder, den ich kenne.

Auf den Seiten 183-184 findest du weitere Erklärungen und Beispiele zu den Adverbien der Art und Weise.

Modern communication

3a   grammar: adverbs of manner (R) p. 183

Copy the sentences and fill in the gaps with adverbs of manner.

1   I can text very ???. (fast)
2   I can keep in touch with my family ??? via video calls. (easy)
3   I reply to text messages very ???. (quick)
4   You should think ??? about what you post online. (careful)

3b   grammar: comparison of adverbs p. 184, workbook p. 48/4

Copy the sentences and fill in the gaps with the comparative forms of the adverbs of manner. You can find help in the box.

1   I can contact my family ??? over the phone than by writing letters. (easy)
2   I live my life ??? in the real world than online. (happy)
3   Texting allows me to choose my words ???. (careful)
4   I can concentrate ??? when I switch my smartphone off. (good)
5   Students who spend a lot of time online often do ??? in school than students who do not. (bad)

> better ·
> more carefully ·
> worse ·
> more happily ·
> more easily

Who?

4   grammar: comparison of adverbs p. 184, workbook p. 48/5

Copy the questions into your exercise book and answer them.

1   Who can sing most beautifully – you or your friend?
2   Who can draw best in your class?
3   Who cooks worst in your family?

DIGITAL+ practise more 12-14

ACTIVATE   **PRACTISE**   DEVELOP   PRACTISE   APPLY

Emoji misunderstandings

5a skill: talking with people p. 154

What is your favourite emoji and what do you use it for? Talk about it with a partner.

5b

Read the article. What is new to you? Talk about it in class.

You can say:

To me, it is new that …

What about you?

Emojis – a universal language?

1 **Why are they called emojis?**
We are very familiar with the little yellow hands and faces we often see in our digital communication –
5 emojis. But do you know where the word "emoji" comes from? While we often use emojis to help express our emotions, it does not come from the word "emotion". "Emoji" is a
10 combination of two Japanese words: picture (绘 pronounced "eh") and character (文字 pronounced "moji").

History of the emoji
In 1999, the first set of Japanese
15 emojis had just 176 icons. Today, there are over 3,000 emojis. They are used so often that the "face with tears of joy" emoji 😂 was named the Oxford Dictionary's "word of the year" in 2015!

20 **Different interpretations**
Many people think that emojis are like a universal language, but for example the angel emoji 😇 is seen in the west as a symbol of innocence or doing a good deed, whereas in
25 China it can be a signal for death! The hand sign 👌 which is used to mean "OK" in many European countries is an insult in Brazil! A less harmful example of different emoji interpretations is the folded hands 🙏 . In
30 Japanese culture, this represents gratitude or a prayer before a meal, but many people have been using it to represent a high five! There are so many small cultural differences in emoji use, that in 2017 the world's first emoji
35 translator was hired!
What are their limits?
So, you should be aware that there is no guarantee that emojis are understood by everybody! 😉

5c CHOOSE YOUR LEVEL skill: reading p. 156

Ⅰ **Where does the word "emoji" come from? Take notes.**
Ⅱ **What do you learn about the folded hands emoji from the article? Take notes.**
Ⅲ **What emojis are mentioned in the article? What do you learn about them? Take notes.**

5d workbook p. 49/6, 7

Do you think it is helpful to use emojis? Give reasons for your answer.

You can write:

In my opinion, emojis …

I think so because …

Communicating online

6a

Look at the pictures and the headline of the article. What do you think the article is about?

6b

Read the article. Were you right in 6a?

Getting connected

1   In a world where many of us are beginning to feel more comfortable communicating online than offline, what changes in our relationships?

The advantages of digital communication

"There are some advantages," says
5 sociologist Savannah Redford. "We can easily reach our loved ones via a text or a phone call. Also, we can share more of our lives with more people – such as posting holiday photos instead of sending
10 a postcard."

Digital communication is also a cheap and time-saving way to keep in touch with friends and family, which can often mean older relatives feel less alone.
15 For young people, online environments can be a chance to make new friends or find people who share the same hobbies or interests. Marcus, a 15-year-old from Texas, agrees: "I am quite shy at school
20 which means I haven't made many friends there, but when I come home, I have plenty of friends to talk to online. We have met a few times in person, but I prefer talking to them online."

25 **The disadvantages of digital communication**

While the digital age of communication has some benefits, it is important to think about how else it is affecting us.
30 "We now have different expectations of how connected we should be," says Savannah. "We used to have clear boundaries between school or work, home life and friendships. Now people expect that they can contact
35 us at all times and that we respond immediately. I don't think this is always a good thing."

Digital media can also affect our social skills. Without face-to-face interaction,
40 misunderstandings can happen easily, and people can act carelessly.

Laura, a 14-year-old from Philadelphia, has learned that the hard way. "I lost a best friend because of something I said
45 to her online. In real life, I would not have said it, but without having the person right there in front of you, it can be easier to say something offensive."

How to maintain good relationships
50 **online**

The digital world is still a part of our offline lives, and we should act responsibly in both environments. "My top tips for maintaining good relationships are all about respect,"
55 says Savannah. "Think carefully about what

you are saying and how you are saying it. You wouldn't shout all the time in a real conversation, so you shouldn't write in an aggressive way, you shouldn't use all capital
60 letters or too many exclamation points or question marks. Always be polite, even if it means that you have to check your messages again before you click send. And most of all – be yourself.
65 Digital communication should make our life better, not harm it."

6c CHOOSE YOUR LEVEL skill: reading p. 156

I Read the article again. Name two advantages of digital communication.

II Read the article again. What are the advantages and disadvantages of digital communication? Take notes.

III Read the article again. Take notes on what it says about:
- the advantages of digital communication.
- the disadvantages of digital communication.
- how to maintain good relationships online.

6d wordbank: (digital) communication p. 167, expressing opinions p. 168

In class, collect all the advantages and disadvantages you found in 6c. You can add more. Discuss: what do you think are the biggest advantages and disadvantages of digital communication?

You can say:

In my opinion, the biggest advantage is …
I think the biggest disadvantage is …
…

6e skill: writing p. 155, media worksheet 15, workbook p. 50/8

What do you think: are there more advantages of digital communication or more disadvantages? Write a comment.

You can write:

Some people say …, but I think …
I'm not so sure that …
On the one hand …, but on the other hand …
…

School rules

7a   skill: mediation p. 157

An exchange student from the US is at your school. You are showing her how to use your school's online communication platform. Explain to her the following rules in English.

- Achte auf die Lesbarkeit deiner Nachrichten. Benutze nicht zu viele Emojis oder Abkürzungen.
- Vermeide Missverständnisse, indem du klar kommunizierst.
- „Schreie" andere nicht an, indem du nur Großbuchstaben verwendest.
- Schreibe keine albernen oder überflüssigen Nachrichten in Gruppenchats.
- Teile und poste Fotos von anderen nur mit deren Erlaubnis.
- Denke immer daran, dass du für gepostete Inhalte verantwortlich bist.

7b   workbook p. 50/9, 10

Which rule or rules do you find most important? Why?

You can say:
I think it is most important (not) to …

An interview about cyberbullying

8a   audio 2/8

**Listen to the interview.
Why is cyberbullying a topic that is very important to Asher?**

8b   skill: listening p. 153

Listen again. Name two things that Asher says about how to protect yourself and others against cyberbullying. Take notes.

8c   workbook p. 51/11, 12

**What do you think: which piece of advice from Asher is the most important?
Talk about it in class.**

You can say:
In my opinion, …
    … is the most important piece of advice.
I think …

Texting

9   GET TOGETHER

Work with a partner. Text each other to make plans for the afternoon.

Partner A
▍ Go to page 131.
▍▍ Go to page 134.
▍▍▍ Go to page 137.

Partner B
▍ Go to page 140.
▍▍ Go to page 143.
▍▍▍ Go to page 146.

ACTIVATE   PRACTISE   **DEVELOP**   PRACTISE   APPLY

Writing an email

10a 📺 video 13, skill: watching a video clip p. 158

Watch the video clip. What is important when you write a formal email? Make a list.

10b ▨📺 skill: writing p. 155, media worksheet 14

Work with a partner. Choose one or more of these situations and write an email.

1 **You are going on a trip to London with your family.** You would like to stay at a youth hostel. You need a family room for four people from 4 July to 8 July. Your little sister needs a small children's bed and your father is a vegan.

2 **You are taking part in an exchange programme.** You would like to ask your host family if they will pick you up from the airport, and if you should bring anything such as a sleeping bag.

3 **You would like to take part in a dance workshop** with a famous American choreographer. You started dancing five years ago, and you are not sure if you are good enough. You would also like to know how much the workshop costs.

10c

Swap your emails and give each other feedback. You can find a feedback sheet at www.westermann.de/webcode if you enter the webcode WES-128207-001.

Communication

11 CHOOSE YOUR TASK

A **Work with a partner. Send your partner a text message in which you describe your day. Only use emojis. Then "translate" the emoji message into an English text about each other's day and read out your texts to each other.**

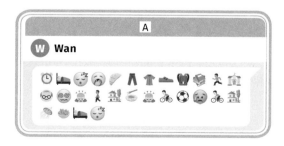

C **What do you find annoying about other people's communication behaviour? Why? Write a short text about it.**

B **Write a polite text message or email to tell your teacher that you cannot come to the class party. Think of a very good or funny reason.**

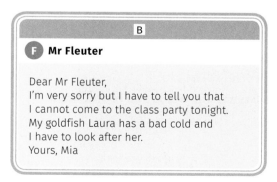

You can write:

I hate it when someone always …

I don't like it / find it annoying when …

Non-stop communication

12a audio 2/10, skill: listening p. 153

Listen to Sofia talking about her friend Liam. What does she find annoying about his behaviour?

12b CHOOSE YOUR LEVEL wordbank: seeking and giving advice p. 166, workbook p. 52/13

▌ **Listen again. What does Sofia say about Liam? Take notes.**

You can write:
doesn't stop sending messages, wants to …

▌▌ **Listen again. What do you think Sofia should do? Send her a text message with one piece of advice.**

You can write:
Hi Sofia, I think you should …

▌▌▌ **Listen again. What do you think Sofia should do? Write a text message to Sofia with advice on what she could do and say.**

What's the opposite?

13a skill: working with words p. 152

Copy the words in the box into your exercise book and write down their opposites by adding a prefix. You can use a dictionary for help.

friendly · polite · healthy · possible · important · advantage · agree

You can write:
*friendly — **un**friendly*
…

13b workbook p. 52/14

Underline the prefixes in your exercise book. What are the different prefixes that can change the meaning of a word to the opposite?

How to pronounce *ea*

14a audio 2/12

Listen to the words and repeat them.

easily · healthy · break up · spread · reason · reach · threat · great

14b

Make lists in your exercise book and listen again. Write the words in your lists.

/e/	/iː/	/eɪ/
healthy	easily	break up
…	…	…

14c audio 2/13, workbook p. 52/15

Listen and check your lists.

DIGITAL+ practise more 12-14

ACTIVATE PRACTISE DEVELOP **PRACTISE** APPLY

Tips for online communication TARGET TASK

15 workbook p. 53/16, wordbank: seeking and giving advice p. 166, skill: presentations p. 160, media worksheet 4

Your task is to collect tips for online communication and present them.
Before you start, look at these steps:

STEP 1

What is important in order to communicate respectfully online?
Get together with a partner or in a small group. Collect your ideas and make notes.

STEP 2

Use your notes to write down a list of tips.

> *Tips for online communication*
>
> *It's important to think first before sending …*
> *You should …*
> *You shouldn't …*
> *Never …*
> *…*

STEP 3

Decide how to present your tips. It could be:

- a poster
- a digital presentation
- a short video
- …

STEP 3

Create your work. Edit it if necessary.

STEP 4

Present your work.

STEP 5

As a class, compare the different tips from the groups. Together, decide on the five most important tips. If you like, you can create a poster and put it up in your classroom.

Check out

1. Kannst du persönliche Aussagen zum Thema Freundschaft verstehen?	Workbook, p. 54
2. Kannst du wiedergeben, was jemand gesagt hat?	Workbook, p. 55
3. Kannst du deine Meinung in einer kurzen Aussage ausdrücken?	Workbook, p. 55
4. Kannst du kurze Zeitungsartikel zum Thema digitale Kommunikation verstehen?	Workbook, p. 56
5. Kannst du ein Interview zum Thema Mobbing im Internet verstehen?	Workbook, p. 56
6. Kannst du eine förmliche E-Mail schreiben?	Workbook, p. 57

Every Day

1 *Each morning, A wakes up in a different body. There's never any warning about who it will be, but A is used to that. Never get too attached.*

5 *And that's fine – until A wakes up in the body of Justin and meets Justin's girlfriend, Rhiannon. Suddenly A has found someone he wants to be with – every day …*

Day 5994

10 I wake up.

Immediately I have to figure out who I am. It's not just the body – opening my eyes and discovering whether the skin on my arm is light or dark, whether my hair is long or

15 short, whether I'm fat or thin, boy or girl, scarred or smooth. (…)

Every day I am someone else. I am myself – I know I am myself – but I am also someone else.

20 It has always been like this.

The information is there. I wake up, open my eyes, understand that it is a new morning, a new place. (…)

Today I am Justin. (…)

25 I'm never the same person twice, but I've certainly been this type before. Clothes everywhere. Far more video games than books. Sleeps in his boxers. (…)

"Good morning, Justin," I say. Checking

30 out his voice. Low. The voice in my head is always different.

Justin doesn't take care of himself. His scalp itches. His eyes don't want to open. He hasn't gotten much sleep.

35 Already I know I'm not going to like today. It's hard being in the body of someone you don't like, because you still have to respect it. (…) So I try to be careful.

From what I can tell, every person I inhabit

40 is the same age as me. I don't hop from being sixteen to being sixty. Right now, it's only sixteen. I don't know how this works. Or why. I stopped trying to figure it out a long time ago. (…)

45 The alarm goes off. I reach for a shirt and some jeans, but something lets me see that it's the same shirt he wore yesterday. I pick a different shirt. I take the clothes with me to the bathroom, dress after showering. His

50 parents are in the kitchen now. They have no idea that anything is different.

Sixteen years is a lot of time to practice. I don't usually make mistakes. Not anymore. I read his parents easily: Justin doesn't

55 talk to them much in the morning, so I don't have to talk to them. (…) I shovel down some cereal, leave the bowl in the sink without washing it, grab Justin's keys and go.

---

warning = *Warnung*; to get attached = *sich binden*; to figure out = *verstehen, begreifen*; skin = *Haut*; light = *hell*; scarred = *vernarbt*; smooth = *glatt*; low = *tief*; scalp = *Kopfhaut*; to itch = *jucken*; to inhabit = *bewohnen*; to hop = *springen*; alarm = *Wecker*; to go off = *klingeln*; to reach for = *greifen nach*; to pick = *aussuchen*; to shower = *duschen*; to shovel = *schaufeln*; sink = *Spülbecken*; key = *Schlüssel*

(…)

60 I access [Justin's] memory to show me
the way to school. (…) As I take Justin's
books out of his locker, I can feel someone
hovering on the periphery. I turn, and the
girl standing there is transparent in her
65 emotions – tentative and expectant, nervous
and adoring. I don't even have to access
Justin to know that this is his girlfriend. (…)
Her name is Rhiannon. And for a moment –
just the slightest beat – I think that, yes, this
70 is the right name for her. I don't know why. I
don't know her. But it feels right.
This is not Justin's thought. It's mine. I try
to ignore it. I'm not the person she wants to
talk to. (…)

75 *A and Rhiannon spend the day together and*
both feel that there is something special going
on between them.

This is hard for me.
I have gotten so used to what I am, and how
80 my life works.
I never want to stay. I'm always ready to
leave.
But not tonight.
(…) I want to stay.

85 *A tells Rhiannon that they wake up in a*
different body every day. After not believing
it at first, Rhiannon finally accepts what A's
life is like, and the two try to see each other
as often as possible. A very much wants to
90 *be in a real relationship with Rhiannon and*
sometimes it seems to be working. But there
are other days when it is difficult.

Day 6005

(…) "You never get involved in the people's
95 lives? The ones you're inhabiting."
I shake my head.
"You try to leave the lives the way you found
them."
"Yeah."
100 "But what about Justin? What made that so
different?"
"You," I say.

Day 6016

"(…) Are you really not a boy or a girl?" (…)
105 "I'm just me," I tell her. "I always feel at
home and I never feel at home. That's just
the way it is."

Day 6026

"(…) I mean, you're a different person every
110 day. And I just can't love every single person
you are equally. I know it's you (…). I know
it's just the package. But I can't, A.
(…) I want you to know, if you were a guy I
met – if you were the same guy every day, if
115 the inside was the outside – there's a good
chance I could love you forever. This isn't
about the heart of you – I hope you know
that. But the rest is too difficult. (…) I just
can't do it."

**What do you think: can a relationship like
this work? Why? Why not?**

---

to hover *(informal)* = *herumstehen*; **periphery** = *Rand*; **to turn** = *sich umdrehen*; **transparent** = *durchschaubar*; **tentative** = *zaghaft*; **expectant**
= *erwartungsvoll*; **adoring** = *hingebungsvoll*; **tonight** = *heute Abend*; **to get involved in** = *sich engagieren*; **package** = *Paket*; **guy** = *Kerl, Typ*;
inside = *Inneres*; **outside** = *Äußeres*; **forever** = *ewig, für immer*

Cyberbullying – FAQs

1 How do you tell the difference between a joke and bullying?

If you feel hurt or think others are laughing at you instead of with you, then the joke has
5 gone too far. If they don't stop even after you've asked them to stop, then this could be bullying. Whether it is happening online or offline, if you are not happy about it, you should not have to put up with it.

10 **Who should I talk to if someone is bullying me online? Why is reporting important?**

If you think you're being bullied, seek help from someone you trust. If you are not
15 comfortable talking to someone you know, search for a helpline to talk to a professional counsellor.

If the bullying is happening on a social platform, consider blocking the bully and
20 formally reporting their behaviour on the platform itself. Social media companies must keep their users safe.

How do we stop cyberbullying without giving up access to the Internet?

25 If you experience cyberbullying, you may want to delete certain apps or stay offline for a while. But this is not a long-term solution. You did nothing wrong, so why should you be disadvantaged?
30 We all want cyberbullying to stop, which is one of the reasons reporting cyberbullying is so important. But creating the Internet we want is more than calling out bullying. We need to be kind to one another online
35 and in real life. It's up to all of us!

Is there a punishment for cyberbullying?

Schools take bullying seriously and will take action against it. If you are being cyberbullied by other students, report it to
40 your school.

Laws against cyberbullying are relatively new and still do not exist everywhere. It is important to remember that punishment is not always the most effective way to
45 change the behaviour of bullies. Sometimes, focusing on repairing the harm and mending the relationship can be better.

Are there any online anti-bullying tools for children or young people?

50 Each social platform offers different tools that allow you to restrict who can comment on or view your posts and to report cases of bullying. Also, the defence against cyberbullying could be you. Think about
55 ways you can help – by raising your voice, calling out bullies, reaching out to trusted adults or by raising awareness of the issue.

> If you are worried about your safety or something that has happened to you online, you must speak to an adult you trust!

---

cyberbullying = *Cybermobbing*; FAQs = *häufig gestellte Fragen*; to tell the difference = *den Unterschied erkennen*; joke = *Witz*; to put up with = *sich abfinden mit*; to report = *melden*; counsellor = *Berater/in*; to consider = *in Betracht ziehen*; formally = *offiziell*; access = *Zugang*; punishment = *Bestrafung, Strafe*; to take seriously = *ernst nehmen*; to restrict = *beschränken*; to raise one's voice = *seine Stimme erheben*

1. What can you see in the pictures? Talk about them in class.
2. What do you think the pictures have to do with "Our world tomorrow"?
3. Do the pictures relate to your hopes and dreams for the future? How?

Our world tomorrow

Part A The power of hope

- Du sprichst über Hoffnungen und Träume.
- Du liest über Menschen, die sich für eine bessere Zukunft einsetzen.
- Ihr präsentiert eure Ideen über eine ideale Zukunft.

Part B The world of work

- Du sprichst über verschiedene Jobs.
- Du findest etwas über *Hard Skills* und *Soft Skills* heraus.
- Du gestaltest eine Seite für ein Infoblatt über Jobs.

Talking about the future

1   wordbank: hopes and dreams p.169, skill: talking with people p.154, workbook p.58/1

What are your hopes and dreams for your personal future? What are your hopes and dreams for the future of the world? Talk to a partner.

You can say:

I wish I …

I hope that …

Hopes and dreams

2a   skill: reading p.156

Read what these teenagers say about their hopes and dreams for the future. Write down two or three keywords for each person.

You can write:

Los Angeles, famous director, …

…

2b

Tell a partner your keywords and let them guess which person you are talking about. Take turns.

1   I'm Chenoa. That's "white dove" in Navajo.
     I'm 15 and I live in Los Angeles with my parents.
     My dream for the future is to become a famous
     director and create movies that make people
5   dream and inspire and motivate them.
     If I had the choice, I would go to the California
     Institute of the Arts but I would have to win a
     scholarship. My family cannot afford the fees.

     My name is José. I'm 13 years old and I want to
10   become a teacher. My parents are from Honduras.
     They came to the USA before I was born because
     they got jobs here. They work a lot, but they don't
     earn very much money.
     But I'm really glad they emigrated to the USA.
15   If we were still living in Honduras, things would be
     more difficult. I wouldn't have the chances I have
     here. Even if I don't win a scholarship for a really
     good college, I could still go to community college.
     Sometimes I dream about what I would do if I was
20   rich. If I had a billion dollars, I would try to help
     students all over the world to get a good education.

ACTIVATE PRACTISE DEVELOP PRACTISE APPLY

My name is Robert. I'm 17 and I would love to become a professional paraclimber. I use a wheelchair, so I had to find a gym with special equipment to start climbing.

25 I've been climbing for three years now, and I love it. There is a large paraclimbing community in the USA, so I can take part in competitions and share my experiences with other people. I'm also really grateful to my family. They always support me. My dad drives me to all my competitions and my mom and my

30 brothers watch me as often as they can and cheer for me. It would be so cool if paraclimbing became a Paralympic sport. Not just because it's my sport but also to show that a disability does not always mean that you cannot do what you want to do!

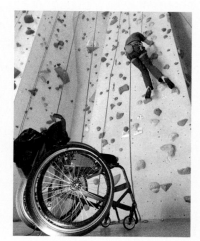

35 I'm Miriam and I'm 15 years old. My dream is to make the world a better place, especially by fighting against climate change. After school I want to train as a sustainability manager because I hope to really change something then. I became a member of the student council at my school last

40 year, and I really like to see our ideas and actions having at least a small impact. At the moment, we try to become a "Green School". I know that this won't stop climate change, but at least we're doing something. I wish that things would change faster. If it didn't take so much time to make

45 politicians listen to young people, a lot of things would improve faster. If I was the president of the United States, I would definitely make better climate laws.

2c CHOOSE YOUR LEVEL

▌ **Read the statements again. What do the teenagers hope and dream?**

▌▌ **Read the statements again. What are the teenagers' hopes and dreams? What are they doing to reach their goals? What are they planning to do?**

▌▌▌ **Read the statements again. What are the teenagers' hopes and dreams? What are they doing to reach their goals? What are they planning? What problems do they talk about?**

2d workbook p. 58/2

If you had a lot of money, which one of the teenagers would you like to help? Why? How?

You can say:
If I had a lot of money, I would like to help …
  because …
I would support …

GRAMMAR HELP   conditional clauses type 2 p. 185

Conditional clauses type 1 kennst du schon. Du benutzt sie, um zu sagen, was unter bestimmten Bedingungen höchstwahrscheinlich geschehen wird, z. B.: *If you miss the bus, you will be late.*

Conditional clauses type 2 verwendest du, um auszudrücken, was unter einer nur gedachten Bedingung passieren würde. Dies ist nicht so wahrscheinlich wie bei den *conditional clauses type 1*. Was fällt dir bei den Beispielen auf?

If I had the choice, I would go to the California Institute of the Arts.	Wenn ich die Wahl hätte, würde ich zum *California Institute of the Arts* gehen.
If I had a billion dollars, I would try to help.	Wenn ich eine Milliarde Dollar hätte, würde ich versuchen zu helfen.
If it did not take so much time, a lot of things would improve.	Wenn es nicht so viel Zeit bräuchte, würden sich viele Dinge verbessern.

Auf Seite 185 findest du weitere Beispiele und Erklärungen zu den *conditional clauses type 2*.

If …

3a   grammar: conditional 2 p. 185

Match the sentence parts and write down the sentences.

1 If Chenoa was a famous director,
2 If paraclimbing became a Paralympic sport,
3 If José and his parents still lived in Honduras,
4 If it did not take so much time to make politicians listen,

A he would not be able to go to college.
B things would be better.
C it would show that people with a disability can do a lot of things.
D she would create films that make people dream.

3b   grammar: conditional 2 p. 185, workbook p. 59/3

Complete these conditional sentences (type 2) with the verb forms from the box.

1 If Chenoa was a student at the California Institute of the Arts, she ??? (learn) how to make films.
2 If there ??? (not be) a paraclimbing community in the USA, Robert would not be able to take part in competitions.
3 If there weren't any gyms with special equipment, Robert ??? (not be able to) do his dream sport.
4 If José's parents ??? (have) a college education, they ??? (get) better jobs.
5 If Miriam ??? (can) change the world, she ??? (make) better climate laws.

> could · wasn't · would learn · had · would make · would not be able to · would get

If I had the chance …

4   grammar: conditional 2 p. 185, workbook p. 59/4

What would you do if you had the chance? Make notes, then talk to a partner.

You can say:

If I had the chance, I would …
… ride my bike around the world. / …

DIGITAL+ practise more 15

ACTIVATE   **PRACTISE**   DEVELOP   PRACTISE   APPLY

Working towards change

5a skill: reading p. 156

Read this article from an American magazine. What does it say about imagination? Do you agree?

5b

In class, collect ideas for actions that you can take on each of the four levels of climate action.

Working towards change – the four levels of climate action

1 **Thinking about the future and challenges like climate change can make us feel helpless.**

If you feel like this too, it can help to know that you are not alone. Many of us feel that 5 way about the climate crisis. There is even a name for it: climate anxiety. The best way to do something about it? Climate action!

But what can we do to make a difference? First, we need to imagine a better future in order to 10 be able to work towards it. Our imagination is a powerful tool. Try to imagine what a green and livable future would look like to you. Also find out what experts say and what we can do about climate change.

15 Before you get going, it is helpful to know the four levels of climate action and decide on which level you can get involved.

LEVEL 1 is about individual action, for example when you decide to eat less meat or buy fewer 20 new clothes in order to reduce the CO_2 output that you are responsible for. Every action for reducing our ecological footprint counts.

LEVEL 2 is action in your direct circle, for example when your family decides to use 25 public transport as often as possible.

On **LEVEL 3**, you take actions to your community. One example for this is establishing a recycling system at your school. Your actions can influence many people in a 30 positive way, for example if others copy the system.

LEVEL 4 is the systemic level. It is about trying to change the system as a whole. You could sign petitions or join an existing movement. 35 Actions on this level usually have the biggest impact, for example when a whole country decides to ban short-distance flights. Actions on this level are often the ones that you need the most stamina and patience for.

40 LEVELS OF CLIMATE ACTION

LEVEL 1: Individual action

LEVEL 2: Our direct circle

LEVEL 3: Community action

LEVEL 4: Systemic action

45 Although action is needed to save our planet, fighting climate change can be exhausting, so remember to take breaks.

5c CHOOSE YOUR LEVEL skill: writing p. 155, wordbank: seeking and giving advice p. 166, workbook p. 60/5-7

What could you tell someone who feels helpless about climate change?
Read the article again to get ideas.

▎ **Write a message of about 40 words and tell them what actions they could take.**
▎▎ **Write a message of about 60 words and tell them what actions they could take.**
▎▎▎ **Write a message of about 80 words and tell them what actions they could take.**

Turning a vision into reality

6a
Look at the pictures and the headline. What do you expect to read about in the article?

6b
Read the article. What was the "spark" that is mentioned in the headline?

The spark that led to a global movement

1 *Americans buy nearly 3 billion batteries every year for their radios, toys, cell phones, watches and laptops. But what happens with these batteries when they are empty? After learning of the potential dangers of batteries, a young boy from New Jersey decided to take action.*

How did it all begin?

5 In 2019, right around his 10th birthday, Sri Nihal Tammana was watching the news about a huge fire in a Californian waste disposal plant that caused not only millions of dollars worth of damage but also massive harm to the environment. The fire was
10 started by a battery. He asked his dad how to prevent this from happening again. His dad told him that you could prevent that if all people recycled their batteries instead of just throwing them away in their household garbage.
15 In the following weeks, Sri Nihal saw more stories about batteries causing fires around the world, and he found out how the chemicals in different kinds of batteries cause terrible pollution when they end up in landfills instead of being taken to recycling plants.
20 He also learned that as many as 15 billion batteries are thrown away each year although they contain valuable chemicals and rare metals that can be used again.

First steps

Sri Nihal decided he had to do something to help.
25 He began by collecting batteries in his school and community and taking them to free recycling points. Eventually, he collected so many that he was told he couldn't use the bins anymore.
So, in June 2019, he started his own non-profit
30 organization "Recycle My Battery." He put up free-to-use battery bins in his school in Edison, New Jersey, which were successful right away.

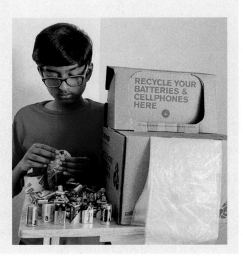

ACTIVATE   PRACTISE   **DEVELOP**   PRACTISE   APPLY

Thinking further

Collecting the batteries was a good starting point.
35 But Sri Nihal realized that real change was only
going to happen if more people knew about
the dangers of batteries. Because of that, he
also started running awareness campaigns to
teach both adults and young people about the
40 importance of battery recycling.
He also told his friends and family and encouraged
them to join him for his campaign.

Where they are today

By today, he and his friends have collected and
45 recycled more than 300,000 used batteries, keeping
them out of landfills. They have also reached an
estimated 15 million people via their campaigns
and recruited over 500 volunteer kids from schools
around the world.
50 Back in 2019, he never believed his little idea about
recycling batteries would grow the way it has.
People just began listening and joining in. This shows that everyone can be a changemaker –
even young people. So if you care about something, first believe that you can change things,
and second, take the first step to make that change happen.

6c   CHOOSE YOUR LEVEL   skill: reading p. 156

I **Read the article again.**
What are the problems with batteries?
Take notes from the text.

You can write:

potential dangers, ...

II **Read the article again. What are the problems with batteries? How can they be solved?**
Take notes from the text.

III **Read the article again. What are the problems with batteries? What did Sri Nihal and**
his friends do to help solve these problems? What have they achieved so far? Take notes
from the text.

6d

What did you find out about Sri Nihal and his project from the article? Talk about it in class.

6e   workbook p. 60/8, 9

Sri Nihal had a vision. Look at the four levels of action on page 85 again.
Which level has Sri Nihal reached with his organization?

Changing the world

7 CHOOSE YOUR TASK   B+C: skill: searching the internet p. 159, media worksheet 6, wordbank: presenting something p. 168

A **What could be done in your neighbourhood to make it more environmentally friendly? Collect ideas and present them in class.**

B **There are many songs about how to change the world. Find and present one or more to your class.**

C **All over the world, you can find people who are changing things for the better. Do some research. Find a good example and tell your class about it.**

LAND & LEUTE 5

Schülervertretungen in den USA

In den USA gibt es an vielen Schulen Schüler-vertretungen, die in der Schule mitbestimmen können. Sie helfen dabei, die Anliegen von Schülerinnen und Schülern bei den Lehrkräften und Schulleitungen vorzubringen und ihre Interessen zu vertreten.

Häufig sammeln sie auch Gelder für gemeinnützige Zwecke oder Aktivitäten, oder sie organisieren Lebensmittel-Sammel-Aktionen, Partys oder Wohltätigkeitsläufe.

Ein wichtiger Aspekt der Arbeit von Schülervertre-tungen ist nicht nur ihre Hilfe zur Verbesserung des

Schullebens, sondern auch, dass hier Schülerinnen und Schüler etwas über Demokratie und Verantwortung lernen.

Gibt es an eurer Schule eine Schülerver-tretung? Was macht sie? Hältst du eine Schülervertretung für eine gute Idee?

A charity run

8   skill: mediation p. 157, workbook p. 62/10, 11

Your little brother's school is organizing a charity run. Your American aunt, Mia, who is staying with your family, does not understand what your brother, Eric, is asking for. Help them.

Eric: Kannst du Tante Mia fragen, ob sie mich sponsert?
(1) You: *Mia, would you sponsor …?*
Mia: Oh, I'd love to, but what for?
(2) You: *Sie möchte wissen, …*
Eric: Für unseren Wohltätigkeitslauf! Mama macht schon mit, und ich rufe Oma gleich an.
(3) You: …
Mia: A charity run, that sounds cool. I think it's great that he's taking part. So, what would I have to do?

(4) You: …
Eric: Sie muss sich überlegen, wie viel sie für jede Runde, die ich laufe, spenden möchte. Das muss sie dann auf diesem Formular eintragen und unterschreiben.
(5) You: …
Mia: OK. What about €1.50?
(6) You: …
Eric: Das wäre toll. Vielen Dank, Mia. Jetzt habe ich schon zwei Sponsoren!
(7) You: …
Mia: You're welcome.

The power of hope

9a

What do you know about Michelle Obama?
What was her job from 2009 to 2017?
Talk about her in class.

9b

Read this excerpt from a speech by Michelle Obama.
What are the topics she addresses?
You can find help in the box.

1   (...) So for all the young people in this room (...) know that this country belongs to you — to all of
you, from every background (...). If you or your parents are immigrants, know that you are part
of a proud American tradition (...), generation after generation (...). If your family doesn't have
much money, I want you to remember that in this country, plenty of folks, including me and my
5   husband — we started out with very little. But with a lot of hard work and a good education,
anything is possible — even becoming President. That's what the American Dream is all about.
(...) Right now, you need to (...) prepare yourself to be informed and engaged as a citizen, to
serve and to lead, to stand up for our proud American values and to honor them in your daily
lives. And that means getting the best education possible so you can think critically, so you can
10   express yourself clearly, so you can get a good job and support yourself and your family, so you
can be a positive force in your communities.
　　And when you encounter obstacles, (...) when you are struggling and you start thinking about
giving up, I want you to remember something (...) and that is the power of hope — the belief that
something better is always possible if you're willing to work for it and fight for it.(...)

hard work · good education · hope · engagement · information · ...

9c   CHOOSE YOUR LEVEL   skill: reading p. 156

▌ **Read the first six lines again. How is anything possible according to Michelle Obama?**
In which line does she say so?
▌▌ **Read the first eight lines again and copy the words that express the main idea best.**
In which lines did you find them?
▌▌▌ **Read the excerpt again and copy the words that express the main idea best.**
In which lines did you find them?

9d   media worksheet 18, workbook p. 62/12

Find a video clip of the speech on the
Internet and watch it. Do you think it is
a good speech? Why or why not?

You can say:
I think it is a ... speech because ...
I like ... / I don't like ...

Word pairs

10a

Combine words from box A and box B to make expressions from this unit. Write them down.

A   climate · ecological · battery ·
non-profit · awareness

B   footprint · change · campaign ·
organization · recycling

10b

Look at the texts in this unit again and find three or more two-word expressions like that. Write them down.

What would happen if …?

11   CHOOSE YOUR LEVEL grammar: conditional 2 p. 185

▌ Copy the sentences and fill in the gaps with words from the box.

1   If more people ??? (recycle) batteries, it ??? (be) good for the environment.
2   If politicians ??? (take) action, things ??? (change) faster.
3   If more people ??? (fight) climate change, the impact ??? (be) bigger.

would change ·
would be ·
would be · fought ·
took · recycled

▌▌ Write about what you would do if …

1   If people ??? (grow) more trees, our cities ??? (become) greener.
2   If politicians ??? (make) better climate laws, things ??? (change) faster.
3   If people ??? (use) public transport more often, there ??? (be) fewer cars on the streets.

▌▌▌ Write about what you would do if …

1   you could wish for three things.
2   a thousand people were willing to help you make the world a better place.
3   you were the president of the United States.

The world in 50 years

12a   🔊 audio 2/18

Listen to the people talking about the future. Which of these topics do they talk about?

schools · houses · travelling ·
food · animals · work

12b   skill: listening p. 153, workbook p. 63/13, 14

Listen again and take notes. What do the people say about the topics?

You can write:

John: in 50 years there might be …

Sarah: there could be …

…

🖥 **DIGITAL+** practise more 15

ACTIVATE   PRACTISE   DEVELOP   **PRACTISE**   APPLY

My ideal future world TARGET TASK

13 ▨▣ workbook p.64/15, wordbank: hopes and dreams p.169

Your task is to present your ideas about your ideal future world.
Before you start, look at these steps:

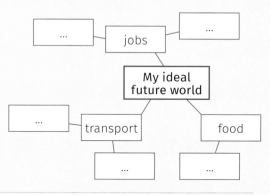

STEP 1

Imagine your ideal world. What does it look like?
You could:
· make notes
· make a drawing
· create a digital word web
· find pictures and make a digital mood board
· ...

STEP 2

Prepare a presentation of your ideas.
Make notes on what you would like to say about your ideal world.

STEP 3

Use your notes to present your work to your classmates.

You can say:
In my ideal future world, there would be no more ...
There would be ... / less ... / more ...
...

Jobs

1a

Work with a partner. Write down all the jobs you know in English. You have three minutes.

1b

How many jobs have you collected? Compare your lists in class.

1c   audio 2/20, skill: listening p. 153, workbook p. 65/1, 2

Listen to the job descriptions and match them to the pictures.

animal keeper

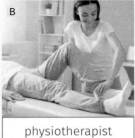

physiotherapist

You can say:

Description number … matches picture …

electrician

gardener

nursery teacher

construction worker

What do they do for a living?

2a

Read the statements. Which job do you find the most interesting? Give reasons.

1 I work in a hospital in a small town in Ohio on the children's ward as a **nurse**. We look after children aged two to twelve with all sorts of problems here. I take blood samples, change wound dressings, take temperatures and try to make our patients feel as comfortable as possible. I'm also allowed to carry out and interpret tests. I can't prescribe any medication though, only

Damian

doctors are allowed to do that. I like working here. It's always great when a kid can leave the hospital because we've helped them get better. The only thing that's sometimes a bit difficult for me is that I have to work shifts.

2 I really like fashion – that's why I became a **fashion designer**. My job is very creative and I design clothing and accessories. I create original new designs or adapt fashion trends. I work with different materials. For example, I have recently started working with recycled and sustainable materials. I hope I will be able to present my own designs in a big fashion show one day – but I know that I will have to work hard.

Cody

3 I am a **forest worker** in Oregon. There are many forests here, and I do lots of different things. For example, I cut down trees, load them onto big tractors and drag them out of the forest. That's why I must be able to drive big trucks and tractors. I can also operate machines that drag logs. We also create areas without trees where forest fires can be stopped. We remove sick trees as well so that the forest stays healthy. I like my job because it is outdoors and it is very physical. I also like the fact that I'm able to do something useful for the ecological system.

John

4 **Surf instructors** teach people surfing techniques. You need to be a very good swimmer and you also have to know a lot about safety and have life-saving skills. I had to get a number of safety certifications before I was allowed to become a surf instructor. Two years ago, I was able to start my own surf school in Santa Cruz, California, so I'm my own boss now which I really like. But that also means that I have to do a lot of office work like planning, advertising and managing surfing courses. I love my job because I can do what I really love for a living, and I meet new people all the time which is very inspiring.

Tamara

2b CHOOSE YOUR LEVEL skill: reading p. 156, workbook p. 65/3-5

▌ **What do Damian and Cody do in their jobs? Take notes.**
▌▌ **What do the people do in their jobs? Take notes.**
▌▌▌ **What do the people do in their jobs? Why do they like their jobs? Take notes.**

You can write:
Damian: works in …
Cody: designs …
…

My future job

3a wordbank: the world of work p. 170

What is important to you in a job? Talk to a partner.
Think about:
· money and working hours
· working indoors or outdoors
· working in a team or on your own
· …

You can say:
I think it is important that …
In my opinion, …
I prefer … to …

3b skill: working with words p. 152

Together with your partner, collect ideas for jobs that each of you could do that fit your ideas from 3a. Look up the names of the jobs in a dictionary if you need help.

GRAMMAR HELP   modal verbs (R) p. 186

Du hast bereits verschiedene Modalverben kennengelernt. Für die Modalverben *must* und *can* gibt es Ersatzformen. Schau dir die folgenden Beispielsätze an.

I will have to **work hard**.	Ich werde **hart arbeiten** müssen.
I had to **get a number of safety certifications**.	Ich musste **eine Menge Sicherheitszertifikate machen**.
I hope I will be able to **present my own designs** one day.	Ich hoffe, dass ich eines Tages **meine eigenen Entwürfe** werde **präsentieren** können.
Two years ago, I was able to **start my own surf school**.	Vor zwei Jahren konnte ich **meine eigene Surfschule eröffnen**.
Only doctors are allowed to **prescribe medication**.	Nur Ärztinnen und Ärzte dürfen **Medikamente verschreiben**.
I had to **get a number of safety certifications** before I was allowed to **become a surf instructor**.	Ich musste **eine Menge Sicherheitsqualifizierungen machen,** bevor ich **Surflehrerin werden** durfte.

Auf Seite 186 findest du weitere Erklärungen und Beispiele zu den Modalverben und ihren Ersatzformen.

Talking about jobs

4   grammar: modal verbs (R) p. 186

Copy the sentences and fill the gaps with modal verbs from the box.

1 In order to become a vet, you ??? study at university.
2 I study medicine so I hope I ??? work as a doctor some day.
3 I ??? start my own business three months ago.
4 I can speak French so I hope I ??? find a job in France in the future.
5 I ??? do lots of different courses before I ??? become a nurse last year.
6 In my old job, I had to go to the office every day. I ??? work from home.

> will be able to ·
> will be able to ·
> was able to ·
> was able to ·
> wasn't allowed to ·
> have to ·
> had to

Asking questions

5   grammar: modal verbs (R) p. 186, workbook p. 67/6

Unscramble the questions. Then look at the texts on page 92 and 93 again and answer them.

1 are you – do at work? – allowed to – Damian, what
2 will be able to do – Cody, what do – one day? – you hope you
3 operate? – John, what kind – able to – are you – of machines
4 your own – able to start – were you – Tamara, when – surf school?

What's the job?

6a audio 2/22

Listen to the job words and repeat them. Where is the stress? Make three lists.

first syllable	second syllable	third syllable
gardener	*photographer*	*electrician*
…	…	…

6b workbook p. 67/7

Choose three or more of the job words from 6a. Write one sentence each explaining what people in the jobs do.

DIGITAL+ practise more 16-17
ACTIVATE **PRACTISE** DEVELOP PRACTISE APPLY

Everybody has skills

7a skill: reading p.156

Read this article from an American magazine and take notes. Work with a partner and summarize the main points in German.

Everybody has skills

1 *Employers usually look for two kinds of skills: soft skills and hard skills. Everybody has soft and hard skills – but what exactly are they?*

Hard skills are skills that help you do particular jobs. Examples are: computer software knowledge, being able
5 to repair cars or bicycles, foreign languages, or computer programming.

People learn hard skills at school, on the job or from life experience. You can even try and teach yourself skills.

Soft skills have to do with your personality, attitude and
10 manners. Examples are: politeness, good communication, reliability, and the ability to work in a team.

hard skills

soft skills

Recognizing your hard and soft skills

As a high school student you may have learned skills through school, volunteering, or sport. If you play a
15 sport, you probably have good teamwork skills.
Are you good at presentations? Your communication skills are likely to be great!
Do you babysit for neighbors? For that you have to be reliable and responsible.

Improving your skills

You can always improve your hard and soft skills! To practice soft skills, talk to friends and
20 family and ask them for feedback. To practice or learn hard skills, take a course, buy a book or watch tutorials. And when it comes to applying for a job, don't just list these skills in your application – make sure you show how you have used them and give examples to show what you can do. Good luck!

7b CHOOSE YOUR LEVEL workbook p.67/8-10

▌ **Read the article again. Make one list with examples of hard skills and one list with examples of soft skills.**

▌ **Make one list with examples of hard skills and one list with examples of soft skills mentioned in the article. Try to add your own examples.**

▌ **Collect the examples of hard and soft skills mentioned in the article. Try to add your own examples. Explain the difference between the two types of skills.**

A soft skill check

8a

Find out if you have good soft skills! What would you do in each situation?
Write down the letters. Then check your result on page 223.

1   You're late for school.
    a) You enter the classroom without saying anything and sit down.
    b) You enter the classroom and say good morning to everyone.
    c) You apologize to the teacher and promise it won't happen again.

2   You start group work in class.
    a) You choose some good classmates so that you don't have to work so hard.
    b) You choose classmates that you know you can work well with.
    c) You ask your teacher for an individual task.

3   Your class has to tidy the school grounds every day for a week.
    a) You wait and hope that others will do the work.
    b) You immediately say that you will do it.
    c) You say you won't do it.

4   Your teacher wants to explain something to the whole class.
    a) You listen carefully and ask questions.
    b) You quietly talk to your neighbour and don't listen at all.
    c) You don't pay much attention and look out of the window.

5   Some of your classmates are arguing on the school bus.
    a) You don't do anything but you later complain to your friends at school.
    b) You try to end the argument.
    c) You shout at your classmates and tell them to stop arguing.

6   Your group work is due tomorrow. Some of you haven't done the work.
    a) You help the others in order to get a good individual and group result.
    b) You work all night long on your own and your partners' work.
    c) You just do your own part of the presentation.

8b

Look at the soft skill check again. What soft skills do you need in each situation? Discuss.

> organisational skills · taking initiative ·
> ability to work in a team · politeness ·
> being on time · listening skills · …

8c   skill: talking with people p. 154

Which skills do you need to improve?
How could you do that? Talk to a partner.

You can say:

I need to work on being on time. I could …

What about you?

What to do?

9a audio 2/24

Nick, a 17-year-old high school student, is talking to his aunt Leah. Listen and read along. What are they talking about?

Leah: Hi Nick, how are you doing? What are you up to?

Nick: Hi Auntie Leah. I want to go to that cool music festival in summer, but the tickets are so expensive. I really need to find a job to add to my pocket money.

Leah: What kind of job are you looking for?

Nick: Well, it needs to be something I can do after school or on the weekends. I was thinking about filling shelves at a supermarket or helping people pack their bags at the cash register. Do you have any other ideas?

Leah: Yes, I do actually. You could mow people's lawns or you could get a job as a paper boy – those jobs are before or right after school. I heard that supermarket jobs are often in the evenings, and I know that you have trouble getting up in the mornings anyway!

Nick: I really don't like getting up early. So I don't think working as a paper boy is for me.

Leah: Hmm, let me think: what about working at a restaurant? Your dad did that when he was a teenager.

Nick: I know – and he hated it! So much hard work, and the pay was really bad – and

I don't think that has changed much. I'd much rather work outside and keep fit at the same time. Dog walking for example! I love dogs, and I am quite good with them.

Leah: Yes, that's a good idea! You're also fun around younger kids. Babysitting could be for you. Or how about tuition? You are good at math and French – and you are patient. Why not help students who are struggling at school?

Nick: That is an awesome idea! Why have I never thought about that until now? I used to help my neighbor with his homework, and I liked it. Well, you have given me some really good ideas. Thanks, Auntie Leah!

Leah: I'm always happy to help! Now good luck, and don't forget to update me!

9b CHOOSE YOUR LEVEL skill: reading p. 156

|| **Look at the dialogue again. List the jobs that Nick and Leah mention.**

||| **Look at the dialogue again. Which jobs does Nick like? What does he like about them? Which jobs does he not like?**

||||| **Look at the dialogue again. What are the advantages and disadvantages of the jobs that Nick and Leah mention?**

9c workbook p. 68/11

What soft skills does Nick need for the jobs? Which skill that Leah mentions is a hard skill?

A job application form

10a

Read Nick's application form. What kind of job is he applying for?

APPLICATION FORM

Name: *Nick Adams*

Address: *12 Washington Rd, Philadelphia, PA 19147*

Phone: ~~517 28763~~

Email: *N.Adams@xyyy.com*

Age: *17*

Current grade at high school: *12th grade*

Subjects you feel comfortable tutoring / last grade achieved in report: *French (A), math (A)*

Grades you feel comfortable tutoring: *up to 11th grade*

Experience in tutoring: *helping my neighbor with his homework*

Other relevant experience: *boy scout camp counselor at the age of 17 (boy scout since the age of 7), spent 2 months in French-speaking Canada last summer, member of the Mathletics club at high school*

Why do you want to work with us? *I like helping others and can work well with younger students. I enjoyed helping my younger neighbor do his homework and prepare for tests. That is why I would enjoy working as a tutor for Top Tutoring.*

References: *Mr. Curtis from Boys Scouts of America and Mrs. Newman, my neighbor*

TOP TUTORING
Working towards better grades

10b   workbook p. 69/12

Do you think that Nick is the right person for the job? Why or why not?

You can say:
In my opinion, Nick is ... because ...
It's very good that he ...

A job interview

11a   wordbank: seeking and giving advice p. 166

Nick is invited to a job interview at Top Tutoring. What tips can you give Nick for his interview? What should he do or say during the interview?

You can say:
During the job interview, Nick should ...
He must ...
He should ...

11b   audio 2/25, workbook p. 69/13

Listen to Nick's interview. Did he follow the tips? Would you give him the job?

ACTIVATE   PRACTISE   **DEVELOP**   PRACTISE   APPLY

LAND & LEUTE 6 📺 video 14

Berufsvorbereitungskurse in den USA

In vielen amerikanischen Highschools können Schülerinnen und Schüler an Kursen teilnehmen, die sie aufs Berufsleben vorbereiten. In diesen Kursen lernen sie besondere Fertigkeiten und gewinnen praktische Erfahrungen, die sie auf eine Anstellung oder eine Ausbildung nach der Highschool vorbereiten. Schülerinnen und Schüler können beispielsweise in Werkstätten, Farmen, Büros oder Krankenhäusern arbeiten.

Dort gewinnen sie einen Eindruck davon, wie es ist, in einem solchen Bereich zu arbeiten. Während es in Deutschland ein sehr gutes duales Ausbildungssystem mit festgelegten Standards gibt, ist dies in den USA nicht der Fall.
Generell fangen weniger Absolventinnen und Absolventen einer Highschool eine Lehre an als ans College oder an eine Universität zu gehen.

Welche praktische Ausbildung würdest du gern in der Schule bekommen?

Help wanted

12 skill: mediation p. 157

An American exchange student sees this ad and asks you what it is about. Tell them the most important information in English.

Helfende Hand gesucht!
Du bist Schülerin oder Schüler und möchtest dein Taschengeld aufbessern? Du bist 14 Jahre oder älter und kannst gut mit Menschen umgehen?
Dann melde dich bei uns. Wir suchen für meine Mutter (76 Jahre) jemanden, der für ein paar Stunden in der Woche kleinere Tätigkeiten für sie übernimmt, wie z. B. einkaufen gehen oder den Hund ausführen. Wir bezahlen gut.
Näheres erfährst du in einem persönlichen Gespräch (Tel.: ▮▮▮▮▮▮▮▮▮).
Wir freuen uns auf deinen Anruf!

The world of work

13 CHOOSE YOUR TASK A+B: skill: searching the internet p. 159, C: wordbank: expressing opinions p. 168

A **What is your dream job? Write a short text and describe it.**
B ▨▨ 📺 **Do some research on unusual jobs, for example a toy doctor, a diamond cutter, a video game tester or an animal hairdresser, and present your top three in class.**
C **Do you think it is a good idea to turn your hobby into a profession? Write a short text about the pros and cons.**

A role play

14 GET TOGETHER

**Get together with a partner.
Do a role play of a job interview.**

Partner A	Partner B
Ⅰ Go to page 132.	Ⅰ Go to page 141.
Ⅱ Go to page 135.	Ⅱ Go to page 144.
Ⅲ Go to page 138.	Ⅲ Go to page 147.

A very bad job interview

15 grammar: conditional 3 (optional) p. 187, workbook p. 70/14, 15

Read about Ella's job interview. Write down some tips for Ella to use in the future.

1 Ella was late for the interview. If she hadn't missed the bus, she would have been on time.

2 Ella's clothes were not good. If her trousers hadn't been full of holes, she would have made a better impression.

3 Ella didn't ask any questions. If she had asked some questions, it would have been better.

4 Ella didn't know much about the company. If she had done some research, she would have known more about the company.

You can write:

Be on time.

Wear …

…

Skills and jobs

16   CHOOSE YOUR LEVEL   wordbank: the world of work p. 170, workbook p. 70/16

▌ **Read what the people say about themselves. What could be a good job for each person? Why?**

▌▌ **Read what the people say about themselves. Take notes on what they like or dislike and what they are good at. What could be a good job for each person?**

▌▌▌ **Read what the people say about themselves. Describe their personalities and skills. What could be a good job for each person?**

Rebecca: My favourite subject at school is art, and I've never been really good at sports. I love using my imagination to create and invent new things. I enjoy making things with my own hands. I wouldn't like working outdoors.

Aaron: It's very important to me that I can help other people. My friends say that I'm a friendly and patient person, and I love being around people. I also see myself as a team player. I wouldn't like doing a job where I have to sit alone at a desk in an office the whole day.

Reza: I like solving problems, and I'm really good with computers. If something isn't working, I won't stop until I've found and solved the problem. At school, I'm in the maths club. I have never really liked history, and I'm not very good at art or music.

Jasmine: I just love sports. I go running almost every day, and I'm also really good at sports at school. My favourite team sport is basketball, and I've started training young children. I really like helping other people improve their skills. It's important to me to be active.

DIGITAL+ practise more 18

ACTIVATE   PRACTISE   DEVELOP   **PRACTISE**   APPLY

Our job booklet TARGET TASK

17 workbook p. 71/17, wordbank: the world of work p. 170

Your task is to create one page for a (digital) booklet about jobs for people with different personalities and skills. Before you start, look at these steps:

STEP 1

In class, make a list of jobs you would like to include in your booklet.

STEP 2

Get together in small groups. Choose the job you would like to write about. Make sure that each job is only presented once in the booklet.

STEP 3

Collect information about the job.
Think about:
- what you do in the job
- where you work
- what hard and soft skills you need
- …

STEP 4

Create your page. Add pictures and / or photos.

STEP 5

Put all your pages together in a (digital) booklet.

> **Tip**
>
> Your page will be good if you …
> - keep information short.
> - present information clearly.
> - use headings.
> - use different colours.
> - use pictures and / or photos.
> - do not overload it with too much information.

Physiotherapist

A physiotherapist
- helps people after an operation
- helps people to improve movement
- gives massages

Hard skills needed:
- medical knowledge

Soft skills needed:
- listening skills and good communication
- ability to understand patients' feelings

Check out

1. Kannst du einem Zeitschriftenartikel wichtige Informationen entnehmen?   Workbook, p. 72
2. Kannst du ausdrücken, was unter bestimmten Bedingungen passieren würde?   Workbook, p. 73
3. Kannst du in einem Gespräch zwischen zwei Personen sprachlich aushelfen?   Workbook, p. 73
4. Kannst du darüber sprechen, was dir bei einem Job wichtig ist?   Workbook, p. 74
5. Kannst du beschreiben, welche Fähigkeiten und Kenntnisse man für einen Job braucht?   Workbook, p. 74
6. Kannst du ein Bewerbungsgespräch verstehen?   Workbook, p. 75

Interview

"Hope is a discipline": youth climate case plaintiff on why he's suing the US government   Dharna Noor

Nathan Baring of Alaska is part of a group of young activists suing the US, which they say "willfully ignored" dangers of fossil fuels

Nathan Baring is [an] Alaskan climate activist. He is also a plaintiff in Juliana v United States, a lawsuit (…) brought by 21 young Americans. [Lawsuits in the USA are named after at least one of the plaintiffs, in this case Kelsey Juliana.]

How did you become aware of the climate crisis?

(…) It's incredible the changes that have happened within my lifetime. When I was growing up, it used to be very normal to have two-week periods of 40-below temperatures during the winter. Now it seems like it's rare that we get those temperatures at all. (…)

How did you get involved in climate organizing? Tell me a little bit about your political journey.

(…) When I was 12 or 13, I attended some climate-science discussions at the University of Alaska, Fairbanks. (…) At that point, I got involved in an organization called *Alaska Youth for Environmental Action* (…). Julia Olson, the head lawyer for the Juliana case, reached out to my organization. (…)

Students Nathan Baring and Avery McRae participate in a Senate Climate Change Task Force.

You're the only Juliana plaintiff from Alaska. Could you tell me a little bit about what that's like?

The organizations I was part of growing up were almost exclusively led by Indigenous organizers who always centered (…) climate justice. (…) But in Juliana, there are a number of plaintiffs who are Indigenous and grew up with much more of that cultural background than I did as a white person.

youth = *Jugendliche/r*; plaintiff = *Kläger/in*; to sue = *verklagen*; activist = *Aktivist/in*; willfully *(AE)* = *absichtlich, mutwillig*; fossil fuel = *fossiler Brennstoff*; Alaskan = *aus Alaska*; v (= versus) = *gegen*; to bring a lawsuit = *Anklage erheben*; to become aware of = *sich bewusst werden*; period = *Zeitraum*; temperature = *Temperatur*; environmental = *Umwelt-*; head lawyer = *leitende/r Anwalt/Anwältin*; to reach out = *Kontakt aufnehmen*; exclusively = *ausschließlich*; to lead = *leiten*; indigenous = *einheimisch, indigen*; to center = *die Aufmerksamkeit richten auf*; to participate in = *teilnehmen an*; senate = *Senat*; task force = *Arbeitsgruppe*

Kelsey Juliana, a plaintiff in Juliana v United States, speaks outside the Supreme Court in Washington, D.C.

I also (…) focus on labor justice because
Alaska is probably the most oil-dependent
state in the nation. The state is largely paid
40 for by taxes on the oil industry. (…)
I have friends that don't believe in climate
change. I have friends who work in the oil
industry (…) or have family members who do.
(…) they've been given no vision for a future
45 without oil. (…)

**We recently saw a landmark victory for
youth climate suits out of Montana,
which like Alaska is a fossil fuel-rich red
state. What did you make of the Montana
50 victory?**
(…) I was absolutely thrilled for them. (…)
This win in a state like Montana, which is, in
a lot of ways, economically similar to Alaska,
it's especially exciting. (…) It came from a
55 state with a really rich coal industry. (…)
The Montana case really emphasized the (…)
importance of a trial. (…) We need that kind
of sunlight. (…)

Juliana could go to trial sometime soon.
60 **How are you feeling about that prospect?**
(…) It's been eight years of pushing for a trial.
I sunk to quite a low in February 2020, (…).
And then boom, March 2020, was the
beginning of Covid. I had to de-center a lot of
65 my own grief and big feelings about climate
change. It's like that famous quote: "Hope
is a discipline." (…) Still, it would be nice to
finally have a trial! In a funny way, the longer
we've waited, the stronger we've become. The
70 evidence of climate change is so clear now. (…)

Protesters outside the Supreme Court in support of the Juliana v United States lawsuit.

What levels of activism does Nathan talk about? How is he trying to change the world?

labor (AE) = Arbeit; justice = Gerechtigkeit; dependent = abhängig; largely = größtenteils; landmark = Meilenstein; suit = Zivilprozess; red state = Bundesstaat, in der die Mehrheit der Menschen die Republikanische Partei unterstützt; to be thrilled = sich wahnsinnig freuen; win = Sieg; economically = wirtschaftlich; coal = Kohle; to emphasize = hervorheben; trial = Prozess, Gerichtsverhandlung; to go to trial = vor Gericht gehen; prospect = Aussicht; to sink to a low = auf einen Tiefpunkt sinken; grief = Kummer; evidence = Beweis; Supreme Court = Oberstes Bundesgericht; in support of = zur Unterstützung; lawsuit = Gerichtsverfahren

Unusual jobs

1 Snake milker

About 4.5 million people are bitten by
snakes every year, and about 120,000 of
them die. That makes the jobs of snake
5 milkers very important. They "milk" snakes
for their venom, which can then be used to
produce an antidote.

Train pusher

The first train pushers worked in New York
10 City. They made sure that people did not get
caught in the doors. Automatic door technology
replaced them about 100 years ago. Today, you
can meet professional train pushers in Tokyo.
Their job is to get as many people as possible
15 into every subway train during rush hour.

Ethical hacker

When you think of hackers, you probably
think of cybercrime. But there are also "good
hackers" who hack into computer programs
20 to find security gaps. They also test software
for big companies to make it as safe as
possible.

Water slide tester

When a hotel or water park gets a new slide,
25 someone has to make sure that it's safe to
use, so you need a water slide tester.
You have to be at least 18 years old, love
a good adrenaline rush, and have great
attention to detail so you can notice and
30 report potential dangers.

What do you think: which of these jobs is the most important? Why?
Which one would you like or not like to do? Why?

---

snake milker = *Schlangenmelker/in;* **are bitten** = *werden gebissen;* **snake** = *Schlange;* **to milk** = *melken;* **venom** = *Gift;* **antidote** = *Gegenmittel;*
train pusher = *jemand, der Menschen in U-Bahnen und Züge schiebt;* **to get caught** = *eingeklemmt werden;* **automatic** = *automatisch;* **rush**
hour = *Stoßzeit;* **ethical** = *ethisch;* **cybercrime** = *Internetkriminalität;* **to hack** = *hacken;* **water slide** = *Wasserrutsche;* **adrenaline rush** =
Adrenalinstoß; **to have great attention to detail** = *große Aufmerksamkeit fürs Detail haben;* **potential** = *möglich*

1. Look at the pictures. What can you see?
2. Where do you think the people are?
3. Choose one of the people in the pictures and write a speech bubble for them.

New horizons

Part A Immigration

· Du liest verschiedene Einwanderungs-
  geschichten.
· Du siehst dir eine Präsentation über
  Statistiken zu Immigration in die USA an.
· Du schreibst einen Text vom Standpunkt
  eines Immigranten / einer Immigrantin.

Part B The Republic of Ireland

· Du hörst Menschen zu, die über ihr Leben
  in Irland berichten.
· Du findest etwas über Sehenswürdigkeiten
  in Irland heraus.
· Du hältst einen fünfminütigen Vortrag über
  einen interessanten Aspekt Irlands.

Leaving home

1a

What do you think: why do people leave their home and begin a new life in a different country? Work in small groups and write down possible reasons.

> flee from war ·
> go and live with a partner ·
> go to university · ...

1b   workbook p.76/1

Share your ideas in class and talk about them.

You can say:

I think people leave their home because …
A reason could be that they want to …

A new beginning

2a   skill: reading p.156

Scan the stories of three immigrants to the USA. What countries did they come from?

Mary in New York in 1858

1 My name is Mary O'Donnell and I'm from Kilkenny in Ireland.
There, I lived on a small farm with my parents and two brothers. In
1846, we lost our complete harvest because of a potato disease.
The same happened in the next years – not only to us but to
5 farmers all over Ireland. By 1851, we were desperate. We couldn't
pay the rent for the farm. We couldn't grow anything else because
of the quality of the soil. Without potatoes we were literally
starving. But we were lucky. My dad's brother, Uncle Joe,
had emigrated to America in 1839, and in 1852 he managed to
10 buy prepaid tickets to New York for all of us. The journey from Cork
to New York on a sailing ship in cold and stormy weather took one
month. The boat was overcrowded, many were seasick, there was little fresh air, our cabin was
tiny and the food was horrible. We were so happy when we arrived in New York!

Simon in the USA in 1943

My name is Simon Goldschmidt, and I was born in Germany in
15 1925. When I was eight years old, my whole life changed when
the Nazis came to power.
Because we are Jewish, my father was not allowed to practice as
a doctor anymore, and I had to leave school. In the beginning,
my mother told us that it would all be over soon. But it only got
20 worse, and it didn't take us long to realize that staying in Germany
would be dangerous for us. After the November Pogrom of 1938, it
was clear that we had to leave to save our lives. It took until 1940
to get visas to the USA. On May 11th 1940, we boarded a ship in
Hamburg. Although it was terrible that I had to leave all my friends
25 and I was worried for my grandparents in Berlin, I was happy to escape.

My name is Ji-Hoon Choi. I was born in South Korea in 1951 and lived there until I was 23.

Korea was a very poor country at that time.

The unemployment rate was very high, and my father advised me to
30 try to find work in the USA. Thanks to my parents' help, I was able to leave Korea. I moved to Los Angeles in 1974. I did not speak much English then, so I was glad that I found a job in a small shop that belonged to a Korean family. I worked in their shop for five years and saved as much money as I could. In 1979, I was able to open my own
35 shop. By then I had married. My wife is Korean, too. She came here in 1977. We worked in the shop together until our two children had finished university.

My wife and I sold our shop in 2016 and retired. We decided to stay here with our children and grandchildren. My grandson has
40 just started college, and my granddaughter is going to finish high school in two years. Leaving home was very hard for me in the beginning, but when I look at my children and grandchildren today, I'm glad that my parents told me to come here.

Ji-Hoon and his wife in 1978

2b CHOOSE YOUR LEVEL

▌ **Read Mary's story and match the sentence parts. In which line did you find the information?**

1 Mary lived on a small farm in Ireland
2 They lost their complete harvest in 1846
3 The same happened to farmers all over
4 Without potatoes, they couldn't pay the

A Ireland in the next couple of years.
B rent for the farm and were starving.
C because of a potato disease.
D with her parents and two brothers.

▌▌ **Read the stories and finish the sentences. In which line did you find the information?**

1 Mary's family lost their harvests because of ...
2 By 1851, they were literally ...
3 Simon Goldschmidt's life changed when ...
4 His family left Germany because ...
5 Ji-Hoon went to the USA to ...
6 Today, he is glad ...

▌▌▌ **Read the stories and finish the sentences. In which line did you find the information?**

1 When Mary O'Donnell's family lost their harvests, they ...
2 In 1852, Mary's uncle Joe managed to ...
3 The boat to New York was ...
4 Simon Goldschmidt's life changed in 1933 because they ...
5 Simon and his parents realized that ...
6 When he left Germany, Simon was ...
7 In the 1970s, Korea was ...
8 Ji-Hoon first worked ...
9 After they retired, Ji-Hoon and his wife decided ...

2c workbook p. 76/2

What do you think: how did Mary and Simon's lives go on? Collect ideas in class.

You can say:

I can imagine that …

Perhaps …

Maybe …

GRAMMAR HELP reported commands p. 188

Wenn du einen Befehl, eine Bitte, eine Aufforderung oder eine Warnung wiedergeben möchtest, bildest du einen indirekten Befehlssatz. Schau dir die Beispiele an. Was fällt dir auf?

Uncle Joe: "**Come** to the USA."

Uncle Joe told us **to come** to the USA.
Onkel Joe sagte uns, wir sollten in die USA **kommen**.

Ji-Hoon's father: "**Try** to find work in the USA."

My father advised me **to try** to find work in the USA.
Mein Vater riet mir, **zu versuchen**, in den USA Arbeit zu finden.

Weitere Erklärungen zu indirekten Befehlssätzen findest du auf Seite 188.

Boarding the ship

3a grammar: reported commands p. 188

It is very noisy at the harbour. Mary's mother asks Mary to repeat what they are told to do when they board the ship.

1 Please board the ship.
2 Bring your suitcase with you.
3 Go to the first cabin on the left.
4 Stay below deck during storms.

You can write:

1. *They told us to board the ship.*
2. ...

3b grammar: reported commands p. 188, workbook p. 77/3, 4

Report what the passengers are told not to do.

1 Do not fall overboard.
2 Please do not use too much fresh water.
3 Do not start a fire.
4 Do not walk around on deck.

You can write:

1. *They warned us not to fall overboard.*
2. *They asked us ...*
3. ...

Verbs and nouns

4a skill: working with words p. 152

Look at the verbs in the box. Find nouns from the same word family and write down the verbs and nouns. There can be more than one solution. Use a dictionary for help.

emigrate · begin · live · rent ·
change · escape · use · work

You can write:

verbs	nouns
emigrate	*emigration*
...	...

4b

Choose four or more of the verbs and write sentences using them. You can look at the texts on page 106 and 107 for help.

DIGITAL+ practise more 19

ACTIVATE **PRACTISE** DEVELOP PRACTISE APPLY

The USA, an immigration country

5a wordbank: numbers p.171

Look at this graph about immigration to the USA. Has there been an increase or decrease in the number of immigrants over the years? What could be the reasons?

You can say:

There has been an increase in the number …

I think one reason is maybe …

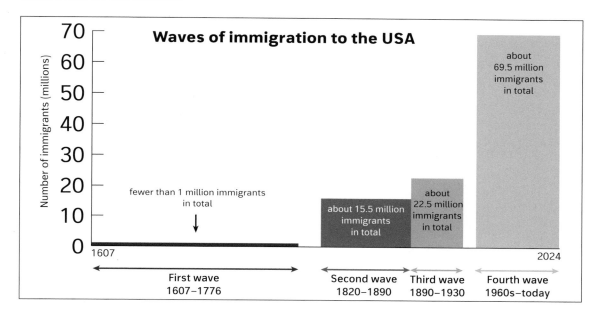

5b CHOOSE YOUR LEVEL video 15, skill: watching a video clip p.158, workbook p.77/5

Watch the presentation and take notes. Then match the sentence parts.

1 The USA has always seen itself
2 Since the first European settlers arrived, the
3 When you look at immigration statistics,
4 Between the 1930s and the 1960s,

A there were not many immigrants.
B you can make out four waves of immigration.
C as a nation of immigrants.
D number of immigrants has increased.

Watch the presentation and take notes. Then complete the sentences.

1 There have been four ??? of immigration to the USA.
2 From 1820 to 1890, most immigrants came from ???, ??? and Scandinavia.

3 During the third immigration wave, the number of people who immigrated to the USA from Eastern and Southern ??? increased.
4 In ???, a quota system was introduced.
5 In 2022, most immigrants came from ???.

Watch the presentation and take notes. Then answer the questions.

1 How many waves of immigration to the USA have there been?
2 Why did many people emigrate from Ireland to the USA in the 1840s and 1850s?
3 When did the second immigration wave peak?

4 What per cent of immigrants came from Italy during the third wave?
5 Why did immigration decrease after 1924?
6 Where did most immigrants come from in 2022?

Elizabeth Flynn – diary of an immigrant

6a

Look at the pictures. What do you expect to read about?

6b

Read the diary entries. Were you right in 6a?

New Orleans, Louisiana, May 1st, 1889
Our ship from Dublin arrived in New Orleans after five
horrible weeks of travel. **I'm so glad to be back on land!**

New Orleans, May 2nd, 1889
We were questioned by immigration officials and had a medical inspection.
One family had to return home! **Thank God we are all healthy and fit!**

New Orleans, July 4th, 1889
The Americans celebrated Independence Day today.
There were fireworks, a parade and a band.
I have never seen anything so wonderful!

St. Louis, July 10th, 1889
We took a steamboat up the Mississippi river to St. Louis
because Father couldn't find work in New Orleans.
The south is very hot and humid. There are alligators
and poisonous snakes there. It is strange and exciting.

St. Louis, July 17th, 1889
We are going southwest to Oklahoma Territory in a wagon
train tomorrow. Father saw an advertisement promising free
farmland in Oklahoma. He said that we will have fresh air and
a farm. My parents bought a wagon, oxen to pull it, a milk cow,
a horse and some chickens. Everything we own is in the wagon:
food, clothes, tools, guns and a few books. I'm so excited!

6c skill: reading p. 156

**Read the diary entries again. What places
and events does Elizabeth mention?**

You can write:

May 1st, 1889: ship from Dublin arrived in ...
May 2nd: ...

Mississippi · Dublin · parade · St. Louis ·
medical inspection · free farmland · band ·
New Orleans · steamboat · Oklahoma · southwest ·
fireworks · ship · poisonous snakes ·
Independence Day · alligators · ...

6d workbook p. 78/6, 7

Do you keep a diary of your life? If you do, in what form? Talk about it in class.

ACTIVATE   PRACTISE   **DEVELOP**   PRACTISE   APPLY

A letter home

7a skill: reading p.156

Scan Elizabeth's letter home to Ireland. What are the elements that show you that this is a letter?

7b

Read Elizabeth's letter. Where is she now? What topics does she write about?

West of Oklahoma City, March 3rd, 1890

Dear family,

I hope you're all well. It took us most of August and September to reach Oklahoma Territory. The Great Plains are beautiful. There is green grass everywhere. We saw lots of bison, deer and rabbits. At night the wolves and coyotes were howling. The weather was very hot and dry, but we had some rain and even a thunderstorm once. The thunder and lightning were very scary.

Life in a wagon train was hard. Emily and I walked to Oklahoma, over 500 miles. Mama and baby James rode in the wagon, and Father rode the horse. After the first week on the trail, I understood why we shouldn't take unnecessary things with us. Every day, we saw what people had left behind: chairs, tables and even a piano!

We had a daily routine. Every day we woke up before the sun. Emily and I collected buffalo chips for our fire. Father milked the cow while mother was cooking breakfast. Then we rode 10 or 15 miles and made camp again. Once, we had to fix a wagon wheel that had broken. We finally made it to Oklahoma City in September, and we survived the winter. Now it is spring. Yesterday, Father got a good piece of farmland. Now we will build a house and barn, plant a vegetable garden and start farming.

Hope to hear from you soon. Give all our love to family and friends.

Love,

Elizabeth

7c CHOOSE YOUR LEVEL

I Read the letter again. What does Elizabeth tell her family about nature? Take notes.

II Read the letter again. What does Elizabeth tell her family about nature and life on the trail? Take notes.

III Read the letter again. What does Elizabeth tell her family about nature, life on the trail and the family's plans for the future? Take notes.

7d workbook p.79/8-10

If you had to leave to start a new life somewhere else and could only pack one bag, what would you take with you? Write a list and talk about it with a partner.

LAND & LEUTE 7 video 16, workbook p. 80/11

Ellis Island

Millionen von Immigranten sahen als Erstes in den USA die Freiheitsstatue und Ellis Island im Hafen von New York. Die Freiheitsstatue gilt als Symbol des Willkommens für Immigranten, die in die USA kamen, weil sie dort auf ein besseres Leben hofften.

Während die Passagiere aus der ersten und zweiten Klasse direkt mit kleinen Booten zum Hafen in New York gebracht wurden, mussten die Passagiere aus der dritten Klasse ab 1892 die Einwanderungsstation auf Ellis Island durchlaufen.

Ellis Island

Es gingen schätzungsweise mehr als 12 Millionen Einwanderer durch die Tore von Ellis Island, bis die Station 1954 geschlossen wurde.

Einwanderungsbeamte schrieben dort Informationen wie Namen, Alter oder Herkunftsland etc. auf, und jeder musste sich einer medizinischen Untersuchung unterziehen. Fiel man an einer Stelle durch, wurde man zurückgeschickt. Deshalb wurde Ellis Island auch bekannt als „Insel der Tränen".

Heute ist Ellis Island ein Museum, das „Ellis Island Immigration Museum".

Wie haben sich die Menschen deiner Meinung nach vor und während ihrer Reise und nach erfolgreicher Untersuchung auf Ellis Island gefühlt?

Medizinische Untersuchung auf Ellis Island

A meme

8a

Look at the meme.
Who could the man be?
Who do you think he is addressing?
What is the message of the meme?

8b

What do you think about the message of the meme?
Talk about it in German.

SO YOU'RE AGAINST IMMIGRATION?

SPLENDID! WHEN DO YOU LEAVE?

ACTIVATE PRACTISE **DEVELOP** PRACTISE AP

On the move

9 CHOOSE YOUR TASK   B: skill: searching the internet p. 159, media worksheet 6, wordbank: presenting something p. 168

A **If you could choose any country in the world to emigrate to, where would you go? Why? Write a short text about your reasons.**

B  **Choose one of the people on pages 106 to 107. Find out more about the situation in their home country around the time they emigrated and present your findings.**

C **Make your own family tree. Ask your parents and grandparents about your family and where everyone came from.**

Life in the USA

10a   audio 3/2

**Listen to Roberto's story. Where does he live?
Where does his family live?
Why did he move to the USA?**

10b CHOOSE YOUR LEVEL   skill: listening p. 153

I Listen again and complete the sentences.
1 Roberto's father ??? (has a farm / works in a factory).
2 Roberto has a ??? (small / big family).
3 Life in Paraguay is not ??? (easy / difficult).
4 Roberto studies in ??? (North Carolina / South Carolina).

II Listen again and complete the sentences.
1 Roberto's father ??? (keeps animals / works in a factory).
2 Roberto's mother is a ??? (teacher / secretary).
3 Life in Paraguay is ??? (easy / difficult).
4 Roberto ??? (can / cannot) see his family very often.
5 Roberto tutors students in ??? (French / Spanish) to earn some extra money.

III Listen again and complete the sentences.
1 Roberto is in the USA in order to ???.
2 He managed to get a scholarship from a ???.
3 Roberto likes to ??? with his friends.
4 Roberto likes to listen to ???.
5 Roberto will be away from home for ??? years.
6 After his studies, Roberto plans to ???.

10c   skill: talking with people p. 153, workbook p. 81/12

**What do you miss when you are away from home? Do you get homesick?
Talk about it with a partner.**

What was going on?

11 grammar: past progressive (R) p. 189, workbook p. 81/13

Copy the sentences and fill in the correct verb forms. Decide whether to use the simple past or the past progressive.

1 While he ??? (live) in Paraguay, Roberto ??? (go) to a small school in his village.
2 While the passengers ??? (board) the ship, a suitcase suddenly ??? (fall) into the water.
3 Elizabeth's parents ??? (work) on the field when it ??? (start) to rain.
4 Mary's uncle ??? (wait) at the harbour when the ship ??? (arrive) at Ellis Island.

You can write:

1. While he was living in Paraguay, Roberto went to …

Adjectives and more

12 CHOOSE YOUR LEVEL   workbook p. 81/14

❙ Copy the sentences and add adjectives to make the sentences more interesting. You can use words from the box or think of your own.

1 Carlos took a ??? plane to the USA.
2 The ??? journey to the airport had taken six hours.
3 He was thinking about the ??? town that he had left to start a ??? life in the USA.
4 He felt ??? when the plane landed in Los Angeles.

happy · big · small · long · new · difficult · excited

❙❙ Choose five of the adjectives and write them down with nouns to make expressions that could be used in a story about immigration.

sad · poor · expensive · new · slow · friendly · cold · difficult · tiny

❙❙❙ Copy the adjectives and add opposites. Then choose five of the adjectives and write sentences that could be used in a story about immigration.

sad · legal · poor · expensive · new · slow · healthy · friendly · cold · difficult · tiny

Countries

13 skill: working with words p. 152, wordbank: around the world p. 162

Write down six or more names of countries and add the matching adjectives. Use a dictionary or look at page 162 if you need help. Compare your list with a partner.

You can write:

Ireland — Irish

China — …

DIGITAL+ practise more 20-21

ACTIVATE   PRACTISE   DEVELOP   **PRACTISE**   APPLY

An immigration story TARGET TASK

14 workbook p. 83/15, skill: writing p. 155, wordbank: around the world p. 162, media worksheet 1, 9–16

Your task is to write a text from the point of view of someone who moved to another country. Before you start, look at these steps:

STEP 1

Collect ideas for your text, for example in a list, a word web, a table, a (digital) mood board, ...
Keep the following questions in mind:
· Who moved?
· When did they move?
· Where did they move to?
· Why did they move?
· What ...?
· How ...?
· What happened then?

STEP 2

Decide what kind of text you would like to write:
diary entries, a letter, an email, a blog post, ...
You can go to www.westermann.de/webcode and enter the webcode WES-128207-001
to find worksheets if you need help.

STEP 3

Make a draft of your text.
Ask a classmate for feedback and
edit it if necessary.

STEP 4

Write your text. Check it for mistakes.
You can add pictures or photos if you like.

STEP 5

Present your text to the class.

> *My immigration story*
>
> *Three years ago, I moved from England to Japan.*
> *I got a job offer from a company in Tokyo. I've always been interested in Japanese culture, so I moved to Tokyo.*
> *In my free time I'm taking part in language classes. I do lots of sightseeing and I like to experience the cultural differences. Japan is an amazing country and I love living here!*
> *Find more details on my website:*
> *#emma_e_intokyo*

A map of Ireland

1   workbook p. 83/1

What do you know about Ireland? What can you find out by looking at this map?
Talk about it in class.

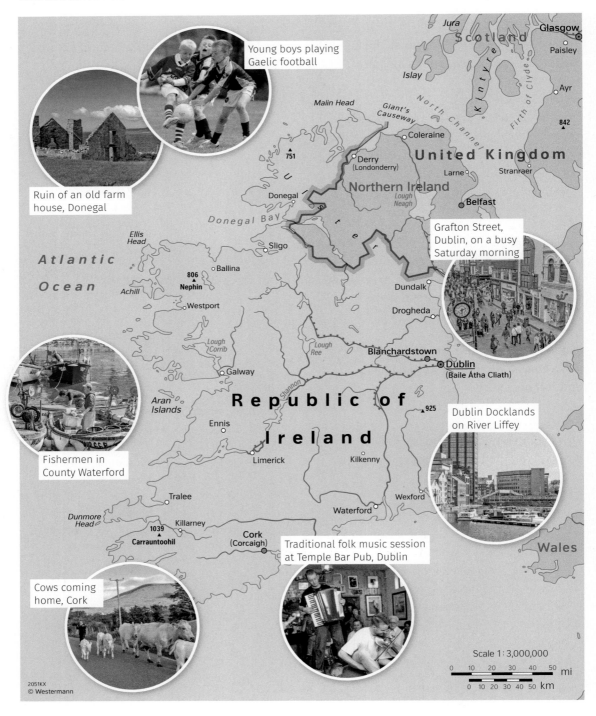

Young boys playing Gaelic football

Ruin of an old farm house, Donegal

Grafton Street, Dublin, on a busy Saturday morning

Fishermen in County Waterford

Dublin Docklands on River Liffey

Cows coming home, Cork

Traditional folk music session at Temple Bar Pub, Dublin

Scale 1 : 3,000,000

0 10 20 30 40 50 mi

0 10 20 30 40 50 km

2051KX
© Westermann

Ireland

2a 🔊 audio 3/4

Listen to the people and read along. Where do they live?

Hello, I'm Finn and I'm from Galway. I'm a Gaelic football player. My team is the St John's Juniors, and I'm the goalkeeper.
You haven't heard of Gaelic football? There are 15 players on each team, and the players can throw, kick and carry the ball. It's the best game in the world!
I'm still in school. I spend all of my time on the football field. My dream is to play in the All-Ireland Senior Championship one day.

My name's Patrick O'Toole. I'm from the USA, and I'm visiting Ireland for the first time in my life. Tonight, I'm in Limerick, but I will travel all over the island during the next few weeks. I want to find out all about my family history. My great-great-grandparents emigrated from Wexford to the USA over a hundred years ago. I have been trying to find out more about them for years. It's very exciting to find out where they came from and to discover this beautiful country.

Hi, I'm Declan. I have a band with my friends Noah and Lucy – the Shamrocks!
We mostly play Irish folk. I've been playing the fiddle since I was a child. We make our money playing in pubs all over Cork, our home town. My favourite concerts are the ones we play for our family and friends. It's a wonderful feeling to play the songs we have known all our lives and to hear our family and friends sing along. That is Ireland to me. That is home to me.

I'm Anna. I'm 34 years old and I live in Sligo. I was born in Poland but moved to Dublin with my parents when I was a little child. Did you know that Polish is the largest non-Irish nationality in Ireland?
I think you could say that I feel Polish and Irish at the same time. For a few months, my partner has been talking about moving to another country, but I know that I want to stay. Ireland will always be my home.

2b CHOOSE YOUR LEVEL skill: reading p. 156

▌ **Choose two or more of the texts and read them again. What do you learn about the people? Take notes.**

▌▌ **Choose three or four of the texts and read them again. What do you learn about the people? Take notes.**

▌▌▌ **Read the texts again. What do you learn about the people? Take notes.**

You can write:

name	what they do	other info
...		

2c workbook p. 83/2

Share your notes in class and talk about the people.

GRAMMAR HELP

the present perfect progressive p. 190-191

Das *present perfect progressive* verwendest du, wenn du über etwas sprechen möchtest, das in der Vergangenheit begonnen hat und immer noch andauert bzw. immer noch zutrifft. Schau dir die Beispiele an und beschreibe, wie die Formen gebildet werden.

I have been trying to find out more about my great-great-grandparents for years.	Ich versuche seit Jahren, mehr über meine Ur-Ur-Großeltern herauszufinden.
I've been playing the fiddle since I was a child.	Ich spiele Geige, seit ich ein Kind war.

Auf den Seiten 190 und 191 findest du weitere Erklärungen und Beispiele zum *present perfect progressive*.

What have they been doing?

3 grammar: present perfect progressive p. 190, workbook p. 84/3

Copy the sentences and complete them with the verb forms from the box.

1 Finn ??? his homework since he came back from football training this afternoon.
2 Finn and his best friend ??? football in the same team for five years.
3 Patrick O'Toole ??? facts about his family history for a long time.
4 Patrick ??? around Limerick for two hours.

> has been trying to find out · have been playing · has been walking · has been doing

Since or for?

4a grammar: present perfect progressive p. 190

Look at the pictures. Write down what the people have been doing or have not been doing.

Patrick – has been travelling – for 7 hours

Anna – has not been watching TV – for 2 hours

Finn – has not been playing Gaelic football – since 5 o'clock

Declan – has been giving a concert – since 8 o'clock

4b grammar: present perfect progressive p. 190

Decide if you have to use "since" or "for". Then copy the sentences into your exercise book.

1 The Shamrocks have been playing in pubs ??? (since / for) six years.
2 Finn has been dreaming about playing in the All Ireland Senior Championship ??? (since / for) he was ten.
3 Anna has been living in Sligo ??? (since / for) three years.
4 Anna's partner has been talking about moving to another country ??? (since / for) a while.

DIGITAL+ practise more 22-23

ACTIVATE **PRACTISE** DEVELOP PRACTISE APPLY

Sightseeing in Ireland

5a   audio 3/5

Listen to the descriptions and match the names of Irish sights to the pictures.

A Powerscourt Estate   C Lemon Rock   E Dingle Peninsula   G Sea Adventure
B Hook Lighthouse   D Blarney Castle   F Connemara National Park   Waterpark

You can say:

Powerscourt Estate is
* picture number …*
…

5b   CHOOSE YOUR LEVEL   skill: listening p. 153

▌ Listen again and take notes. Complete the sentences with the correct information.

1 Powerscourt Estate is ??? minutes away from Dublin.	A 13	B 30
2 At Blarney Castle, you can listen to the mystical story about the Blarney ???.	A stone	B horse
3 Dingle is the perfect place for ??? lovers.	A car	B animal
4 Connemara National Park is on the ??? coast.	A Atlantic	B Pacific

▌▌ Listen again and take notes. Then match the information with the sights from 5a.

1 Here you can see magnificent gardens.
2 At this sight, you should kiss a stone.
3 Some people say that ghosts live here.
4 Some scenes in a famous film were filmed here.

5 Here you can choose one of many hiking trails.
6 If you want to watch dolphins or seals, you should come here.

▌▌▌ Listen again and take notes. What do you learn about the sights? Write down one or more fact for each of the sights.

5c   workbook p. 84/4

Which of the sights would you like to visit? Tell a partner and say why.

What to do in Dublin

6a   wordbank: descriptions p. 163

Look at these photos from a travel guide. Talk about what you see.

6b

Read the texts. Which sights do you find interesting? Where would you like to go?

Right at the heart of Dublin, you will find the beautiful campus of **Trinity College**. About 20,000 students from Ireland and all around the world study here.
Trinity College is not only Ireland's oldest and most famous university, it is also the home of the Book of Kells, a beautifully illustrated manuscript of the bible which dates back to around the year 800. Over a million tourists come to see it every year.

Go shopping in **Grafton Street**. Spend your money on the latest fashion or buy some traditional Irish sweaters. Listen to the many street musicians playing music.
Have some cake at Bewley's, Dublin's most famous café, or relax at St Stephen's Green, a big public park next to Grafton Street.

If you like cool arts and music, visit **Temple Bar**. This area in the centre of Dublin has arts centres and theatres, a fashion and design market, hip second-hand shops and lots of pubs and bars. Temple Bar is a lively centre of activity for young people and tourists.

ACTIVATE   PRACTISE   **DEVELOP**   PRACTISE   APPLY

Visit **EPIC, the Irish Emigration Museum,** and find out about the many Irish people who left the island and made their mark in the USA and all over the world.
Explore what "being Irish" means in Ireland and all around the world.

Do you like swords, shields and historic battles? Check out **Dublinia Viking Museum**!
Try Viking clothes, find out about life on a Viking ship and learn to fight like a Viking warrior. Learn about Dublin's medieval past by getting to know the city as it was 700 years ago. Play medieval games, find out about medieval food and walk along a medieval Dublin street.

Follow in the footsteps of those who fled the potato famine. 2,500 of them sailed across the Atlantic on the **Jeanie Johnston**.
Travel back in time, find out about the horrible living conditions on board a famine ship and hear the stories of the people who had to leave their home country in order to escape starvation.

6c CHOOSE YOUR LEVEL skill: reading p. 156

| **Choose at least two of the attractions. Write down one or two keywords for each.**
|| **Choose at least three of the attractions. Write down one or two keywords for each.**
||| **Choose at least four of the attractions. Write down one or two keywords for each.**

6d workbook p. 85/5, 6

Work with a partner. Can they guess which attraction your keywords describe? Take turns.

LAND & LEUTE 8  video 17, workbook p.86/7

Irland

Irland ist unterteilt in Nordirland, das zum Vereinigten Königreich gehört, und die Republik Irland mit der Hauptstadt Dublin. Irland stand 750 Jahre lang unter britischer Herrschaft.

Viele Iren wollten, dass Irland unabhängig sein solle, aber es gab auch eine starke Minderheit, die Teil des Vereinigten Königreichs bleiben wollte. Dies waren hauptsächlich Protestanten in Nordirland. Im Jahr 1922, nach dem *Irish War of Independence*, wurden die 26 Grafschaften im südlichen Teil Irlands als *Irish Free State* unabhängig, während die sechs Grafschaften im Norden Teil des Vereinigten Königreichs blieben. Lange Zeit war das

Anlass von Unruhen und Gewalt, vor allem in Nordirland zwischen den 1960er Jahren und 1998. Diese Zeit ist als *The Troubles* bekannt.

1948 wurde der offizielle Name *Republic of Ireland* eingeführt, und 1973 wurde die Republik Irland Teil der Europäischen Union. Seit dem Brexit 2020 ist Irland neben Malta das einzige EU-Mitglied mit Englisch als offizieller Sprache.

Seht euch das Video an. Über welchen Aspekt der irischen Geschichte würdet ihr gern mehr erfahren?

A song for Ireland

7a

Listen to the "Song for Ireland" by Phil and June Colclough and read the first few lines of the lyrics. What do you think the person speaking is like? What situation are they in?

Walking all the day	Talking all the day
Near tall towers where falcons build their nests	With true friends, who try to make you stay
Silver-winged they fly	Telling jokes and news
They know the call of freedom in their breasts	Singing songs to pass the night away
Soar Black Head against the sky	Watched the Galway salmon run
Where twisted rocks run down to the sea	Like silver dancing darting in the sun
Living on your western shore	Living on your western shore
Saw summer sunsets asked for more	Saw summer sunsets asked for more
I stood by your Atlantic sea	I stood by your Atlantic sea
And sang a song for Ireland	And sang a song for Ireland (...)

7b wordbank: feelings p.166

How does the song make you feel? Write down at least three words that describe your feelings.

7c workbook p.86/8, 9

Share your words with a partner. Explain to each other why you chose them.

ACTIVATE   PRACTISE   **DEVELOP**   PRACTISE   APPLY

Gaelic football

8   skill: mediation p. 155, workbook p. 87/10

Imagine you and your friend are talking to Finn, the Gaelic football player. Your friend is very interested in Gaelic football, but his English is not as good as yours. Help him and Finn understand each other.

Your friend: Ich wüsste schon gerne, ob Gaelic Football das Gleiche wie Fußball ist.
(1) You: *Finn, is Gaelic football the same as …?*

Finn: It's a bit like football, but it is also like rugby and basketball.
(2) You: *Es ist ein bisschen …*

Your friend: Spielen da denn 11 Spieler mit?
(3) You: …

Finn: No, there are 15 players on the field.
(4) You: …

Your friend: Und wenn das ein bisschen wie Basketball ist, gibt es dann auch Körbe?
(5) You: …
Finn: No, there are no baskets. The players

kick or punch the ball into or above a goal.
(6) You: …

Your friend: Und wie lange dauert so ein Spiel?
(7) You: …

Finn: A game has two halves of 30 minutes and a short half-time break.
(8) You: …

Your friend: Ich kann mir das alles immer noch nicht vorstellen. Frag ihn bitte, ob wir mal zu einem Spiel kommen können.
(9) You: …

Finn: That's an epic idea! Why don't you come to our game on Friday?
(10) You: …

Planning a trip

9 GET TOGETHER

Get together with a partner.
Read the travel information about Ireland and make a travel itinerary.

Partner A	Partner B
Ⅰ **Go to page 132.**	Ⅰ **Go to page 141.**
Ⅱ **Go to page 135.**	Ⅱ **Go to page 144.**
Ⅲ **Go to page 138.**	Ⅲ **Go to page 147.**

More about Ireland

10 CHOOSE YOUR TASK A: wordbank: travelling p. 163, B+C: skill: searching the internet p. 159, C: wordbank: descriptions p. 163

A **Design a poster advertising Ireland as a holiday destination.**
B   **Do some research on the languages spoken in Ireland and present your findings in class.**
C   **Find information about a famous Irish person (actor, musician, writer, …) and tell your class about them.**

Facts about Ireland

11   CHOOSE YOUR LEVEL workbook p. 87/11, 12

▍▌ Choose the correct words to complete the sentences. Write them down.

1 Dublin is the capital of **The Republic of Ireland** / **Northern Ireland**.
2 Trinity College is Ireland's most famous **church** / **university**.
3 There are lots of **street musicians** / **actors** in Grafton Street.
4 Temple Bar is an area with many **schools and shopping centres** / **arts centres and theatres**.

▍▌ Match the sentence parts and write down the sentences.

1 Dublin is
2 The river in Dublin
3 The Republic of Ireland
4 Ireland is
5 Northern Ireland

A an island.
B belongs to the UK.
C is called the river Liffey.
D is a member of the European Union.
E the capital of the Republic of Ireland.

▍▍▍ Unscramble the sentences and write them down.

1 part of – Northern Ireland – the UK. – is
2 Cork – Ireland. – in the south of – is a city
3 Ireland – and hills. – its green fields – is known for
4 is – an important part of – Music – Irish culture.
5 is – Gaelic football – one of the most popular – in Ireland. – sports
6 the official – of the Republic of Ireland. – English and Irish – languages – are

Preparing a talk

12   workbook p. 88/13, 14

Read the phrases. Then copy them into your exercise book in the order in which you would hear them in a talk.

A Thank you very much for listening.

B Hello everyone. Today, I would like to talk about …

C Finally, I would like to talk about …

D Have you got any questions?

E My next point is …

F To sum everything up, …

G First, let me show you …

■ DIGITAL+ practise more 22-23

ACTIVATE   PRACTISE   DEVELOP   **PRACTISE**   APPLY

A five-minute talk TARGET TASK

13 ▨ ▣ workbook p. 89/15, skill: presentations p. 160, wordbank: presenting something p. 168, media worksheet 4

Your task is to give a five-minute talk about one interesting aspect of Ireland.
Before you start, look at these steps:

STEP 1

Decide what you would like to talk about. Think about:

· music   · people
· food   · sights
· history   · ...

STEP 2

Do your research.
· Do some research on your topic.
· Do not forget to list your sources.
· Choose texts in English which are easy to understand.
· Take notes on the most important facts.

STEP 3

Prepare your presentation.
· Read through your findings. What is important? Leave out what is not important.
· How do you want to present the facts? In which order do you want to present them?
· Find some good pictures.
· You can make a (digital) presentation or a poster and show pictures or videos during your talk.
· Make notes on cue cards.

STEP 4

Practise your talk with a partner.
· Use your notes.
· Give each other feedback.

STEP 5

Give your talk.

Check out

1. Kannst du Schaubildern wichtige Informationen entnehmen?	Workbook, p. 90
2. Kannst du verstehen, was Immigrantinnen und Immigranten über ihr Leben erzählen?	Workbook, p. 91
3. Kannst du einen Text mit Adjektiven interessanter machen?	Workbook, p. 91
4. Kannst du Texte aus einem Reiseführer verstehen?	Workbook, p. 92
5. Kannst du über Sehenswürdigkeiten in Irland sprechen?	Workbook, p. 92
6. Kennst du nützliche Redewendungen für eine Präsentation?	Workbook, p. 93

Enrique's journey

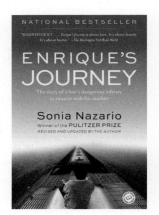

1 *Every year, more than one million immigrants come to the USA. About*
500,000 of them enter the USA illegally, and about 120,000 of these are
"unaccompanied minors" – children who travel without an adult. Most of
them come across the southern border from Mexico after a long journey in
5 *constant fear of being caught and sent back home. One of these minors was*
Enrique, who left Honduras in the year 2000 to look for his mother.
In 2002, his story, reported and written by Sonia Nazario, was published as
a six-part series in the Los Angeles Times and later made into a book.

In Honduras

10 The boy does not understand.
His mother is not talking to him. She will not even look at him. (...)

Lourdes [his mother] knows. She understands, as only a mother can, the terror she is about to
inflict, the ache Enrique will feel and finally the emptiness.
What will become of him? (…)

15 They live on the outskirts of Tegucigalpa, in Honduras. She can barely afford food for him and
his sister, Belky, who is 7. Lourdes, 24, scrubs other people's laundry in a muddy river. She fills a
wooden box with gum and crackers and cigarettes, and she finds a spot where she can (...) sell the
items to passersby. (…)
They have a bleak future. He and Belky are not likely to finish (...) school. Lourdes cannot afford
20 uniforms or pencils. Her husband is gone. A good job is out of the question. So she has decided:
She will leave. She will go to the United States and make money and send it home. She will be gone
for one year, less with luck, or she will bring her children to be with her. It is for them she is leaving,
she tells herself, but still, she feels guilty.
She kneels and kisses Belky and hugs her tightly. (…)
25 But Lourdes cannot face Enrique. He will remember only one thing that she says to him: "Don't
forget to go to church this afternoon."
It is Jan. 29, 1989. His mother (…) walks away.
"Donde esta mi mami?" Enrique cries, over and over. "Where is my mom?"
His mother never returns.

30 *In the following years, Enrique lives first with his father, then with his grandmother. He talks to his*
mother on the phone from time to time. She is able to send money but never comes back and Enrique
misses her. Eleven years after his mother left Honduras, when he is 16 years old, Enrique decides to
leave home and try to get to the USA on his own. Because they have little to no money, many people
trying to get to the USA from Central America ride on freight trains – a dangerous thing to do.

---

illegally = ungesetzlich, illegal; unaccompanied = unbegleitet; minor = Minderjährige/r; border = Grenze; constant = ständig; terror =
Schrecken; to be about to do something = Im Begriff sein, etwas zu tun; to inflict = zufügen; ache = Schmerz; emptiness = Leere; outskirts (pl) =
Randbezirke; barely = kaum; to afford = sich leisten; to scrub = schrubben; laundry = Wäsche; muddy = matschig; wooden box = Holzkiste; gum
= Kaugummi; cracker = Kräcker; cigarette = Zigarette; passersby = Vorübergehende; bleak = trostlos; to be out of the question = nicht in Frage
kommen; guilty = schuldig; to kneel = knien; to hug = umarmen; tightly = fest; Central America = Mittelamerika; freight train = Güterzug

Facing the beast

Enrique looks ahead on the train. Men and boys are
hanging on to the sides of tank cars, trying to find
a spot to sit or stand. Some of the youngsters could
not land their feet on the ladders and have pulled
themselves up rung by rung on their knees, which are
bruised and bloodied.
Suddenly, Enrique hears screams.
Three cars away, a boy, 12 or 13 years old, has
managed to grab the bottom rung of a ladder on
a fuel tanker, but he cannot haul himself up. Air
rushing beneath the train is sucking his legs under
the car. It is tugging at him harder, drawing his feet
toward the wheels.
"Don't let go!" a man shouts. He and others crawl
along the top of the train to a nearby car. They shout again.
The boy dangles from the ladder. He struggles to keep his grip.
Carefully, the men crawl down and reach for him. Slowly, they lift him up.
The rungs batter his legs, but he is alive. He still has his feet.

*Enrique tries several times to get to Mexico. On his journey, he is robbed, beaten, caught by the
immigration police and sent back, but he never gives up. On his eighth try he finally makes it as far
as the Rio Grande, the river that forms part of the border between Mexico and the USA. There he
stays in a camp with other people who wait for a chance to cross the river into US territory. Enrique
manages to call his mother, who is living in North Carolina by now, and she sends him money so he
can pay smugglers to take him to Texas.*

Across the border

Lourdes has not slept. (…)
Now a female smuggler is on the phone. The woman says: "We have your son in Texas, but $1,200 is
not enough. $1,700." Lourdes grows suspicious. (…)
"Put him on the line." she demands.
"He is out shopping for food," the smuggler says.
Lourdes will not be put off. "He is asleep," the smuggler says.
"How can he be both?" Lourdes demands to talk to him.
Finally, the smuggler gives the phone to Enrique.
"Sos tu?" his mother asks anxiously. "Is it you?"
"Si, Mami, it's me."

What do you think: how does the story go on?

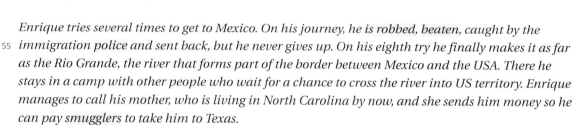

beast = *Bestie*; ahead = *voraus*; to hang on = *sich festhalten an*; ladder = *Leiter*; rung = *Sprosse*; bruised = *geprellt*; bloodied =
blutverschmiert; scream = *Schrei*; bottom = *untere(r, s)*; fuel = *Benzin*; tanker = *Tankwagen*; to haul = *ziehen*; beneath = *unter*; to suck =
saugen; to tug at = *zerren an*; to draw = *ziehen*; toward = *in Richtung*; to let go = *loslassen*; to crawl = *kriechen*; to dangle = *herabhängen*;
grip = *Griff*; to batter = *böse zurichten*; to be robbed = *beraubt werden*; to be beaten = *geschlagen werden*; police = *Polizei*; smuggler =
Schmuggler/in; suspicious = *misstrauisch*; to demand = *verlangen*; to be put off = *sich vertrösten lassen*; anxiously = *besorgt*

Annie Moore

1 After the opening of the new immigration building on Ellis Island on 1 January 1892, the New York Times reported that the "first immigrant to register was fifteen-year-old Annie Moore, from Cork, Ireland."

5 Annie had arrived on the steamboat *Nevada* with her two younger brothers, Anthony and Philip. They were going to join their parents and two older siblings, who had arrived in New York two years earlier.

Ellis Island was decorated in red, white and blue that 10 day to celebrate its opening. Whistles and foghorns were blowing, and it must have been overwhelming to a young girl coming from Ireland. She did not know that she was the first of twelve million people to enter the United States through Ellis Island to look for a 15 better life and that she would become a symbol of Irish immigration to the USA in the years to come.

THE FIRST TO LAND.

Opening of the New Immigration Building at Ellis Island.

New York, Jan. 1.—The opening of the new federal immigration building at Ellis Island took place this morning. Superintendent Colonel John B. Webber and his corps of assistants received the first batch of immigrants, 107 in number, from the steamship Nevada.

The first immigrant to register was fifteen-year-old Annie Moore, from Ireland, who has come over to her brother, John Moore, of this city.

The first immigrant to buy a ticket was Mrs. Ellen King, from Linsmore, who is going to Dorchester, Neb. The building is perfect in detail and 7,000 immigrants can be handled daily with ease.

The article that appeared in the New York Times on January 2, 1892

Today, you can see statues of Annie Moore in New York, inside the Ellis Island National Museum of Immigration and in Cobh, a small town just outside Cork in Ireland, the place where Annie and her brothers set off on their journey to the USA.

20 The sculpture at Cobh is of Annie and her two brothers, the one in New York shows Annie holding a small suitcase in one hand and looking 25 expectantly at the scene before her.

In 1993, Irish sculptor Jeanne Rynhart created two statues of Annie Moore. One stands at the Cobh Heritage Centre in Cork ...

... the other in Ellis Island, New York

opening = Eröffnung; **New York Times** = *Name einer Tageszeitung*; **to register** = *sich anmelden*; **sibling** = *Geschwister*; **whistle** = *Pfeife*; **foghorn** = *Nebelhorn*; **to blow** = *ertönen*; **overwhelming** = *überwältigend*; **to set off** = *sich auf den Weg machen*; **sculpture** = *Skulptur*; **expectantly** = *erwartungsvoll*; **sculptor** = *Bildhauer/in*

Isle of Hope, Isle of Tears

1 *Annie's story inspired writers and musicians.*
One of the most famous songs about her
is "Isle of Hope, Isle of Tears" by Brendan
Graham.

5 On the first day of January
Eighteen ninety-two
They opened Ellis Island
And they let the people through
And the first to cross the threshold
10 Of that Isle of hope and tears
Was Annie Moore from Ireland
Who was only fifteen years

Isle of Hope, Isle of Tears
Isle of Freedom, Isle of Fears
15 But it's not the Isle you left behind
That Isle of Hunger, Isle of Pain
Isle you'll never see again
But the Isle of home is always on your mind

In a little bag she carried
20 All her past and history
And her dreams for the future
In the Land of Liberty
And courage is the passport
When your old world disappears
25 But there's no future in the past
When you're fifteen years

Isle of Hope, Isle of Tears
Isle of Freedom, Isle of Fears
But it's not the Isle you left behind
30 That Isle of Hunger, Isle of Pain
Isle you'll never see again
But the Isle of home is always on your mind

When they closed down Ellis Island
In Nineteen Forty-Three
35 Seventeen million people
Had come there for Sanctuary
And in springtime when I came here
And I stepped onto its piers
I thought of how it must have been
40 When you're fifteen years

Isle of Hope, Isle of Tears
Isle of Freedom, Isle of Fears
But it's not the Isle you left behind
That Isle of Hunger, Isle of Pain
45 Isle you'll never see again
But the Isle of home is always on your mind

Isle of Hope, Isle of Tears
Isle of Freedom, Isle of Fears
But it's not the Isle you left behind
50 That Isle of Hunger, Isle of Pain
Isle you'll never see again
But the Isle of home is always on your mind

What do you think: how did Annie feel when she arrived in the USA? Write her diary entry.

isle = *kleine Insel*; threshold = *(Tür)schwelle*; to leave behind = *zurücklassen*; pain = *Schmerz*; to be on one's mind = *an etwas denken*; courage = *Mut*; passport = *(Reise)pass*; to close down = *schließen*; sanctuary = *Zufluchtsort*; springtime = *Frühling*

At Grand Central Station

9 UNIT 1, p. 27 PARTNER A, wordbank: travelling p. 163, skill: performing a scene p. 161

You work at the ticket office at Grand Central Station in New York.
Your partner would like to go to New Haven.
Look at the boxes and do a role play. You are the first to start.

---

1 Sage Hallo und frage, wie du helfen kannst.
You can say:
Hello. How can I ...?

---

2 Partner B möchte Fahrkarten kaufen.

---

3 Sage, dass das kein Problem ist und frage, wie viele Personen fahren möchten.
You can say:
That's ... How many ...?

---

4 Partner B antwortet.

---

5 Sage, dass es ein Sonderangebot für Familien gibt und frage, wie alt die Kinder sind.
You can say:
There's a special offer for ...
How old ...?

---

6 Partner B antwortet.

---

7 Sage, dass die Fahrkarten für Kinder zwischen 5 und 11 nur 1 Dollar kosten.
You can say:
Tickets for children between ...
are only ...

---

8 Partner B hat eine weitere Frage.

---

9 Sage, dass Hin- und Rückfahrkarten für alle 75 Dollar kosten.
You can say:
Return tickets are ...

---

10 Partner B reagiert.

---

11 Überreiche die Fahrkarten und frage, ob Partner B mit Karte oder Bargeld zahlen möchte.
You can say:
Here you are. Would you like to pay with card or cash?

---

12 Partner B hat noch eine Frage.

---

13 Sage, dass der nächste Zug um 11.45 Uhr auf Gleis 17 fährt.
You can say:
... leaves at ... from platform ...

---

14 Partner B reagiert.

---

15 Verabschiede dich.

Exchange challenges

10 UNIT 2, p. 51   PARTNER A, wordbank: seeking and giving advice p. 166, skill: performing a scene p. 161

Imagine you are an exchange student at an American high school and you are unhappy. You want to talk to the school counsellor. Choose one problem or more from the list. Talk to your partner about your situation.

Problems
→ *I have no friends at my new school.*
→ *My host parents are always at work.*
→ *I don't like the food.*
→ *...*

You can say:
I'm unhappy because ...
I have a problem. I ...
...

Texting

9 UNIT 3, p. 74   PARTNER A

You and your partner are texting each other to make plans for the afternoon. Look at the ideas below and write two or more messages to your partner. You are the first to start.

Cinema
watch film and
buy pizza later

Swimming
go to the pool

Gaming
play video
games

???

You can write:
What about ...?
Let's ...
Do you have another idea?
...

Arguments for
→ *It's fun.*
→ *It's cheap.*
→ *You can meet friends there.*
→ *It's nice outside.*
→ *...*

Arguments against
→ *It's boring.*
→ *I don't like it.*
→ *It's expensive.*
→ *The weather is not good enough.*
→ *...*

A role play

14 UNIT 4, p. 99   PARTNER A, wordbank: the world of work p. 170, skill: performing a scene p. 161

You are applying for a job as a dogsitter. Your partner is looking for a dogsitter. Use your role card and do a role play. Your partner is the first to start.

Role card partner A

- You have some experience because your grandmother has dogs.
- You are free on Tuesdays and Thursdays.
- You can sometimes work at the weekend.
- …

You can say:

I love dogs.
I have some experience with dogs.
I sometimes look after my …
I can work …
…

Planning a trip

9 UNIT 5, p. 123 PARTNER A, skill: talking with people p. 154

Read the flyers and tell your partner about the sights. Then listen to what partner B tells you about *Dolphin Discovery Boat Trips* and *Marble Arch Caves* – two tourist attractions in Ireland. Decide on two sights you would both like to visit.

The Ring of Kerry

This route in County Kerry takes you to some of the most beautiful places in Ireland. Here are some:
- Derrynane Beach, one of the world's cleanest beaches
- Cahergal, a stone ringfort from the Iron Age
- Torc Waterfall

You can do the tour by car or bus, but there are walking paths, too.

You can say:

At … there is …
You can see …
I would like to go to … because …
I don't like …
…

The Zoological Museum Dublin

- An exhibition of animals from Ireland and abroad.
- Learn how scientists in Australia are trying to recreate the Tasmanian Wolf.
- Have your photograph taken through the jaws of a Great White Shark.

At Grand Central Station

9a UNIT 1, p. 27 PARTNER A, wordbank: travelling p. 163, skill: performing a scene p. 161

▌ **You work at the ticket office at Grand Central Station in New York.**
Your partner would like to go to New Haven.
Look at the boxes and do a role play. You are the first to start.

1 Begrüße deinen Kunden / deine Kundin und frage, wie du helfen kannst. You can say: *Hello. How can I ...?*	**9** Sage, dass Hin- und Rückfahrkarten für alle $75 kosten. You can say: *Return tickets are ...*
2 Partner B möchte Fahrkarten kaufen.	**10** Partner B reagiert.
3 Sage, dass das kein Problem ist und frage, wie viele Personen fahren möchten. You can say: *... How many ...?*	**11** Überreiche die Fahrkarten und frage, ob Partner B mit Karte oder Bargeld zahlen möchte. You can say: *Would you like to pay with card or cash?*
4 Partner B antwortet.	**12** Partner B hat noch eine Frage.
5 Sage, dass es ein Sonderangebot für Familien gibt und frage, wie alt die Kinder sind. You can say: *There's a special offer for ...* *How old ...?*	**13** Sage, dass der nächste Zug um 11:45 auf Gleis 17 fährt. You can say: *... leaves at ... from platform ...*
6 Partner B antwortet.	**14** Partner B reagiert.
7 Sage, dass die Fahrkarten für Kinder zwischen 5 und 11 nur $1 kosten, wenn sie mit einem Erwachsenen zusammen fahren. You can say: *Tickets for children between ... are only ... if they are travelling with an adult.*	**15** Verabschiede dich.
8 Partner B hat eine weitere Frage.	

Exchange challenges

10 UNIT 2, p. 51 PARTNER A, wordbank: seeking and giving advice p. 166, skill: performing a scene p. 161

Imagine you are an exchange student at an American high school and you are unhappy. You have made an appointment with the school counsellor. Choose one problem or more from the list below or make up your own. Talk to your partner about your situation.

Problems
→ I haven't made any friends at my new school yet.
→ My host parents are always at work and I'm alone all the time.
→ I don't like the food my host parents cook.
→ I'm homesick.
→ …

You can say:
I'm very unhappy because …
I have a problem. I …
I don't know how to tell them that …
…

Texting

10a UNIT 3, p. 74 PARTNER A

You and your partner are texting each other to make plans for the afternoon.
Look at the ideas below and write two or more messages to your partner.
You are the first to start.

Cinema
watch film and
go for pizza afterwards

Swimming
spend the afternoon
at the pool

Gaming
play video
games

???

You can write:
What about …?
Let's …
Why don't we …?
Do you have another idea?
…

Arguments for
→ It's fun.
→ It's not too expensive.
→ We've never tried it before.
→ You can meet friends there.
→ It's so nice outside.
→ …

Arguments against
→ It's boring.
→ I didn't like it last time.
→ It's too expensive.
→ My parents will never say yes.
→ The weather is not good enough.
→ …

A role play

14 UNIT 4, p. 99   PARTNER A, wordbank: the world of work p. 170, skill: performing a scene p. 161

You are applying for a job as a dogsitter. Your partner is looking for a dogsitter. Use your role card and do a role play. Your partner is the first to start.

Role card partner A

· You have some experience because your grandmother has always had dogs.
· You are free on Tuesdays and Thursdays.
· You can also sometimes work at the weekend.
· ...

You can say:
I love dogs.
I have some experience with dogs.
I used to look after ...
...

Planning a trip

9 UNIT 5, p. 123   PARTNER A, skill: talking with people p. 154

Read the flyers and tell your partner about the sights. Then listen to what partner B tells you about *Dolphin Discovery Boat Trips* and *Marble Arch Caves* – two tourist attractions in Ireland. Decide on two sights you would both like to visit.

The Ring of Kerry

This route in County Kerry takes you to some of the most beautiful places in Ireland. Here are some:
· Derrynane Beach, one of the world's cleanest beaches
· Cahergal, a stone ringfort from the Iron Age
· 110-metre long Torc Waterfall
You can do the tour by car or bus, but there are walking paths, too.

You can say:
At ... there is ...
You can see ...
I would like to go to ... because ...
I don't like ... that much. I'd rather go to ...
...

The Zoological Museum Dublin

· An interactive exhibition of animals from Ireland and abroad.
· Learn how scientists in Australia are trying to use DNA to recreate the Tasmanian Wolf.
· Have your photograph taken through the jaws of a Great White Shark.

At Grand Central Station

9a UNIT 1, p. 27 PARTNER A, wordbank: travelling p. 163, skill: performing a scene p. 161

▌▌▌ You work at the ticket office at Grand Central Station in New York.
Your partner would like to go to New Haven.
Look at the boxes and do a role play. You are the first to start.

1 Begrüße deinen Kunden / deine Kundin und frage, wie du helfen kannst.
You can say:
Hello. How …?

2 Partner B möchte Fahrkarten kaufen.

3 Sage, dass das kein Problem ist und frage, wie viele Personen fahren möchten.
You can say:
… How …?

4 Partner B antwortet.

5 Sage, dass es ein Sonderangebot für Familien gibt und frage, wie alt die Kinder sind.
You can say:
There's a special offer …
How …?

6 Partner B antwortet.

7 Sage, dass die Fahrkarten für Kinder zwischen 5 und 11 nur $1 kosten, wenn sie mit einem Erwachsenen zusammen fahren.
You can say:
Tickets … between … are only …
if they … with an adult.

8 Partner B hat eine weitere Frage.

9 Sage, dass Hin- und Rückfahrkarten für alle $75 kosten.
You can say:
Return tickets are …

10 Partner B reagiert.

11 Überreiche die Fahrkarten und frage, ob Partner B mit Karte oder Bargeld zahlen möchte.
You can say:
… with card or cash?

12 Partner B hat noch eine Frage.

13 Sage, dass der nächste Zug um 11:45 auf Gleis 17 fährt.
You can say:
… from platform …

14 Partner B reagiert.

15 Verabschiede dich.

Exchange challenges

10 UNIT 2, p. 51 PARTNER A, wordbank: seeking and giving advice p. 166, skill: performing a scene p. 161

III Imagine you are an exchange student at an American high school and you are unhappy. You have made an appointment with the school counsellor. Choose one problem or more from the list below or make up your own. Talk to your partner about your situation.

Problems

→ *I haven't made any friends at my new school yet.*

→ *My host parents are always at work and I'm alone all the time.*

→ *I don't like the food my host parents cook.*

→ *I'm homesick.*

→ *My host brother is not very nice.*

→ *...*

Texting

9 UNIT 3, p. 74 PARTNER A

III You and your partner are texting each other to make plans for the afternoon. Look at the ideas below and write two or more messages to your partner. You are the first to start.

| **Cinema** watch film and go for pizza afterwards | **Swimming** spend the afternoon at the pool |
| **Gaming** play video games | **???** |

You can write:

What about ...?

Let's ...

Why don't we ...?

...

Arguments for

→ *fun*

→ *not too expensive*

→ *never tried it before*

→ *can meet friends there*

→ *good for your health*

→ *weather so good*

→ *...*

Arguments against

→ *boring*

→ *too expensive*

→ *didn't like it last time*

→ *what we always do*

→ *people there I don't want to meet*

→ *parents will never say yes*

→ *...*

A role play

14 UNIT 4, p. 99   PARTNER A, wordbank: the world of work p. 170, skill: performing a scene p. 161

▮▮▮ You are applying for a job as a dogsitter. Your partner is looking for a dogsitter. Use your role card and do a role play. Your partner is the first to start.

Role card partner A

· You have some experience because your grandmother has always had dogs.
· You are free on Tuesdays and Thursdays.
· You can also sometimes work at the weekend.
· …

Planning a trip

9 UNIT 5, p. 123   PARTNER A, skill: talking with people p. 154

▮▮▮ Read the flyers and tell your partner about the sights. Then listen to what partner B tells you about *Dolphin Discovery Boat Trips* and *Marble Arch Caves* – two tourist attractions in Ireland. Decide on two sights you would both like to visit.

The Ring of Kerry

This 179-kilometre-long route takes you to some of the most beautiful places in County Kerry, Ireland. Here are just a few:
· Derrynane Beach, near the village of Caherdaniel, is one of the world's cleanest beaches.
· Make sure to go to Cahergal, a stone ringfort from the Iron Age.
· Torc Waterfall is a 110-metre long waterfall surrounded by fantastic woodland.
You can do the tour by car or bus, but there are walking paths, too.

The Zoological Museum Dublin

· A collection of animals from Ireland and abroad in an interactive exhibition.
· Learn how scientists in Australia are trying to use DNA to recreate the Tasmanian Wolf.
· Hold one of the world's strangest teeth.
· Have your photograph taken through the jaws of a Great White Shark.

At Grand Central Station

9 UNIT 1, p. 27   PARTNER B, wordbank: travelling p. 163, skill: performing a scene p. 161

You are at the ticket office at Grand Central Station in New York and would like to go to New Haven. Look at the boxes and do a role play. Your partner is the first to start.

1   Partner A begrüßt dich.

2   Sage Hallo und sage, dass du gern Fahrkarten nach New Haven kaufen möchtest.
You can say:
Hello. I would like to buy …, please.

3   Partner A fragt dich etwas.

4   Sage, dass zwei Erwachsene und zwei Kinder fahren möchten.
You can say:
… adults and …

5   Partner A hat noch eine Frage.

6   Sage, dass die Kinder 7 und 9 Jahre alt sind.
You can say:
They are …

7   Partner A reagiert.

8   Sage, dass das großartig ist und frage, wie teuer Fahrkarten für die Hin- und Rückfahrt für die ganze Familie sind.
You can say:
Great.
How much are return tickets for …?

9   Partner A beantwortet deine Frage.

10   Sage, dass du die Fahrkarten kaufen möchtest.
You can say:
OK. Then I'd like to …

11   Partner A fragt dich etwas.

12   Sage, dass du mit Karte zahlen möchtest. Zahle und frage, wann und wo der nächste Zug nach New Haven fährt.
You can say:
With card, please. Here you are.
Thank you very much. When does … leave? From which platform does …?

13   Partner A reagiert.

14   Bedanke und verabschiede dich.

15   Partner A reagiert.

Exchange challenges

10 UNIT 2, p. 51 PARTNER B, wordbank: seeking and giving advice p. 166, skill: performing a scene p. 161

Imagine you are a school counsellor at an American high school. An exchange student from Germany is unhappy and has come to talk to you. Give them some advice.

Advice
→ *join a school club or a sports team*
→ *talk to your host family but stay polite and friendly*
→ *cook for your host family or go shopping for food with them*
→ *...*

You can say:
Why don't you ...?
You could ...
...

Texting

9 UNIT 3, p. 74 PARTNER B

You and your partner are texting each other to make plans for the afternoon.
Look at the ideas below and write two or more messages to your partner.
Your partner is the first to start.

| **Studying** | **Hanging out** |
| prepare for maths test | meet friends and chill |

| **Biking** | **???** |
| go on a bike tour | |

You can write:
What about ...?
Let's ...
Why don't we ...?
Do you have another idea?
...

Arguments for
→ *I really need a good mark in maths.*
→ *It's fun.*
→ *It's cheap.*
→ *It's nice outside.*
→ *...*

Arguments against
→ *It's boring.*
→ *I don't like it.*
→ *It's too expensive.*
→ *The weather is not good.*
→ *...*

A role play

14 UNIT 4, p. 99   PARTNER B, wordbank: the world of work p. 170, skill: performing a scene p. 161

You are looking for a dogsitter. Your partner has applied for the job and has come to your place for a job interview. Use your role card and do a role play. You are the first to start.

Role card partner B

- You have a new job and now you don't have enough time for your dog.
- You are looking for a dogsitter with experience.
- You need someone who takes your dog for walks on at least two afternoons a week and sometimes at the weekend.
- …

You can say:

*What's your experience with dogs or
    other pets?*
When can you take my dog …?
Could you …?
…

Planning a trip

9 UNIT 5, p. 123   PARTNER B, skill: talking with people p. 154

Read the flyers. Then listen to what your partner tells you about the *Ring of Kerry* and the *Zoological Museum* in Dublin – two tourist attractions in Ireland.
Tell your partner about the *Marble Arch Caves* and the *Dolphin Discovery Boat Trip*.
Together, decide on two sights you both would like to visit.

Marble Arch Caves

- Explore a natural underworld of rivers and passages.
- Our guides take you on exciting tours through the caves.
- Take a ride on one of our electric boats along a river through the caves.

You can say:

At … there is …
You can see …
I would like to go to … because …
…

Dolphin Discovery Boat Trip

- There is a group of bottlenose dolphins where the river Shannon flows into the Atlantic Ocean.
- We take you on a tour to watch them and their family.

At Grand Central Station

9 UNIT 1, p. 27 PARTNER B, wordbank: travelling p. 163, skill: performing a scene p. 161

You are at the ticket office at Grand Central Station in New York and would like to go to New Haven. Look at the boxes and do a role play. Your partner is the first to start.

---

1 Partner A begrüßt dich.

---

2 Begrüße den Ticketverkäufer / die Ticketverkäuferin und sage, dass du gern Fahrkarten nach New Haven kaufen möchtest.
You can say:
Hello. I would like to …, please.

---

3 Partner A benötigt weitere Informationen.

---

4 Sage, dass vier Personen fahren möchten, zwei Erwachsene und zwei Kinder.
You can say:
… adults and …

---

5 Partner A hat noch eine Frage.

---

6 Sage, dass die Kinder 7 und 9 Jahre alt sind.
You can say:
They are …

---

7 Partner A reagiert.

---

8 Sage, dass das großartig ist und frage, wie teuer Fahrkarten für Hin- und Rückfahrt für die ganze Familie sind.
You can say:
Great.
So how much are return tickets for …?

---

9 Partner A beantwortet deine Frage.

---

10 Sage, dass du die Fahrkarten kaufen möchtest.
You can say:
OK. Then I'd like to …

---

11 Partner A reagiert.

---

12 Sage, dass du mit Karte zahlen möchtest und frage, wann und wo der nächste Zug nach New Haven fährt.
You can say:
With card, please. Here …
When … leave?
From which …?

---

13 Partner A reagiert.

---

14 Bedanke und verabschiede dich.

---

15 Partner A reagiert.

Exchange challenges

10 UNIT 2, p. 51 PARTNER B, wordbank: seeking and giving advice p. 166, skill: performing a scene p. 161

II Imagine you are a school counsellor at an American high school. An exchange student from Germany is unhappy and has come to talk to you. Give them some advice.

Advice
→ *join school club or sports team*
→ *talk to host family, stay polite and friendly*
→ *cook your favourite food for host family, go shopping for food with them*
→ *...*

You can say:

Why don't you ...?

You could ...

It can be helpful if you ...

...

Texting

9 UNIT 3, p. 74 PARTNER B

II You and your partner are texting each other to make plans for the afternoon.
Look at the ideas below and write two or more messages to your partner.
Your partner is the first to start.

Studying prepare for maths test	**Hanging out** meet friends and just chill
Biking go on a bike tour and enjoy nature	**???**

You can write:

What about ...?

Let's ...

Why don't we ...?

Do you have another idea?

...

Arguments for
→ *I really need a good mark in maths.*
→ *It's fun.*
→ *It's not too expensive.*
→ *We've never tried it before.*
→ *It's so nice outside.*
→ *...*

Arguments against
→ *It's boring.*
→ *I didn't like it last time.*
→ *It's too expensive.*
→ *My parents will never say yes.*
→ *The weather is not good enough.*
→ *...*

A role play

14   UNIT 4, p. 99   PARTNER B, wordbank: the world of work p. 170, skill: performing a scene p. 161

‖ **You are looking for a dogsitter. Your partner has applied for the job and has come to your place for a job interview. Use your role card and do a role play. You are the first to start.**

Role card partner B

· You have a new job and now you don't have enough time for your dog anymore.
· You are looking for a dogsitter with some experience.
· You need someone who takes your dog for walks on at least two afternoons a week and sometimes at the weekend.
· ...

You can say:

What's your experience with dogs or other pets?

When can you take my dog ...?

Could you ...?

...

Planning a trip

9   UNIT 5, p. 123   PARTNER B, skill: talking with people p. 154

‖ **Read the flyers. Then listen to what your partner tells you about the *Ring of Kerry* and the *Zoological Museum* in Dublin – two tourist attractions in Ireland. Tell your partner about the *Marble Arch Caves* and the *Dolphin Discovery Boat Trip*.**
Together, decide on two sights you both would like to visit.

Marble Arch Caves

· Explore a natural underworld of rivers, waterfalls and passages.
· Our guides take you on exciting tours through the caves.
· Take a ride on one of our electric boats along a river through the caves.

You can say:

At ... there is ...

You can see ...

I would like to go to ... because ...

I don't like ... that much. I'd rather go to ...

...

Dolphin Discovery Boat Trip

· Where the river Shannon flows into the Atlantic Ocean lives a group of bottlenose dolphins.
· We take you on a tour to watch them and their calves.

At Grand Central Station

9 UNIT 1, p. 27   PARTNER B, wordbank: travelling p. 163, skill: performing a scene p. 161

III You are at the ticket office at Grand Central Station in New York and would like to go to New Haven. Look at the boxes and do a role play. Your partner is the first to start.

1   Partner A begrüßt dich.

2   Begrüße den Ticketverkäufer / die Ticketverkäuferin und sage, dass du gern Fahrkarten nach New Haven kaufen möchtest.
You can say:
…, please.

3   Partner A benötigt weitere Informationen.

4   Sage, dass vier Personen fahren möchten, zwei Erwachsene und zwei Kinder.
You can say:
… adults and …

5   Partner A hat noch eine Frage.

6   Sage, dass die Kinder 7 und 9 Jahre alt sind.
You can say:
They …

7   Partner A reagiert.

8   Sage, dass das großartig ist und frage, wie teuer Fahrkarten für Hin- und Rückfahrt für die ganze Familie sind.
You can say:
… are return tickets for …?

9   Partner A beantwortet deine Frage.

10   Sage, dass du die Fahrkarten kaufen möchtest.
You can say:
OK. Then I'd …

11   Partner A reagiert.

12   Sage, dass du mit Karte zahlen möchtest und frage, wann und wo der nächste Zug nach New Haven fährt.
You can say:
With card, please.
When …? From which …?

13   Partner A reagiert.

14   Bedanke und verabschiede dich.

15   Partner A reagiert.

Exchange challenges

10 UNIT 2, p. 51 PARTNER B, wordbank: seeking and giving advice p. 166, skill: performing a scene p. 161

||| **Imagine you are a school counsellor at an American high school. An exchange student from Germany is unhappy and has come to talk to you. Give them some advice.**

Advice
→ *join school club or sports team, try to be more open*
→ *talk to host family, stay polite and friendly*
→ *cook your favourite food for host family, go shopping for food with them*
→ *...*

You can say:

Why don't you ...?

It can be helpful if you ...

...

Texting

9 UNIT 3, p. 74 PARTNER B

||| **You and your partner are texting each other to make plans for the afternoon.
Look at the ideas below and write two or more messages to your partner.
Your partner is the first to start.**

Studying prepare for maths test	**Hanging out** meet friends and just chill
Biking go on a bike tour and enjoy nature	**???**

You can write:

What about ...?

Let's ...

Why don't we ...?

...

Arguments for
→ *need a good mark in maths*
→ *fun*
→ *not too expensive*
→ *never tried it before*
→ *so nice outside*
→ *...*

Arguments against
→ *boring*
→ *didn't like it last time*
→ *too expensive*
→ *parents will never say yes*
→ *weather is not good enough*
→ *...*

A role play

14 UNIT 4, p. 99 PARTNER B, wordbank: the world of work p. 170, skill: performing a scene p. 161

||| **You are looking for a dogsitter. Your partner has applied for the job and has come to your place for a job interview. Use your role card and do a role play. You are the first to start.**

Role card partner B

- You have a new job and now you don't have enough time for your dog anymore.
- You are looking for a dogsitter with some experience.
- You need someone who takes your dog for walks on at least two afternoons a week and sometimes at the weekend.
- ...

Planning a trip

9 UNIT 5, p. 123 PARTNER B, skill: talking with people p. 154

||| **Read the flyers. Then listen to what your partner tells you about the *Ring of Kerry* and the *Zoological Museum* in Dublin – two tourist attractions in Ireland. Tell your partner about the *Marble Arch Caves* and the *Dolphin Discovery Boat Trip*. Together, decide on two sights you both would like to visit.**

Marble Arch Caves

- Explore a natural underworld of rivers, waterfalls and winding passages.
- Our guides take you on exciting tours through the caves.
- Take a ride on one of our electrically powered boats along a river that flows through the caves.

Dolphin Discovery Boat Trip

- Where the river Shannon flows into the Atlantic Ocean lives Ireland's only resident group of bottlenose dolphins.
- Book a tour on one of our five boats and enjoy an afternoon of watching them and their calves.

Hollywood ◼ DIGITAL+

Introduction

Hollywood is a neighbourhood in Los Angeles and the heart of the world-famous American film industry. It is home to many big film companies and attracts creative people who want to try their luck in the entertainment industry.
Take a closer look at what lies behind the glitz and glamour of the red carpet and find out more about Hollywood and the American film industry!

Plan it

1 In class, think about what you would like to do in your project. You can collect ideas in a list, for example:

- Prepare a presentation or a podcast about the history of the film industry in Hollywood.
- Present a famous Hollywood film director, producer, film music composer, actor or actress.
- Write about jobs in the film industry.
- Prepare a presentation or a podcast about important film awards.
- Present facts about a famous Hollywood film in a fact file.
- Write a film review about a Hollywood production.
- …

> **Tip**
>
> You can make a class product, for example a film magazine: every group creates one page, and then you can put everything together at the end.

2 Now get together in small groups and make a detailed plan. Write down:

- what information you need
- how you can find information
- how you want to present your work
- what material you need for your project work
  (for example: computer, paper, glue, ...)
- who does what and when

> **Tip**
>
> When you as a group have a plan about what to do and how to present your work, you can ask your classmates from other groups for feedback on your plan.

Do it skill: searching the Internet p. 159, media worksheet 6

And ... action! Do research, collect pictures, write texts, ... and create an interesting film review, fact file, poster, computer presentation, ... Here is an example of a film review:

Film review: La La Land

United States, 2016
Running time: 128 minutes
Cast: Ryan Gosling, Emma Stone, John Legend, Rosemarie DeWitt
Director: Damien Chazelle
Genres: romance, comedy, drama, musical

The film is about an actress (Mia, played by Emma Stone) and a jazz musician (Sebastian, played by Ryan Gosling). They meet in Los Angeles several times. They are both trying to make their dreams come true – Mia wants to star in big films and Sebastian wants to play music at his own concerts. They fall in love, but trying to make their dreams come true takes a lot of energy, and they find that they don't have any energy left for their relationship.

"La La Land" is a lovely film with lots of singing and dancing. I enjoyed it because it shows the world of Hollywood in an exciting way. Some people don't like the film because of how some of the acting is done, but I think you should form your own opinion about it!

★★★☆☆

Check it

Check everything. Are there any spelling or grammar mistakes? Are the pictures big enough? Is everything easy to understand? If you want to give a presentation, practise it before you give it.

Present it skill: presentations p. 160

Present your work. You can ask your classmates for feedback after the presentation.

Green cities ⬚ DIGITAL+

Introduction

Cities not only in the US, but all around the world are trying to become "greener" in order to improve their citizens' quality of life, become more sustainable and fight climate change. So how can cities become "greener", and what are good examples?
Do some research and find out more!

Plan it

1 In class, collect ideas for topics you could work on. You can make notes in a word web. Here is an example:

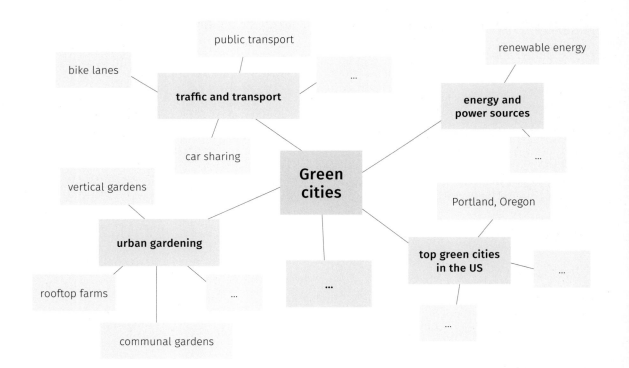

2 Now collect ideas about what you could create. For example:

- fact files
- articles
- podcasts
- posters
- ...

Urban gardening in NYC – The 'edible' city

There are more than 700 urban farms and gardens in New York City – and they're not only on the ground. Many are high above the streets on rooftops! These urban farms are growing fresh fruit and vegetables right in the city. They're good for the environment and they look nice. But there's more to urban gardening than fresh vegetables, fruit, beautiful flowers and bees. Gardens like these help people to live a better life because it's also about creating a community, about caring and sharing.

3 Now get together in small groups and make a detailed plan. Write down:

- what information you need
- how you can get the information
- how you want to present your work
- what material you need for your project work (for example: computer, paper, glue, ...)
- who does what and when

Tip

When you as a group have a plan about what to do and how to present your work, you can ask your classmates from other groups for feedback on your plan.

Do it 🔳 🔳 skill: searching the Internet p. 159, media worksheet 6

Do research, collect pictures, write texts, ... and create an interesting fact file, article, ...

Check it

Check everything. Are there any spelling or grammar mistakes? Are the pictures big enough?
Is everything easy to understand? If you want to give a presentation, practise it before you give it.

Present it skill: presentations p. 160

Present your work. You can ask your classmates for feedback after the presentation.

1 WORKING WITH WORDS
Wortschatzarbeit

Im *Dictionary* ab Seite 224 kannst du die Wörter aus diesem Buch und die Lernwörter aus den vorigen Bänden nachschlagen. Wenn du ein Wort suchst, das dort nicht steht, kannst du ein Wörterbuch benutzen. Oft kannst du dir aber auch ein Wort erschließen, weil du schon ein ähnliches Wort kennst.

Wörterbücher

▶ Die Wörter sind alphabetisch geordnet. Du darfst nicht nur auf den ersten Buchstaben achten, sondern musst auch die folgenden Buchstaben angucken: *face* steht beispielsweise vor *false*.

▶ Hinter den Einträgen stehen Lautschrift und Wortart. Dann folgen in einsprachigen Wörterbüchern eine Definition oder Erklärung des Wortes, in zweisprachigen Wörterbüchern die Übersetzung und Beispiele zur Verwendung des Wortes.

▶ Du musst immer alle Einträge durchlesen. Dann entscheidest du, welche Übersetzung am besten passt. Wenn du zum Beispiel ein Rezept liest und dort das Wort *season* findest, schlag im Wörterbuch unter „s", dann „se" / „sea" usw. nach, bis du das Wort findest.

> *Method:*
> *1. Cut the chicken into slices. Then season the chicken with salt, pepper and curry powder.*

▶ *season* als Nomen mit der Bedeutung „Jahreszeit" oder „Saison" ergibt hier keinen Sinn. Weiter unten findest du das Verb *season*. Dort steht unter anderem der Eintrag „würzen" – das passt hier gut als Übersetzung.

Erschließungsmethoden

▶ Manche Wörter musst du gar nicht nachschlagen, denn du kannst sie dir herleiten. Du kennst beispielsweise *„friendly"* – *„unfriendly"* ist das Gegenteil. Oder du kennst *„organization"* – *„organize"* ist das zugehörige Verb.

▨▨ 🔲 **Tipp: Nutze elektronische Hilfsmittel!** (media worksheet 3)

· Im Internet gibt es viele Seiten, auf denen du Wörter nachschlagen und dir die richtige Aussprache anhören kannst. Oft gibt es Erklärungen zu den unterschiedlichen Bedeutungen in verschiedenen Zusammenhängen.

2 LISTENING
Hören

Folgende Strategien für Hörübungen können dir helfen, Hörtexte
besser zu verstehen:

1. Vor dem Hören

▶ Gibt es eine Höraufgabe im Buch? Lies sie dir genau durch. Was sollst du herausfinden?

▶ Wie lautet die Überschrift des Hörtextes? Welche Hinweise gibt sie dir?

▶ Gibt es Bilder? Was ist darauf zu sehen?

▶ Überlege: Worum könnte es gehen? Was weißt du schon über das Thema?

2. Während des Hörens

▶ Höre dir den Hörtext einmal ganz an. Wer spricht? Was passiert? Du musst nicht jedes einzelne
Wort verstehen. Versuche erst einmal herauszufinden, worum es ganz allgemein geht
(listening for gist).

▶ Achte auch auf die Stimmen der Sprechenden und auf Hintergrundgeräusche. Sie können dir
helfen zu verstehen, worum es geht.

▶ Sieh dir noch einmal die Aufgabe an. Dann höre wieder zu.
Achte diesmal auf Details *(listening for detail)* und mache dir Notizen.

Who?	Where?	When?	What?
Wer spricht? Um wen geht es?	Wo findet das Gespräch / die Geschichte statt?	Wann findet das Gespräch / die Geschichte statt?	Was wird besprochen? Was passiert?

3. Nach dem Hören

▶ Vergleicht eure Ergebnisse. Was habt ihr herausgefunden?

🔲 **Tipp: Nutze jede Gelegenheit, um Englisch zu hören!**

· Alle Hörtexte zum Buch findest du, wenn du auf www.westermann.de/webcode den Webcode
WES-128207-001 eingibst oder den QR-Code scannst, den du auf Seite 2 findest.
· Es gibt verschiedene Möglichkeiten, sich Texte in verschiedenen Geschwindigkeiten vorlesen zu
lassen. Du kannst probieren, das Tempo nach und nach zu erhöhen.

3 Mit anderen sprechen

TALKING WITH PEOPLE

Sprich so viel Englisch wie möglich mit deinen Mitschülerinnen und Mitschülern.

1. Versuche, so viel wie möglich auf Englisch auszudrücken

▸ Lerne Ausdrücke auswendig, die du im Gespräch verwenden kannst, z. B. *"There is … / There are … / What about …? / Thank you. / You're welcome."*
 Auch in den *wordbanks* ab Seite 162 findest du nützliche Ausdrücke.

▸ Wenn dir ein Wort, z. B. „*spoon*", nicht einfällt, kannst du es umschreiben:
 "Excuse me, could you pass me the … erm … it's not a fork or a knife. You can eat soup with it."

2. Merke dir Redewendungen und Sätze

▸ Es gibt eine Reihe von Redewendungen und Sätzen, die du im Englischunterricht häufig verwenden kannst. Viele davon findest du bei den *classroom phrases* auf den Seiten 172-173.

3. Wenn du Interviews durchführst

▸ Schreibe deine Fragen auf.

▸ Stelle Fragen, auf die man nicht nur mit „ja" oder „nein" antworten kann: Verwende Fragewörter wie *what, when, where, who, how* oder *why*.

▸ Wenn du etwas nicht richtig verstanden hast, bitte um Wiederholung:
 "Can you say that again, please?" oder: *"Can you repeat that, please?"*

4. Sprich so oft Englisch, wie du kannst

▸ Höre dir die Hörtexte aus deinem Englischbuch an und lies die Texte laut mit. Versuche, die Aussprache der Sprecherinnen und Sprecher nachzuahmen.

▸ Singe englischsprachige Lieder mit.

▸ Unterhalte dich auf Englisch mit jemandem, der ebenfalls Englisch sprechen kann.

▨ ▩ **Tipp: Nimm dich auf!** (media worksheet 2, 5, 17)

· Lies einen Text aus dem Buch laut vor oder sprich Englisch und nimm dich auf. Dann kannst du dich selbst anhören und überprüfen, wie dein Englisch klingt.

· Wenn ihr zu zweit zusammenarbeitet, könnt ihr Dialoge und Interviews aufnehmen und gemeinsam prüfen, ob es noch etwas zu verbessern gibt.

4 WRITING
Schreiben

Es ist wichtig, dass du deinen Text planst und nach dem Schreiben überarbeitest.

1. Planen

▷ Auf www.westermann.de/webcode kannst du den Webcode WES-128207-001 eingeben und dort Anleitungen zu verschiedenen Textsorten, z.B. Brief, E-Mail oder Blogeintrag, finden.

▷ Wenn du eine Geschichte schreiben willst, kannst du mithilfe von *who, what, where, when* und *why* Ideen sammeln und die Geschichte planen.

▷ Du kannst in einem *word web* oder in einer Liste passende Wörter sammeln. Sieh in den *wordbanks* ab Seite 162 nach, wenn du Hilfe brauchst.

▷ Überlege: Was sollte am Anfang stehen? Was folgt darauf? Wie könnte das Ende sein? Wie kannst du den Text interessant machen? Wenn du einen Artikel oder Bericht schreibst, solltest du dir vorher überlegen, wie du ihn gliedern möchtest.

2. Schreiben und überarbeiten

▷ Schreibe zuerst einen Entwurf.
▷ Überlege dir eine passende Überschrift.
▷ Wenn du Bilder einfügen möchtest, vergiss nicht, anzugeben, wo du sie gefunden hast.
▷ Überarbeite und verbessere dann deinen Text. Du kannst auch andere um Hilfe bitten.
▷ Schreibe dann deinen Text sauber ab. Das kannst du handschriftlich oder mithilfe eines Textverarbeitungsprogramms am Computer machen.

3. Veröffentlichen

▷ Zeige deinen fertigen Text deiner Lehrkraft, einem Mitschüler, einer Mitschülerin oder der Klasse.
▷ Du kannst deinen Text in deinem (digitalen) Portfolio aufbewahren.

▨▣ Tipp: Texte digital erstellen und veröffentlichen (media worksheet 1, 9-16)

· Wenn du einen Text am Computer schreibst, kannst du zunächst Ideen und nützliche Wörter in einem Dokument sammeln und speichern. Du kannst deine Ideen und deinen Text jederzeit ändern und ergänzen.
· Ihr könnt eure Texte auch zu einem Klassenprodukt zusammenfügen. Vielleicht gibt es die Möglichkeit, dieses Produkt auf der Schul- oder Klassenwebseite zu veröffentlichen.

5 READING
Lesen

Es gibt viele Strategien, die dir helfen können, einen englischen Text zu verstehen. Sieh dir vor allem erst einmal die **Überschrift** und die **Bilder** an, die dir schon viel über den Inhalt verraten. Beim Text selbst kannst du zum Beispiel eine der folgenden Strategien anwenden:

1. Skimming

Beim *skimming* überfliegst du den Text erst einmal. Du verschaffst dir schnell einen Überblick: Worum geht es? Was passiert? Wer ist dabei? Du musst nicht jedes Wort verstehen.

2. Reading for detail

Du liest den Text gründlich, um möglichst viele Details herauszufinden. Mache dir Notizen. Auf Kopien oder in deinen eigenen Büchern kannst du auch wichtige Textstellen markieren. Die *wh*-Fragen können dir helfen: Who? Where? When? What?

SWIMMING IS HIS LIFE

This young man is going to make it to the top. Leroy Haffner will soon be one of Britain's best swimmers! Leroy was born in Bristol, UK. Swimming has always been his greatest love. He started swimming at the age of four. Three years later he had already won medals for his local club. He took part in

one national competition after another. Then last year, Leroy had an injury and couldn't swim for nearly two months. But Leroy didn't give up. He started swimming again – and with great success. Next week, Leroy will participate in the National Championships. His coach, Ted Henley, knows that "Leroy will do really, really well".

---

3. Scanning

Beim *scanning* suchst du einen Text gezielt nach ganz bestimmten Informationen ab.
Wenn es wichtige Wörter gibt, die du nicht kennst, probiere Folgendes aus:

▶ Kennst du einzelne Teile eines langen Wortes oder ähnliche Wörter aus dem Deutschen oder aus einer anderen Sprache? Versuche, dir den Sinn des Wortes herzuleiten.

▶ Kannst du dir die Bedeutung eines unbekannten Wortes aus dem Textzusammenhang herleiten?
Erst wenn das nicht funktioniert, solltest du das Wort in einem Wörterbuch nachschlagen.

Tipp: Suche dir englische Texte zu Themen, die dich interessieren!

· Du kannst im Internet und in Büchereien nach interessanten Texten auf Englisch suchen.
· Lies so viel du kannst. Am Ende jeder Unit in diesem Buch findest du eine Kurzgeschichte und einen Sachtext oder ein Gedicht.

6 MEDIATION
Sprachmittlung

Manchmal gibt es Situationen, in denen du jemandem helfen musst, der deine Muttersprache oder eine Fremdsprache nicht so gut kann wie du.

1. Gib den Sinn wieder
Übersetze nicht alles Wort für Wort. Wichtiger ist es, den Sinn wiederzugeben.

2. Fasse dich kurz
Bilde einfache, kurze Sätze. Unwichtige Einzelheiten kannst du weglassen.

Was gibt es heute Besonderes?

Our special recommendation today is fresh fish. Our chef was able to get some fresh trout that was caught this morning. We serve it with a lemon cream sauce, a side dish of rice and a light salad.

Es gibt frischen Fisch in Zitronensauce mit Reis und Salat.

Was steht denn da?

**Science Museum –
New section open now**
Don't miss our brand new exhibition section on the history of the computer. From a model of Konrad Zuse's Z3, the first working computer in the world, to the latest tablets, there's a lot to see, learn and try out.

Sie haben eine neue Abteilung zur Geschichte des Computers eröffnet.

Tipp: Keine Angst vor Fehlern!

· Wenn dir ein wichtiges Wort nicht einfällt, kannst du es umschreiben.
· Versuche, dich an Redewendungen zu erinnern. Zum Beispiel kannst du mit *"What about …?"* Vorschläge machen oder mit *"There is … / There are …"* etwas beschreiben.

7 WATCHING A VIDEO CLIP
Videoclips verstehen

Englischsprachige Videoclips anzuschauen macht Spaß und ist auch eine tolle Möglichkeit, die Sprache besser zu lernen. Dabei solltest du einige Dinge beachten:

1. Bevor es losgeht
▶ Gibt es Bilder aus dem Videoclip? Was ist zu sehen?
▶ Lies den Titel des Videoclips. Welche Hinweise gibt er auf den Inhalt?
▶ Worum könnte es gehen? Stelle Vermutungen an.

2. Währenddessen
▶ Schaue dir den Videoclip in Ruhe an. Was ist dein erster Eindruck? Mache dir Notizen.

Who?   Wer ist zu sehen? Um wen geht es?
What?   Worum geht es? Was passiert?
Where?   Wo findet es statt?
When?   Wann findet es statt?

▶ Es ist nicht schlimm, wenn du nicht alles verstehst. Achte auf die Stimmen, Körpersprache und Gesichtsausdrücke der Personen im Videoclip.

▶ Gibt es eine Aufgabe zu dem Videoclip? Behalte sie im Kopf, während du ein zweites Mal zuschaust. Konzentriere dich stärker auf das, was du hörst. Gibt es Wörter, die immer wieder vorkommen? Notiere sie dir.

▶ Versuche, gleich danach die Frage zu beantworten. Wenn nötig, schaue dir dann den Clip ein weiteres Mal an. Überprüfe dabei deine Antworten.

3. Hinterher
▶ Tausche dich mit deinen Mitschülerinnen und Mitschülern aus.

Tipp: Schaue dir Videoclips und Filme auf Englisch an (media worksheet 8)

· Alle Videoclips zum Buch findest du, wenn du auf www.westermann.de/webcode den Webcode WES-128207-001 eingibst oder den QR-Code scannst, den du auf Seite 2 findest.
· Sieh dir Filme, Serien oder Berichte zu Themen, die dich interessieren, auf Englisch an.
· Auf DVDs oder bei Streaming-Diensten kannst du fast immer den englischen Ton und englische Untertitel einschalten. Nach und nach lernst du so besser zu verstehen, was gesagt wird.

8 SEARCHING THE INTERNET
Im Internet recherchieren

Hier erfährst du, wie du im Internet zu einem Thema recherchieren kannst.

1. Benutze eine Suchmaschine

▷ Gute Suchbegriffe erleichtern dir die Suche im Internet. Versuche, auf Englisch möglichst genau zu formulieren, wonach du suchst.

▷ Gib die Suchbegriffe in eine Suchmaschine ein. Bei vielen Suchmaschinen kannst du Englisch als Sprache wählen. Dann steht dir der nötige Wortschatz gleich zur Verfügung.

▷ Es kann sein, dass die Suchmaschine sehr viele Treffer anzeigt. Oft genügt es, sich die ersten 10 bis 20 Suchergebnisse anzuschauen.

▷ Es gibt Webseiten, auf denen du Informationen in einfacherem Englisch finden kannst. Deine Lehrkraft kann dir helfen, sie zu finden.

2. Halte nützliche Informationen fest

▷ Überfliege erst einmal die Seiten, die dir interessant erscheinen. Du brauchst nicht jedes Wort zu verstehen.

▷ Dann kannst du dir Notizen zu den Inhalten machen.

▷ Denke daran, dir das Datum deiner Recherche aufzuschreiben und die Quelle abzuspeichern.

▷ Wenn du Textausschnitte unverändert aus dem Internet übernimmst, musst du zeigen, dass es Zitate sind. Setze sie in deinem Text in Anführungszeichen und gib die Quelle und das Datum an, an dem du sie gefunden hast.

3. Sei kritisch

▷ Informationen, die du im Internet findest, sind nicht immer richtig.

▷ Sei deshalb kritisch und überprüfe die Informationen noch einmal auf anderen Seiten oder in einem Lexikon.

Tipp: Nutze digitale Tools (media worksheet 6, 7)

· Es gibt viele sinnvolle Tools im Internet. Du kannst zum Beispiel Währungen und Maßeinheiten umrechnen oder dir Entfernungen anzeigen lassen.

· Viele englischsprachige Einrichtungen, vor allem Museen, bieten virtuelle Rundgänge an. Du kannst auch virtuell durch britische Städte spazieren.

9 PRESENTATIONS
Präsentationen halten

Hier findest du einige Tipps und Tricks für gelungene Präsentationen.

1. Bevor du etwas präsentierst

▶ Überlege: Was möchtest du zu deinem Thema sagen?
Wie viel Zeit hast du?

▶ Gliedere deinen Vortrag: Überlege, in welcher Reihenfolge
du was sagen und wie du anfangen möchtest.

▶ Fertige ein Poster oder eine Computerpräsentation an,
um deinen Vortrag anschaulich zu machen. Wenn du
Bilder oder Texte aus dem Internet oder aus einem Buch
kopiert hast, dann schreibe immer dazu, wo und wann
du sie gefunden hast.

▶ Notiere Stichpunkte zu dem, was du sagen möchtest,
auf Karteikarten.

▶ Nützliche Redewendungen findest du in der *wordbank*
auf Seite 168.

▶ Übe deinen Vortrag vor dem Spiegel, vor Freunden oder
vor deiner Familie.

> *So sieht ein gelungenes*
> *Vortragsposter aus*
>
> ▸ *treffende Überschrift*
> ▸ *interessante Informationen*
> ▸ *verständliche Sätze, aber*
>   *nicht zu viel Text*
> ▸ *große Bilder und Schrift:*
>   *Jeder im Raum muss sie*
>   *sehen und lesen können.*
> ▸ *saubere Schrift*
> ▸ *Bilder mit Bildunter-*
>   *schriften*

2. Während du präsentierst

▶ Sprich langsam und deutlich.

▶ Sieh deine Zuhörerinnen und Zuhörer an, wenn du sprichst. Achte zum Beispiel bei einer
Computerpräsentation darauf, nicht ständig auf den Bildschirm zu schauen.

▶ Versuche, frei zu sprechen. Du kannst die wichtigsten Punkte von deinen Karteikarten
oder deinem Poster ablesen.

3. So wird dein Vortrag spannend und lebendig

▶ Musik, Videoclips, interessante Bilder oder Zitate machen deinen Vortrag abwechslungsreich.

▶ Achte darauf, dass dein Vortrag nicht klingt, als würdest du einen Text ablesen.

▶ Zeige deinen Zuhörerinnen und Zuhörern auf deinem Poster oder auf den Seiten deiner
Computerpräsentation, worüber du gerade sprichst.

Tipp: Schau dir Tutorials an (media worksheet 4)

· Zum Präsentieren gibt es viele Tutorials im Internet. Schau dir einige an und überlege,
was bei dir schon gut klappt und was du noch verbessern könntest.

· Zum Thema Computerpräsentationen kannst du dir ein passendes Arbeitsblatt herunterladen
und dir Tutorials anschauen. Gehe dazu auf www.westermann.de/webcode und gib den
Webcode WES-128207-001 ein.

10 PERFORMING A SCENE
Eine Szene vorspielen

Szenische Lesungen, Rollenspiele und Theaterstücke sind eine gute Methode, um Englisch zu trainieren. Denke immer daran, laut und deutlich und nicht zu schnell zu sprechen, damit man dich gut verstehen kann.

1. Szenische Lesung

▶ Für ein *dramatic reading* musst du deinen Text nicht auswendig lernen. Du solltest ihn aber so gut kennen, dass du auf deine Aussprache, Lautstärke, Betonung und deinen Gesichtsausdruck achten kannst, ohne den Faden zu verlieren.

▶ Achte darauf, dass Aussprache, Lautstärke, Betonung und Gesichtsausdruck zu dem passen, was du liest.

2. Rollenspiele

▶ Halte beim Sprechen Augenkontakt zu deinem Gegenüber.

▶ Versetze dich in die Person hinein, die du darstellst. Denke beim Sprechen an den passenden Gesichtsausdruck und die passende Körpersprache.

▶ Wechselt auch mal die Rollen und übt mit anderen Partnern. So lernt ihr, spontan zu reagieren.

▶ Wenn ihr *cue cards* verwendet, denkt daran, nur Stichworte zu notieren, keine ganzen Sätze!

3. Theaterstücke

▶ Bei Theaterstücken geht es noch mehr als bei Rollenspielen um das Schauspielern. Du solltest deinen Text gut auswendig lernen, damit du dich besser auf das Spielen konzentrieren kannst. Mit der Methode *read – look up – speak* kannst du deine Rolle auswendig lernen: Du liest deinen Satz still, siehst dann auf und sprichst ihn.

▶ Versetze dich in die Person hinein, die du darstellst. Denke beim Sprechen an den passenden Gesichtsausdruck und die passende Körpersprache.

▶ Mit passenden Gegenständen auf der Bühne und Kostümen fällt es leichter, in eine Rolle hineinzuschlüpfen.

4. Präsentieren

▶ Mit Rollenspielen, kleinen Szenen, Sketchen und Theaterstücken könnt ihr zeigen, wie viel Englisch ihr schon könnt. Bei einem Schulfest oder an einem Tag der offenen Tür könnt ihr Eltern oder andere Klassen zu einer Vorführung einladen.

▨ ▤ **Tipp: Schaut euch selbst zu** (media worksheet 2, 5)

· Rollenspiele könnt ihr aufnehmen und so gemeinsam überprüfen, ob es noch etwas zu verbessern gibt.

Around the world

Writing and talking about places

The capital of ... is ...

... is huge / small. It covers an area of ... km².

It has a population of ...

The longest river / highest mountain is ...

... is known as ... / famous for ... / also called ...

I would describe ... as a ... place.

When I think of ..., ... comes to mind.

In this area, you can see ...

... is a must-see / a perfect place to ... / an ideal ...

... is located / situated in ...

... is the biggest / best / least / one of the most ...

Countries and nationalities

Korea – Korean · Italy – Italian ·
Wales – Welsh · Scotland – Scottish ·
Poland – Polish · Paraguay – Paraguayan ·
Turkey / Türkiye – Turkish · France – French ·
England – English · Ireland – Irish ·
Germany – German · China – Chinese ·
the USA – US-American · Japan – Japanese · ...

There is / are ...

deserts · beaches · forests ·
cities · towns · villages ·
mountain peaks · tropical wetlands ·
long stretches of farmland · islands ·
a wide variety of climate zones ·
diverse ecosystems · natural beauty ·
different landscapes · national parks ·
a number of landmarks · natural wonders ·
interesting sights · cool events · ...

Places can be ...

awesome · sunny · covered with snow ·
huge · amazing · big · fantastic · small ·
noisy · breathtaking · stunning · charming ·
rich in history · cool · busy · quiet ·
historic · great · loud · large ·
fascinating · boring · lively · dirty ·
impressive · clean · famous ·
pretty · multicultural · dangerous · lovely ·
a home · magnificent · a hotspot · ...

I left my home ...

... because I found a job in a different place.

... to find new opportunities.

... to start a new life.

... to get away from a difficult situation.

... because I wanted to be with my family.

... to search for a better life.

... to travel around the world.

... to flee from war.

Travelling

I would like to go to … / How do I get to …?

I would like to buy a ticket to …, please.

What's the quickest way to …?

How much is a single ticket / return ticket to …, please?

When does the next train / plane for … leave?

From which platform does the train to … leave?

There is a special offer for children between the ages of … and … travelling with an adult.

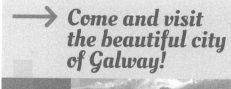

Come and visit the beautiful city of Galway!

- Discover **Galway's rich history**.
- Join a **food tour** and explore our restaurants, cafés, bistros and pubs.
- Visit the **beautiful beaches** in the Galway city area.
- Don't miss out on the **Galway festivals**.

Descriptions

Describing people

was born in … · got married in … ·
is famous because … · invented … ·
had … children · fought for … · worked … ·
went to school / university in … ·
encouraged other people to … · died in …

People can be …

kind · happy · tall ·
angry · clever · smart · friendly · small ·
cool · funny · lazy · mean · active · …

Objects and things can be …

bright · colourful · big · small · cool
made of plastic / wood / paper / … · boring ·
expensive · cheap · interesting · …

A situation or atmosphere can be …

exciting · interesting · scary · inspiring ·
special · boring · happy · lively ·
relaxed · electric · …

Walt Disney

Walt Disney was an American film producer. He was born on December 5, 1901 in Chicago and is probably most famous for creating the cartoon character 'Mickey Mouse' in 1928.

Another famous cartoon character he invented is 'Dumbo', but he also produced films with real people such as the musical film 'Mary Poppins' in 1964.

Walt Disney died on December 15, 1966.

Talking about pictures

In the picture, there is / are … ·
It shows … · I can see … ·
In the photo, you can see that … · …

School life

High school students in the USA …

… often have a homecoming week at the beginning of the school year.

There is a homecoming king and queen. There are special events like a football game, a dance and performances by different clubs.

… usually go to school by bus or by car.

… do not have to wear uniform at school.

… have to carry their school ID card with them at all times.

… keep their bags and books in lockers.

… get their schedule / timetable at the registrar's office.

… go to homeroom for their first period. There their homeroom teacher checks attendance.

… begin their school day with the Pledge of Allegiance.

… can choose from a wide variety of electives such as art, foreign languages or video game development.

… can join a lot of different school clubs such as glee club, marching band or model congress.

… collect credits in order to graduate.

… celebrate graduation with a formal dance called prom.

Electives

robotics · business law · marketing · movie production · woodworking · maintenance · plumbing · culinary art · computer repairing · women's studies · light and sound technology · welding · IT · auto body repair · world literature · fashion design · personal finance · …

School clubs

library club · fundraiser club · history club · mathletics club · drama / theater group · debating society · chemistry club · FBLA (future business leaders of America) · yearbook club · …

American and British English

American English	British English
aside from	apart from
auditorium	assembly hall
on the weekend	at the weekend
fall	autumn
tailgate / trunk	car boot
parking lot	car park
French fries	chips
chips	crisps
movie	film
apartment	flat
soccer	football
vacation	holiday
period	lesson
grade	grade / mark
grade	year
cell (phone)	mobile (phone)
gym	PE
elementary school	primary school
trash / garbage	rubbish
store	shop
schedule	timetable
subway	underground

American English	British English
color / neighbor	colour / neighbour
favorite / to honor	favourite / to honour
to practice	to practise
center / theater	centre / theatre
percent	per cent
traveled	travelled
math	maths
pajamas	pyjamas
program	programme
learned / dreamed	learnt / dreamt

Tipp

Es gibt ein paar Unterschiede zwischen dem Englisch, das in Großbritannien gesprochen wird *(BE)*, und dem Englisch, das in den USA gesprochen wird *(AE)*. Einige Wörter werden unterschiedlich buchstabiert, wobei es in manchen Fällen Regelmäßigkeiten gibt.

So werden Wörter aus dem Britischen Englisch wie *favourite* oder *harbour* im Amerikanischen Englisch nur mit *o* geschrieben: *favorite* oder *harbor*. Wörter mit der Endung *-re* (z. B. *centre* oder *theatre*) enden im Amerikanischen Englisch auf *-er* (*center, theater*). Bei anderen Wörtern muss man sich die Unterschiede einfach merken, wie zum Beispiel bei *per cent (BE)* / *percent (AE)*. Das gleiche gilt für einige Verben, deren Vergangenheitsformen im Amerikanischen Englisch regelmäßig sind *(learned, dreamed)*, im Britischen aber unregelmäßig *(learnt, dreamt)*.

Dann gibt es noch eine Gruppe von Wörtern, die komplett unterschiedlich sind, z. B. *fall (AE)* und *autumn (BE)*. In einigen Fällen sind die Unterschiede nicht mehr so groß. Beeinflusst durch amerikanische Filme und Musik werden heutzutage auch im britischen Sprachraum Wörter wie *kid, movie* oder *post* verwendet. Auch Wörter, die im Britischen Englisch eigentlich mit *s* geschrieben werden (z. B. *organise, realise*), liest man mittlerweile häufig auch in Großbritannien in der amerikanischen Schreibweise mit *z*.

Du kannst dir die britische und amerikanische Aussprache der Wörter aus den Listen auf dieser Seite im Audiotrack anhören.

Feelings

People can be feeling …

depressed · lonely · happy · helpless ·
excited · angry · glad · upset ·
worried · unhappy · sad · cheerful · …

They look like they are really angry.
Maybe they are having an argument.

I am feeling sad because
my best friend won't talk
to me anymore.

Friends are people you …

| … can trust. | … like to spend time with. |
| … can rely on. | … can talk to about anything. |

The girl in the yellow T-shirt seems
to be very cheerful. I think she is
happy to be with her friends.

When you love someone, …

… you would
do anything for
them.

… you will
be there for
them.

… you will
listen to their
problems.

Seeking and giving advice

I need your help with …

I don't think you should worry about it
too much because you'll find a solution.

If I were you,
I would …

Can you please give me
some advice on …?

You shouldn't / should …

I'm having problems with …

Why don't you …?

What should I do when …?

Have you tried talking
to someone?

What's your advice on …?

Make sure you don't make
the same mistake twice.

What about finding new friends?

Don't … /
Never …

I think it would be
a good idea if you …

It's important to … /
Be careful not to …

(Digital) communication

Digital communication is a good thing ...

- ... because it is a cheap and time-saving way to keep in touch with friends and family – even if they are far away from you.
- ... because it helps you to share pictures and memories easily.
- ... because you can meet new people online, even if you are very shy offline.
- ... because you can meet people who share your hobbies and interests.

Digital communication is a bad thing ...

- ... because people often spend too much time online.
- ... because of cyberbullying.
- ... because you can meet new people online who might be dangerous.
- ... because the boundaries between school or work and home life are not clear and you are expected to be online at all times.
- ... because misunderstandings are more likely to happen.

Digital communication can ...   It makes people ...   The best / worst thing about online communication is ...

You can't ... without using ...   It causes ...   ... is a negative side of online communication because ...

Writing a letter

Dear ...

How are you?
I am writing to you from ...
I want to tell you all about ...
Today we ...

Lots of love/Love from,

Writing a text message

Hi Ben!
I'm at ...
There are ... It's ...
You should ...
See you soon! :)

Writing an email

New message   _ □ ×
To
Subject

Dear ... / Hello ...

I am writing to ...
I would like to ...
Could you tell me more about ...?

Many thanks, ...
Best wishes, ...

Expressing opinions

I think that … because …   In my opinion it's … because …   I believe that … because …

When you look at … you can see that …   One of the reasons for that is …   If you ask me, …

Another important point is that …   The pros are …

I think it's just as important to … as to …

I agree with that because …   So I agree with … the most.

On the one hand, you can say that …, on the other hand, …

However, you could say that …   The cons are …

I don't think you can …   I think … is more important than …   I disagree with …

I'd have to think some more about it.   I can't decide if I'm for or against it.   I cannot agree with …

I'm not sure what I agree with.   To sum it all up, …   Summarizing, I would say that …

Presenting something

Hello and welcome to my presentation about …
Today, I am going to talk about …
I would like to tell you about …
First, I would like to introduce the topic of …
In the second part of my presentation, I will …
After that, I will talk about …
Finally, I will look at …
I will first give some information on …
Here is an example of …
On this slide, you can see …
This is a photo of …
This picture shows that …
In this picture, you can clearly see …
The most important point is …
It is also important to mention that …
You should know that …
This shows how …
The last aspect is …
Thanks for listening. Are there any questions?

Hopes and dreams

I hope to ...

have a good life · have a family ·
make the most out of life · travel the world ·
make a difference · help people ·
have some fun · be able to go abroad ·
change the world · improve things ·
make lots of money · become ... · ...

My hopes and dreams!

When I grow up, I'll ...
When I have finished school, I ...
My dream is to ...
I want to ...
I hope to ...
I could ...
If I ..., I would ...
It would be ... if I had ...

I am planning on doing ... / going to ...
I dream of being ...

being successful in my job ·
doing something useful ·
becoming a vet / teacher / ... ·
living in another country · ...

starting my own business ·
getting rich ·
achieving my goals ·
having my own flat · ...

Talking about the future

It would be great if there were ...

In the future, I'll ...

I think that more people will ... in the future.

There will be more / less ...

My ideal world in the future would look like this: ...

I don't think there will be ... anymore.

The world of work

Different jobs

> doctor · teacher · lawyer · police officer · nursery teacher ·
> photographer · electrician · gardener · waiter / waitress ·
> engineer · nurse · bike mechanic · physiotherapist · coach ·
> vet · dentist · fashion designer · forest worker · surf instructor ·
> pilot · actor / actress · construction worker · …

You can work …

> outdoors · indoors · in an office ·
> on your own · in a team · with people ·
> at a desk · from home · in a factory ·
> in a hospital · at a school · with animals · …

A job should …

> be fun · be interesting · pay well ·
> have regular working hours · …

Soft skills

> **I can …**
> communicate ·
> be a team leader · be a team member · …

> **I have …**
> lots of ideas · good manners · …

> **I am …**
> open to new ideas · creative · organized ·
> good at … · good with people · polite ·
> always on time · reliable · responsible · …

Hard skills

> **I can …**
> speak another language · repair cars ·
> teach English · drive a car · …

> **I have …**
> knowledge of IT programs ·
> presentation skills · experience in / with … · …

A job interview

> Thank you for inviting me.

> Your application form looks very good.

> I would like to get the job because …

> Why don't you tell me a little about yourself?

> I'm interested in / good at …

> Why would you like to work for us?

> I've worked for …

> Do you prefer working indoors or outdoors?

> What about working hours?

> Have you got any more questions?

> How much money will I earn?

> Do you like working in a team or on your own?

> How many days paid holiday do I get?

Numbers

Dates

by 1733 · until 1865 · in 1805 · after 1924 ·
between 1820 and 1890 · till 1783 ·
around 1,000 AD · about 20,000 years ago ·
in the 19th century · from 1820 to 1890 ·
during World War I · since the 1960s · ...

Statistics

This graph clearly shows that ...
increased.
There is an increase in ...

In this graph you can see that
... decreased. The number of
... became smaller. There is a
decrease in ...

This bar chart displays the
number of people who ... from
... to ...

This bar chart shows the
development between ...
and ...

This pie chart shows that
25 per cent of ... are ...
There are fewer ... than ...

Here you can see that there are
more ... than ....
The number of ... is bigger.

There was a rise from ... to ...
The wave ... then peaked in ...
and fell after ...

The statistics prove/show that ...

Tipp

you write	you say
1st March or 1 March	the first of March
2nd April or 2 April	the second of April
12th October	the twelfth of October

Tipp

Jahreszahlen sprichst du so aus:
1492	fourteen ninety-two
1939	nineteen thirty-nine
1951	nineteen fifty-one
2010	two thousand and ten

Tipp

**Daten schreibst du im britischen
Englisch so:**
1 August, 2 January, 5 November
oder so:
1st / 1st August, 2nd / 2nd January,
5th / 5th November
**Eine Jahreszahl schreibst du einfach
dahinter:**
1 August 2024 oder 01/08/24
**Im amerikanischen Englisch ist es
umgekehrt! Hier schreibt man den
Monat VOR dem Tag:**
August 1, August 1st oder 08/01/2024

Tipp

**Du verwendest im Englischen Kommata,
wenn du Ziffern gruppieren möchtest,
keine Punkte!**
The distance between New York and
Los Angeles is 4,490 km.

Measurements

This box is 11cm
wide, 6cm deep
and 1cm tall.

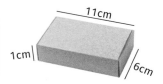

Classroom phrases

Which topic have you chosen?	Welches Thema hast du dir ausgesucht?
Which topic are you going to work on?	An welchem Thema hast du vor zu arbeiten?
Who is going to work on topic A / B / … ?	Wer hat vor, an Thema A / B / … zu arbeiten?
I haven't decided yet.	Ich habe mich noch nicht entschieden.
I can't make up my mind.	Ich kann mich nicht entscheiden.
Do you want to work with me?	Willst du mit mir zusammenarbeiten?
You're good at … Why don't you …?	Du kannst gut … Warum machst du nicht …?

Sorry, I haven't got … with me.	Tut mir leid, ich habe … nicht dabei.
Sorry, I forgot to bring …	Tut mir leid, ich habe vergessen, … mitzubringen.

I've got a question.	Ich habe eine Frage.
Can you help me, please?	Können Sie / Kannst du mir bitte helfen?
I don't understand this.	Ich verstehe das hier nicht.
What's … in English / German?	Was heißt … auf Englisch / Deutsch?
What does … mean?	Was bedeutet …?
Can you spell that, please?	Kannst du das bitte buchstabieren?
Can you say that again, please?	Kannst du das bitte noch einmal sagen?
Sorry, I don't know.	Tut mir leid, das weiß ich nicht.
What page is it on?	Auf welcher Seite ist das?

Let's do the activities together.	Lass uns die Aktivitäten zusammen machen.
Let's compare …	Lass uns … vergleichen.
What do you think?	Was meinst du?
Whose turn is it?	Wer ist dran?

Are we allowed to use a dictionary?	Dürfen wir ein Wörterbuch benutzen?
Let's look it up in the dictionary.	Lass es uns im Wörterbuch nachschlagen.
What else do we need?	Was brauchen wir noch?

First we have to read up on ... /
investigate the idea about ... / ...

Als Erstes müssen wir uns über ... informieren /
die Idee über ... untersuchen / ...

I think we should first watch ... /
read ... / explore ... / ...

Ich meine, wir sollten zuerst ... anschauen /
... lesen / ... untersuchen / ...

Do you know how to use the webcode?

Weißt du, wie man den Webcode benutzt?

Why don't we have a look at the website /
on the Internet / ... ?

Warum schauen wir nicht auf der Website /
im Internet / ... nach?

Who wants to keep the word list / take notes /
prepare the fact file / ... ?

Wer will die Wortliste führen / Notizen machen /
den Steckbrief vorbereiten / ... ?

Who is doing the presentation?

Wer übernimmt die Präsentation?

Who is writing down the results?

Wer notiert die Ergebnisse?

What do you think is the biggest problem /
the most important fact / ... ?

Was hältst du für das größte Problem /
die wichtigste Tatsache / ... ?

I think it would be a good idea to ...

Ich finde, es wäre eine gute Idee, wenn wir ...

Can I be the one to call / do the interview with /
talk to / ... ?

Kann ich ... anrufen / das Interview mit ... führen /
mit ... sprechen / ... ?

Let me give you an example.

Lass mich dir ein Beispiel geben.

Well, it's a fact that ...

Es ist nun mal eine Tatsache, dass ...

I think that's a good point.

Ich denke, das ist ein guter Hinweis.

I wouldn't say so.

Das würde ich nicht sagen.

I see what you mean, but ...

Ich verstehe, was du meinst, aber ...

Sorry, I don't agree with you.

Tut mir leid, aber ich stimme dir nicht zu.

I'd rather focus on ...

Ich würde mich lieber auf ... konzentrieren.

We should do some more research on ...

Wir sollten ... besser untersuchen.

I'm sure there's more to it.

Ich glaube, da steckt mehr dahinter.

Only two of us seem to think that it's
best to ...

Nur zwei von uns scheinen der Ansicht zu sein,
dass es am besten ist, wenn wir ...

I agree with your idea / suggestion / ...

Ich stimme deiner Idee / deinem Vorschlag / ... zu.

You could make your text more interesting
if you ...

Du könntest deinen Text interessanter machen,
wenn du ...

I would use a different word here.

Ich würde hier ein anderes Wort verwenden.

We are running out of time.

Uns läuft die Zeit davon.

Well done!

Gut gemacht!

1 THE SIMPLE PAST: STATEMENTS (REVISION)
Die einfache Vergangenheit: Aussagen *(revision)*

In the holidays, I went to Poland with my family. We visited my grandma. It was great!

We didn't go abroad, we stayed in the UK. The weather wasn't bad so we went outside a lot.

Das *simple past* verwendet man, wenn man über etwas spricht, das in der Vergangenheit liegt und abgeschlossen ist.

a) Formen und bejahte Aussagesätze im *simple past*

Bei den regelmäßigen Verben hängst du -ed an die Grundform an:

DIGITAL+ video 18, 19

stay + **ed** → stay**ed** /steɪd/   look + **ed** → look**ed** /lʊkt/   visit + **ed** → visit**ed** /ˈvɪzɪtɪd/

Achte auf die Rechtschreibung: Endet die Grundform des Verbs auf -e, dann wird nur -d angehängt.

arriv**e** → arriv**ed** /əˈraɪvd/

Endet das Verb auf einen kurzen betonten **Vokal + Konsonant**, dann wird der Konsonant verdoppelt.

sto**p** → sto**pped** /stɒpt/

Endet das Verb auf **Konsonant + y**, dann wird aus dem -y ein -i und die Endung lautet -ied.

tid**y** → tid**ied** /ˈtaɪdid/

Unregelmäßige Verben haben im *simple past* eine eigene Form (siehe Seite 263-265).

have → **had**   I **had** a great holiday.
go → **went**   We **went** to Yellowstone National Park.
do → **did**   We **did** lots of things.

Das Verb *be* hat zwei Formen im *simple past*: I / he / she / it **was** – you / we / they **were**

I **was** in New York last week, but my friends **were** in Boston.
Ich **war** letzte Woche in New York, aber meine Freunde **waren** in Boston.

b) Verneinte Aussagesätze im *simple past*

Sätze im *simple past* verneinst du im Allgemeinen mit *didn't (= did not)*.
Didn't ist bei allen Personen gleich. Danach kommt dann das Verb in der Grundform.

I **didn't go** to Boston last week. Ich **fuhr** letzte Woche nicht nach Boston.

Bei *was* und *were* hängst du nur *not* oder die Kurzform *n't* an.

I **wasn't** in Boston last week, and my friends **weren't** in New York.
Ich **war** letzte Woche **nicht** in Boston, und meine Freunde **waren nicht** in New York.

2 THE SIMPLE PAST: QUESTIONS (REVISION)
Die einfache Vergangenheit: Fragen *(revision)*

Did you go to Bristol in the holidays?

Yes, I did.

Was it good?

Yes, it was.

Fragen im *simple past* bildest du in den meisten Fällen mit *did*. Eine Ausnahme sind Sätze mit *was* oder *were*.

a) Entscheidungsfragen und Kurzantworten im *simple past*

DIGITAL+ video 18, 19

Bei Entscheidungsfragen im *simple past* stellst du *did* an den Satzanfang.
Did ist bei allen Personen gleich.
Achte auch hier darauf, das Verb danach in der Grundform zu verwenden.
In der Kurzantwort wird *did* wieder aufgegriffen.

Entscheidungsfrage	Kurzantwort	Kurzantwort
Did you go to Yellowstone?	Yes, I did.	No, I didn't.
Did your friends come with you?	Yes, they did.	No, they didn't.

Bei Fragen mit *was* und *were* brauchst du kein *did*.
Hier steht *was* oder *were* am Satzanfang.
In der Kurzantwort wird *was* bzw. *were* wieder aufgegriffen.

Entscheidungsfrage	Kurzantwort	Kurzantwort
Were your parents in New York last year?	Yes, they were.	No, they weren't.
Was the weather good?	Yes, it was.	No, it wasn't.

b) Fragen mit Fragewort im *simple past*

Bei Sätzen mit Fragewort steht das Fragewort am Satzanfang. Es steht vor *did*.

What did you do in the holidays?
Where did you go?

Bei Fragen mit *who* braucht man jedoch kein zusätzliches *did*, wenn *who* nach dem Subjekt fragt.

Who went to the USA? – My parents went to the USA.

Bei Fragen mit *was* oder *were* brauchst du ebenfalls kein *did*.

How was your holiday?
What were your favourite places?

3 THE PRESENT PERFECT: STATEMENTS (REVISION)
Das Perfekt: Aussagen *(revision)*

Das *present perfect* verwendest du, wenn etwas irgendwann in einem Zeitraum von der Vergangenheit bis zur Gegenwart passiert ist. Der genaue Zeitpunkt ist dabei nicht wichtig.
Du verwendest es auch, wenn ein Vorgang in der Vergangenheit noch Auswirkungen auf die Gegenwart hat.

I have already finished my homework.
Can I go out now?

a) Bejahte Aussagesätze im *present perfect*

📱 **DIGITAL+** video 20

Das *present perfect* bildest du mit *have / has* + Partizip Perfekt *(past participle)*.
Statt *have* bzw. *has* kannst du auch die entsprechende Kurzform benutzen.

I **have climbed** to the top.	Ich **bin** an die Spitze **geklettert**.
I**'ve done** lots of sightseeing so far.	Ich **habe** bisher viel Sightseeing **gemacht**.
He **has finished** his dinner.	Er **hat** sein Abendessen **beendet**.
He**'s** just **seen** a fantastic Broadway show.	Er **hat** gerade eine fantastische Show auf dem Broadway **gesehen**.

Bei regelmäßigen Verben bildest du das Partizip Perfekt, indem du an die Grundform des Verbs die Endung *-ed* anhängst. Beachte auch die Besonderheiten bei der Schreibung und Aussprache der *ed*-Endungen (siehe. auch Grammatik-Kapitel 1 auf Seite 174).

Grundform	*simple past*	*past participle*
climb	climbed	climbed
visit	visited	visited
stop	stopped	stopped
tidy	tidied	tidied
arrive	arrived	arrived

Die Formen der unregelmäßigen Verben musst du wie Vokabeln auswendig lernen.

Auf den Seiten 263-265 findest du hierzu eine Liste und auf Seite 265 einen Tipp, wie du die unregelmäßigen Formen gruppieren kannst, um sie dir leichter einzuprägen.

Grundform	*simple past*	*past participle*
be	was / were	been
do	did	done
have	had	had
buy	bought	bought

b) Verneinte Aussagesätze im *present perfect*

Die Verneinung bildest du mit *have not / has not* + Partizip Perfekt bzw. mit den Kurzformen *haven't / hasn't* + Partizip Perfekt.

I **have not been** to New York yet.	Ich **bin** noch **nicht** in New York **gewesen**.
He **hasn't finished** his dinner yet.	Er **hat** sein Abendessen noch **nicht beendet**.
We **haven't eaten** lunch yet.	Wir **haben** noch **nicht** zu Mittag **gegessen**.

4 THE PRESENT PERFECT: QUESTIONS (REVISION)
Das Perfekt: Fragen *(revision)*

Mit einer Entscheidungsfrage im *present perfect* kannst du z.B. fragen, ob jemand etwas irgendwann in der Vergangenheit schon einmal gemacht hat. Der genaue Zeitpunkt ist dabei nicht so wichtig.

Have you ever been to the USA?

No, I haven't, but I'd like to go there one day.

a) Entscheidungsfragen und Kurzantworten im *present perfect*

Entscheidungsfragen im *present perfect* bildest du, indem du *have* bzw. *has* an den Satzanfang stellst.

DIGITAL+ video 20

Entscheidungsfrage	Kurzantwort	Kurzantwort
Have you ever been to New York?	Yes, I have.	No, I haven't.
Has Ben ever seen a Broadway show?	Yes, he has.	No, he hasn't.
Have the children ever cycled across Brooklyn Bridge?	Yes, they have.	No, they haven't.

b) Fragen mit Fragewort im *present perfect*

Bei Fragen mit Fragewort steht das Fragewort am Satzanfang.

What have you done?   *Was* hast du gemacht?
Where have you been?   *Wo* bist du gewesen?
Why hasn't she arrived yet? *Warum* ist sie noch nicht angekommen?

c) Adverbien der unbestimmten Zeit

Beim *present perfect* ist es nicht wichtig, wann genau in der Vergangenheit etwas passiert ist. Man betrachtet stattdessen den Zeitraum von der Vergangenheit bis zur Gegenwart. Daher werden bei Fragen und Aussagen im *present perfect* häufig Adverbien der unbestimmten Zeit verwendet, z.B. *ever* (= jemals), *never* (= nie), *already* (= schon), *just* (= gerade), *yet* (= schon) und *not yet* (= noch nicht).
Die meisten Adverbien stehen dann direkt vor dem Partizip Perfekt.

*Have you **ever** been to the USA? – No, I've **never** been there.*
*Bist du **jemals** in den USA gewesen? – Nein, ich bin **noch nie** dort gewesen.*
*Has Suri **already** eaten? – Yes, she has **just** finished.*
*Hat Suri **schon** gegessen? – Ja, sie ist **gerade** fertig geworden.*

Beachte die Ausnahme: *yet* steht am Satzende.
*Have you been to Central Park **yet**? – No, I haven**'t** been there **yet**.*
*Bist du **schon** im Central Park gewesen? – Nein, ich bin **noch nicht** dort gewesen.*

5 THE PASSIVE (REVISION)
Das Passiv *(revision)*

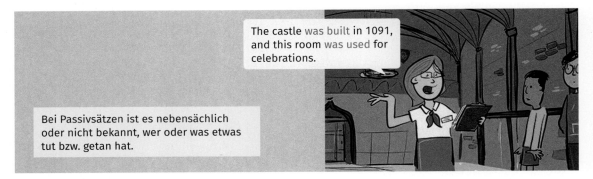

> The castle was built in 1091, and this room was used for celebrations.

> Bei Passivsätzen ist es nebensächlich oder nicht bekannt, wer oder was etwas tut bzw. getan hat.

Aktivsätze sagen uns, wer oder was handelt bzw. gehandelt hat.
In folgendem Beispiel sind das *thousands of workers*.

DIGITAL+ video 21

*Thousands of workers **built** the Empire State Building between 1930 and 1931.*
*Tausende von Arbeitern **bauten** das Empire State Building zwischen 1930 und 1931.*

Wenn aber nicht betont werden soll oder wenn nicht bekannt ist, wer etwas tut oder getan hat, kannst du einen Passivsatz verwenden.

*The Empire State Building **was built** between 1930 and 1931.*
*Das Empire State Building **wurde** zwischen 1930 und 1931 **gebaut**.*

Das Objekt aus dem Aktivsatz, hier *the Empire State Building*, wird zum Subjekt des Passivsatzes.

	Subjekt	Verb	Objekt	
Aktivsatz:	Thousands of workers	built	the Empire State Building	between 1930 and 1931.
Passivsatz:	The Empire State Building	was built		between 1930 and 1931.

Das Passiv bildest du so: Form von **be** + **Partizip Perfekt** *(past participle)*

Englisch	Deutsch
English is spoken all over the world.	Englisch wird überall auf der Welt gesprochen.
My computer was made in China.	Mein Computer wurde in China hergestellt.
Since its opening, the museum has been visited by lots of tourists.	Seit seiner Eröffnung ist das Museum von vielen Touristen besucht worden.
The building will be renovated / is going to be renovated next year.	Das Gebäude wird nächstes Jahr renoviert werden.
The museum is being renovated at the moment.	Das Museum wird gerade renoviert.

In der Liste mit den unregelmäßigen Verben auf den Seiten 263-265 findest du das Partizip Perfekt *(past participle)* in der dritten Spalte.

Wenn du in einem Passivsatz doch einmal die handelnde Person oder die Ursache für etwas nennen willst, hängst du sie mit **by** („von", „durch") an den Satz an:

*The Empire State Building was built **by** thousands of workers between 1930 and 1931.*
*Das Empire State Building wurde **von** Tausenden von Arbeitern zwischen 1930 und 1931 gebaut.*

6 THE PAST PERFECT
Die Vorvergangenheit

Yesterday at 8am

Du verwendest das *past perfect* z. B., wenn du über eine Handlung sprechen möchtest, die vor einer anderen Handlung in der Vergangenheit stattgefunden hat. Beide Handlungen sind dabei abgeschlossen.

After Noah **had taken** a shower, he **brushed** his teeth.

a) Aussagesätze im *past perfect*

Das *past perfect* bildest du mit *had* + Partizip Perfekt *(past participle)*.

DIGITAL+ video 22

Eric Johnson **had read** the most books.	Eric Johnson **hatte** die meisten Bücher **gelesen**.
Katie Miller **had trained** intensively.	Katie Miller **hatte** intensiv **trainiert**.

Das Partizip Perfekt kennst du schon vom *present perfect* (siehe Grammatik-Kapitel 3 auf Seite 176).
Bei regelmäßigen Verben endet das Partizip Perfekt auf *-ed*.
Bei unregelmäßigen Verben musst du die Formen auswendig lernen. Auf den Seiten 263-265 findest du eine Liste mit unregelmäßigen Verben.

Wenn du über zwei abgeschlossene Handlungen in der Vergangenheit sprechen möchtest, verwendest du für die weiter zurückliegende Handlung das *past perfect* und für die darauf-folgende Handlung das *simple past*.

1. Handlung *(past perfect)*	2. Handlung *(simple past)*
After the formal dinner **had ended**,	the party **continued** with the traditional dance.
Once the cheerleaders **had finished** their dance,	there **was** a fantastic football game.

Die Verneinung bildest du mit *had not* + Partizip Perfekt *(past participle)* bzw. mit der Kurzform *hadn't* + Partizip Perfekt *(past participle)*.

Eric **hadn't expected** to win the prize.   Eric **hatte nicht erwartet**, den Preis zu gewinnen.

b) Fragen im *past perfect*

Entscheidungsfragen im *past perfect* bildest du, indem du *had* an den Satzanfang stellst.
In der Kurzantwort wird *had* wieder aufgegriffen.

Had Katie **trained** intensively? – Yes, she **had**. / No, she **hadn't**.
Hatte Katie intensiv **trainiert**? – Ja. / Nein.

Bei Fragen mit Fragewort steht das Fragewort am Satzanfang.

How many books **had** Eric **read**?
Wie viele Bücher **hatte** Eric **gelesen**?

7 CONDITIONAL CLAUSES TYPE 1 (REVISION)
Bedingungssätze Typ 1 *(revision)*

If you like math, you'll enjoy the Mathletics club.

> Mit Bedingungssätzen kannst du sagen, was unter bestimmten Bedingungen passieren wird bzw. passieren kann.

Ein Bedingungssatz besteht aus einem *if*-Satz und einem Hauptsatz. Der *if*-Satz nennt eine Bedingung. Der Hauptsatz drückt aus, was passiert, wenn die Bedingung erfüllt ist.
Im *if*-Satz vom Typ 1 steht das *simple present*, im Hauptsatz meist das *will-future*.

DIGITAL+ video 23

if-Satz (Bedingung: Wenn ...)	Hauptsatz (Folge: ... dann ...)
If you miss the bus,	you will be late.
If it rains,	the children won't go outside.

Bedingungssätze können entweder mit dem *if*-Satz oder mit dem Hauptsatz beginnen.
Wenn sie mit dem *if*-Satz beginnen, werden sie mit einem Komma getrennt.
Wenn sie mit dem Hauptsatz beginnen, verwendest du kein Komma.

If you go to the concert**, I'll** come with you.
Falls / Wenn du zum Konzert gehst, **werde** ich mit dir kommen.

I'**ll** come with you **if** you go to the concert.
Ich **werde** mit dir kommen, **falls / wenn** du zum Konzert gehst.

Im Hauptsatz kannst du auch Modalverben (z. B. *can, must, should, could)* oder den Imperativ verwenden.

If you want, we **can go** to the concert together.
Wenn du willst, **können** wir zusammen zum Konzert **gehen**.
If you like acting, you **could join** the drama club.
Wenn du das Schauspielern magst, **könntest** du der Theater-AG **beitreten**.
If you have any questions, **ask** the teacher.
Falls du irgendwelche Fragen hast, **frag** die Lehrkraft.

8 REFLEXIVE PRONOUNS
Reflexivpronomen

Du verwendest Reflexivpronomen, wenn das Subjekt und das Objekt in einem Satz dieselbe Person bezeichnen.

Lucy was very proud of herself.

Reflexivpronomen beziehen sich auf das Subjekt in einem Satz.

*I enjoyed **myself** at the party. Ich habe **mich** auf der Party amüsiert.*

*My friends enjoyed **themselves**, too.*

*Meine Freunde haben **sich** auch amüsiert.*

*Ben was really proud of **himself**.*

*Ben war wirklich stolz auf **sich**.*

Personalpronomen	Reflexivpronomen
I	myself
you	yourself
he	himself
she	herself
it	itself
we	ourselves
you	yourselves
they	themselves

Im Englischen werden Reflexivpronomen auch benutzt, um ein Nomen oder Pronomen besonders zu betonen. Sie bedeuten dann im Deutschen „selbst" oder „selber".

*I can't repair this **myself**. – Ich kann das nicht selber reparieren.*
*You said that **yourself**. – Du hast das selbst gesagt.*

Nicht immer sind Verben, die im Deutschen reflexiv sind, auch im Englischen reflexiv.

Ich kann mich nicht konzentrieren. – I can't concentrate. (sich konzentrieren = concentrate)
Die Freunde trafen sich in der Schule. – The friends met at school. (sich treffen = meet)

9 REPORTED SPEECH 2
Indirekte Rede 2

... and then he told me that he liked me and that he would call me next weekend.

Wenn du berichten willst, was jemand sagt oder gesagt hat, verwendest du indirekte Rede *(reported speech)*.

Indirekte Rede besteht aus einem Begleitsatz und der wiedergegebenen Aussage. Beide Satzteile können durch *that* verbunden werden.
Wenn im Begleitsatz das Verb in der Gegenwart steht, ändert sich die Zeitform in der wiedergegebenen Aussage nicht.

DIGITAL+ video 24

	Begleitsatz	wiedergegebene Aussage
Emily: "Chloe is angry with me."	Emily says (that)	Chloe is angry with her.

Oft steht jedoch das Verb im Begleitsatz in der Vergangenheit. Dann rückt die Zeitform sozusagen eine Stufe weiter in die Vergangenheit (Zeitverschiebung = *backshift of tenses*).

	Begleitsatz	wiedergegebene Aussage
Tom: "Most of my classmates seem OK."	Tom told me (that)	most of his classmates seemed OK.
Tom: "The first week was really boring."	Tom mentioned (that)	the first week had been really boring.
Tom: "I haven't made any new friends yet."	Tom told me (that)	he hadn't made any new friends yet.
Linh: "Ruby and Anne aren't talking to each other."	Linh said (that)	Ruby and Anne weren't talking to each other.

Denke daran, Bezugswörter, die nur aus dem Zusammenhang richtig zu verstehen sind, wenn nötig in der wiedergegebenen Aussage anzupassen, wie z. B. Personalpronomen, Zeit- und Ortsangaben.
Tom: *"I will call you again tomorrow."* → Tom told Lucia that *he* would call *her* again *the next day*.
Tom: „*I werde dich morgen wieder anrufen."* → Tom sagte Lucia, dass *er sie am nächsten Tag* wieder anrufen werde.

Aus diesen Tabellen kannst du ablesen, wie sich die Zeiten sowie Zeit- und Ortsangaben verändern.

Direkte Rede		Indirekte Rede		Direkte Rede		Indirekte Rede
simple present	→	simple past		today	→	that day
simple past	→	past perfect		yesterday	→	the day before
present perfect	→	past perfect		last week	→	the week before
present progressive	→	past progressive		tomorrow	→	the next day
will	→	would		next Friday	→	the following Friday
can	→	could		here	→	there

10 ADVERBS OF MANNER (REVISION)
Adverbien der Art und Weise *(revision)*

Lily is dancing happily.

Wenn du beschreiben möchtest, wie jemand etwas tut oder wie etwas geschieht, kannst du Adverbien der Art und Weise benutzen.

Adverbien der Art und Weise beziehen sich auf Verben und beschreiben, wie jemand etwas tut oder wie etwas geschieht. Diese Adverbien beschreiben also Tätigkeiten.

📷 **DIGITAL+** video 25

Adjektiv: *Lily is **happy**.*

Adverb: *Lily is dancing **happily**.*

Ein Adverb der Art und Weise bildest du, indem du an das Adjektiv die Endung *-ly* anhängst.

Adjektiv	Adverb
loud	loudly
bad	badly
slow	slowly

Manchmal ändert sich die Schreibweise, wenn *-ly* angehängt wird:
-y wird zu *-ily*
-le wird zu *-ly*
-l wird zu *-lly*.
-ic wird zu *-ically*

Adjektiv	Adverb
easy	easily
terrible	terribly
beautiful	beautifully
fantastic	fantastically

Einige Adverbien haben Sonderformen, die du wie Vokabeln lernen musst.
Manche Adjektive und Adverbien haben die gleiche Form (z. B. *fast* und *hard*)

Adjektiv	Adverb
good	well
fast	fast
hard	hard

Vorsicht: Nach einigen Verben der Sinneswahrnehmung (z. B. *look*, *taste*, *smell* und *feel*) verwendet man kein Adverb, sondern ein Adjektiv.

*This website **looks interesting**. Diese Webseite sieht interessant aus.*
*The cake **tastes delicious**. Der Kuchen schmeckt lecker.*
*The fish doesn't **smell good**. Der Fisch riecht nicht gut.*
*I **feel great**. Ich fühle mich großartig.*

11 THE COMPARISON OF ADVERBS
Die Steigerung von Adverbien

> The girl in the middle can run faster than the other girls.

Auch Adverbien, die beschreiben, wie jemand etwas tut, kann man steigern. Hier gelten die gleichen Regeln wie bei der Steigerung von Adjektiven.

a) Formen

Einsilbige Adverbien (z.B. *fast* und *hard*) werden durch das Anhängen von *-er* und *-est* gesteigert.

*Olivia trains **harder** than her friends.*
*Olivia trainiert **härter** als ihre Freunde.*
*Olivia trains **the hardest**.*
*Olivia trainiert **am härtesten**.*

	Komparativ	Superlativ
fast	**faster**	(the) **fastest**
hard	**harder**	(the) **hardest**

Es gibt auch unregelmäßige Steigerungs-formen, die du wie Vokabeln lernen musst.

*Tony skates **better** than all the others.*
*Tony skatet **besser** als alle anderen.*
*He skates **the best**. Er skatet **am besten**.*

	Komparativ	Superlativ
well	better	(the) best
badly	worse	(the) worst
much	more	(the) most

Zwei- und mehrsilbige Adverbien, die auf *-ly* enden, steigerst du mit *more* und *most*.

*Janet talks **more quickly** than Liz.*
*Janet spricht **schneller** als Liz.*
*Emily talks **the most quickly**.*
*Emily spricht **am schnellsten**.*

	Komparativ	Superlativ
slowly	more **slowly**	(the) most **slowly**
quickly	more **quickly**	(the) most **quickly**
loudly	more **loudly**	(the) most **loudly**
happily	more **happily**	(the) most **happily**
beautifully	more **beautifully**	(the) most **beautifully**

b) Vergleichssätze

Vergleichssätze bildest du wie bei den Adjektiven mit *than* oder mit *as … as*:

*Ann sings more beautifully **than** Janet.*   *Ann singt schöner als Janet.*
*Jason sings **as** beautifully **as** Ann.*   *Jason singt genauso schön wie Ann.*

12 CONDITIONAL CLAUSES TYPE 2
Bedingungssätze Typ 2

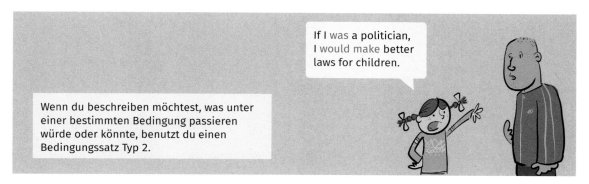

If I was a politician, I would make better laws for children.

Wenn du beschreiben möchtest, was unter einer bestimmten Bedingung passieren würde oder könnte, benutzt du einen Bedingungssatz Typ 2.

Bedingungssätze können realistische oder unrealistische Bedingungen nennen. Ist eine Bedingung erfüllbar, verwendet man den Bedingungssatz Typ 1 (siehe auch Grammatik-Kapitel 7 auf Seite 180).

DIGITAL+ video 26

*If I **study** hard, maybe I **will win** a scholarship.*
*Wenn ich viel **lerne**, **werde** ich vielleicht ein Stipendium **bekommen**.*

Ist eine Bedingung jedoch unwahrscheinlich oder unmöglich, verwendet man den Bedingungssatz Typ 2.

*If I **had** a billion dollars, I **would support** people all over the world.*
*Wenn ich eine Milliarde Dollar **hätte**, **würde** ich Menschen überall auf der Welt **unterstützen**.*

Da die Person das Geld nicht hat, ist die Bedingung nicht erfüllbar.
Bei dieser zweiten Art von Bedingungssätzen steht der *if*-Satz im *simple past*.
Im Hauptsatz steht *would* (oder *could*) mit einem Hauptverb im Infinitiv.

if-Satz *(simple past)* (Bedingung: Wenn …)	Hauptsatz *(would/could + infinitive)* (Folge: … dann …)
If Robert's family **wasn't** so supportive,	it **would be** more difficult for him.
If politicians **listened** more to young people,	maybe things **would change** more quickly.
If I **had** more time,	I **could train** even more.

Übrigens: Statt "*If I was …*" wird oft "*If I were …*" gebraucht. Beide Formen sind hier richtig.

***If I were** still in Honduras, things would be more difficult.* Oder:
***If I was** still in Honduras, things would be more difficult.*
***Wenn** ich immer noch in Honduras **wäre**, wären die Dinge schwieriger.*

Bedingungssätze können entweder mit dem *if*-Satz oder mit dem Hauptsatz beginnen.
Wenn sie mit dem *if*-Satz beginnen, werden sie mit einem Komma getrennt.
Wenn sie mit dem Hauptsatz beginnen, verwendest du kein Komma.
*Things would be more difficult **if I was** still in Honduras.*

13 MODAL VERBS (REVISION)
Modalverben *(revision)*

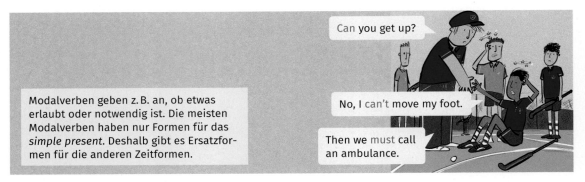

Modalverben geben z. B. an, ob etwas erlaubt oder notwendig ist. Die meisten Modalverben haben nur Formen für das *simple present*. Deshalb gibt es Ersatzformen für die anderen Zeitformen.

> Can you get up?
>
> No, I can't move my foot.
>
> Then we must call an ambulance.

a) Fähigkeit: *can / be able to*

DIGITAL+ video 27

Wenn du sagen willst, dass jemand fähig ist, etwas zu tun, verwendest du *can* und die Ersatzform *be able to*. Im *simple past* kannst du auch *could* benutzen.

*John **can** cut down trees.*   *John **could / was able to** stop a fire yesterday.*

*Tamara **will be able to** offer more surf courses in the future.*

b) Erlaubnis: *can, may / be allowed to*

Mit *can*, *may* und der Ersatzform *be allowed to* kannst du ausdrücken, dass etwas erlaubt ist.

***May** I open the window?* ***Can** I open the window?*

*Cody hopes that one day he **will be allowed to** present his designs in a fashion show.*

c) Verbot: *may not / can't / mustn't / not be allowed to*

Mit *may not*, *can't*, *mustn't* und der Ersatzform *not be allowed to* kannst du ein Verbot ausdrücken. Achtung! *mustn't* klingt wie im Deutschen „muss nicht", heißt aber „darf nicht"!

*Damian **can't** prescribe medication. = Damian **isn't allowed to** prescribe medication.*

*The patient **won't be allowed to** do sports for three weeks. The patient **may not** do sports.*

d) Notwendigkeit: *must / have to*

Mit *must* und der Ersatzform *have to* kannst du ausdrücken, dass etwas getan werden muss.

*A surf instructor **must** know a lot about safety. = A surf instructor **has to** know a lot about safety.*

*I **had to** get a number of safety certifications.*   *I **will have to** work hard.*

Mit *needn't* und der Ersatzform *don't have to* kannst du sagen, dass etwas nicht notwendig ist.

*You **needn't** say that again. = You **don't have to** say that again.*

e) Empfehlung: *should / shouldn't*

Mit *should / shouldn't* drückst du aus, was deiner Meinung nach (nicht) passieren sollte.

*You **should** study for the test.*   *You **shouldn't** talk behind your friend's back.*

f) Möglichkeit: *may / may not*

Mit *may / may not* drückst du aus, was vielleicht passiert.

*It **may** rain today.*   *He is not feeling well. He **may not** come to school today.*

14 CONDITIONAL CLAUSES TYPE 3 (OPTIONAL)
Bedingungssätze Typ 3 *(optional)*

If she had left the house earlier, she would have caught the bus.

Wenn du beschreiben möchtest, was in der Vergangenheit unter einer bestimmten Bedingung hätte passieren können, aber nicht passiert ist, benutzt du einen Bedingungssatz Typ 3.

Bedingungssätze Typ 1 und 2 kennst du bereits (siehe Grammatik-Kapitel 7 auf Seite 180 und Grammatik-Kapitel 12 auf Seite 185).

 **DIGITAL+** video 28

Bei der dritten Art von Bedingungssätzen ist die Bedingung im *if*-Satz nicht mehr erfüllbar. Der *if*-Satz steht hier im *past perfect*.
Im Hauptsatz steht *would* (oder *could*) + *have* + Partizip Perfekt *(past participle)*.

if-Satz *(past perfect)* (Bedingung: Wenn …)	Hauptsatz *(would/could + have + past participle)* (Folge: … dann …)
If Ella **hadn't missed** the bus, Wenn Ella den Bus **nicht verpasst hätte**,	she **would have been** on time. **wäre** sie pünktlich **gewesen**.
If Ella **had prepared** well for the interview, Wenn Ella sich **gut** auf das Interview **vorbereitet hätte**,	maybe she **would have got** the job. **hätte** sie den Job vielleicht **bekommen**.

Bedingungssätze können entweder mit dem *if*-Satz oder mit dem Hauptsatz beginnen.
Wenn sie mit dem *if*-Satz beginnen, werden sie mit einem Komma getrennt.
Wenn sie mit dem Hauptsatz beginnen, verwendest du kein Komma.

*She **would have been** on time **if** she **hadn't missed** the bus.*

15 REPORTED COMMANDS
Indirekte Befehlssätze

Mit einem indirekten Befehlssatz kannst du zum Beispiel einen Befehl, eine Bitte, eine Aufforderung oder eine Warnung wiedergeben.

My mum is asking me to get some bread from the shop.

Wenn du einen Befehlssatz in der indirekten Rede wiedergeben willst, benutzt du den Infinitiv mit *to*.

Befehlssatz (direkte Rede)	Indirekter Befehlssatz
Uncle Joe: "**Come** to the USA."	Mary: "Uncle Joe told us **to come** to the USA."
Uncle Joe: „**Kommt** in die USA."	Mary: „Uncle Joe sagte uns, wir **sollen** in die USA **kommen**."
Mary's mother: "**Pack** your bag."	Mary: "My mother told me **to pack** my bag."
Marys Mutter: „**Pack** deine Tasche."	Mary: „Meine Mutter sagte mir, ich **solle** meine Tasche **packen**."

Um einen Befehl oder eine Aufforderung wiederzugeben, kannst du im indirekten Befehlssatz das Verb *tell* verwenden.

Bitten kannst du mit *ask*, Warnungen mit *warn* und Ratschläge mit *advise* wiedergeben.

Wenn der Originalsatz negativ ist, steht im indirekten Befehlssatz *not* vor dem Infinitiv mit *to*:

Befehlssatz (direkte Rede)	Indirekter Befehlssatz
Uncle Joe: "**Don't wait** too long."	Mary: "Uncle Joe warned us **not to wait** too long."
Onkel Joe: „**Wartet nicht** zu lange."	Mary: „Onkel Joe warnte uns, **nicht** zu lange **zu warten**."
Mary's mother: "Please **don't put** too many things into your bag."	Mary: "My mother asked me **not to put** too many things into my bag."
Marys Mutter: „Bitte **steck nicht** zu viele Dinge in deine Tasche."	Mary: „Meine Mutter bat mich, **nicht** zu viele Dinge in meine Tasche **zu stecken**."

Denke auch daran, gegebenenfalls Bezugswörter anzupassen.

Befehlssatz (direkte Rede)	Indirekter Befehlssatz
Mary's mother: "Please give **me your** bag."	Mary: "My mother told me to give **her my** bag."
Marys Mutter: „Gib **mir** bitte **deine** Tasche."	Mary: „Meine Mutter sagte mir, ich solle **ihr meine** Tasche geben."
Officer: "Give **me your** documents, please."	Mary: "The officer told us to give **him our** documents."
Beamter: „Geben Sie **mir** bitte **Ihre** Papiere."	Mary: „Der Beamte sagte mir, ich solle **ihm unsere** Papiere geben."

16 THE PAST PROGRESSIVE (REVISION)
Die Verlaufsform der Vergangenheit *(revision)*

Mit dem *past progressive* kannst du ausdrücken, was zu einem bestimmten Zeitpunkt in der Vergangenheit gerade passierte.

Yesterday at 5pm

At 5pm, the girls were setting up their tent.

a) Bejahte Aussagesätze im *past progressive*

Das *past progressive* bildest du mit *was / were* + *ing*-Form.

DIGITAL+ video 29

*The people **were boarding** the ship. A child **was crying**.*
*Die Menschen **gingen (gerade)** an Bord des Schiffes. Ein Kind **weinte (gerade)**.*

So kannst du beschreiben, was gerade vor sich ging, als plötzlich etwas anderes geschah:

past progressive	simple past
While the people were leaving the ship, Während die Menschen das Schiff verließen,	it started to rain. fing es zu regnen an.

was gerade passierte:
past progressive

neues Ereignis:
simple past

b) Verneinte Aussagesätze im *past progressive*

Für die Verneinung fügst du **not** hinter die Form von *be* (**was** bzw. **were**) ein bzw. verwendest die entsprechenden Kurzformen.

*Elizabeth **wasn't** sleeping. Her parents **weren't sleeping** either.*
*Elizabeth **schlief nicht**. Ihre Eltern **schliefen** auch **nicht**.*

c) Entscheidungsfragen und Kurzantworten im *past progressive*

Entscheidungsfragen im *past progressive* bildest du, indem du *was* bzw. *were* an den Satzanfang stellst. In der Kurzantwort wird *was* bzw. *were* aufgegriffen.

***Was** Elizabeth **sleeping**?*	–	*Yes, she **was**. / No, she **wasn't**.*
***Were** her parents **cooking** breakfast?*	–	*Yes, they **were**. / No, they **weren't**.*

d) Fragen mit Fragewort im *past progressive*

Bei Fragen mit Fragewörtern stellst du das Fragewort an den Satzanfang.

***What was** Elizabeth **doing**?*   *Was tat Elizabeth (gerade)?*
***Where were** the people **going**?*   *Wohin gingen die Leute (gerade)?*

17 THE PRESENT PERFECT PROGRESSIVE: STATEMENTS
Die Verlaufsform des Perfekts: Aussagen

Das *present perfect progressive* verwendest du, wenn du über etwas sprechen möchtest, das in der Vergangenheit begonnen hat und immer noch andauert.

She has been sleeping for an hour.

a) Bejahte Aussagesätze im *present perfect progressive*

Das *present perfect progressive* bildest du mit *have / has* + *been* + *ing*-Form.
Statt *have* bzw. *has* kannst du auch die entsprechende Kurzform benutzen.

DIGITAL+ video 30

I **have been doing** homework for hours. Ich **mache** schon seit Stunden Hausaufgaben.
We**'ve been listening** to the concert all evening. Wir **haben** den ganzen Abend dem Konzert **zugehört**.
Liam **has been playing** football all day. Liam **spielt** schon den ganzen Tag Fußball.

b) Verneinte Aussagesätze im *present perfect progressive*

Bei Verneinungen fügst du *not* hinter *have* oder *has* ein bzw. verwendest die entsprechenden Kurzformen.

I **haven't been working** for long. Ich **habe** noch nicht lange **gearbeitet**.
He **hasn't been practising** the guitar for a long time. Er **hat** noch nicht lange Gitarre **geübt**.

c) Die Zeitangaben *since* und *for*

Sätze im *present perfect progressive* enthalten oft eine Zeitangabe mit *since* oder *for*.

Since verwendest du, wenn es um einen genauen Zeitpunkt geht, an dem etwas begonnen hat, z.B. *since 2021, since ten o'clock, since I was six years old.*
Dabei muss diese Tätigkeit nicht durchgängig stattgefunden haben.

Declan has been playing the fiddle **since he was a child**.
Declan spielt Geige, **seit er ein Kind war**.

Bei einem Zeitraum benutzt du *for*, z.B. *for six months, for ten years, for a long time.*

Declan has been playing the fiddle **for many years**.
Declan spielt schon **viele Jahre lang** Geige.

18

THE PRESENT PERFECT PROGRESSIVE: QUESTIONS

Die Verlaufsform des Perfekts: Fragen

Have **you** been playing hockey for a long time?

Yes, I have. I've been playing hockey for eight years now.

Mit einer Entscheidungsfrage im *present perfect progressive* kannst du z. B. fragen, ob jemand etwas schon seit längerem tut.

a) Entscheidungsfragen im *present perfect progressive*

Entscheidungsfragen im *present perfect progressive* bildest du, indem du *have* bzw. *has* an den Satzanfang stellst.
Have bzw. *has* wird in den Kurzantworten aufgegriffen.

DIGITAL+ video 30

Entscheidungsfrage	Kurzantwort	Kurzantwort
Have you been waiting for a long time? Wartest du schon lange?	Yes, I have. Ja.	No, I haven't. Nein.
Has Patrick been travelling a lot during the last weeks? Ist Patrick während der letzten Wochen viel gereist?	Yes, he has. Ja.	No, he hasn't. Nein.
Have the children been playing all day? Spielen die Kinder schon den ganzen Tag?	Yes, they have. Ja.	No, they haven't. Nein.

b) Fragen mit Fragewort im *present perfect progressive*

Bei Fragen mit Fragewort steht das Fragewort am Satzanfang.

What have you been doing all day?   *Was* hast du den ganzen Tag gemacht?
How long has Anna been living in Ireland?   *Wie lange* lebt Anna schon in Irland?

Nach Vokabeln suchen

Alphabetische Wortliste *(Dictionary)*: Du suchst nach der Bedeutung eines einzelnen englischen Wortes, das im Textbook vorgekommen ist? Dann nutze die alphabetische Wortliste ab Seite 224. Hier findest du auch unbekannte Wörter aus den Projekten, aus den *Wordbanks* und von den *Get together*-Seiten. Einige englische Wörter, die im Englischen und im Deutschen gleich sind, findest du auf Seite 194.

Wortlisten nach Kapiteln *(Vocabulary)*: Du möchtest die Vokabeln zu einem ganzen Abschnitt im Buch lernen? Dann nutze die chronologische Wortliste ab Seite 195. Nach Kapiteln und Seitenzahlen sortiert findest du hier alle Wörter, die neu im Buch vorkommen.

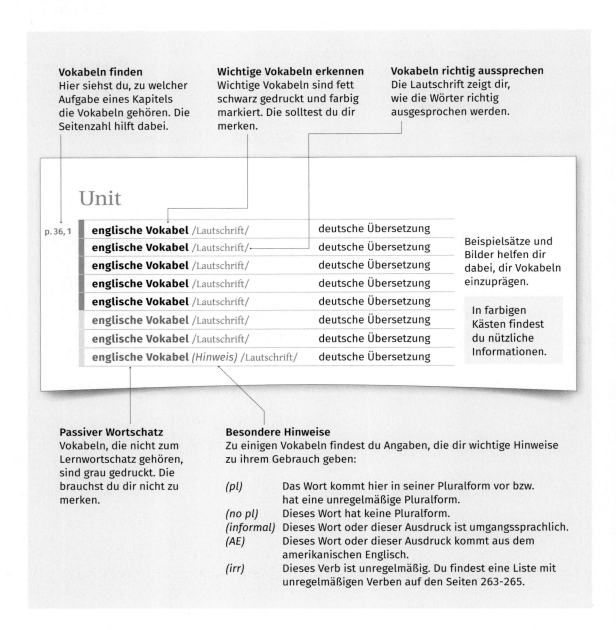

Vokabeln finden
Hier siehst du, zu welcher Aufgabe eines Kapitels die Vokabeln gehören. Die Seitenzahl hilft dabei.

Wichtige Vokabeln erkennen
Wichtige Vokabeln sind fett schwarz gedruckt und farbig markiert. Die solltest du dir merken.

Vokabeln richtig aussprechen
Die Lautschrift zeigt dir, wie die Wörter richtig ausgesprochen werden.

Unit

p. 36, 1

englische Vokabel /Lautschrift/	deutsche Übersetzung
englische Vokabel /Lautschrift/	deutsche Übersetzung
englische Vokabel /Lautschrift/	deutsche Übersetzung
englische Vokabel /Lautschrift/	deutsche Übersetzung
englische Vokabel /Lautschrift/	deutsche Übersetzung
englische Vokabel /Lautschrift/	deutsche Übersetzung
englische Vokabel /Lautschrift/	deutsche Übersetzung
englische Vokabel *(Hinweis)* /Lautschrift/	deutsche Übersetzung

Beispielsätze und Bilder helfen dir dabei, dir Vokabeln einzuprägen.

In farbigen Kästen findest du nützliche Informationen.

Passiver Wortschatz
Vokabeln, die nicht zum Lernwortschatz gehören, sind grau gedruckt. Die brauchst du dir nicht zu merken.

Besondere Hinweise
Zu einigen Vokabeln findest du Angaben, die dir wichtige Hinweise zu ihrem Gebrauch geben:

(pl)   Das Wort kommt hier in seiner Pluralform vor bzw. hat eine unregelmäßige Pluralform.

(no pl)   Dieses Wort hat keine Pluralform.

(informal)   Dieses Wort oder dieser Ausdruck ist umgangssprachlich.

(AE)   Dieses Wort oder dieser Ausdruck kommt aus dem amerikanischen Englisch.

(irr)   Dieses Verb ist unregelmäßig. Du findest eine Liste mit unregelmäßigen Verben auf den Seiten 263-265.

Die richtige Aussprache

Im Englischen spricht man Wörter oft anders aus als man sie schreibt.
Die Aussprache der Wörter wird mithilfe der Lautschrift in jedem Wörterbuch angegeben.
Man kann so auch neue Wörter richtig aussprechen, ohne sie vorher gehört zu haben.
Die Lautschrift ist eine Schrift, deren Symbole jeden Laut genau bezeichnen.
Hier ist eine Liste mit den Symbolen dieser Lautschrift zusammen mit Beispielwörtern.

The English alphabet

a	/eɪ/
b	/biː/
c	/siː/
d	/diː/
e	/iː/
f	/ef/
g	/dʒiː/
h	/eɪtʃ/
i	/aɪ/
j	/dʒeɪ/
k	/keɪ/
l	/el/
m	/em/
n	/en/
o	/əʊ/
p	/piː/
q	/kjuː/
r	/ɑː/
s	/es/
t	/tiː/
u	/juː/
v	/viː/
w	/ˈdʌbljuː/
x	/eks/
y	/waɪ/
z	/zed/

English sounds

Vokale

/ɑː/	**arm**
/ʌ/	**but**
/e/	**desk**
/ə/	**a, an**
/ɜː/	**girl, bird**
/æ/	**apple**
/ɪ/	**in, it**
/i/	**happy**
/iː/	**easy, eat**
/ɒ/	**orange, sorry**
/ɔː/	**all, call**
/ʊ/	**look**
/u/	**January**
/uː/	**boot**

Doppellaute

/aɪ/	**eye, by, buy**
/aʊ/	**our**
/eə/	**air, there**
/eɪ/	**take, they**
/ɪə/	**here**
/ɔɪ/	**boy**
/əʊ/	**go, old**
/ʊə/	**tour**

Konsonanten

/b/	**bag, club**
/d/	**duck, card**
/f/	**fish, laugh**
/g/	**get, dog**
/h/	**hot**
/j/	**you**
/k/	**can, duck**
/l/	**lot, small**
/m/	**more, mum**
/n/	**now, sun**
/ŋ/	**song, long**
/p/	**present, top**
/r/	**red, around**
/s/	**sister, class** *(stimmlos)*
/z/	**nose, dogs** *(stimmhaft)*
/t/	**time, cat**
/ʒ/	**television**
/dʒ/	**sausage**
/ʃ/	**fresh**
/tʃ/	**child, cheese**
/ð/	**these, mother** *(stimmhaft)*
/θ/	**bathroom, think** *(stimmlos)*
/v/	**very, have**
/w/	**what, word**

Betonungszeichen für die folgende Silbe

/ˈ/	**Hauptbetonung**
/ˌ/	**Nebenbetonung**

Bekannte Wörter

Viele Wörter sind im Englischen und im Deutschen so gut wie gleich. Manche unterscheiden sich nur durch die Groß- bzw. Kleinschreibung – im Englischen werden die meisten Nomen kleingeschrieben. Viele dieser Wörter, die in deinem Buch vorkommen, findest du hier. Bei denen, die anders ausgesprochen werden als im Deutschen, ist die Lautschrift farbig hervorgehoben.

action /'ækʃn/
adverb /'ædvɜːb/
alligator /'ælɪˌɡeɪtə/
anorak /'ænəræk/
anti- /'ænti/
app /æp/
arm /ɑːm/
audio /'ɔːdiəʊ/
baby /'beɪbi/
babysitting /'beɪbiˌsɪtɪŋ/
ball /bɔːl/
band /bænd/
bar /bɑː/
base /beɪs/
baseball /'beɪsˌbɔːl/
basketball /'bɑːskɪtˌbɔːl/
bistro /'biːstrəʊ/
block /blɒk/
blog /blɒɡ/
boom /buːm/
boss /bɒs/
bowling /'bəʊlɪŋ/
bronze /brɒnz/
burger /'bɜːɡə/
bus /bʌs/
café /'kæfeɪ/
cafeteria /ˌkæfə'tɪəriə/
camping /'kæmpɪŋ/
car sharing /'kɑː ˌʃeərɪŋ/
cartoon /kɑː'tuːn/
champion /'tʃæmpjən/
chance /tʃɑːns/
chat /tʃæt/
cheerleader /'tʃɪəˌliːdə/
cheerleading /'tʃɪəˌliːdɪŋ/
clever /'klevə/
clip /klɪp/
collage /'kɒlɑːʒ/
computer /kəm'pjuːtə/
cool /kuːl/
deck /dek/
demonstration /ˌdemən'streɪʃn/
designer /dɪ'zaɪnə/
digital /'dɪdʒɪtl/
DJ /'diːˌdʒeɪ/
DNA /ˌdiː_en_'eɪ/
dollar /'dɒlə/
drama /'drɑːmə/

element /'elɪmənt/
email /'iːmeɪl/
emoji /ɪ'məʊdʒi/
engagement /ɪn'ɡeɪdʒmənt/
ensemble /ɒn'sɒmbl/
episode /'epɪsəʊd/
etc. (= et cetera) /et 'setrə/
fair /feə/
film /fɪlm/
finger /'fɪŋɡə/
fit /fɪt/
flyer /'flaɪə/
food truck /'fuːd ˌtrʌk/
form /fɔːm/
gaming /'ɡeɪmɪŋ/
generation /ˌdʒenə'reɪʃn/
glamour /'ɡlæmə/
global /'ɡləʊbl/
gold /ɡəʊld/
hacker /'hækə/
hamburger /'hæmˌbɜːɡə/
hand /hænd/
high five /ˌhaɪ 'faɪv/
hip-hop /'hɪp hɒp/
hobby /'hɒbi/
hot dog /ˌhɒt 'dɒɡ/
hotel /həʊ'tel/
hunger /'hʌŋɡə/
icon /'aɪkɒn/
ideal /aɪ'dɪəl/
illegal /ɪ'liːɡl/
info /'ɪnfəʊ/
instrument /'ɪnstrʊmənt/
international /ˌɪntə'næʃnəl/
Internet /'ɪntəˌnet/
interpretation /ɪnˌtɜːprɪ'teɪʃn/
interview /'ɪntəˌvjuː/
IT /ˌaɪ 'tiː/
jazz /dʒæz/
jeans /dʒiːnz/
Jr. (= junior) /'dʒuːniə/
lacrosse /lə'krɒs/
land /lænd/
laptop /'læpˌtɒp/
layout /'leɪaʊt/
legal /'liːɡl/
live /laɪv/
make-up /'meɪk ˌʌp/

mama /'mæmə/
manager /'mænɪdʒə/
marketing /'mɑːkɪtɪŋ/
material /mə'tɪəriəl/
meme /miːm/
million /'mɪljən/
mini /'mɪni/
mini golf /'mɪni ɡɒlf/
minute /'mɪnɪt/
modern /'mɒdən/
moment /'məʊmənt/
multiple-choice /ˌmʌltɪpl 'tʃɔɪs/
museum /mju'ziːəm/
musical /'mjuːzɪkl/
name /neɪm/
national /'næʃnəl/
nest /nest/
normal /'nɔːml/
offline /ˌɒf'laɪn/
OK, okay /ˌəʊ'keɪ/
online /'ɒnlaɪn/
outfit /'aʊtfɪt/
parade /pə'reɪd/
park /pɑːk/
partner /'pɑːtnə/
party /'pɑːti/
patient /'peɪʃnt/
person /'pɜːsn/
pier /pɪə/
pilot /'paɪlət/
pizza /'piːtsə/
plan /plæn/
planet /'plænɪt/
podcast /'pɒdˌkɑːst/
pogrom /'pɒɡrəm/
pool /puːl/
pop /pɒp/
popcorn /'pɒpkɔːn/
post, poster /pəʊst, 'pəʊstə/
problem /'prɒbləm/
professor /prə'fesə/
quiz /kwɪz/
radar /'reɪdɑː/
radio /'reɪdiəʊ/
recycling /riː'saɪklɪŋ/
region /'riːdʒn/
regional /'riːdʒnəl/
reporter /rɪ'pɔːtə/

rest /rest/
restaurant /'restrɒnt/
revolution /ˌrevə'luːʃn/
routine /ruː'tiːn/
rugby /'rʌɡbi/
sandwich /'sænwɪdʒ/
semester /sə'mestə/
service /'sɜːvɪs/
show /ʃəʊ/
sightseeing /'saɪtˌsiːɪŋ/
signal /'sɪɡnl/
simulation /ˌsɪmjʊ'leɪʃn/
situation /ˌsɪtʃu'eɪʃn/
skyline /'skaɪˌlaɪn/
slogan /'sləʊɡən/
smartphone /'smɑːtˌfəʊn/
so /səʊ/
software /'sɒfˌweə/
standard /'stændəd/
statue /'stætʃuː/
stunt /stʌnt/
symbol /'sɪmbl/
system /'sɪstəm/
T-shirt /'tiː ʃɜːt/
team /tiːm/
teamwork /'tiːmˌwɜːk/
teen(ager) /tiːn, 'tiːnˌeɪdʒə/
terrorist /'terərɪst/
test /test/
text, texting /tekst, 'tekstɪŋ/
ticket /'tɪkɪt/
toast /təʊst/
tour, tourist /tʊə, 'tʊərɪst/
tradition /trə'dɪʃn/
training /'treɪnɪŋ/
trend /trend/
tutorial /tjuː'tɔːriəl/
uniform /'juːnɪfɔːm/
verb /vɜːb/
video /'vɪdiəʊ/
video call /'vɪdiəʊ kɔːl/
vlog /vlɒɡ/
web /web/
webcode /'webˌkəʊd/
website /'webˌsaɪt/
winter /'wɪntə/
workshop /'wɜːkˌʃɒp/
zone /zəʊn/
zoo /zuː/

Quiz

p. 6	**state** /steɪt/	(der) Staat, (der) Bundesstaat
	capital /ˈkæpɪtl/	(die) Hauptstadt
	president /ˈprezɪdənt/	(der/die) Präsident/in
	billion /ˈbɪljən/	(die) Milliarde
	award /əˈwɔːd/	(der) Preis, (die) Auszeichnung
	America /əˈmerɪkə/	Amerika
	(the) US (= the United States) /ðə ˌjuːˈes, ðə juːˌnaɪtɪd ˈsteɪts/	US, Vereinigte Staaten (von Amerika); US-
	(to) fight *(irr)* /faɪt/	kämpfen
	equal /ˈiːkwəl/	gleich
	US-American /ˌjuːˌesˌəˈmerɪkən/	(der/die) US-Amerikaner/in; US-amerikanisch
	(to) make *(irr)* /meɪk/	*hier:* ergeben
	the Oscars /ðiˈɒskəz/	*amerikanischer Filmpreis*
	Thanksgiving /ˈθæŋksˌgɪvɪŋ/	Thanksgiving *(amerikanisches Erntedankfest)*
	Independence Day /ˌɪndɪˈpendəns deɪ/	(der) Unabhängigkeitstag
	Pancake Day /ˈpænkeɪk deɪ/	(der) Pfannkuchentag
	the Statue of Liberty /ðə ˌstætʃuːˌəvˈlɪbəti/	(die) Freiheitsstatue
	the very first /ðə ˌveri ˈfɜːst/	der/die/das allererste
	Antarctica /ænˈtɑːktɪkə/	(die) Antarktis
	Asia /ˈeɪʒə/	Asien
	Australia /ɒˈstreɪliə/	Australien
	Olympic /əˈlɪmpɪk/	olympisch
p. 7	medal /ˈmedl/	(die) Medaille
	European /ˌjʊərəˈpiːən/	(der/die) Europäer/in; europäisch
	(to) shout /ʃaʊt/	rufen, schreien
	Spanish /ˈspænɪʃ/	(das) Spanisch
	moccasin /ˈmɒkəsɪn/	(der) Mokassin
	kayak /ˈkaɪæk/	(der) Kajak
	indigenous /ɪnˈdɪdʒənəs/	(ein)heimisch, indigen
	Asian /ˈeɪʒn/	(der/die) Asiat/in; asiatisch
	stadium *(pl stadiums or stadia)* /ˈsteɪdiəm, ˈsteɪdiəmz, ˈsteɪdiə/	(das) Stadion
	(to) originate /əˈrɪdʒəneɪt/	entstehen, seinen Anfang nehmen
	Super Bowl /ˈsuːpə bəʊl/	*(das) Finale der US-amerikanischen American Football-Profiliga*
p. 8	**landscape** /ˈlænˌskeɪp/	(die) Landschaft
	desert /ˈdezət/	(die) Wüste
	ride /raɪd/	(die) Fahrt
	surfing /ˈsɜːfɪŋ/	(das) Surfen
	dog sled /ˈdɒg sled/	(der) Hundeschlitten
	farmland /ˈfɑːmˌlænd/	(das) Ackerland

The **capital** is the most important city of a **state**.

You can win an **award** for doing something great.

equal = the same

the Statue of Liberty

People who come from Europe are known as **Europeans**.

A **desert** is a large area of dry land. There are not many plants in a desert.

Unit 1 | Part A Impressions of the USA

p. 9	**impression** /ɪmˈpreʃn/	(der) Eindruck
p. 10, 2	**east** /iːst/	(der) Osten
	west /west/	(der) Westen
	wide /waɪd/	groß, breit, enorm
	variety /vəˈraɪəti/	(die) Vielfalt, (die) Auswahl
	climate /ˈklaɪmət/	(das) Klima
	island /ˈaɪlənd/	(die) Insel
	snow /snəʊ/	(der) Schnee
	innovation /ˌɪnəʊˈveɪʃn/	(die) Neuerung
	factory /ˈfæktri/	(die) Fabrik
	(to) **extend** /ɪkˈstend/	sich erstrecken
	man *(pl **men**)* /mæn, men/	(der) Mensch
	(to) **develop** /dɪˈveləp/	erarbeiten, (sich) entwickeln
	artificial intelligence (= AI) /ɑːtɪˌfɪʃl̩ ɪnˈtelɪdʒns, ˌeɪ ˈaɪ/	(die) künstliche Intelligenz
	spotlight /ˈspɒtˌlaɪt/	(der) Scheinwerfer
	area /ˈeəriə/	(die) Fläche
	square /ˈskweə/	quadratisch, Quadrat-
	tropical /ˈtrɒpɪkl̩/	tropisch
	stretch /stretʃ/	*hier:* (der) Abschnitt
	California /ˌkælɪˈfɔːniə/	Kalifornien
	peak /piːk/	(der) Gipfel, (die) Bergspitze
	all year round /ˌɔːl ˈjɪə raʊnd/	das ganze Jahr lang
	(to) **install** /ɪnˈstɔːl/	aufstellen, installieren
	assembly line /əˈsembli laɪn/	(das) Fließband
	(to) **set foot on** *(irr)* /ˌset ˈfʊt‿ɒn/	betreten
	information technology (= IT) /ˌɪnfəˌmeɪʃn tekˈnɒlədʒi, ˌaɪ ˈtiː/	(die) Informationstechnologie, (die) IT
p. 11, 2	(to) **establish** /ɪˈstæblɪʃ/	gründen, einführen
	politician /ˌpɒləˈtɪʃn/	(der/die) Politiker/in
	(to) **preserve** /prɪˈzɜːv/	erhalten
	natural /ˈnætʃrəl/	natürlich
	beauty /ˈbjuːti/	(die) Schönheit
	diverse /daɪˈvɜːs/	vielfältig, unterschiedlich
	ecosystem /ˈiːkəʊˌsɪstəm/	(das) Ökosystem
	(to) **provide** /prəˈvaɪd/	zur Verfügung stellen
	(to) **influence** /ˈɪnfluəns/	beeinflussen
	ingredient /ɪnˈgriːdiənt/	(die) Zutat
	wetlands *(pl)* /ˈwetlændz/	(das) Sumpfgebiet
	eating habit /ˈiːtɪŋ ˌhæbɪt/	(die) Essgewohnheit
	eating /ˈiːtɪŋ/	(das) Essen

A **factory** is a place where things are made, mostly by machines.

„**Man**" in der Bedeutung „Mensch" wird meist in der Literatur verwendet und gilt heute als veraltet. In der Bedeutung „Menschheit" hat es keine Pluralform.

square kilometre (= km²) /ˌskweə ˈkɪləˌmiːtə/ (der) Quadratkilometer
square mile /ˌskweə ˈmaɪl/ (die) Quadratmeile

A **politician** is someone whose job it is to work in politics, for example as a member of a parliament or in a local government.

diverse = very different from something

to **provide** = to give

	(to) inspire /ɪnˈspaɪə/	inspirieren
	country music /ˈkʌntri ˌmjuːzɪk/	(die) Countrymusik
	(to) come up *(irr)* /ˈkʌm ˌʌp/	aufkommen
	hotspot /ˈhɒtˌspɒt/	*(der) angesagte Ort*
	birthplace /ˈbɜːθˌpleɪs/	(der) Geburtsort
	youth culture /ˈjuːθ ˌkʌltʃə/	(die) Jugendkultur
p. 12, 3	irregular /ɪˈreɡjʊlə/	unregelmäßig
	greetings *(pl)* /ˈɡriːtɪŋz/	Grüße
p. 12, 4	(to) unscramble /ʌnˈskræmbl/	ordnen, in die richtige Reihenfolge bringen
p. 12, 5	**according to** /əˈkɔːdɪŋ ˌtuː/	nach, gemäß
p. 13, 6	**destination** /ˌdestɪˈneɪʃn/	(das) Ziel, (das) Reiseziel
	trip /trɪp/	(die) Reise
	foot *(pl feet)* /fʊt, fiːt/	Fuß *(Maßeinheit, 1 Fuß = 0,3048 Meter)*
	edge /edʒ/	(der) Rand
	(to) **experience** /ɪkˈspɪəriəns/	erleben, kennenlernen
	independence /ˌɪndɪˈpendəns/	(die) Unabhängigkeit
	hall /hɔːl/	(die) Halle
	wonder /ˈwʌndə/	(das) Wunder
	breathtaking /ˈbreθˌteɪkɪŋ/	atemberaubend
	endless /ˈendləs/	endlos
	must-see /ˌmʌst ˈsiː/	*etwas, das man unbedingt sehen muss*
	lover /ˈlʌvə/	(der/die) Liebhaber/in
	magnificent /mæɡˈnɪfɪsnt/	wunderbar, großartig
	ultimate /ˈʌltɪmət/	höchste(r, s); stärkste(r, s)
	thrill /θrɪl/	(der) Nervenkitzel, (der) Kick
	(to) step out /ˌstepˈaʊt/	heraustreten
	canyon /ˈkænjən/	(die) Schlucht
	stunning /ˈstʌnɪŋ/	toll, fantastisch
	charming /ˈtʃɑːmɪŋ/	charmant
	(to) step back in time /ˌstepˌbækˌɪn ˈtaɪm/	sich in die Vergangenheit zurück-versetzen
	gold rush /ˈɡəʊld rʌʃ/	(der) Goldrausch
	era /ˈɪərə/	(die) Epoche, (das) Zeitalter
	(to) take a ride *(irr)* /ˌteɪkˌə ˈraɪd/	eine Fahrt machen
	magic /ˈmædʒɪk/	(die) Magie, (der) Zauber
	historic /hɪˈstɒrɪk/	historisch
p. 14, 7	(to) **claim** /kleɪm/	Anspruch erheben auf, behaupten
	(to) **settle** /ˈsetl/	sich niederlassen
	east /iːst/	östlich, Ost-
	coast /kəʊst/	(die) Küste
	political /pəˈlɪtɪkl/	politisch
	economic /ˌiːkəˈnɒmɪk/	wirtschaftlich
	freedom /ˈfriːdəm/	(die) Freiheit

Country music is a type of music in the traditional style of the southern USA.

The glass is dangerously close to the **edge** of the table.

A **hall** is a very large room.

She is a book **lover**.

stunning = great, fantastic

The **coast** is very nice in this part of the country.

among /əˈmʌŋ/	unter; zwischen
ship /ʃɪp/	(das) Schiff
settler /ˈsetlə/	(der/die) Siedler/in
Native American /ˌneɪtɪv_əˈmerɪkən/	Native American *(Selbstbezeichnung der ersten Bevölkerungen in den USA)*
nation /ˈneɪʃn/	(die) Nation, (das) Land; (das) Volk
violence /ˈvaɪələns/	(die) Gewalt
disease /dɪˈziːz/	(die) Krankheit
familiar /fəˈmɪliə/	vertraut, bekannt
colony /ˈkɒləni/	(die) Kolonie
tax /tæks/	(die) Steuer, (die) Abgabe
(to) **declare** /dɪˈkleə/	verkünden; erklären
independent /ˌɪndɪˈpendənt/	unabhängig
glimpse /glɪmps/	(der) flüchtige Blick
continent /ˈkɒntɪnənt/	(der) Kontinent
Scandinavia /ˌskændɪˈneɪviə/	Skandinavien
North America /ˌnɔːθ_əˈmerɪkə/	Nordamerika
settlement /ˈsetlmənt/	(die) Siedlung
Canada /ˈkænədə/	Kanada
the Caribbean /ðə ˌkærɪˈbiən/	(die) Karibik, karibische Inseln
Spain /speɪn/	Spanien
colonization /ˌkɒlənaɪˈzeɪʃn/	(die) Kolonisierung
pilgrim /ˈpɪlgrɪm/	(der/die) Pilger/in
way of living /ˌweɪ_əv ˈlɪvɪŋ/	(die) Lebensweise
(to) govern /ˈgʌvən/	regieren
War of Independence /ˌwɔːr_əv_ˌɪndɪˈpendəns/	(Amerikanischer) Unabhängigkeitskrieg
(to) **force** /fɔːs/	zwingen, erzwingen
condition /kənˈdɪʃn/	(die) Bedingung, (der) Zustand
Civil War /ˌsɪvl ˈwɔː/	(der) Bürgerkrieg
industrialized /ɪnˈdʌstriəlaɪzd/	industrialisiert
agricultural /ˌægrɪˈkʌltʃrəl/	landwirtschaftlich
southern /ˈsʌðən/	südliche(r, s); Süd-
(to) **be involved in** *(irr)* /ˌbi_ɪnˈvɒlvd_ɪn/	beteiligt sein an
(to) **enter** /ˈentə/	eintreten in
presence /ˈprezns/	(die) Anwesenheit, (die) Präsenz
(to) **lead** *(irr)* /liːd/	führen
institution /ˌɪnstɪˈtjuːʃn/	(die) Einrichtung, (die) Institution
civil rights *(pl)* /ˌsɪvl ˈraɪts/	(die) Bürgerrechte
movement /ˈmuːvmənt/	(die) Bewegung
leader /ˈliːdə/	(der/die) Anführer/in
attack /əˈtæk/	(der) Angriff
(to) **serve** /sɜːv/	dienen; eine Amtszeit durchlaufen
historical /hɪˈstɒrɪkl/	geschichtlich, historisch

p. 15, 7

Sidebar notes:

A **nation** is a country that has its own government and land.
The word can also refer to all of the people in a country.

A **disease** is an illness.

to **declare** = to state

Scandinavia is a region in north-west Europe.

Spain is a country in south-west Europe.

An **industrialized** country has lots of developed industries.

southern ≠ northern

Man verwendet „**historic**", wenn man ausdrücken will, dass etwas „historisch bedeutsam" ist, und „**historical**", wenn etwas „die Vergangenheit betreffend" ist.

	slavery /ˈsleɪvəri/	(die) Sklaverei
	slave /sleɪv/	(der/die) Sklave/Sklavin
	Africa /ˈæfrɪkə/	Afrika
	field of work /ˌfiːld_əv ˈwɜːk/	(der) Arbeitsbereich
	fighting /ˈfaɪtɪŋ/	(die) Kämpfe, (die) Gefechte
	ally /ˈælaɪ/	(der/die) Verbündete, (der/die) Alliierte
	military /ˈmɪlɪtri/	militärisch
	mid- /mɪd/	Mitte
	racial segregation /ˌreɪʃl segrɪˈgeɪʃn/	(die) Rassentrennung
	(to) hijack /ˈhaɪdʒæk/	entführen
	(to) rebuild (irr) /ˌriːˈbɪld/	wieder aufbauen
	complex /ˈkɒmpleks/	(der) Komplex
	African American /ˌæfrɪkən_əˈmerɪkən/	(der/die) Afroamerikaner/in; afroamerikanisch
	chronological /ˌkrɒnəˈlɒdʒɪkl/	chronologisch
and und Leute 1	**tear** /tɪə/	(die) Träne
	trail /treɪl/	(der) Weg, (der) Pfad
p. 16, 8	(to) commemorate /kəˈmeməreɪt/	(einer Person oder Sache) gedenken
p. 16, 9	one-minute /ˌwʌnˈmɪnɪt/	einminütig
	sportsperson /ˈspɔːtsˌpɜːsn/	(der/die) Sportler/in
	flag /flæg/	(die) Fahne, (die) Flagge
p. 17, 10	**quote** /kwəʊt/	(das) Zitat
	opportunity /ˌɒpəˈtjuːnəti/	(die) Chance, (die) Möglichkeit, (die) Gelegenheit
	choice /tʃɔɪs/	(die) Auswahl, (die) Wahl
	(to) **give a reason** (irr) /ˌgɪv_ə ˈriːzn/	einen Grund nennen
	education /ˌedjʊˈkeɪʃn/	(die) Bildung, (die) Ausbildung; (die) Erziehung
	security /sɪˈkjʊərəti/	(die) Sicherheit
	peace /piːs/	(der) Frieden
	passage /ˈpæsɪdʒ/	(die) (Text)passage, (der) Gang, (die) Überfahrt
	entry /ˈentri/	(der) Eintrag
	such as /ˈsʌtʃ_æz/	wie
	democracy /dɪˈmɒkrəsi/	(die) Demokratie
	equality /ɪˈkwɒləti/	(die) Gleichberechtigung, (die) Gleichheit
	social /ˈsəʊʃl/	gesellschaftlich; sozial
	origin /ˈɒrɪdʒɪn/	(der) Ursprung, (die) Herkunft
	(to) **disagree** /ˌdɪsəˈgriː/	nicht zustimmen
	(to) **achieve** /əˈtʃiːv/	erreichen
	born /bɔːn/	geboren
	historian /hɪˈstɔːriən/	(der/die) Historiker/in
	(to) **rank** /ræŋk/	einstufen, anordnen

World War I (= **the First World War**) /ˌwɜːld ˌwɔː ˈwʌn, ðə ˌfɜːst ˌwɜːld ˈwɔː/ (der) Erste Weltkrieg
World War II (= **the Second World War**) /ˌwɜːld ˌwɔː ˈtuː, ðə ˌsekənd ˌwɜːld ˈwɔː/ (der) Zweite Weltkrieg

There are **tears** running down his face.

A **one-minute** presentation should last 60 seconds.

When you **give a reason**, you explain why you have a certain opinion.

Education is the process or activity of teaching people.

When you write something into a diary, you make a diary **entry**.

to **achieve** something = to be successful at doing something

tolerance /ˈtɒlərəns/	(die) Toleranz	
set /set/	*hier:* (die) Reihe	
regardless of /rɪˈɡɑːdləs‿əv/	trotz, ungeachtet	
greatness /ˈɡreɪtnəs/	(die) Bedeutsamkeit	
themselves /ðəmˈselvz/	sich; selbst	
(to) **be situated** *(irr)* /ˌbiː ˈsɪtʃueɪtɪd/	liegen, gelegen sein	
known /nəʊn/	bekannt	
silver /ˈsɪlvə/	(das) Silber	
bracket /ˈbrækɪt/	(die) Klammer	
bean /biːn/	(die) Bohne	
economy /ɪˈkɒnəmi/	(die) Wirtschaft	
writer /ˈraɪtə/	(der/die) Schriftsteller/in	
suitable /ˈsuːtəbl/	geeignet, passend	

p. 18, 11 — **themselves**
p. 18, 12 — (to) **be situated**
p. 19, 13 — **economy**

The village **is situated** between two mountains.

mixed /mɪkst/ gemischt
baked /beɪkt/ gebacken

writer = author

Unit 1 | Part B New York City

noisy /ˈnɔɪzi/	laut	
fascinating /ˈfæsɪneɪtɪŋ/	faszinierend	
lively /ˈlaɪvli/	lebhaft, lebendig	
at the back of /ˌæt ðə ˈbæk‿əv/	am Ende von, hinten in	
awesome /ˈɔːsm/	beeindruckend; super	
production /prəˈdʌkʃn/	(die) Produktion	
crown /kraʊn/	(die) Krone	
ferry /ˈferi/	(die) Fähre	
harbor *(AE)* = **harbour** *(BE)* /ˈhɑːbə/	(der) Hafen	
across /əˈkrɒs/	über, quer durch	
theater *(AE)* /ˈθɪətə/	(das) Theater	
stop /stɒp/	(der) Halt	
bike lane /ˈbaɪk leɪn/	(der) Fahrradweg	
(to) tour /tʊə/	bereisen, erkunden	
lovely /ˈlʌvli/	schön, herrlich	
calm /kɑːm/	ruhig, friedlich	
in the middle of /ˌɪn ðə ˈmɪdl‿əv/	in der Mitte von, mitten in	
(to) **hit** *(irr)* /hɪt/	treffen, stoßen gegen	
since then /sɪns ˈðen/	seitdem, seither	
former /ˈfɔːmə/	ehemalige(r, s); frühere(r, s)	
skyscraper /ˈskaɪˌskreɪpə/	(der) Wolkenkratzer	
all around /ˌɔːl‿əˈraʊnd/	rundherum, überall (in/auf)	
moving /ˈmuːvɪŋ/	bewegend, ergreifend	
(to) **learn** *(irr)* /lɜːn/	erfahren	
borough /ˈbʌrə/	(der) Bezirk, (der) Stadtteil	
(to) **build a park** *(irr)* /ˌbɪld‿ə ˈpɑːk/	einen Park anlegen	
all day long /ˌɔːl deɪ ˈlɒŋ/	den ganzen Tag lang	
(to) **rent** /rent/	mieten	

p. 20, 1 — **noisy**
p. 20, 2 — **at the back of**
p. 21, 2 — **lovely**

noisy = loud

at the back of ≠ in the front

„Lady Liberty" ist ein Spitzname für die Freiheitsstatue in New York.

There are often lots of **skyscrapers** in big cities.

present perfect /ˌpreznt ˈpɜːfɪkt/ das Perfekt
simple past /ˌsɪmpl ˈpɑːst/ die einfache Vergangenheit

	memorial /məˈmɔːriəl/	(das) Denkmal, (das) Ehrenmal
	Twin Towers /ˌtwɪn ˈtaʊəz/	*Zwillingstürme in New York City*
	footprint /ˈfʊtˌprɪnt/	(der) Fußabdruck, (die) Standfläche
p. 22, 4	follow-up question /ˈfɒləʊˌʌp ˌkwestʃn/	(die) Folgefrage
p. 23, 5	**floor** /flɔː/	(das) Stockwerk
	(to) **turn into** /ˌtɜːn_ˈɪntʊ/	umwandeln in
	railroad /ˈreɪlˌrəʊd/	*hier:* (das) Eisenbahngelände
p. 24, 6	(to) **make money** *(irr)* /ˌmeɪk ˈmʌni/	Geld verdienen
	high school *(AE)* /ˈhaɪ skuːl/	(die) Highschool, (die) weiterführende Schule
	(to) **be proud of** *(irr)* /ˌbiː ˈpraʊd_əv/	stolz sein auf
	cultural, culturally /ˈkʌltʃərəl, ˈkʌltʃərəli/	kulturell
	whenever /wenˈevə/	wann auch immer
	Lebanon /ˈlebənən/	der Libanon
	neighborhood *(AE)* /ˈneɪbəˌhʊd/	(das) Viertel, (die) Nachbarschaft
	apartment *(AE)* /əˈpɑːtmənt/	(die) Wohnung
	brownstone (house) /ˈbraʊnˌstəʊn haʊs/	*(das) Haus aus rötlich braunem Sandstein*
	downtown *(AE)* /ˌdaʊnˈtaʊn/	in der Innenstadt, im Zentrum
	sidewalk *(AE)* /ˈsaɪdˌwɔːk/	(der) Bürgersteig
	store *(AE)* /stɔː/	(der) Laden
	Hispanic /hɪˈspænɪk/	(der/die) Hispanoamerikaner/in; hispanisch
	crime rate /ˈkraɪm reɪt/	(die) Kriminalitätsrate
p. 25, 7	**extract** /ˈekstrækt/	(der) Auszug, (das) Exzerpt
	diversity /daɪˈvɜːsəti/	(die) Vielfalt
	electric /ɪˈlektrɪk/	elektrisierend, spannungsgeladen
	(to) **test** /test/	prüfen, testen
	pretty /ˈprɪti/	hübsch
	(to) **reject** /rɪˈdʒekt/	ablehnen, zurückweisen
	(to) **accept** /əkˈsept/	anerkennen, akzeptieren
	lyrics *(pl)* /ˈlɪrɪks/	(der) Liedtext
	speaker /ˈspiːkə/	(der/die) Sprecher/in
	(to) **address** /əˈdres/	ansprechen, adressieren
	character /ˈkærəktə/	(das) Wesen, (der) Charakter
	NYC (= New York City) /ˌen waɪ ˈsiː, ˌnjuː jɔːk ˈsɪti/	*die Stadt New York*
	(to) **come to mind** *(irr)* /ˌkʌm tə ˈmaɪnd/	einfallen, in den Sinn kommen
	the Battery /ðə ˈbætri/	*Park in New York*
	Middle-Eastern /ˌmɪdl_ˈiːstən/	(der) Mensch aus dem Nahen Osten; Nahost-, nahöstlich
	Latin /ˌlætɪn_əˈmerɪkən/	(der/die) Lateinamerikaner/in; lateinamerikanisch
	Black /blæk/	*politische Selbstbezeichnung Schwarzer Menschen in den USA*

Das Erdgeschoss ist in den USA „first floor", in Großbritannien „ground floor". Der erste Stock heißt in den USA „second floor", in Großbritannien „first floor".

„them" wird benutzt, wenn man vermeiden möchte, **„him"** oder **„her"** zu sagen. Man kann **„they"** sagen, wenn man vermeiden möchte, **„he"** oder **„she"** zu sagen.

downtown *(AE)* = city (centre) *(BE)*
store *(AE)* = shop *(BE)*

The **speaker addresses** the people who are listening to him.

White /waɪt/	(der/die) Weiße/r	
(to) make happen *(irr)* /ˌmeɪk ˈhæpən/	möglich machen	
water tower /ˈwɔːtə ˌtaʊə/	(der) Wasserturm	
prizefighter /ˈpraɪzˌfaɪtə/	(der/die) Preisboxer/in	
Wall Street /ˈwɔːl striːt/	*Straße in New York, auf der sich viele Banken und die weltgrößte Wertpapierbörse befinden*	
trader /ˈtreɪdə/	(der/die) Händler/in	The British English word for **"subway"** is "underground".
subway *(AE)* /ˈsʌbˌweɪ/	(die) U-Bahn	
car *(AE)* /kaː/	(der) Waggon, (der) Wagen	
unified /ˈjuːnɪfaɪd/	vereint	
whoever /huːˈevə/	wer auch immer	
(to) do well *(irr)* /ˌduː ˈwel/	erfolgreich sein	
hell /hel/	(die) Hölle	
(to) give thanks *(irr)* /ˌgɪv ˈθæŋks/	Dank sagen	to **give thanks** = to thank
(to) pass /paːs/	*hier:* durchgehen	
drove /drəʊv/	(die) Herde	
love letter /ˈlʌv ˌletə/	(der) Liebesbrief	
(to) bring together *(irr)* /ˌbrɪŋ təˈgeðə/	zusammenbringen	
lifelong /ˈlaɪfˌlɒŋ/	lebenslang	
(to) dedicate /ˈdedɪkeɪt/	widmen	
(to) blend /blend/	vermischen	'cause (= because) /kɔːz, bɪˈkɒz/ weil, da
(to) mend /mend/	reparieren, in Ordnung bringen	ain't (= am/are/is not) *(informal)* /eɪnt/
9/11 /ˌnaɪn ˌɪˈlevn/	*Terrorangriffe am 11. September 2001*	nicht sein
gritty /ˈgrɪti/	grob; mutig, tapfer	
peoples *(pl)* /ˈpiːplz/	(die) Völker	
wherever /werˈevə/	wo(her) auch immer	
landmark /ˈlænˌmaːk/	(das) Wahrzeichen	
(to) **vary** /ˈveəri/	variieren, verschieden sein	to **vary** = to be different
in advance /ˌɪn ədˈvaːns/	im Voraus	
admission /ədˈmɪʃn/	(der) Eintritt, (der) Eintrittspreis	
above /əˈbʌv/	darüber	
under /ˈʌndə/	darunter	**under** ≠ **above**
within /wɪðˈɪn/	innerhalb, innen	
including /ɪnˈkluːdɪŋ/	einschließlich	
electronic /ˌelekˈtrɒnɪk/	elektronisch	Your name, a photograph of yourself and your place of birth are on your **ID card**.
the media /ðə ˈmiːdiə/	(die) Medien	
ID (= ID card) /ˌaɪˈdiː, ˌaɪˈdiː kaːd/	(der) Ausweis	
due to /ˈdjuː tʊ/	wegen	
special offer /ˌspeʃl̩ ˈɒfə/	(das) Sonderangebot	
(to) take a tour *(irr)* /ˌteɪk ə ˈtʊə/	eine Tour machen	
tour guide /ˈtʊə gaɪd/	(der/die) Reiseführer/in	
senior /ˈsiːniə/	(der) ältere Mensch; ältere(r, s)	
aged *(after noun)* /eɪdʒd/	im Alter von	

p. 26, 8

	architecture /ˈɑːkɪˌtektʃə/	(die) Architektur
	sculpture /ˈskʌlptʃə/	(die) Bildhauerei
	photography /fəˈtɒɡrəfi/	(die) Fotografie
	print /prɪnt/	(der) Druck
	full-time /ˌfʊl ˈtaɪm/	Vollzeit-
	renovation /ˌrenəˈveɪʃn/	(die) Renovierung, (die) Sanierung
	monument /ˈmɒnjʊmənt/	(das) Denkmal
p. 27, 9	Grand Central Station /ˌɡrænd ˌsentrəl ˈsteɪʃn/	*Bahnhof in Manhattan*
p. 27, 10	**essential** /ɪˈsenʃl/	unbedingt erforderlich, unverzichtbar
	(to) **represent** /ˌreprɪˈzent/	präsentieren, vertreten
	nationality /ˌnæʃəˈnæləti/	(die) Nationalität
	heritage /ˈherɪtɪdʒ/	(das) Erbe
	(to) honor *(AE)* = honour *(BE)* /ˈɒnə/	ehren
	legacy /ˈleɡəsi/	(das) Vermächtnis, (das) Erbe
	host /həʊst/	*hier:* (der/die) Podcast-Host
	walking tour /ˈwɔːkɪŋ tʊə/	(die) Wanderung
	Mexican /ˈmeksɪkən/	(der/die) Mexikaner/in; mexikanisch
	amusement park /əˈmjuːzmənt pɑːk/	(der) Freizeitpark
p. 27, 11	acrostic /əˈkrɒstɪk/	(das) Akrostichon, (der) Leistenvers
	nickname /ˈnɪkˌneɪm/	(der) Spitzname, (der) Kosename
p. 28, 12	**passive** /ˈpæsɪv/	(das) Passiv
p. 28, 13	**curious** /ˈkjʊəriəs/	neugierig
	(to) **complete** /kəmˈpliːt/	fertigstellen
p. 28, 14	center *(AE)* /ˈsentə/	(das) Zentrum
	favorite *(AE)* /ˈfeɪvrət/	Liebling; Lieblings-
p. 29, 15	**travel guide** /ˈtrævl ɡaɪd/	(der) Reiseführer *(Buch)*

He is creating a **monument**.

When something is **essential**, it is extremely important and necessary.

There is an **amusement park** on Brighton Pier.

travel guide

Unit 2 | Part A Welcome to high school!

p. 33	after-school /ˌɑːftə ˈskuːl/	Nachmittags-
p. 34, 2	**exchange** /ɪksˈtʃeɪndʒ/	(der) Austausch; Austausch-
	(to) **welcome** /ˈwelkəm/	willkommen heißen
	host *(before nouns)* /həʊst/	Gast-
	reader /ˈriːdə/	(der/die) Leser/in
	Congratulations! /kənˌɡrætʃʊˈleɪʃnz/	Glückwunsch!, Gratuliere!
	once /wʌns/	sobald; wenn; als
	football *(AE)* /ˈfʊtˌbɔːl/	American Football
	support /səˈpɔːt/	(die) Unterstützung, (die) Hilfe
	championship /ˈtʃæmpiənʃɪp/	(die) Meisterschaft
	fall *(AE)* /fɔːl/	(der) Herbst
	yearbook /ˈjɪəˌbʊk/	(das) Jahrbuch
	program *(AE)* /ˈprəʊɡræm/	(das) Programm
	vacation *(AE)* /vəˈkeɪʃn/	(die) Ferien, (der) Urlaub

traveled *(AE)* = travelled *(BE)*

had travelled war(en) gereist
had read hatte(n) gelesen
had finished hatte(n) beendet
had graduated hatte(n) die Abschlussprüfung bestanden

program *(AE)* = programme *(BE)*

	grade *(AE)* /greɪd/	(die) Klasse
	in total /ˌɪn ˈtəʊtl/	insgesamt
	read /riːd/	(die) Lektüre
	homecoming *(no pl, AE)* /ˈhoʊm‚kʌmɪŋ/	(das) Ehemaligentreffen
	(to) graduate *(AE)* /ˈɡrædʒueɪt/	die (Highschool-)Abschlussprüfung bestehen
	(to) crown /kraʊn/	krönen
	marching band /ˈmɑːtʃɪŋ bænd/	(die) Marschkapelle
	(to) come second *(irr)* /ˌkʌm ˈsekənd/	Zweite/r werden
	(to) be in full swing *(irr)* /ˌbi_ɪn ˌfʊl ˈswɪŋ/	in vollem Gang sein
p. 35, 2	**after** /ˈɑːftə/	nachdem
	record /ˈrekɔːd/	(der) Rekord
	energy /ˈenədʒi/	(die) Energie, (die) Kraft
	(to) **raise** /reɪz/	beschaffen, sammeln
	college /ˈkɒlɪdʒ/	(das) College *(Bildungseinrichtung, die zu einem eher praxisorientierten Bachelor-Abschluss hinführt)*
	success /sək'ses/	(der) Erfolg
	suit /suːt/	(der) Anzug
	formal /ˈfɔːml/	formell; offiziell
	(to) **continue** /kən'tɪnjuː/	andauern, weitergehen
	freshman *(pl freshmen) (AE)* /ˈfreʃmən, ˈfreʃmən/	*(der/die)* Schüler/in einer Highschool im ersten Jahr
	demonstration /ˌdemən'streɪʃn/	(die) Vorführung, (die) Demonstration
	tournament /ˈtʊənəmənt/	(das) Turnier
	(to) practice *(AE)* /ˈpræktɪs/	üben, trainieren; praktizieren
	cheer basics *(pl)* /ˈtʃɪə ˌbeɪsɪks/	*Grundkenntnisse beim Cheerleading*
	(to) cheer for /ˈtʃɪə fə/	anfeuern
	athlete /ˈæθliːt/	(der/die) Athlet/in
	single /ˈsɪŋɡl/	*hier:* (der) Einzelwettwerb
	final /ˈfaɪnl/	(das) Endspiel, (das) Finale
	fundraising /ˈfʌndreɪzɪŋ/	(das) Spendensammeln
	fundraiser /ˈfʌnd‚reɪzə/	(der/die) Spendensammler/in
	graduate /ˈɡrædʒuət/	(der/die) Absolvent/in
	prom *(AE)* /prɒm/	*(der) Ball am Ende des Jahres in einer amerikanischen Highschool*
	graduation /ˌɡrædʒu'eɪʃn/	(der) Schulabschluss
	prom king *(AE)* /ˈprɒm kɪŋ/	(der) Ballkönig
	prom queen *(AE)* /ˈprɒm kwiːn/	(die) Ballkönigin
p. 36, 3	(to) **underline** /ˌʌndə'laɪn/	unterstreichen
p. 36, 4	(to) **lie down** *(irr)* /ˌlaɪ ˈdaʊn/	sich hinlegen
	(to) **fall asleep** *(irr)* /ˌfɔːl_ə'sliːp/	einschlafen
	(to) **dream** *(irr)* /driːm/	träumen
p. 37, 5	(to) **call** /kɔːl/	nennen
	difference /ˈdɪfrəns/	(der) Unterschied

had practised
hatte(n) geübt/trainiert
had trained
hatte(n) trainiert
had ended
hatte(n) geendet

The man is wearing a **suit**.

to practice *(AE)* =
to practise *(BE)*
Im britischen Englisch ist „practice" mit „c" das Hauptwort: die Übung, das Training.

athlete = sportsperson

She **has fallen asleep** in the park.

	pie /paɪ/	(die) Pastete, (der) Kuchen
	dress code /ˈdres kəʊd/	(die) Bekleidungsvorschriften
	French fries *(AE, pl)* /ˌfrentʃ ˈfraɪz/	(die) Pommes frites
p. 38, 6	**cereal** /ˈsɪəriəl/	(die) Frühstücksflocken
	bus stop /ˈbʌs‿stɒp/	(die) Bushaltestelle
	hardly /ˈhɑːdli/	kaum
	over here /ˌəʊvə ˈhɪə/	hier (drüben)
	locker /ˈlɒkə/	(das) Schließfach, (der) Spind
	republic /rɪˈpʌblɪk/	(die) Republik
	liberty /ˈlɪbəti/	(die) Freiheit
	justice /ˈdʒʌstɪs/	(die) Gerechtigkeit
	(to) **stare at** /ˈsteər‿æt/	anstarren
	(to) **feel uncomfortable** *(irr)* /ˌfiːl‿ʌnˈkʌmftəbl/	sich unwohl fühlen
	(to) blog /blɒg/	bloggen
	the ones /ðə ˈwʌnz/	diejenigen; diese
	schoolchild *(pl* schoolchildren) /ˈskuːl,tʃaɪld, ˈskuːl,tʃɪldrən/	(das) Schulkind
	registrar's office /ˌredʒɪstrɑːz‿ˈɒfɪs/	(das) Sekretariat
	registrar /ˌredʒɪˈstrɑː/	(der/die) Sekretär/in
	schedule *(AE)* /ˈske,dʒul, ˈʃedjuːl/	(der) Stundenplan
	homeroom /ˈhəʊmruːm/	(der) Klassenraum, (die) Klassenlehrkraftstunde
	attendance /əˈtendəns/	(die) Anwesenheit
	(to) give out *(irr)* /ˌgɪv‿ˈaʊt/	bekannt geben, verteilen
	first thing *(informal)* /ˌfɜːst ˈθɪŋ/	als Erstes
	the Pledge of Allegiance /ˌpledʒ‿əv‿əˈliːdʒns/	*(der) Treueschwur*
	(to) pledge /pledʒ/	versprechen, schwören
	allegiance /əˈliːdʒns/	(die) Loyalität, (die) Ergebenheit
	God /gɒd/	(der) Gott
	indivisible /ˌɪndɪˈvɪzəbl/	unteilbar
p. 39, 6	**apart from** /əˈpɑːt frəm/	abgesehen von
	elective /ɪˈlektɪv/	(das) Wahlpflichtfach
	(to) **carry** /ˈkæri/	tragen
	math *(AE, informal)* /mæθ/	Mathe *(Schulfach)*
	period *(AE)* /ˈpɪəriəd/	(die) Stunde
	gym *(AE)* /dʒɪm/	(der) Sportunterricht
	robotics /rəʊˈbɒtɪks/	(die) Robotertechnik
	study period /ˈstʌdi ˌpɪəriəd/	(die) Lernstunde, (die) Übungsstunde
	study hall /ˈstʌdi hɔːl/	(der) Lernraum, (der) Übungsraum
	lab /læb/	(das) Labor
	hallway /ˈhɔːl,weɪ/	(der) Korridor, (der) Flur
	organic /ɔːˈgænɪk/	aus biologischem Anbau, Bio-

The people are waiting at the **bus stop**.

They **are staring at** each other through the glass.

to **feel umcomfortable** = to not feel good in a situation

The British English word for **"schedule"** is "timetable".

An **elective** is a subject you can choose to do at school but don't have to do.

freshman *(AE)* /ˈfreʃmən/ *(der/die) Schüler/in einer Highschool im ersten Jahr*
sophomore *(AE)* /ˈsɒfə,mɔː/ *(der/die) Schüler/in einer Highschool im zweiten Jahr*
junior *(AE)* /ˈdʒuːniə/ *(der/die) Schüler/in einer Highschool im vorletzten Jahr*
senior *(AE)* /ˈsiːniə/ *(der/die) Schüler/in einer Highschool im letzten Jahr*

	locally /ˈləʊkli/	am Ort, vor Ort
p. 40, 7	**credit** /ˈkredɪt/	(der) Schein, (der) Leistungsnachweis
	robot /ˈrəʊbɒt/	(der) Roboter
	(to) **program** /ˈprəʊgræm/	programmieren
	piece of paper /ˌpiːs_əv ˈpeɪpə/	(das) Blatt Papier
	business /ˈbɪznəs/	(das) Geschäft, (der) Handel
	literature /ˈlɪtrətʃə/	(die) Literatur
	(to) **videochat** /ˈvɪdiəʊtʃæt/	einen Videochat machen
	(to) **be behind** *(irr, informal)* /ˌbiː bɪˈhaɪnd/	hinterher sein, zurückliegen
	optional /ˈɒpʃnəl/	optional, fakultativ
	business law /ˈbɪznəs lɔː/	(das) Wirtschaftsrecht
	auto body repair /ˌɔːtəʊ ˌbɒdi rɪˈpeə/	(die) Karosseriereparatur
	law /lɔː/	(die) Rechtswissenschaft
	a different one /ə ˈdɪfrənt wʌn/	ein anderer/eine andere/ein anderes
	guidance counsellor /ˈgaɪdns ˌkaʊnslə/	(der/die) Beratungslehrer/in
	plumbing /ˈplʌmɪŋ/	(das) Klempnern
	women's studies /ˈwɪmɪnz ˌstʌdiz/	*(das) Schulfach, das die Rolle der Frau in Geschichte, Gesellschaft und Literatur untersucht*
p. 41, 8	**finance** /ˈfaɪnæns/	(die) Finanzwirtschaft, (das) Geldwesen
	(to) **manage** /ˈmænɪdʒ/	verwalten, organisieren
	finances *(pl)* /ˈfaɪnænsɪz/	(die) Finanzen
	product /ˈprɒdʌkt/	(das) Produkt
	movie *(AE)* /ˈmuːvi/	(der) Film
	(to) **get to know** *(irr)* /ˌget tə_ˈnəʊ/	kennenlernen
	skill /skɪl/	(die) Fertigkeit, (die) Kompetenz
	preparation /ˌprepəˈreɪʃn/	(die) Vorbereitung; (die) Zubereitung
	(to) **market** /ˈmɑːkɪt/	vermarkten
	maintenance /ˈmeɪntənəns/	(die) Pflege, (die) Wartung
	repair /rɪˈpeə/	(die) Reparatur
	household /ˈhaʊsˌhəʊld/	(der) Haushalt
	culinary art /ˌkʌlɪnriˈɑːt/	(die) Kochkunst
	woodworking /ˈwʊdˌwɜːkɪŋ/	(das) Tischlern
	processing /ˈprəʊsesɪŋ/	(das) Bearbeiten
	safety precaution /ˈseɪfti prɪˌkɔːʃn/	(die) Sicherheitsvorkehrung
p. 41, 10	commercial /kəˈmɜːʃl/	(der) Werbespot
p. 42, 11	**whether** /ˈweðə/	ob
p. 42, 12	**device** /dɪˈvaɪs/	(das) Gerät, (der) Apparat
	household machine /ˈhaʊsˌhəʊld məˌʃiːn/	(das) Haushaltsgerät
	(to) **last** /lɑːst/	halten
p. 42, 13	(to) **cover** /ˈkʌvə/	abdecken, sich befassen mit
p. 43, 14	**matching** /ˈmætʃɪŋ/	passend
	headline /ˈhedˌlaɪn/	(die) Überschrift, (die) Schlagzeile

robot

Literature is books or poems that people see as art.

I'm fine. Es geht mir gut.
I'm doing OK. *(informal)*
Es läuft ganz gut.

A **product** is something that is made so that you can sell it.

to **get to know** = to meet

He has invented an interesting **device**.

A **headline** is the title of a newspaper story.

welding /ˈweldɪŋ/	(das) Schweißen	
light technology /ˈlaɪt_tek,nɒlədʒi/	(die) Lichttechnik	
sound technology /ˈsaʊnd_tek,nɒlədʒi/	(die) Tontechnik	
gallery walk /ˈgæləri wɔːk/	*(die) Gruppendiskussion in Stationsarbeit*	

Unit 2 | Part B After-school activities

p. 44, 2	**brain** /breɪn/	(das) Gehirn	
	(to) **succeed** /səkˈsiːd/	erfolgreich sein	
	debate /dɪˈbeɪt/	(die) Debatte, (die) Diskussion	A **debate** is a special kind of discussion.
	future /ˈfjuːtʃə/	zukünftig	
	career /kəˈrɪə/	(die) Karriere, (die) Laufbahn	
	mathletics club *(informal)* /mæθˈletɪks klʌb/	(die) Mathe-AG	
	(to) stretch /stretʃ/	dehnen, spannen	He **is stretching** his back.
	mathematics /,mæθəˈmætɪks/	(die) Mathematik	
	pitcher /ˈpɪtʃə/	(der/die) Werfer/in	
	catcher /ˈkætʃə/	(der/die) Fänger/in	
	glee club /ˈgliː klʌb/	(die) Gesangs-AG	
	singing /ˈsɪŋɪŋ/	(das) Singen, (der) Gesang	
	congress /ˈkɒŋgres/	(der) Kongress	
	role-playing /ˈrəʊl ,pleɪɪŋ/	(das) Rollenspiel	
	(to) debate /dɪˈbeɪt/	diskutieren, debattieren	
	(to) improvise /ˈɪmprəvaɪz/	improvisieren	
	auditorium *(AE)* /,ɔːdɪˈtɔːriəm/	(der) Vortragssaal, (die) Festhalle	
	debating society /dɪˈbeɪtɪŋ sə,saɪəti/	(die) Debattiergesellschaft	The boy has **fewer** apples than the girl.
p. 45, 2	**fewer** /ˈfjuːə/	weniger *(bei zählbaren Nomen)*	
	(to) be up to something *(irr)* /,bi_,ʌp tə ˈsʌmθɪŋ/	etwas vorhaben	
	lunchtime /ˈlʌntʃtaɪm/	(die) Mittagszeit, (die) Mittagspause	
	elementary school *(AE)* /elɪˈmentri skuːl/	(die) Grundschule	
	primary school /ˈpraɪməri skuːl/	(die) Grundschule	In the United States, children start school at an **elementary school** when they are about 6 years old until they are about 12 years old. In Great Britain, a **primary school** is for children between about 4 or 5 and 11 years.
	(to) drop out /,drɒp_ˈaʊt/	abbrechen	
	chemistry /ˈkemɪstri/	(die) Chemie	
	business /ˈbɪznəs/	(der) Handel, (das) Geschäft	
p. 46, 4	**type** /taɪp/	(der) Typ	
	conditional (clause) /kənˈdɪʃnəl klɔːz/	(das) Konditional, (der) Konditionalsatz	
p. 47, 6	tailgate party *(AE)* /ˈteɪlgeɪt ,pɑːti/	*(das) Picknick von der Ladefläche oder aus dem Kofferraum eines Autos während einer Sportveranstaltung oder eines Konzerts*	
	parking lot *(AE)* /ˈpɑːkɪŋ lɒt/	(der) Parkplatz	
	chilli *(pl chillies)* /ˈtʃɪli, ˈtʃɪliz/	(der) Chili, (die) Peperoni	
	baked potatoes *(pl)* /,beɪkt pəˈteɪtəʊz/	(die) Ofenkartoffeln	A **car park** is an area where people can leave their cars.
p. 48, 7	**car park** /ˈkɑː pɑːk/	(der) Parkplatz	

(to) **take out** *(irr)* /ˌteɪk_ˈaʊt/	herausnehmen		
(to) **unpack** /ʌnˈpæk/	auspacken	to **unpack** ≠ to pack	
(to) **smell** *(irr)* /smel/	riechen		
seat /siːt/	(der) Sitz		
professional /prəˈfeʃnəl/	professionell, beruflich		
not at all /ˌnɒt_ət_ˈɔːl/	überhaupt nicht		
anyway /ˈeniweɪ/	sowieso		
(to) **seem** /siːm/	scheinen		
(to) **enjoy oneself** /ɪnˈdʒɔɪ wʌnˌself/	sich amüsieren	When something is **incredible**, you can hardly believe it.	
incredible /ɪnˈkredəbl/	unglaublich		
spirit /ˈspɪrɪt/	(der) Geist, (die) Stimmung		
pattern /ˈpætən/	(das) Muster		
complicated /ˈkɒmplɪˌkeɪtɪd/	kompliziert	**complicated** = not easy	
both ... and ... /ˈbəʊθ ænd/	sowohl ... als auch ...		
(to) hashtag /ˈhæʃˌtæg/	mit einem Hashtag versehen		
opening act /ˈəʊpənɪŋ ˌækt/	(die) Eröffnungsfeier		
tailgate *(AE)* /ˈteɪlgeɪt/	(die) Heckklappe, *hier:* (der) Kofferraum		
car boot /ˈkɑː ˌbuːt/	(der) Kofferraum		
trunk *(AE)* /trʌŋk/	(der) Kofferraum		
confusing /kənˈfjuːzɪŋ/	verwirrend		
chips *(pl, AE)* /tʃɪps/	(die) Chips		
crisps *(pl)* /krɪsps/	(die) Chips	They love to **barbecue** at the weekends.	
(to) barbecue /ˈbɑːbɪˌkjuː/	grillen		
playing field /ˈpleɪɪŋ ˌfiːld/	(der) Sportplatz		
half-time /ˌhɑːf ˈtaɪm/	(die) Halbzeit		
jump /dʒʌmp/	(der) Sprung		
flip /flɪp/	(der) Salto		
(to) do one's best *(irr)* /ˌduː wʌnz ˈbest/	sein Bestes geben	They are having fun at **carnival**.	
carnival /ˈkɑːnɪvl/	(das) Volksfest, (der) Karneval		
chant /tʃɑːnt/	(der) Sprechgesang		
clap /klæp/	(das) Klatschen		
(to) go crazy *(irr)* /ˌgəʊ ˈkreɪzi/	verrückt werden; *hier:* ausrasten	When you take part in a competition and you want to win, your **aim** is to win.	
Opening Day /ˈəʊpənɪŋ deɪ/	(der) Eröffnungstag		
aim /eɪm/	(das) Ziel		
up (to) /ˈʌp tuː/	bis (zu)		
full-contact sport /ˌfʊl ˈkɒntækt spɔːt/	*(die) Vollkontakt-Sportart*		
kind /kaɪnd/	freundlich	A **kind** person is friendly.	
jam /dʒæm/	(die) Marmelade		
aside from *(AE)* /əˈsaɪd frəm/	abgesehen von	**myself** (ich) selbst **yourself** (du) selbst	
yourselves /jɔːˈselvz/	euch; selbst	**himself** (er) selbst; sich **herself** (sie) selbst; sich	
reflexive pronoun /rɪˌfleksɪv ˈprəʊnaʊn/	(das) Reflexivpronomen	**ourselves** (wir) selbst	
pronoun /ˈprəʊnaʊn/	(das) Pronomen, (das) Fürwort	**yourselves** (ihr) selbst	
(to) thank /θæŋk/	danken, sich bedanken	**themselves** (sie) selbst	

p. 49, 7

Land und Leute 4
p. 50, 8

p. 51, 11

p. 52, 12

p. 52, 13

Unit 3 | Part A Relationships

p. 57	**relationship** /rɪˈleɪʃn̩ʃɪp/	(die) Beziehung
p. 58, 2	**depressed** /dɪˈprest/	deprimiert
	glad /glæd/	glücklich, froh
	unhappy /ʌnˈhæpi/	unglücklich
p. 58, 3	BFF (= best friend forever) *(informal)* /ˌbiːˌefˈef, ˌbest ˌfrend fərˈevə/	(der/die) allerbeste Freund/in
	that way /ˈðæt weɪ/	so, auf diese Weise
	(to) stand somebody *(irr)* /ˈstænd ˌsʌmbədi/	jemanden leiden können
p. 59, 3	**though** *(nachgestellt)* /ðəʊ/	jedoch
	close /kləʊs/	nah(e); eng
	point of view /ˌpɔɪnt̬ əvˈvjuː/	(die) Ansicht, (die) Perspektive
	(to) be into *(informal, irr)* /ˌbiˈɪntrəstɪd ɪn/	interessiert sein an
	(to) hang out *(informal, irr)* /ˌhæŋˈaʊt/	rumhängen, Zeit mit jemandem verbringen
	lately /ˈleɪtli/	in letzter Zeit, kürzlich
p. 60, 4	**report (to)** /rɪˈpɔːt/	berichten, wiedergeben
p. 61, 6	weakness /ˈwiːknəs/	(die) Schwäche
p. 61, 7	(to) **rely on** /rɪˈlaɪ ɒn/	sich verlassen auf
	comment /ˈkɒment/	(der) Kommentar, (die) Bemerkung
	(to) **sum up** /ˌsʌmˈʌp/	zusammenfassen
	(to) make *(irr)* /meɪk/	*hier:* ausmachen
	loyal /ˈlɔɪəl/	treu, loyal
p. 62, 8	**research** /rɪˈsɜːtʃ/	(die) Forschung
	out of /ˈaʊt̬ əv/	von
	rare /reə/	selten
	(to) **act** /ækt/	sich verhalten
	mean /miːn/	gemein; bösartig
	(to) **ignore** /ɪgˈnɔː/	ignorieren
	hurt /hɜːt/	verletzt, gekränkt
	however /haʊˈevə/	aber, wie auch immer
	(to) **remember** /rɪˈmembə/	bedenken, denken an
	common /ˈkɒmən/	üblich, weit verbreitet
	(to) **make sense** *(irr)* /ˌmeɪk ˈsens/	sinnvoll sein
	(to) **remind somebody** /rɪˈmaɪnd ˌsʌmbədi/	jemanden erinnern
	(to) **forgive** *(irr)* /fəˈgɪv/	vergeben, verzeihen
	(to) **be sorry** *(irr)* /ˌbiː ˈsɒri/	bedauern; sich entschuldigen
	apart /əˈpɑːt/	getrennt
	responsible /rɪˈspɒnsəbl/	verantwortungsbewusst, verantwortlich
	behavior *(AE)* = **behaviour** *(BE)* /bɪˈheɪvjə/	(das) Benehmen, (das) Verhalten

„(to) stand somebody" wird meistens negativ verwendet: I can't **stand** my new neighbours! I just don't like them!

When a person **reports** something, they give information about what they have seen or heard.

glad = happy

unhappy ≠ happy

They are doing **research**.

rare = not often

A **common** problem is a problem many people have.

to **be sorry** = to apologize

	(to) send in *(irr)* /ˌsendˈɪn/	einsenden	to **send in** ≠ to get
	psychologist /saɪˈkɒlədʒɪst/	(der/die) Psychologe/Psychologin	
	swim practice /ˈswɪm ˌpræktɪs/	(das) Schwimmtraining	
	for a long time /fərˌə ˈlɒŋ taɪm/	lange	
	(to) pick up (on) /ˌpɪkˈʌp/	anknüpfen an	
p. 63, 8	(to) **behave** /bɪˈheɪv/	sich verhalten, sich benehmen	They don't **agree with** each
	(to) **agree with** /əˈgriː wɪð/	einer Meinung sein mit, übereinstimmen mit	other so they are having a fight.
p. 64, 9	**stranger** /ˈstreɪndʒə/	(der/die) Fremde	
	painfully /ˈpeɪnfli/	schmerzlich	
p. 64, 11	(to) **dislike** /dɪsˈlaɪk/	nicht mögen	
	saying /ˈseɪɪŋ/	(das) Sprichwort	
p. 65, 12	**empty** /ˈempti/	leer	The cinema is nearly **empty**.
	(to) **keep from doing something** *(irr)* /ˌkiːp frəm ˈduːɪŋ ˌsʌmθɪŋ/	etwas unterlassen, sich etwas verkneifen	
	umbrella /ʌmˈbrelə/	(der) Regenschirm	
	hat /hæt/	(der) Hut	
	(to) **look away** /ˌlɒkˌəˈweɪ/	wegsehen	
	shape /ʃeɪp/	(die) Form, (die) Gestalt	
	fat /fæt/	dick	
	(to) **fall in love** *(irr)* /ˌfɔːlˌɪn ˈlʌv/	sich verlieben	
	(to) **lie** *(irr)* /laɪ/	liegen	
	sky /skaɪ/	(der) Himmel	
	cloud /klaʊd/	(die) Wolke	People who **argue** speak
	(to) **argue** /ˈɑːgju/	sich streiten	to each other in an angry way.
	smile /smaɪl/	(das) Lächeln	
	on /ɒn/	*hier:* über	
	discomfort /dɪsˈkʌmfət/	(das) Unbehagen	
	(to) tell *(irr)* /tel/	*hier:* bemerken	
	wallpaper /ˈwɔːlpeɪpə/	(die) Tapete	
	crack /kræk/	(der) Riss	
	ceiling /ˈsiːlɪŋ/	(die) Zimmerdecke	
	iced tea /ˌaɪstˈtiː/	(der) Eistee	
	light bulb /ˈlaɪt bʌlb/	(die) Glühbirne	
	standing lamp /ˈstændɪŋ læmp/	(die) Stehlampe	
	fan /fæn/	(der) Ventilator	
	whale /weɪl/	(der) Wal	
	elephant /ˈelɪfənt/	(der) Elefant	
	trunk /trʌŋk/	(der) Rüssel	The **trunk** is the long nose of an **elephant**.
	(to) lower /ˈləʊə/	senken	
	plaster /ˈplɑːstə/	(der) Verputz	When you **fall in love**,
p. 66, 13	**tense** /tens/	(die) Zeitform	you can **ask** the
	(to) **ask on a date** /ˌɑːsk ɒnˌə ˈdeɪt/	um eine Verabredung bitten	person **on a date**.
	romantic /rəʊˈmæntɪk/	romantisch	

	comedy /ˈkɒmədi/	(die) Komödie
p. 66, 14	**particular** /pəˈtɪkjʊlə/	bestimmt; besondere(r, s)
	(to) be connected (to) *(irr)* /ˌbi: kəˈnektɪd_tə/	verbunden sein (mit), in Verbindung stehen (mit)
	unknown /ʌnˈnəʊn/	unbekannt
p. 67, 15	(to) read out *(irr)* /ˌri:d_ˈaʊt/	(laut) vorlesen

unknown ≠ known

Unit 3 | Part B Digital communication

p. 68, 1	**channel** /ˈtʃænl/	(der) Kanal
	voice message /ˈvɔɪs ˌmesɪdʒ/	(die) Sprachnachricht
p. 68, 2	**virtual** /ˈvɜ:tʃʊəl/	virtuell
	connection /kəˈnekʃn/	(die) Verbindung
	further /ˈfɜ:ðə/	weiter
	little /ˈlɪtl/	wenig
	compared to /kəmˈpeəd_tʊ/	im Vergleich zu
	since /sɪns/	da, weil
	right away /ˌraɪt_əˈweɪ/	sofort, gleich
	(to) access /ˈækses/	zugreifen auf
	study /ˈstʌdi/	(die) Studie
	majority /məˈdʒɒrəti/	(die) Mehrheit
	average /ˈævərɪdʒ/	durchschnittlich
	in fact /ɪnˈfækt/	tatsächlich, in Wirklichkeit
	(to) respond to /rɪˈspɒnd_tə/	antworten auf, reagieren auf
	(to) receive /rɪˈsi:v/	erhalten; empfangen
	(to) message /ˈmesɪdʒ/	eine Nachricht schicken
	addict /ˈædɪkt/	(der/die) Abhängige
	pillow /ˈpɪləʊ/	(das) Kissen
	easily /ˈi:zɪli/	leicht, mühelos
	(to) glue /glu:/	kleben
	cell phone *(AE)* /ˈsel fəʊn/	(das) Handy
	(to) be far from reach *(irr)* /ˌbi: ˌfɑ: frəm ˈri:tʃ/	außer Reichweite sein
p. 69, 2	**(to) bully** /ˈbʊli/	mobben
	nasty /ˈnɑ:sti/	böse, gemein
	threat /θret/	(die) Bedrohung
	rumor *(AE)* = **rumour** *(BE)* /ˈru:mə/	(das) Gerücht
	social media /ˌsəʊʃl ˈmi:diə/	soziale Medien
	major /ˈmeɪdʒə/	bedeutend, wichtig; Haupt-
	proof /pru:f/	(der) Beweis
	(to) ban /bæn/	verbieten; ausschließen
	(to) block /blɒk/	blockieren
	account /əˈkaʊnt/	(das) Benutzerkonto
	age /eɪdʒ/	(das) Zeitalter

The girl has **little** water. She has less water than the boy.

When you **respond to** something, you answer or react to it.

to **message** = to send a message

cell phone *(AE)* = mobile phone *(BE)*

A **threat** is a situation or activity that could result in danger.

major = important

survey /'sɜːveɪ/	(die) Umfrage	
via /'vaɪə/	über	
(to) **admit** /əd'mɪt/	zugeben, eingestehen	
shocked /'ʃɒkt/	schockiert, entsetzt	
(to) harass /'hærəs/	belästigen	
(to) humiliate /hjuː'mɪlieɪt/	erniedrigen	
(to) spread *(irr)* /spred/	verteilen, verbreiten	
apparently /ə'pærəntli/	offensichtlich	
cyberbullying /'saɪbə‚bʊliɪŋ/	(das) Cybermobbing	
bully /'bʊli/	*(die) Person, die mobbt*	
(to) expel /ɪk'spel/	von der Schule verweisen	
constantly /'kɒnstəntli/	ständig, dauernd	**constantly** = all the time
(to) break up *(irr)* /‚breɪk‿'ʌp/	Schluss machen	
face-to-face /‚feɪs tə 'feɪs/	persönlich	"Loudly", "badly" and "quickly" are **adverbs of manner.**
p. 70, 3 · adverb of manner /‚ædvɜːb‿əv 'mænə/	(das) Adverb der Art und Weise	
comparative /kəm'pærətɪv/	(der) Komparativ	
p. 71, 5 · **emotion** /ɪ'məʊʃn/	(das) Gefühl, (die) Emotion	
character /'kærəktə/	(das) Zeichen, (das) Schriftzeichen	
set /set/	(der) Satz, (die) Garnitur	
whereas /weər'æz/	während; wohingegen	
death /deθ/	(der) Tod	
harmful /'hɑːmfl/	schädlich	
limit /'lɪmɪt/	(die) (Höchst)grenze, (das) Limit	
(to) **be aware of** *(irr)* /‚bi‿ə'weər‿əv/	sich bewusst sein	She **is aware of** the fact that everybody is looking at her.
misunderstanding /‚mɪsʌndə'stændɪŋ/	(das) Missverständnis	
universal /‚juːnɪ'vɜːsl/	allgemein, universell	The language that people speak in Japan is called **Japanese.**
Japanese /‚dʒæpə'niːz/	Japaner/in; japanisch	
joy /dʒɔɪ/	(die) Freude	
angel /'eɪndʒl/	(der) Engel	
innocence /'ɪnəsns/	(die) Unschuld	
deed /diːd/	(die) Tat	
insult /'ɪnsʌlt/	(die) Beleidigung	
Brazil /brə'zɪl/	Brasilien	
folded hands /‚fəʊldɪd 'hændz/	betende Hände	
gratitude /'grætɪtjuːd/	(die) Dankbarkeit	
translator /træns'leɪtə/	(der/die) Übersetzer/in	
guarantee /‚gærən'tiː/	(die) Garantie	
p. 72, 6 · (to) **feel comfortable** *(irr)* /‚fiːl 'kʌmftəbl/	sich wohl fühlen	to **feel comfortable** ≠ to feel uncomfortable
advantage /əd'vɑːntɪdʒ/	(der) Vorteil	
interest /'ɪntrəst/	(das) Interesse, (das) Hobby	**interest** = hobby
disadvantage /‚dɪsəd'vɑːntɪdʒ/	(der) Nachteil	**disadvantage** ≠ advantage
benefit /'benɪfɪt/	(der) Vorteil, (der) Nutzen	

	(to) **affect** /əˈfekt/	betreffen, beeinflussen	
	(to) **respond** /rɪˈspɒnd/	antworten; reagieren	
	immediately /ɪˈmiːdiətli/	sofort	**immediately** = right away
	(to) get connected *(irr)* /ˌget kəˈnektɪd/	sich verbinden, in Kontakt treten	
	sociologist /ˌsəʊsiˈɒlədʒɪst/	(der/die) Soziologe/Soziologin	
	loved ones *(pl)* /ˈlʌvd wʌnz/	(der/die) Angehörige, (die) nahestehenden Personen	**loved ones**: family, relatives and close friends
	phone call /ˈfəʊn kɔːl/	(der) Telefonanruf	
	instead of /ɪnˈsted‿əv/	anstatt	
	time-saving /ˈtaɪm seɪvɪŋ/	zeitsparend	
	plenty of /ˈplenti‿əv/	reichlich, genug	
	in person /ˌɪn ˈpɜːsn/	persönlich	
	expectation /ˌekspekˈteɪʃn/	(die) Erwartung	
	boundary /ˈbaʊndri/	(die) Grenze	
	at all times /æt‿ɔːl ˈtaɪmz/	jederzeit, immer	
p. 73, 6	**offensive** /əˈfensɪv/	beleidigend, ausfallend	
	(to) **maintain** /meɪnˈteɪn/	erhalten, pflegen	
	carefully /ˈkeəfli/	gründlich	
	aggressive /əˈgresɪv/	aggressiv, angriffslustig	The girl on the right seems to be quite **aggressive**.
	interaction /ˌɪntərˈækʃn/	(die) Interaktion, (die) Kommunikation	
	carelessly /ˈkeələsli/	unvorsichtig, gedankenlos	
	responsibly /rɪˈspɒnsəbli/	verantwortungsbewusst	
	capital letter /ˌkæpɪtl ˈletə/	(der) Großbuchstabe	
	exclamation point *(AE)* /ˌekskləˈmeɪʃn pɔɪnt/	(das) Ausrufezeichen	
	question mark /ˈkwestʃn mɑːk/	(das) Fragezeichen	
	(to) harm /hɑːm/	schaden, Schaden zufügen	
p. 74, 8	(to) **protect (from)** /prəˈtekt frəm/	schützen (vor)	
	piece of advice /ˌpiːs‿əv‿ədˈvaɪs/	(der) Rat(schlag)	
p. 75, 10	(to) **swap** /swɒp/	tauschen	The twins can always **swap** places, people never know who is who.
	youth hostel /ˈjuːθ ˌhɒstl/	(die) Jugendherberge	
	sleeping bag /ˈsliːpɪŋ bæg/	(der) Schlafsack	
	choreographer /ˌkɒriˈɒgrəfə/	(der/die) Choreograph/in	
p. 75, 11	(to) translate /trænsˈleɪt/	übersetzen	
p. 76, 12	non-stop /ˌnɒn ˈstɒp/	ununterbrochen	
p. 76, 13	prefix /ˈpriːfɪks/	(die) Vorsilbe, (das) Präfix	"Dis" is the **prefix** of "disagree".
p. 77, 15	respectfully /rɪˈspektfəli/	respektvoll	

Unit 4 | Part A The power of hope

p. 81	(to) **relate to** /rɪˈleɪt‿tʊ/	handeln von; zu tun haben mit	
	hope /həʊp/	(die) Hoffnung	
	power /ˈpaʊə/	(die) Macht, (der) Einfluss	
p. 82, 2	**keyword** /ˈkiːˌwɜːd/	(das) Schlüsselwort, (das) Stichwort	
	director /dəˈrektə/	(der/die) Regisseur/in	Part of a **director**'s job is to tell the actors and actresses what to do in a film.

	dove /dʌv/	(die) Taube
	Navajo /ˈnævəhəʊ/	*(die) Sprache der Navajo*
	(to) motivate /ˈməʊtɪveɪt/	motivieren
	California Institute of the Arts /ˌkælɪˌfɔːniəˌɪnstɪˌtjuːtˌəv ðiˈɑːts/	*private Kunsthochschule in Kalifornien*
	(to) win a scholarship *(irr)* /ˌwɪnˌə ˈskɒləʃɪp/	ein Stipendium bekommen
	(to) afford /əˈfɔːd/	sich leisten
	community college /kəˈmjuːnəti ˌkɒlɪdʒ/	*(das) subventionierte zweijährige College*
p. 83, 2	**grateful** /ˈɡreɪtfl/	dankbar
	(to) **support** /səˈpɔːt/	(unter)stützen
	disability /ˌdɪsəˈbɪləti/	(die) Behinderung, (die) Einschränkung
	climate change /ˈklaɪmət tʃeɪndʒ/	(die) Klimaveränderung, (der) Klimawandel
	(to) **train** /treɪn/	eine Ausbildung machen
	sustainability /səˌsteɪnəˈbɪləti/	(die) Nachhaltigkeit
	impact /ˈɪmpækt/	(die) Auswirkung, (der) Einfluss
	(to) **take time** *(irr)* /ˌteɪk ˈtaɪm/	dauern
	law /lɔː/	(das) Gesetz
	goal /ɡəʊl/	(das) Ziel
	paraclimber /ˈpærəˌklaɪmə/	*(der/die) Kletterer/Kletterin mit Handicap*
	Paralympic /ˌpærəˈlɪmpɪk/	paralympisch
	student council /ˈstjuːdnt ˌkaʊnsl/	(die) Schülervertretung
p. 85, 5	**change** /tʃeɪndʒ/	(die) Veränderung, (der) Wechsel
	imagination /ɪˌmædʒɪˈneɪʃn/	(die) Fantasie, (die) Vorstellungskraft
	(to) **take action** *(irr)* /ˌteɪkˈækʃn/	handeln, Maßnahmen ergreifen
	action /ˈækʃn/	(das) Handeln, (die) Maßnahmen
	crisis *(pl* **crises)** /ˈkraɪsɪs, ˈkraɪsiːz/	(die) Krise
	(to) **make a difference** *(irr)* /ˌmeɪkˌə ˈdɪfrəns/	einen Unterschied machen, verändern
	powerful /ˈpaʊəfl/	mächtig, stark
	(to) **get involved** *(irr)* /ˌɡetˌɪnˈvɒlvd/	sich engagieren
	individual /ˌɪndɪˈvɪdʒuəl/	individuell; einzeln
	ecological footprint /ˌiːkəˌlɒdʒɪkl ˈfʊtprɪnt/	(der) ökologische Fußabdruck
	direct /daɪˈrekt/	direkt
	circle /ˈsɜːkl/	(der) Kreis, (die) Runde
	public transport /ˌpʌblɪk ˈtrænspɔːt/	(das) öffentliche Verkehrsmittel
	stamina /ˈstæmɪnə/	(das) Durchhaltevermögen, (die) Ausdauer
	patience /ˈpeɪʃns/	(die) Geduld
	(to) **take a break** *(irr)* /ˌteɪkˌə ˈbreɪk/	eine Pause machen
	helpless /ˈhelpləs/	hilflos
	anxiety /æŋˈzaɪəti/	(die) Sorge, (die) Angst

When you help someone, the person you help is certainly **grateful**.

It **takes** a long **time** to fly to another continent.

When you make a **change**, you do something different.

to take action = to act

Buses are a type of **public transport**.

to take a break = to relax

livable *(AE)* = liveable *(BE)* /ˈlɪvəbl/	lebenswert	
(to) get going *(irr)* /ˌget ˈgəʊɪŋ/	in Gang bringen	
CO₂ (= carbon dioxide) /ˌsiː ˌəʊ ˈtuː, ˌkɑːbən daɪˈɒksaɪd/	(das) Kohlendioxid	
output /ˈaʊtpʊt/	(der) Ausstoß, (die) Produktion	
systemic /sɪˈstiːmɪk/	systemisch	
as a whole /əz ə ˈhəʊl/	als Ganzes	
petition /pəˈtɪʃn/	(die) Petition, (die) Unterschriftenliste	
short-distance flight /ˈʃɔːtˌdɪstəns ˈflaɪt/	(der) Kurzstreckenflug	

In his dreams he has the **vision** that he can fly.

p. 86, 6

vision /ˈvɪʒn/	(die) Vorstellung, (die) Vision
reality /riˈæləti/	(die) Realität, (die) Wirklichkeit
(to) **cause** /kɔːz/	verursachen
worth /wɜːθ/	wert
damage /ˈdæmɪdʒ/	(der) Schaden
(to) **recycle** /riːˈsaɪkl/	recyceln, wiederaufbereiten
instead of /ɪnˈsted əv/	anstatt
garbage *(AE)* /ˈgɑːbɪdʒ/	(der) Abfall, (der) Müll
pollution /pəˈluːʃn/	(die) Umweltverschmutzung
metal /ˈmetl/	(das) Metall
point /pɔɪnt/	(die) Stelle
organization (= **organisation**) /ˌɔːgənaɪˈzeɪʃn/	(die) Organisation, (die) Vereinigung
spark /spɑːk/	(der) Funke, (der) Auslöser
battery /ˈbætri/	(die) Batterie
potential /pəˈtenʃl/	potenziell, möglich
Californian /ˌkæləˈfɔːniən/	kalifornisch
waste disposal plant /ˌweɪst dɪˈspəʊzl plɑːnt/	(die) Abfallentsorgungsanlage
massive /ˈmæsɪv/	riesig, enorm
harm /hɑːm/	(der) Schaden
chemical /ˈkemɪkl/	(die) Chemikalie
(to) end up /ˌend ˈʌp/	schließlich landen
landfill /ˈlændˌfɪl/	(das) Deponiegelände
recycling plant /riːˈsaɪklɪŋ plɑːnt/	(die) Recyclinganlage
valuable /ˈvæljʊbl/	wertvoll
eventually /ɪˈventʃuəli/	schließlich; irgendwann
non-profit /ˌnɒn ˈprɒfɪt/	nicht gewinnorientiert

Water **pollution** is a threat to the environment.

Früher war die britische Schreibweise von Wörtern mit „-ise", „isation" oder „-iser" eindeutig die mit „s", nur im amerikanischen Englisch wurden alle diese Wörter mit „z" geschrieben. Mittler-weile werden kaum noch Unterschiede gemacht. Viele Briten schreiben „organize, organization, realize, ...". In vielen Wörterbüchern wird sogar die Schreib-weise mit „z" als die häufiger vorkommende gelistet.

p. 87, 6

(to) **run** *(irr)* /rʌn/	durchführen
campaign /kæmˈpeɪn/	(die) Kampagne
importance /ɪmˈpɔːtns/	(die) Bedeutung, (die) Wichtigkeit
(to) **encourage** /ɪnˈkʌrɪdʒ/	ermutigen
starting point /ˈstɑːtɪŋ pɔɪnt/	(der) Ausgangspunkt
awareness /əˈweənəs/	(das) Bewusstsein
used /juːzd/	gebraucht

Her friends **encouraged** her, but she was still afraid.

	estimated /ˈestɪmeɪtəd/	geschätzt
	(to) recruit /rɪˈkruːt/	anwerben
	volunteer /ˌvɒlənˈtɪə/	ehrenamtlich
	changemaker /ˈtʃeɪndʒ ˌmeɪkə/	*jemand, der sich aktiv bemüht, Dinge zu verändern*
	(to) care about /ˈkeər_ə,baʊt/	sich aus etwas etwas machen
	(to) take a step *(irr)* /ˌteɪk_ə ˈstep/	einen Schritt machen
p. 88, 7	**environmentally friendly** /ɪnˌvaɪrənmentli ˈfrendli/	umweltfreundlich
p. 88, 8	charity run /ˈtʃærəti rʌn/	(der) Wohltätigkeitslauf
	(to) sponsor /ˈspɒnsə/	sponsern
p. 89, 9	**speech** /spiːtʃ/	(die) Rede
	citizen /ˈsɪtɪzn/	(der/die) Bürger/in
	value /ˈvælju:/	(der) Wert
	force /fɔːs/	(die) Kraft
	(to) **give up** *(irr)* /ˌgɪv_ˈʌp/	aufgeben
	belief /bɪˈliːf/	(der) Glaube
	excerpt /ˈeksɜːpt/	(der) Auszug, (das) Exzerpt
	folks *(informal)* /fəʊks/	(die) Leute
	(to) start out /ˌstɑːt_ˈaʊt/	anfangen
	anything /ˈeni,θɪŋ/	alles
	informed /ɪnˈfɔːmd/	informiert
	engaged /ɪnˈgeɪdʒd/	beschäftigt; *hier:* engagiert
	(to) stand up for *(irr)* /ˌstænd_ˈʌp fɔː/	sich einsetzen für
	critically /ˈkrɪtɪkli/	kritisch
	(to) encounter /ɪnˈkaʊntə/	treffen, begegnen
	obstacle /ˈɒbstəkl/	(das) Hindernis, (die) Hürde
	(to) struggle /ˈstrʌgl/	sich abmühen, sich quälen
	(to) be willing to *(irr)* /ˌbiː ˈwɪlɪŋ tʊ/	bereit sein
p. 90, 10	(to) **combine** /kəmˈbaɪn/	verbinden
	expression /ɪkˈspreʃn/	(der) Ausdruck
p. 90, 11	(to) wish for /ˈwɪʃ fɔː/	sich wünschen

You do not earn money for a **volunteer** job.

He is giving a **speech**.

Your **belief** is what you believe in.

folks *(informal)* = guys *(informal)*

Ollie **wishes for** a long holiday with lots of spaghetti to eat.

Unit 4 | Part B The world of work

p. 92, 1	**physiotherapist** /ˌfɪziəʊˈθerəpɪst/	(der/die) Physiotherapeut/in
	electrician /ɪˌlekˈtrɪʃn/	(der/die) Elektriker/in
	gardener /ˈgɑːdnə/	(der/die) Gärtner/in
	nursery teacher /ˈnɜːsəri ˌtiːtʃə/	(der/die) Vorschullehrer/in; (der/die) Erzieher/in
	construction worker /kənˈstrʌkʃn ˌwɜːkə/	(der/die) Bauarbeiter/in
	animal keeper /ˈænɪml ˌkiːpə/	(der/die) Tierpfleger/in
p. 92, 2	(to) **do for a living** *(irr)* /ˌduː fər_ə ˈlɪvɪŋ/	seinen Lebensunterhalt verdienen

The **gardener** loves his job.

What does he **do for a living**? He is a teacher.

(to) **carry out** /ˌkæriˈaʊt/	durchführen, betreiben	
ward /wɔːd/	(die) Station	
blood sample /ˈblʌd ˌsɑːmpl/	(die) Blutprobe	
wound dressing /ˈwuːnd ˌdresɪŋ/	(der) Verband	
(to) take somebody's temperature *(irr)* /ˌteɪk ˌsʌmbədiz ˈtemprɪtʃə/	Fieber bei jemandem messen	
(to) interpret /ɪnˈtɜːprɪt/	deuten, interpretieren	
(to) prescribe /prɪˈskraɪb/	verschreiben	
medication /ˌmedɪˈkeɪʃn/	(die) Medikamente *(pl)*	
(to) work shifts /ˌwɜːk ˈʃɪfts/	Schichtdienst machen	Nurses have to **work shifts**.

that's why /ˈðæts ˌwaɪ/	deshalb	
original /əˈrɪdʒnəl/	originell, außergewöhnlich	
recently /ˈriːsntli/	vor Kurzem, neulich	**recently** = not long ago
recycled /riːˈsaɪkld/	wiederverwertet, Recycling-	
sustainable /səˈsteɪnəbl/	nachhaltig	
worker /ˈwɜːkə/	(der/die) Arbeiter/in	
ecological /ˌiːkəˈlɒdʒɪkl/	ökologisch	
(to) **start** /stɑːt/	gründen	
accessory /əkˈsesəri/	(das) Accessoire	
(to) adapt /əˈdæpt/	anpassen, bearbeiten	
(to) cut down *(irr)* /ˌkʌtˈdaʊn/	abholzen, fällen	
tractor /ˈtræktə/	(der) Traktor	**tractor**
(to) drag /dræg/	ziehen, schleifen	
truck *(AE)* /trʌk/	(der) Lastwagen	
(to) operate /ˈɒpəreɪt/	bedienen	
log /lɒg/	(der) Baumstamm	
surf instructor /ˈsɜːf ɪnˌstrʌktə/	(der/die) Surflehrer/in	
technique /tekˈniːk/	(die) Technik	
swimmer /ˈswɪmə/	(der/die) Schwimmer/in	**swimmer**
life-saving skill /ˈlaɪfˌseɪvɪŋ skɪl/	*(die) Kenntnis im Rettungsschwimmen*	
a number of /ə ˈnʌmbər əv/	einige, ein paar	
certification /ˌsɜːtɪfɪˈkeɪʃn/	(die) Qualifizierung; (das) Zertifikat	
planning /ˈplænɪŋ/	(das) Planen	
advertising /ˈædvəˌtaɪzɪŋ/	(die) Werbung	
inspiring /ɪnˈspaɪərɪŋ/	inspirierend, anregend	

working hours *(pl)* /ˈwɜːkɪŋ ˌaʊəz/	(die) Arbeitszeiten	
surf school /ˈsɜːfskuːl/	(die) Surfschule	A **job** can be a task that you have to do or the work for which you are paid.
job /dʒɒb/	(die) Stelle, (der) Job	
each /iːtʃ/	je(weils)	
(to) **summarize** (= summarise) /ˈsʌməraɪz/	zusammenfassen	
employer /ɪmˈplɔɪə/	(der/die) Arbeitgeber/in	
soft skill /ˌsɒft ˈskɪl/	*(die) persönliche, soziale und methodische Kompetenz*	

hard skill /ˌhɑːd ˈskɪl/	*(die) berufstypische Qualifikation*	
knowledge /ˈnɒlɪdʒ/	(die) Kenntnis, (das) Wissen	Learning a **foreign language** is an important **hard skill**.
foreign language /ˌfɒrɪn ˈlæŋɡwɪdʒ/	(die) Fremdsprache	
personality /ˌpɜːsəˈnæləti/	(die) Persönlichkeit	
attitude /ˈætɪˌtjuːd/	(die) Haltung, (die) Einstellung	When you behave badly, you have no **manners**.
manners *(pl)* /ˈmænəz/	(die) Manieren	
politeness /pəˈlaɪtnəs/	(die) Höflichkeit	
reliability /rɪˌlaɪəˈbɪliti/	(die) Zuverlässigkeit	
ability /əˈbɪləti/	(die) Fähigkeit	
(to) **recognize (= recognise)** /ˈrekəɡnaɪz/	erkennen	
likely /ˈlaɪkli/	wahrscheinlich	**likely** = probably
reliable /rɪˈlaɪəbl/	verlässlich, zuverlässig	
(to) **take a course** *(irr)* /ˌteɪk_ə ˈkɔːs/	einen Kurs machen	If you want a job, you have to **apply for** it.
(to) **apply for** /əˈplaɪ fɔː/	sich bewerben um	
bicycle /ˈbaɪsɪkl/	(das) Fahrrad	
programming /ˈprəʊˌɡræmɪŋ/	(das) Programmieren	
volunteering /ˌvɒlənˈtɪərɪŋ/	(das) Verrichten von Freiwilligendienst	
(to) babysit /ˈbeɪbiˌsɪt/	babysitten	
neighbor *(AE)* /ˈneɪbə/	(der/die) Nachbar/in	
(to) **complain (to)** /kəmˈpleɪn/	sich beklagen (bei)	
(to) listen carefully /ˌlɪsn ˈkeəfli/	aufmerksam zuhören	
due /djuː/	fällig	
organizational (= organisational) /ˌɔːɡənaɪˈzeɪʃnəl/	organisatorisch	
(to) **take the initiative** *(irr)* /ˌteɪk ðiː_ɪˈnɪʃətɪv/	die Initiative ergreifen	
(to) **work on** /ˈwɜːk_ɒn/	arbeiten an	You can get a lot of food at a **supermarket**.
supermarket /ˈsuːpəˌmɑːkɪt/	(der) Supermarkt	
pay /peɪ/	(der) Lohn	
patient /ˈpeɪʃnt/	geduldig	
auntie *(informal)* /ˈɑːnti/	(die) Tante	
(to) add to /ˈæd_tʊ/	beitragen	on the weekends *(AE)* = at the weekends *(BE)*
on the weekends *(AE)* /ˌɒn ðə ˈwiːkendz/	an den Wochenenden	
cash register *(AE)* /ˈkæʃ ˌredʒɪstə/	(die) Kasse	
(to) mow /məʊ/	mähen	
lawn /lɔːn/	(der) Rasen	
paper boy /ˈpeɪpə bɔɪ/	(der) Zeitungsjunge	
dog walking /ˈdɒɡ ˌwɔːkɪŋ/	(das) Ausführen von Hunden	
tuition /tjuːˈɪʃn/	*hier:* (die) Nachhilfe	
(to) update /ˌʌpˈdeɪt/	auf den neuesten Stand bringen	When you want to get a job, you have to make an **application**.
application /ˌæplɪˈkeɪʃn/	(die) Bewerbung	
form /fɔːm/	(das) Formular	

p. 96, 8
p. 97, 9
p. 98, 10

	grade /greɪd/	(die) Note	
	age /eɪdʒ/	(das) Alter	
	current /ˈkʌrənt/	gegenwärtig, aktuell	**current** = happening now
	reference /ˈrefrəns/	(die) Referenz, (das) Zeugnis	
	tutoring /ˈtjuːtərɪŋ/	(die) Nachhilfe	
	(to) tutor /ˈtjuːtə/	Nachhilfe geben	
	report /rɪˈpɔːt/	(das) Zeugnis	
	A /eɪ/	*etwa:* Note 1, sehr gut	
	relevant /ˈreləvnt/	relevant; wichtig	
	boy scout /ˌbɔɪ ˈskaʊt/	(der) Pfadfinder	
	counselor *(AE)* = counsellor *(BE)* /ˈkaʊnslə/	*hier:* (der/die) Betreuer/in	
	tutor /ˈtjuːtə/	(der/die) Nachhilfelehrer/in	
p. 98, 11	**job interview (= interview)** /ˈdʒɒb‿ˌɪntəvjuː, ˈɪntəˌvjuː/	(das) Bewerbungsgespräch, (das) Vorstellungsgespräch	In a **job interview**, a future employer talks to someone who is applying for a job.
	(to) **follow** /ˈfɒləʊ/	befolgen	
p. 99, 13	diamond cutter /ˈdaɪəmənd ˌkʌtə/	(der/die) Diamantschleifer/in	
	tester /ˈtestə/	(der/die) Tester/in	
	profession /prəˈfeʃn/	(der) Beruf	
p. 101, 17	**once** /wʌns/	einmal	**once** = one time
	booklet /ˈbʊklət/	(die) Broschüre	

Unit 5 | Part A Immigration

p. 105	**immigration** /ˌɪmɪˈgreɪʃn/	(die) Einwanderung, (die) Immigration	
	the Republic of Ireland /ðə rɪˌpʌblɪk‿əv‿ˈaɪələnd/	(die Republik) Irland	
	horizon /həˈraɪzn/	(der) Horizont	
p. 106, 1	(to) **flee** *(irr)* /fliː/	fliehen	to **flee** = to leave a place very quickly, especially because of a dangerous situation
p. 106, 2	**harvest** /ˈhɑːvɪst/	(die) Ernte	
	farmer /ˈfɑːmə/	(der/die) Bauer/Bäuerin	
	rent /rent/	(die) Miete, (die) Pacht	
	(to) **starve** /stɑːv/	verhungern	
	air /eə/	(die) Luft	
	tiny /ˈtaɪni/	winzig	
	(to) **board a ship** /ˌbɔːd‿ə ˈʃɪp/	ein Schiff besteigen	The people **are boarding the ship**.
	desperate /ˈdesprət/	verzweifelt	
	soil /sɔɪl/	(der) Boden, (die) Erde	
	literally /ˈlɪtrəli/	buchstäblich, wirklich	
	prepaid /ˌpriːˈpeɪd/	im Voraus bezahlt	
	sailing ship /ˈseɪlɪŋ ʃɪp/	(das) Segelschiff	**sailing ship**
	stormy /ˈstɔːmi/	stürmisch	
	overcrowded /ˌəʊvəˈkraʊdɪd/	überfüllt	
	seasick /ˈsiːˌsɪk/	seekrank	

	cabin /ˈkæbɪn/	(die) Kabine
	visa /ˈviːzə/	(das) Visum
p. 107, 2	**unemployment rate** /ˌʌnɪmˈplɔɪmənt reɪt/	(die) Arbeitslosenrate
	(to) **advise** /ədˈvaɪz/	raten, beraten
	grandson /ˈɡrænˌsʌn/	(der) Enkel
	granddaughter /ˈɡrænˌdɔːtə/	(die) Enkelin
	South Korea /ˌsaʊθ kəˈrɪə/	Südkorea
	at that time /æt ˈðæt taɪm/	zu jener Zeit
	thanks to /ˈθæŋks tʊ/	dank, wegen
	then /ðen/	damals
	Korean /kəˈriːən/	(der/die) Koreaner/in; koreanisch
	by then /ˌbaɪ ˈðen/	bis dahin
	(to) retire /rɪˈtaɪə/	in den Ruhestand treten
p. 108, 3	**suitcase** /ˈsuːtˌkeɪs/	(der) Koffer
	storm /stɔːm/	(der) Sturm
	overboard /ˈəʊvəbɔːd/	über Bord
	(to) start a fire /ˌstaːt ə ˈfaɪə/	Feuer machen
p. 108, 4	**emigration** /ˌemɪˈɡreɪʃn/	(die) Auswanderung, (die) Emigration
p. 109, 5	**graph** /ɡraːf/	(das) Diagramm, (der) Graph
	increase /ˈɪŋkriːs/	(der) Anstieg, (das) Wachstum
	decrease /ˈdiːkriːs/	(der) Rückgang
	wave /weɪv/	(die) Welle
	statistics (pl) /stəˈtɪstɪks/	(die) Statistik
	(to) **increase** /ɪnˈkriːs/	ansteigen
	eastern /ˈiːstən/	östlich, Ost-
	quota /ˈkwəʊtə/	(die) Quote
	(to) **peak** /piːk/	den Höhepunkt erreichen
	per cent (BE), **percent** (AE) /pəˈsent/	(das) Prozent
	(to) **decrease** /diːˈkriːs/	abnehmen, zurückgehen
	(to) **make out** (irr) /ˌmeɪk ˈaʊt/	ausmachen
	(to) **immigrate** /ˈɪmɪɡreɪt/	einwandern
p. 110, 6	(to) **return** /rɪˈtɜːn/	zurückkehren, zurückkommen
	southwest /ˌsaʊθˈwest/	in den Südwesten, nach Südwesten
	territory /ˈterətri/	(das) Gebiet, (das) Territorium
	(to) question /ˈkwestʃn/	befragen, verhören
	official /əˈfɪʃl/	(die) Amtsperson
	medical /ˈmedɪkl/	medizinisch
	inspection /ɪnˈspekʃn/	(die) Untersuchung
	thank God /ˌθæŋk ˈɡɒd/	Gott sei Dank
	steamboat /ˈstiːmbəʊt/	(das) Dampfschiff
	humid /ˈhjuːmɪd/	feucht
	poisonous /ˈpɔɪznəs/	giftig
	snake /sneɪk/	(die) Schlange

The **unemployment rate** tells you what per cent of a country's population are without jobs.

suitcase

A **graph** is a picture that shows the relationship between numbers.

to **increase** = to go up in number

The police officer **is questioning** the man.

Many **snakes** are **poisonous**.

	wagon train /ˈwægən treɪn/	(der) Planwagenzug	
	advertisement /ədˈvɜːtɪsmənt/	(die) Werbung, (die) Anzeige	
	wagon /ˈwægən/	(der) Planwagen	
	ox *(pl* oxen*)* /ɒks, ˈɒksn/	(der) Ochse	
	gun /gʌn/	(die) Waffe	
p. 111, 7	**unnecessary** /ʌnˈnesəsəri/	unnötig	**unnecessary** ≠ necessary
	(to) **make** (it/something) *(irr)* /meɪk/	(es/etwas) schaffen	
	(to) **survive** /səˈvaɪv/	überleben	
	west /west/	westlich	
	the Great Plains /ðə ˌɡreɪt ˈpleɪnz/	(die) Great Plains *(Kurzgras-Prärien)*	
	bison *(pl* bison*)* /ˈbaɪsn, ˈbaɪsn/	(das) Bison, (das) Wisent	
	deer *(pl* deer*)* /dɪə, dɪə/	(der) Hirsch, (das) Reh	
	wolf *(pl* wolves*)* /wʊlf, wʊlvz/	(der) Wolf	
	coyote /kaɪˈəʊti/	(der) Kojote	
	(to) howl /haʊl/	brüllen, heulen	
	thunderstorm /ˈθʌndəstɔːm/	(das) Gewitter	
	thunder /ˈθʌndə/	(der) Donner	
	lightning /ˈlaɪtnɪŋ/	(der) Blitz	Even if it is dark at night, you can see when there is **lightning.**
	buffalo chips *(pl)* /ˈbʌfələʊ tʃɪps/	(der) getrocknete Büffelmist	
	(to) milk /mɪlk/	melken	
	(to) make camp *(irr)* /ˌmeɪk ˈkæmp/	das Lager aufschlagen	
	(to) fix /fɪks/	reparieren	
	barn /bɑːn/	(die) Scheune	
	(to) plant /plɑːnt/	pflanzen	Pretty flowers **have been planted** here.
	farming /ˈfɑːmɪŋ/	(der) Ackerbau, (die) Viehzucht	
p. 112, 8	splendid /ˈsplendɪd/	großartig	**splendid** = great
p. 113, 9	on the move /ˌɒn ðə ˈmuːv/	unterwegs	
p. 113, 10	**secretary** /ˈsekrətri/	(der/die) Sekretär/in	
	scholarship /ˈskɒləʃɪp/	(das) Stipendium	
	studies *(pl)* /ˈstʌdiz/	(das) Studium	
	(to) get homesick *(irr)* /ˌget ˈhəʊmˌsɪk/	Heimweh bekommen	
p. 114, 11	past progressive /ˌpɑːst prəʊˈgresɪv/	(die) Verlaufsform der Vergangenheit	
p. 114, 13	**Irish** /ˈaɪrɪʃ/	irisch	When you do something wrong, you make a **mistake.**
p. 115, 14	**mistake** /mɪˈsteɪk/	(der) Fehler	
	(to) keep in mind *(irr)* /ˌkiːp ɪn ˈmaɪnd/	im Gedächtnis behalten	
	worksheet /ˈwɜːkʃiːt/	(das) Arbeitsblatt	

Unit 5 | Part B The Republic of Ireland

p. 116, 1	ruin /ˈruːɪn/	(die) Ruine	Gruppenbezeichnungen wie „team", „family" oder „police" werden von einem Verb in der Pluralform gefolgt, wenn man beschreiben will, was die einzelnen Mitglieder der Gruppe tun. Will man die Einheit der Gruppe betonen, benutzt man ein Verb in der Singularform.
	Gaelic football /ˌgeɪlɪk ˈfʊtbɔːl/	*Ballsportart mit zwei Teams zu je 15 Spielern/Spielerinnen*	
	fisherman *(pl* fishermen*)* /ˈfɪʃəmən/	(der) Fischer, (der) Angler	
	county /ˈkaʊnti/	(der) (Verwaltungs)bezirk; (die) Grafschaft	

	the docklands *(pl)* /ðə ˈdɒkləndz/	(das) Hafenviertel
p. 117, 2	**tonight** /təˈnaɪt/	heute Abend
	goalkeeper /ˈgəʊlˌkiːpə/	(der/die) Tormann/Torfrau
	one day /ˌwʌn ˈdeɪ/	eines Tages
	great-great-grandparents *(pl)* /ˌgreɪt ˌgreɪt ˈgrænˌpeərənts/	(der) Ururgroßeltern
	fiddle /ˈfɪdl/	(die) Geige
	Polish /ˈpəʊlɪʃ/	(das) Polnisch; polnisch
	non- /nɒn/	nicht
p. 119, 5	**Atlantic, Atlantic Ocean** /ətˈlæntɪk, ətˌlæntɪk ˈəʊʃn/	(der) Atlantik, (der) Atlantische Ozean
	Pacific, Pacific Ocean /pəˈsɪfɪk, pəˌsɪfɪk ˈəʊʃn/	(der) Pazifik, (der) Pazifische Ozean
	lighthouse /ˈlaɪtˌhaʊs/	(der) Leuchtturm
	peninsula /pəˈnɪnsjələ/	(die) Halbinsel
	mystical /ˈmɪstɪkl/	mystisch
	(to) kiss /kɪs/	küssen
	hiking trail /ˈhaɪkɪŋ treɪl/	(der) Wanderweg
	dolphin /ˈdɒlfɪn/	(der) Delfin
	seal /siːl/	(der) Seehund, (die) Robbe
p. 120, 6	(to) **date back** /ˌdeɪt ˈbæk/	zurückgehen auf, stammen aus
	sweater /ˈswetə/	(der) Pullover
	campus /ˈkæmpəs/	(die) Universität, (der) Campus
	illustrated /ˈɪləstreɪtɪd/	illustriert, bebildert
	manuscript /ˈmænjuskrɪpt/	(das) Manuskript
	bible /ˈbaɪbl/	(die) Bibel
	hip /hɪp/	hip, cool
p. 121, 6	**living conditions** *(pl)* /ˈlɪvɪŋ kənˌdɪʃnz/	(die) Lebensbedingungen
	(to) **make one's mark** *(irr)* /ˌmeɪk wʌnz ˈmɑːk/	seine Spuren hinterlassen
	sword /sɔːd/	(das) Schwert
	shield /ʃiːld/	(der) Schild
	Viking /ˈvaɪkɪŋ/	(der/die) Wikinger/in; Wikinger-
	warrior /ˈwɒriə/	(der/die) Krieger/in
	medieval /ˌmediˈiːvl/	mittelalterlich
	(to) **follow in somebody's footsteps** /ˌfɒləʊ ɪn ˌsʌmbədiz ˈfʊtsteps/	in jemandes Fußstapfen treten
	the potato famine /ðə pəˈteɪtəʊ ˌfæmɪn/	*Hungersnot in Irland zwischen 1845 und 1849*
	famine /ˈfæmɪn/	(die) Hungersnot
	(to) **sail** /seɪl/	segeln
	on board /ˌɒn ˈbɔːd/	an Bord
	starvation /stɑːˈveɪʃn/	(der) Hungertod
p. 122, 7	**western** /ˈwestən/	West-, westlich
	joke /dʒəʊk/	(der) Witz

present perfect progressive /ˌpreznt ˌpɜːfɪkt prəʊˈgresɪv/ Verlaufsform des Perfekt

dolphin

Their **living conditions** are very good. They can afford to go on a holiday.

When people lack food in a certain region over a period of time, it is a **famine**.

falcon /ˈfɔːlkən/	(der) Falke	
silver /ˈsɪlvə/	silbern	A bird is a **winged** animal.
winged /wɪŋd/	mit Flügeln, geflügelt	
call of freedom /ˌkɔːl‿əv‿ˈfriːdəm/	(der) Ruf der Freiheit	
breast /brest/	(die) Brust	
(to) soar /sɔː/	aufsteigen, sich erheben	
twisted /ˈtwɪstɪd/	verdreht, verschlungen	
shore /ʃɔː/	(die) Küste, (das) Ufer	
sunset /ˈsʌnˌset/	(der) Sonnenuntergang	
(to) stand by (irr) /ˌstænd‿ˈbaɪ/	dabeistehen	
(to) pass away /ˌpɑːs‿ə'weɪ/	verbringen	
salmon /ˈsæmən/	(der) Lachs	
(to) dart /dɑːt/	flitzen, sausen	There are five dogs in the **basket**.
basket /ˈbɑːskɪt/	(der) Korb	
(to) punch /pʌntʃ/	schlagen	
epic (informal) /ˈepɪk/	super, klasse	
itinerary /aɪˈtɪnərəri/	(die) Reiseroute	
(to) **advertise** /ˈædvətaɪz/	für etwas Werbung machen	
Northern Ireland /ˌnɔːðən‿ˈaɪələnd/	Nordirland	
European Union /ˌjʊərəˌpiːən ˈjuːnjən/	(die) Europäische Union	
(to) **give a talk** (irr) /ˌgɪv‿ə ˈtɔːk/	einen Vortrag halten	He **is giving a talk**.

p. 123, 8 (basket)
p. 123, 9 (itinerary)
p. 123, 10 (advertise)
p. 124, 11 (Northern Ireland)
p. 125, 13 (give a talk)

Results for the soft skill check on page 96:

	a	b	c
1	1 point	2 points	3 points
2	2 points	3 points	1 point
3	2 points	3 points	1 point
4	3 points	1 point	2 points
5	1 point	3 points	2 points
6	3 points	2 points	1 point

15 – 18: You have very good soft skills. You are a very responsible, polite and patient person who can work and communicate well with other people.

10 – 14: There is room to improve your soft skills, but in general you are a good team player.

6 – 9: You should work on your soft skills!

Hier findest du alphabetisch sortiert alle Wörter aus dem vorliegenden Buch mit der Angabe der Seite *(p.)*, auf der das Wort das erste Mal vorkommt oder auf der es zum Lernwort gemacht wird. Die Zahl hinter dem Komma bezeichnet die Aufgabe auf der Seite.

Lernwörter aus den vorigen Bänden sind mit „NHG 5", „NHG 6" oder „NHG 7" markiert.

Die **fett** gedruckten Lernwörter solltest du dir merken.

(informal) bedeutet: Dieses Wort oder dieser Ausdruck ist umgangssprachlich.

Folgende Abkürzungen werden verwendet: *(pl)* = (unregelmäßige) Mehrzahlform, *(no pl)* = keine Mehrzahlform, *(irr)* = unregelmäßiges Verb, *(AE)* = amerikanisches Englisch, L&L = Land und Leute

A

a, an /ə/eɪ, ən/ **ein(e)** NHG 5

a /ə/ pro NHG 6

A /eɪ/ *etwa:* Note 1, sehr gut p. 98, 10

ability /əˈbɪləti/ Fähigkeit p. 95, 7

(to) **be able to do something** *(irr)* /ˌbiˌeɪbl tə ˈduː ˌsʌmθɪŋ/ etwas tun können NHG 6

about /əˈbaʊt/ über; an NHG 5; ungefähr NHG 6

(to) **be about** *(irr)* /ˌbiˌəˈbaʊt/ gehen um; handeln von NHG 5

above /əˈbʌv/ über NHG 5; oben, oberhalb NHG 7; darüber p. 26, 8

(to) **go abroad** *(irr)* /ˌgəʊˌəˈbrɔːd/ ins Ausland gehen / fahren NHG 6

absolutely /ˈæbsəluːtli/ absolut NHG 7

accent /ˈæksnt/ Akzent NHG 7

(to) **accept** /əkˈsept/ anerkennen; akzeptieren p. 25, 7

(to) **access** /ˈækses/ zugreifen auf p. 68, 2

accessory /əkˈsesəri/ Accessoire p. 93, 2

accident /ˈæksɪdnt/ Unfall NHG 7

by accident /ˌbaɪˈæksɪdnt/ zufällig; aus Versehen NHG 7

accidentally /ˌæksɪˈdentli/ versehentlich; zufällig NHG 7

according to /əˈkɔːdɪŋ ˌtuː/ nach; gemäß p. 12, 5

account /əˈkaʊnt/ Benutzerkonto p. 69, 2

(to) **achieve** /əˈtʃiːv/ erreichen p.17,10

across /əˈkrɒs/ über, quer durch p. 20, 2

acrostic /əˈkrɒstɪk/ Akrostichon; Leistenvers p. 27, 11

(to) **act** /ækt/ handeln; spielen NHG 6; sich verhalten p. 62, 8

(to) **act out** /ˌæktˌˈaʊt/ nachspielen; vorspielen NHG 5

acting /ˈæktɪŋ/ Schauspielern p. 149

action /ˈækʃn/ Handlung NHG 5; Handeln; Maßnahmen p. 85, 5

(to) **take action** *(irr)* /ˌteɪkˈækʃn/ handeln, Maßnahmen ergreifen p. 85, 5

(to) activate /ˈæktɪveɪt/ aktivieren p. 10, 2

active /ˈæktɪv/ aktiv NHG 7

activity /ækˈtɪvəti/ Aktivität NHG 5

actor/actress /ˈæktə, ˈæktrəs/ Schauspieler/in NHG 6

actually /ˈæktʃuəli/ eigentlich; tatsächlich NHG 6

AD (= Anno Domini) /ˌeɪ ˈdiː, ˌænəʊ ˈdɒmɪnaɪ/ n. Chr. (= nach Christus) NHG 7

(to) adapt /əˈdæpt/ anpassen, bearbeiten p. 93, 2

(to) **add** /æd/ hinzufügen NHG 5

(to) add to /ˈædˌtʊ/ beitragen p. 97, 9

addict /ˈædɪkt/ Abhängige/r p. 68, 2

address /əˈdres/ Adresse NHG 5

(to) **address** /əˈdres/ ansprechen; adressieren p. 25, 7

adjective /ˈædʒɪktɪv/ Adjektiv NHG 6

admission /ədˈmɪʃn/ Eintritt; Eintrittspreis p. 26, 8

(to) **admit** /ədˈmɪt/ zugeben, eingestehen p. 69, 2

adult /ˈædʌlt/ Erwachsene/r NHG 6

in advance /ˌɪnˌədˈvɑːns/ im Voraus p. 26, 8

advantage /ədˈvɑːntɪdʒ/ Vorteil p.72,6

adventure /ədˈventʃə/ Abenteuer NHG 6

adverb of manner /ˌædvɜːb əv ˈmænə/ Adverb der Art und Weise p. 70

advert (= ad) /ˈædvɜːt, æd/ Werbung; Anzeige NHG 7

(to) **advertise** /ˈædvətaɪz/ für etwas Werbung machen p. 123, 10

advertisement /ədˈvɜːtɪsmənt/ Werbung; Anzeige p. 110, 6

advertising /ˈædvəˌtaɪzɪŋ/ Werbung p. 93, 2

advice /ədˈvaɪs/ Rat(schlag) NHG 7

(to) **give advice** *(irr)* /ˌgɪvˌədˈvaɪs/ Rat geben NHG 7

piece of advice /ˌpiːs əvˌədˈvaɪs/ Rat(schlag) p. 74, 8

(to) **seek advice** *(irr)* /ˌsiːkˌədˈvaɪs/ Rat suchen NHG 7

(to) **advise** /ədˈvaɪz/ raten, beraten p. 107, 2

(to) **affect** /əˈfekt/ betreffen; beeinflussen p. 72, 6

(to) **afford** /əˈfɔːd/ sich leisten p. 82, 2

(to) **be afraid of** *(irr)* /ˌbiˌəˈfreɪdˌəv/ Angst haben vor NHG 6

Africa /ˈæfrɪkə/ Afrika p. 15, 7

African American /ˌæfrɪkənˌəˈmerɪkən/ Afroamerikaner/in; afroamerikanisch p. 15, 7

after /ˈɑːftə/ nach NHG 5; nachdem p. 35, 2

after that /ˌɑːftəˈðæt/ danach NHG 7

after-school /ˌɑːftəˈskuːl/ Nachmittags- p. 33

afternoon /ˌɑːftəˈnuːn/ Nachmittag NHG 5

afterwards /ˈɑːftəwədz/ anschließend; später NHG 6

again /əˈgen/ wieder; noch einmal NHG 5

against /əˈgenst/ gegen NHG 6

age /eɪdʒ/ Zeitalter p. 69, 2; Alter p. 98, 10

aged *(after noun)* /eɪdʒd/ im Alter von p. 26, 8

aggressive /əˈgresɪv/ aggressiv, angriffslustig p. 73, 6

... ago /əˈgəʊ/ vor ... NHG 6

(to) **agree** /əˈgriː/ zustimmen NHG 7

(to) **agree on** /əˈgriː ɒn/ sich einigen auf NHG 7

(to) **agree with** /əˈgriː wɪð/ einer Meinung sein mit, übereinstimmen mit p. 63, 8

agricultural /ˌægrɪˈkʌltʃrəl/ landwirtschaftlich p. 15, 7

aim /eɪm/ Ziel p. 50, 8

ain't (= am/are/is not) (informal) /eɪnt/ nicht sein p. 25, 7

air /eə/ Luft p. 106, 2

airport /ˈeəpɔːt/ Flughafen NHG 6

all /ɔːl/ alle; alles; ganz; völlig NHG 5

all around /ˌɔːl əˈraʊnd/ rundherum; überall (in/auf) p. 21, 2

all day long /ˌɔːl deɪ ˈlɒŋ/ den ganzen Tag lang p. 21, 2

all kinds of /ˌɔːl ˈkaɪndz əv/ alle möglichen NHG 6

all over /ˌɔːl ˈəʊvə/ überall NHG 6

all over the world /ˌɔːl ˌəʊvə ðə ˈwɜːld/ auf der ganzen Welt NHG 6

All the best! /ˌɔːl ðə ˈbest/ Alles Gute! NHG 7

all the time /ˌɔːl ðə ˈtaɪm/ die ganze Zeit NHG 6

all year round /ˌɔːl ˈjɪə raʊnd/ das ganze Jahr lang p. 10, 2

allegiance /əˈliːdʒns/ Loyalität; Ergebenheit p. 38, 6

(to) **be allergic to** (irr) /ˌbi əˈlɜːdʒɪk tʊ/ allergisch sein auf NHG 7

(to) **allow** /əˈlaʊ/ erlauben NHG 7

(to) **be allowed (to)** (irr) /ˌbi əˈlaʊd tə/ erlaubt sein, dürfen NHG 6

ally /ˈælaɪ/ Verbündete/r; Alliierte/r p. 15, 7

almost /ˈɔːlməʊst/ fast; beinahe NHG 6

alone /əˈləʊn/ allein NHG 5

along /əˈlɒŋ/ entlang NHG 6

already /ɔːlˈredi/ schon; bereits NHG 5

also /ˈɔːlsəʊ/ auch NHG 5

although /ɔːlˈðəʊ/ obwohl NHG 6

always /ˈɔːlweɪz/ immer NHG 5

am (= ante meridiem) /ˌeɪˈem, ˌænti məˈrɪdiəm/ morgens, vormittags (nur hinter Uhrzeit zwischen Mitternacht und 12 Uhr mittags) NHG 5

amazing (informal) /əˈmeɪzɪŋ/ toll NHG 6

(to) **call an ambulance** /ˌkɔːl ən ˈæmbjʊləns/ einen Krankenwagen rufen NHG 7

America /əˈmerɪkə/ Amerika p. 6

American /əˈmerɪkən/ Amerikaner/in; amerikanisch NHG 7

among /əˈmʌŋ/ unter; zwischen p. 14, 7

amusement park /əˈmjuːzmənt pɑːk/ Freizeitpark p. 27, 10

ancient /ˈeɪnʃnt/ alt; antik NHG 6

and /ænd/ und NHG 5

and so on /ænd ˈsəʊ ɒn/ und so weiter NHG 6

angel /ˈeɪndʒl/ Engel p. 71, 5

angry /ˈæŋgri/ zornig, wütend NHG 6

animal /ˈænɪml/ Tier NHG 5

animal keeper /ˈænɪml ˌkiːpə/ Tierpfleger/in p. 92, 1

ankle /ˈæŋkl/ (Fuß)knöchel NHG 7

announcement /əˈnaʊnsmənt/ Mitteilung; Durchsage NHG 6

annoyed /əˈnɔɪd/ genervt NHG 6

annoying /əˈnɔɪɪŋ/ ärgerlich NHG 7

another /əˈnʌðə/ noch ein/e; ein anderer/ein anderes/eine andere NHG 5

answer /ˈɑːnsə/ Antwort NHG 5

(to) **answer** /ˈɑːnsə/ (be)antworten NHG 5

Antarctica /ænˈtɑːktɪkə/ die Antarktis p. 6

anxiety /æŋˈzaɪəti/ Sorge; Angst p. 85, 5

any /ˈeni/ (irgend)ein(e) NHG 5

any more /ˌeni ˈmɔː/ noch mehr NHG 7

anybody /ˈenibɒdi/ irgendjemand; jede(r, s) NHG 7

anyone /ˈeniwʌn/ jede(r, s); (irgend)jemand NHG 7

anything /ˈeniˌθɪŋ/ irgendetwas NHG 5

anything /ˈeniˌθɪŋ/ alles p. 89, 9

anyway /ˈeniweɪ/ jedenfalls NHG 6; sowieso p. 48, 7

anywhere /ˈeniˌweə/ überall; irgendwo NHG 7

apart /əˈpɑːt/ auseinander NHG 6; getrennt p. 62, 8

apart from /əˈpɑːt frəm/ abgesehen von p. 39, 6

apartment (AE) /əˈpɑːtmənt/ Wohnung p. 24, 6

(to) **apologize (= apologise)** /əˈpɒlədʒaɪz/ sich entschuldigen NHG 7

apparently /əˈpærəntli/ offensichtlich p. 69, 2

(to) **appear** /əˈpɪə/ erscheinen, auftauchen NHG 7

apple /ˈæpl/ Apfel NHG 5

application /ˌæplɪˈkeɪʃn/ Bewerbung p. 98, 10

(to) **apply** /əˈplaɪ/ anwenden p. 10, 2

(to) **apply for** /əˈplaɪ fɔː/ sich bewerben um p. 95, 7

appointment /əˈpɔɪntmənt/ Termin NHG 7

April /ˈeɪprəl/ April NHG 5

architecture /ˈɑːkɪˌtektʃə/ Architektur p. 26, 8

area /ˈeəriə/ Gebiet; Region NHG 5

area /ˈeəriə/ Fläche p. 10, 2

(to) **argue** /ˈɑːgjuː/ sich streiten p. 65, 12

argument /ˈɑːgjʊmənt/ Streit; Argument NHG 7

around /əˈraʊnd/ um; herum; umher NHG 6; ungefähr NHG 7

(to) **arrive** /əˈraɪv/ ankommen NHG 5

art /ɑːt/ Kunst NHG 5

article /ˈɑːtɪkl/ Artikel NHG 5

artificial intelligence (= AI) /ˌɑːtɪfɪʃl ɪnˈtelɪdʒns, ˌeɪ ˈaɪ/ künstliche Intelligenz p. 10, 2

as /əz/ als; wie; während NHG 5

as … as /æz æz/ so … wie NHG 6

as a whole /əz ə ˈhəʊl/ als Ganzes p. 85, 5

as well /əz ˈwel/ auch NHG 6

Asia /ˈeɪʒə/ Asien p. 6

Asian /ˈeɪʒn/ Asiat/in; asiatisch p. 7

aside from (AE) /əˈsaɪd frəm/ abgesehen von p. 51, 11

(to) **ask** /ɑːsk/ fragen; bitten NHG 5

(to) **ask for advice** /ˌɑːsk fər ədˈvaɪs/ um Rat bitten NHG 7

(to) **ask on a date** /ˌɑːsk ɒn ə ˈdeɪt/ um eine Verabredung bitten p. 66, 13

(to) **ask questions** /ˌɑːsk ˈkwestʃnz/ Fragen stellen NHG 5

aspect /ˈæspekt/ Aspekt; Gesichtspunkt NHG 7

assembly /ə'sembli/ (Schüler)
versammlung NHG 5

assembly hall /ə'sembli hɔ:l/ Aula
p. 165

assembly line /ə'sembli laɪn/ Fließ-
band p. 10, 2

at /æt/ an; in; bei; um NHG 5

at all times /ˌæt ˌɔ:l 'taɪmz/ jederzeit,
immer p. 72, 6

at first /ˌæt 'fɜ:st/ zuerst NHG 6

at home /ˌæt 'həʊm/ zu Hause NHG 5

at least /ˌæt 'li:st/ mindestens;
wenigstens NHG 6

at that time /ˌætˌ'ðætˌtaɪm/ zu jener
Zeit p. 107, 2

at the back /ˌæt ðə 'bæk/ hinten
NHG 5

at the back of /ˌæt ðə 'bækˌəv/ am
Ende von; hinten in p. 20, 2

at the doctor's /ˌætˌ_ðə 'dɒktəz/
beim Arzt/bei der Ärztin NHG 7

at the front /ˌæt ðə 'frʌnt/ vorne
NHG 5

at the same time /ˌætˌ_ðə ˌseɪm
'taɪm/ gleichzeitig; zur gleichen
Zeit NHG 7

at the weekend /ˌætˌ_ðə 'wi:kend/
am Wochenende p. 132

athlete /'æθliːt/ Athlet/in p. 35, 2

athletic /æθ'letɪk/ athletisch;
sportlich p. 48, 7

(to) do athletics *(irr)*
/ˌduː_æθ'letɪks/ Leichtathletik
machen NHG 5

Atlantic, Atlantic Ocean /ət'læntɪk,
ətˌlæntɪkˌ_'əʊʃn/ Atlantik, Atlan-
tischer Ozean p. 119, 5

atmosphere /'ætməsˌfɪə/ Atmo-
sphäre NHG 7

attack /ə'tæk/ Angriff p. 15, 7

(to) attend /ə'tend/ besuchen NHG 7

attendance /ə'tendəns/ Anwesenheit p. 38, 6

(to) draw attention to *(irr)*
/ˌdrɔ_ə'tenʃn tə/ Aufmerksamkeit
lenken auf NHG 7

(to) pay attention (to) *(irr)*
/ˌpeɪ_ə'tenʃn tʊ/ aufpassen; achten
auf NHG 6

attitude /'ætɪˌtjuːd/ Haltung;
Einstellung p. 95, 7

(to) attract /ə'trækt/ anziehen
p. 148

attraction /ə'trækʃn/ Attraktion
NHG 6

auto body repair /ˌɔ:təʊ ˌbɒdi
rɪ'peə/ Karosseriereparatur p. 40, 7

auditorium *(AE)* /ˌɔ:dɪ'tɔ:riəm/ Vor-
tragssaal; Festhalle p. 41, 10

August /'ɔ:gəst/ August NHG 5

aunt /ɑ:nt/ Tante NHG 5

auntie *(informal)* /'ɑ:nti/ Tante
p. 97, 9

Australia /ɒ'streɪliə/ Australien p. 6

author /'ɔ:θə/ Autor/in NHG 7

autumn /'ɔ:təm/ Herbst NHG 6

average /'ævərɪdʒ/ durchschnittlich
p. 68, 2

(to) avoid /ə'vɔɪd/ (ver)meiden NHG 7

award /ə'wɔ:d/ Preis; Auszeichnung
p. 6

(to) be aware of *(irr)* /ˌbi_ə'weər_əv/
sich bewusst sein p. 71, 5

awareness /ə'weənəs/ Bewusstsein
p. 87, 6

away /ə'weɪ/ weg NHG 5

(to) go away *(irr)* /ˌgəʊ_ə'weɪ/ weggehen; verschwinden NHG 6

awesome /'ɔ:sm/ beeindruckend;
super p. 20, 2

B

(to) babysit /'beɪbiˌsɪt/ babysitten
p. 95, 7

back /bæk/ zurück NHG 5; Rücken
NHG 7

at the back /ˌæt ðə 'bæk/ hinten
NHG 5

at the back of /ˌæt ðə 'bækˌəv/ am
Ende von; hinten in p. 20, 2

in the back /ˌɪn ðə 'bæk/ hinten
NHG 5

background /'bækˌgraʊnd/ Hinter-
grund NHG 6

bad /bæd/ schlecht; schlimm NHG 5

bag /bæg/ Tasche; Tüte NHG 5

(to) bake /beɪk/ backen NHG 5

baked potatoes *(pl)* /ˌbeɪkt
pə'teɪtəʊz/ Ofenkartoffeln p. 47, 6

baker /'beɪkə/ Bäcker/in NHG 6

balloon /bə'lu:n/ Luftballon NHG 5

(to) ban /bæn/ verbieten p. 69, 2

banana /bə'nɑ:nə/ Banane NHG 5

bandage /'bændɪdʒ/ Verband NHG 7

bar chart /'bɑ: tʃɑ:t/ Säulen-
diagramm p. 171

(to) barbecue /'bɑ:bɪˌkjuː/ grillen
p. 48, 7

bargain /'bɑ:gɪn/ Schnäppchen
NHG 7

barn /bɑ:n/ Scheune p. 111, 7

basic /'beɪsɪk/ grundlegend;
wesentlich NHG 7

basket /'bɑ:skɪt/ Korb p. 123, 8

bat /bæt/ Schläger p. 50, 9

bathroom /'bɑ:θˌru:m/ Badezimmer
NHG 5

battery /'bætri/ Batterie p. 86, 6

the Battery /ðə 'bætri/ *Park in New
York* p. 25, 7

battle /'bætl/ Kampf NHG 7

BC (= before Christ) /ˌbi: 'si:, bɪˌfɔ:
'kraɪst/ v. Chr. (= vor Christus)
NHG 7

(to) be *(irr)* /bi:/ sein NHG 5

(to) be a shame *(irr)* /ˌbi_ə 'ʃeɪm/
schade sein NHG 7

(to) be able to do something *(irr)*
/ˌbi_ˌeɪbl tə 'duː ˌsʌmθɪŋ/ etwas tun
können NHG 6

(to) be about *(irr)* /ˌbi_ə'baʊt/ gehen
um; handeln von NHG 5

(to) be afraid of *(irr)* /ˌbi_ə'freɪd_əv/
Angst haben vor NHG 6

(to) be allergic to *(irr)* /ˌbi_ə'lɜ:dʒɪk
tʊ/ allergisch sein auf NHG 7

(to) be allowed (to) *(irr)*
/ˌbi_ə'laʊd_tə/ erlaubt sein, dürfen
NHG 6

(to) be aware of *(irr)* /ˌbi_ə'weər_əv/
sich bewusst sein p. 71, 5

(to) be behind *(irr, informal)*
/ˌbi: bɪ'haɪnd/ hinterher sein,
zurückliegen p. 40, 7

(to) be born *(irr)* /ˌbi: 'bɔ:n/ geboren
werden NHG 7

(to) be connected (to) *(irr)* /ˌbi:
kə'nektɪd_tə/ verbunden sein (mit),
in Verbindung stehen (mit)
p. 66, 14

(to) be far from reach *(irr)* /ˌbi: ˌfɑ:
frəm 'ri:tʃ/ außer Reichweite sein
p. 68, 2

(to) be good at doing something
(irr) /ˌbi: gʊd_ət 'du:ɪŋ ˌsʌmθɪŋ/ gut
darin sein, etwas zu tun NHG 5

(to) be good at something *(irr)*
/ˌbi: 'gʊd_æt ˌsʌmθɪŋ/ gut in etwas
sein NHG 6

(to) **be (good/great) fun** *(irr)* /ˌbiː ˌɡʊd/ˌɡreɪt ˈfʌn/ (viel/großen) Spaß machen NHG 5

(to) **be into** *(irr, informal)* /ˌbi ˈɪnˈtuː/ interessiert sein an p. 59, 3

(to) **be interested in** *(irr)* /ˌbi ˈɪntrəstɪd ɪn/ interessiert sein an NHG 7

(to) **be involved in** *(irr)* /ˌbi ɪnˈvɒlvd ɪn/ beteiligt sein an p. 15, 7

(to) **be located** *(irr)* /ˌbiː ləʊˈkeɪtɪd/ gelegen sein NHG 7

(to) **be one's turn** *(irr)* /ˌbiː wʌnz ˈtɜːn/ an der Reihe sein NHG 5

(to) **be proud of** *(irr)* /ˌbiː ˈpraʊd əv/ stolz sein auf p. 24, 6

(to) **be right** *(irr)* /ˌbiː ˈraɪt/ recht haben NHG 5

(to) **be situated** *(irr)* /ˌbiː ˈsɪtʃueɪtɪd/ liegen, gelegen sein p. 18, 12

(to) **be sorry** *(irr)* /ˌbiː ˈsɒri/ bedauern; sich entschuldigen p. 62, 8

(to) **be up to something** *(irr)* /ˌbi ˌʌp tə ˈsʌmθɪŋ/ etwas vorhaben p. 45, 2

(to) **be willing to** *(irr)* /ˌbiː ˈwɪlɪŋ tʊ/ bereit sein p. 89, 9

(to) **be worth** *(irr)* /ˌbiː ˈwɜːθ/ (sich) lohnen; wert sein NHG 7

(to) **be wrong** *(irr)* /ˌbiː ˈrɒŋ/ im Unrecht sein NHG 7

(to) **be wrong (with)** *(irr)* /ˌbiː ˈrɒŋ wɪθ/ nicht in Ordnung sein (mit) NHG 7

beach /biːtʃ/ Strand NHG 5

bean /biːn/ Bohne p. 18, 12

beard /bɪəd/ Bart NHG 7

beautiful /ˈbjuːtəfl/ schön NHG 5

beauty /ˈbjuːti/ Schönheit p. 11, 2

because /bɪˈkɒz/ weil; da NHG 5

because of /bɪˈkɒz əv/ wegen NHG 7

(to) **become** *(irr)* /bɪˈkʌm/ werden NHG 6

bed /bed/ Bett NHG 5

bedroom /ˈbedruːm/ Schlafzimmer NHG 5

bee /biː/ Biene NHG 6

before /bɪˈfɔː/ bevor; zuvor, vorher; vor NHG 5

(to) **begin** *(irr)* /bɪˈɡɪn/ anfangen; beginnen NHG 5

beginning /bɪˈɡɪnɪŋ/ Anfang; Beginn NHG 6

(to) **behave** /bɪˈheɪv/ sich verhalten, sich benehmen p. 63, 8

behavior *(AE)* = **behaviour** *(BE)* /bɪˈheɪvjə/ Benehmen; Verhalten p. 62, 8

behind /bɪˈhaɪnd/ hinter NHG 5

(to) be behind *(irr, informal)* /ˌbiː bɪˈhaɪnd/ hinterher sein, zurückliegen p. 40, 7

belief /bɪˈliːf/ Glaube p. 89, 9

(to) **believe (in)** /bɪˈliːv ɪn/ glauben (an) NHG 6

bell /bel/ Glocke NHG 6

(to) **belong (to)** /bɪˈlɒŋ/ gehören (zu) NHG 7

below /bɪˈləʊ/ unten, unter NHG 6

benefit /ˈbenɪfɪt/ Vorteil; Nutzen p. 72, 6

best /best/ beste(r, s) NHG 5

All the best! /ˌɔːl ðə ˈbest/ Alles Gute! NHG 7

the best /ðə ˈbest/ der/die/das beste NHG 5; am besten NHG 6

(to) **like best** /ˌlaɪk ˈbest/ am liebsten mögen NHG 5

(to) do one's best *(irr)* /ˌduː wʌnz ˈbest/ sein Bestes geben p. 48, 7

best wishes /ˌbest ˈwɪʃɪz/ viele Grüße p. 167

better /ˈbetə/ besser NHG 6

(to) **get better** *(irr)* /ˌget ˈbetə/ besser werden; gesund werden NHG 7

between /bɪˈtwiːn/ zwischen NHG 5

BFF (= best friend forever) *(informal)* /ˌbiː ef ˈef, ˌbest ˌfrend fərˈevə/ allerbeste/r Freund/in p. 58, 3

bible /ˈbaɪbl/ Bibel p. 120, 6

bicycle /ˈbaɪsɪkl/ Fahrrad p. 95, 7

big /bɪɡ/ groß NHG 5

bike /baɪk/ Fahrrad NHG 6

(to) **ride a bike** *(irr)* /ˌraɪd ə ˈbaɪk/ Fahrrad fahren NHG 5

bike lane /ˈbaɪk leɪn/ Fahrradweg p. 20, 2

biking /ˈbaɪkɪŋ/ Radfahren p. 140

bill /bɪl/ Rechnung NHG 7

billion /ˈbɪljən/ Milliarde p. 6

bin /bɪn/ Abfalleimer NHG 5

bird /bɜːd/ Vogel NHG 6

birthday /ˈbɜːθdeɪ/ Geburtstag NHG 5

Happy birthday (to you)! /ˌhæpi ˈbɜːθdeɪ tʊ juː/ Herzlichen Glückwunsch zum Geburtstag! NHG 5

birthplace /ˈbɜːθpleɪs/ Geburtsort p. 11, 2

biscuit /ˈbɪskɪt/ Keks NHG 5

bison *(pl bison)* /ˈbaɪsn, ˈbaɪsn/ Bison; Wisent p. 111, 7

a bit /ə ˈbɪt/ ein bisschen NHG 5

black /blæk/ schwarz NHG 5

Black /blæk/ *politische Selbstbezeichnung Schwarzer Menschen in den USA* p. 25, 7

(to) **bleed** *(irr)* /bliːd/ bluten NHG 7

(to) **blend** /blend/ vermischen p. 25, 7

(to) **block** /blɒk/ blockieren p. 69, 2

(to) **blog** /blɒɡ/ bloggen p. 38, 6

blood /blʌd/ Blut NHG 6

blood sample /ˈblʌd ˌsɑːmpl/ Blutprobe p. 92, 2

blue /bluː/ blau NHG 5

board /bɔːd/ Tafel; Brett NHG 5

on board /ˌɒn ˈbɔːd/ an Bord p. 121, 6

(to) **board a ship** /ˌbɔːd ə ˈʃɪp/ ein Schiff besteigen p. 106, 2

board game /ˈbɔːd ɡeɪm/ Brettspiel NHG 6

boat /bəʊt/ Boot NHG 5

body /ˈbɒdi/ Körper NHG 5

book /bʊk/ Buch NHG 5

(to) **book** /bʊk/ buchen, reservieren NHG 6

booklet /ˈbʊklət/ Broschüre p. 101, 17

bookshelf /ˈbʊkʃelf/ Bücherregal NHG 5

bored /bɔːd/ gelangweilt NHG 6

boring /ˈbɔːrɪŋ/ langweilig NHG 5

born /bɔːn/ geboren p. 17, 10

(to) **be born** *(irr)* /ˌbiː ˈbɔːn/ geboren werden NHG 7

borough /ˈbʌrə/ Bezirk; Stadtteil p. 21, 2

(to) **borrow** /ˈbɒrəʊ/ (aus)leihen NHG 5

both /bəʊθ/ beide NHG 7

both ... and ... /ˈbəʊθ ænd/ sowohl ... als auch ... p. 48, 7

bottle /ˈbɒtl/ Flasche NHG 5

bottlenose dolphin /ˈbɒtlnəʊz ˌdɒlfɪn/ Tümmler p. 141

boundary /ˈbaʊndri/ Grenze p. 72, 6

bowl /bəʊl/ Schüssel; Schale NHG 6

box /bɒks/ Kasten; Kiste NHG 5

boy /bɔɪ/ Junge NHG 5

boy scout /ˌbɔɪ ˈskaʊt/ Pfadfinder p. 98, 10

bracket /ˈbrækɪt/ Klammer p. 18, 12

brain /breɪn/ Gehirn p. 44, 2

Brazil /brəˈzɪl/ Brasilien p. 71, 5

bread /bred/ Brot NHG 7

break /breɪk/ Pause NHG 5

(to) **take a break** *(irr)* /ˌteɪk_ə ˈbreɪk/ eine Pause machen p. 85, 5

(to) **break** *(irr)* /breɪk/ brechen; zerbrechen; kaputt machen NHG 6

(to) break up *(irr)* /ˌbreɪk_ˈʌp/ Schluss machen p. 69, 2

breakfast /ˈbrekfəst/ Frühstück NHG 5

breast /brest/ Brust p. 122, 7

breathtaking /ˈbreθˌteɪkɪŋ/ atemberaubend p. 13, 6

bridge /brɪdʒ/ Brücke NHG 6

bright, brightly /braɪt,ˈbraɪtli/ hell; strahlend NHG 6

brilliant /ˈbrɪljənt/ genial, klasse NHG 5

(to) **bring** *(irr)* /brɪŋ/ mitbringen NHG 5

(to) **bring over** *(irr)* /ˌbrɪŋ_ˈəʊvə/ herbeibringen NHG 7

(to) bring together *(irr)* /ˌbrɪŋ təˈɡeðə/ zusammenbringen p. 25, 7

Britain /ˈbrɪtn/ Großbritannien NHG 6

British /ˈbrɪtɪʃ/ britisch NHG 6

brochure /ˈbrəʊʃə/ Broschüre NHG 7

broken /ˈbrəʊkən/ gebrochen; zerbrochen; kaputt NHG 7

brother /ˈbrʌðə/ Bruder NHG 5

brown /braʊn/ braun NHG 5

brownstone (house) /ˈbraʊnˌstəʊn haʊs/ *Haus aus rötlich braunem Sandstein* p. 24, 6

(to) **brush one's teeth** /ˌbrʌʃ wʌnz ˈtiːθ/ sich die Zähne putzen NHG 5

buffalo chips *(pl)* /ˈbʌfələʊ tʃɪps/ getrockneter Büffeldung p. 111, 7

(to) **build** *(irr)* /bɪld/ bauen NHG 5

(to) build a park *(irr)* /ˌbɪld_ə ˈpaːk/ einen Park anlegen p. 21, 2

building /ˈbɪldɪŋ/ Gebäude NHG 6

(to) **bully** /ˈbʊli/ mobben p. 69, 2

bully /ˈbʊli/ *Person, die mobbt* p. 69, 2

bus stop /ˈbʌs_stɒp/ Bushaltestelle p. 38, 6

business /ˈbɪznəs/ Geschäft; Handel p. 40, 7

business law /ˈbɪznəs lɔː/ Wirtschaftsrecht p. 40, 7

busy /ˈbɪzi/ beschäftigt NHG 5; bewegt, ereignisreich; belebt; verkehrsreich NHG 6

but /bʌt/ aber NHG 5; außer NHG 6

(to) **buy** *(irr)* /baɪ/ kaufen NHG 5

by /baɪ/ von; mit NHG 5; bei, an; *hier:* (spätestens) bis NHG 6

by *(+ Verbform mit -ing)* /baɪ/ indem NHG 6

by accident /ˌbaɪ_ˈæksɪdnt/ zufällig; aus Versehen NHG 7

by heart /ˌbaɪ ˈhaːt/ auswendig NHG 7

by then /ˌbaɪ ˈðen/ bis dahin p. 107, 2

bye /baɪ/ tschüs(s) NHG 5

C

cabin /ˈkæbɪn/ Kabine p. 106, 2

cage /keɪdʒ/ Käfig NHG 5

cake /keɪk/ Kuchen NHG 5

calculator /ˈkælkjʊˌleɪtə/ Taschenrechner NHG 5

calendar /ˈkælɪndə/ Kalender NHG 5

calf *(pl* calves*)* /kaːf, kaːv/ Junges p. 144

California /ˌkæləˈfɔːniə/ Kalifornien p. 10, 2

California Institute of the Arts /ˌkæləˌfɔːniəˌɪnstɪˌtjuːt_əv ðiˈaːts/ *private Kunsthochschule in Kalifornien* p. 82, 2

Californian /ˌkæləˈfɔːniən/ kalifornisch p. 86, 6

call /kɔːl/ Anruf; Gespräch NHG 7

(to) **call** /kɔːl/ anrufen NHG 6; nennen p. 37, 5

(to) **call an ambulance** /ˌkɔːl_ən_ˈæmbjʊləns/ einen Krankenwagen rufen NHG 7

call of freedom /ˌkɔːl_əv_ˈfriːdəm/ Ruf der Freiheit p. 122, 7

(to) be called /ˌbiː ˈkɔːld/ heißen, genannt werden NHG 5

calm /ˈkaːm/ ruhig; friedlich p. 21, 2

(to) **calm down** /ˌkaːm ˈdaʊn/ (sich) beruhigen NHG 7

camera /ˈkæmrə/ Kamera; Fotoapparat NHG 6

camp /kæmp/ (Zelt)lager NHG 6

(to) make camp *(irr)* /ˌmeɪk_ˈkæmp/ das Lager aufschlagen p. 111, 7

campaign /kæmˈpeɪn/ Kampagne p. 87, 6

campus /ˈkæmpəs/ Universität; Campus p. 120, 6

can /kæn/ können NHG 5

can /kæn/ Dose; Büchse NHG 7

can't (= cannot) /kaːnt, ˈkænɒt/ nicht können NHG 5

Canada /ˈkænədə/ Kanada p. 14, 7

candle /ˈkændl/ Kerze NHG 5

canyon /ˈkænjən/ Schlucht p. 13, 6

cap /kæp/ Mütze NHG 6

capital /ˈkæpɪtl/ Hauptstadt p. 6

capital letter /ˌkæpɪtl ˈletə/ Großbuchstabe p. 73, 6

caption /ˈkæpʃn/ Bildunterschrift NHG 7

car /kaː/ Auto NHG 5

car *(AE)* /kaː/ Waggon; Wagen p. 25, 7

car boot /ˈkaː ˌbuːt/ Kofferraum p. 48, 7

car boot sale /ˌkaː ˈbuːt seɪl/ *Kofferraum-Flohmarkt* NHG 7

car park /ˈkaː paːk/ Parkplatz p. 48, 7

card /kaːd/ Karte NHG 5

(to) care about /ˈkeər_əˌbaʊt/ sich aus etwas etwas machen p. 87, 6

(to) **take care (of)** *(irr)* /ˌteɪk ˈkeər_əv/ sich kümmern um NHG 6

career /kəˈrɪə/ Karriere; Laufbahn p. 44, 2

careful /ˈkeəfl/ vorsichtig NHG 6

carefully /ˈkeəfli/ vorsichtig NHG 6; gründlich p. 73, 6

(to) listen carefully /ˌlɪsn ˈkeəfli/ aufmerksam zuhören p. 96, 8

carelessly /ˈkeələsli/ unvorsichtig, gedankenlos p. 73, 6

the Caribbean /ðə ˌkærɪˈbiən/ Karibik, karibische Inseln p. 14, 7

caring /ˈkeərɪŋ/ Kümmern p. 151

carnival /ˈkaːnɪvl/ Volksfest; Karneval p. 49, 7

carpet /ˈkaːpɪt/ Teppich p. 148

carrot /ˈkærət/ Möhre; Karotte NHG 5

(to) **carry** /ˈkæri/ tragen p. 39, 6

(to) **carry out** /ˌkæriˈaʊt/ durchführen, betreiben p. 92, 2

case /keɪs/ Fall NHG 6

cash /kæʃ/ Geld; Bargeld NHG 7

cash register (AE) /ˈkæʃ ˌredʒɪstə/ Kasse p. 97, 9

cast /kɑːst/ Gips NHG 7

cast /kɑːst/ Besetzung p. 149

castle /ˈkɑːsl/ Burg; Schloss NHG 6

cat /kæt/ Katze NHG 5

(to) **catch** (irr) /kætʃ/ fangen NHG 5

(to) **catch a cold** (irr) /ˌkætʃ ə ˈkəʊld/ sich erkälten NHG 7

catcher /ˈkætʃə/ Fänger/in p. 44, 2

category /ˈkætəgri/ Kategorie NHG 6

(to) **cause** /kɔːz/ verursachen p. 86, 6

'cause (= because) /kɔːz, bɪˈkɒz/ weil, da p. 25, 7

cave /keɪv/ Höhle p. 132

ceiling /ˈsiːlɪŋ/ Zimmerdecke p. 65, 12

(to) **celebrate** /ˈseləˌbreɪt/ feiern NHG 6

celebration /ˌseləˈbreɪʃn/ Feier NHG 6

cell phone (AE) /ˈsel fəʊn/ Handy p. 68, 2

center (AE) /ˈsentə/ Zentrum p. 28, 14

centre /ˈsentə/ Zentrum NHG 6

shopping centre /ˈʃɒpɪŋ ˌsentə/ Einkaufszentrum NHG 5

century /ˈsentʃəri/ Jahrhundert NHG 6

cereal /ˈsɪəriəl/ Frühstücksflocken p. 38, 6

certainly /ˈsɜːtnli/ sicher; gerne NHG 7

certification /ˌsɜːtɪfɪˈkeɪʃn/ Qualifizierung; Zertifikat p. 93, 2

chain /tʃeɪn/ Kette NHG 6

chair /tʃeə/ Stuhl NHG 5

challenge /ˈtʃæləndʒ/ Herausforderung NHG 5

championship /ˈtʃæmpiənʃɪp/ Meisterschaft p. 34, 2

chance /tʃɑːns/ Möglichkeit; Gelegenheit NHG 7

change /tʃeɪndʒ/ Wechselgeld NHG 5; Veränderung; Wechsel p. 85, 5

(to) **change** /tʃeɪndʒ/ (sich) ändern; verändern NHG 6

(to) **change lines** /ˌtʃeɪndʒ ˈlaɪnz/ umsteigen NHG 6

(to) **change one's mind** /ˌtʃeɪndʒ wʌnz ˈmaɪnd/ seine Meinung ändern NHG 6

changemaker /ˈtʃeɪndʒ ˌmeɪkə/ *jemand, der sich aktiv bemüht, Dinge zu verändern* p. 87, 6

channel /ˈtʃænl/ Kanal p. 68, 1

chant /tʃɑːnt/ Sprechgesang p. 49, 7

character /ˈkærəktə/ Figur; Charakter NHG 6; Wesen p. 25, 7; Zeichen; Schriftzeichen p. 71, 5

charity /ˈtʃærəti/ Wohltätigkeitsorganisation NHG 7

charity run /ˈtʃærəti rʌn/ Wohltätigkeitslauf p. 88, 8

charming /ˈtʃɑːmɪŋ/ charmant p. 13, 6

(to) **chat** /tʃæt/ plaudern; chatten NHG 7

cheap /tʃiːp/ billig NHG 7

check /tʃek/ Überprüfung; Kontrolle NHG 7

(to) **check** /tʃek/ überprüfen; kontrollieren NHG 5

(to) **check out** /ˌtʃek ˈaʊt/ auschecken p. 29, 15

(to) **check out** (informal) /ˌtʃek ˈaʊt/ sich ansehen; ausprobieren NHG 7

cheer basics (pl) /ˈtʃɪə ˌbeɪsɪks/ *Grundkenntnisse beim Cheerleading* p. 35, 2

(to) cheer for /ˈtʃɪə fə/ anfeuern p. 35, 2

cheerful /ˈtʃɪəfl/ fröhlich, vergnügt NHG 7

cheese /tʃiːz/ Käse NHG 5

chemical /ˈkemɪkl/ Chemikalie p. 86, 6

chemistry /ˈkemɪstri/ Chemie p. 45, 2

chess /tʃes/ Schach NHG 7

chicken /ˈtʃɪkɪn/ Huhn NHG 6

child (pl **children**) /tʃaɪld, ˈtʃɪldrən/ Kind NHG 5

(to) **chill** (informal) /tʃɪl/ relaxen, chillen p. 140

chilli (pl chillies) /ˈtʃɪli, ˈtʃɪliz/ Chili; Peperoni p. 47, 6

Chinese /ˌtʃaɪˈniːz/ Chinese/Chinesin; chinesisch NHG 6

chips (pl) /tʃɪps/ Pommes frites NHG 5

chips (AE, pl) /tʃɪps/ Chips p. 48, 7

chocolate /ˈtʃɒklət/ Schokolade NHG 5

choice /tʃɔɪs/ Auswahl; Wahl p. 17, 10

(to) **choose** (irr) /tʃuːz/ wählen; sich entscheiden NHG 5

(to) **chop** /tʃɒp/ hacken NHG 7

chore /tʃɔː/ lästige Aufgabe; Hausarbeit NHG 5

choreographer /ˌkɒriˈɒgrəfə/ Choreograph/in p. 75, 10

Christian /ˈkrɪstʃən/ Christ/in; christlich NHG 6

Christmas /ˈkrɪsməs/ Weihnachten NHG 6

chronological /ˌkrɒnəˈlɒdʒɪkl/ chronologisch p. 15, 7

church /tʃɜːtʃ/ Kirche NHG 6

cinema /ˈsɪnəmə/ Kino NHG 5

circle /ˈsɜːkl/ Kreis; Runde p. 85, 5

citizen /ˈsɪtɪzn/ Bürger/in p. 89, 9

city /ˈsɪti/ Stadt; Innenstadt NHG 5

civil rights (pl) /ˌsɪvl ˈraɪts/ Bürgerrechte p. 15, 7

Civil War /ˌsɪvl ˈwɔː/ Bürgerkrieg p. 15, 7

(to) **claim** /kleɪm/ Anspruch erheben auf; behaupten p. 14, 7

clap /klæp/ Klatschen p. 49, 7

class /klɑːs/ Klasse; Unterrichtsstunde NHG 5

classmate /ˈklɑːsmeɪt/ Klassenkamerad/in; Mitschüler/in NHG 5

classroom /ˈklɑːsruːm/ Klassenzimmer NHG 5

clause /klɔːz/ Satzglied; Satzteil p. 46

clean /kliːn/ sauber NHG 5

(to) **clean (up)** /kliːn, ˌkliːn ˈʌp/ sauber machen NHG 5

clear /klɪə/ klar; deutlich NHG 6

clearly /ˈklɪəli/ klar; deutlich NHG 6

(to) **click on** /ˈklɪk ɒn/ anklicken NHG 7

climate /ˈklaɪmət/ Klima p. 10, 2

climate change /ˈklaɪmət tʃeɪndʒ/ Klimaveränderung; Klimawandel p. 83, 2

(to) **climb** /klaɪm/ auf etwas (hinauf)steigen; klettern NHG 5

clock /klɒk/ Uhr NHG 5

close /kləʊs/ nah(e); eng p. 59, 3

(to) **close** /kləʊz/ zumachen; schließen NHG 5

closed /kləʊzd/ geschlossen NHG 6

(to) take a closer look at (irr) /ˌteɪk ə ˌkləʊsə ˈlʊk ət/ sich genauer ansehen p. 148

clothes *(pl)* /kləʊðz/ Kleider;
Kleidung NHG 5

cloud /klaʊd/ Wolke p. 65, 12

club /klʌb/ AG; Klub NHG 5

CO_2 (= carbon dioxide) /ˌsiː ˌəʊ ˈtuː,
ˌkɑːbən daɪˈɒksaɪd/ Kohlendioxid
p. 85, 5

coach /kəʊtʃ/ Trainer/in NHG 7

coast /kəʊst/ Küste p. 14, 7

coffee /ˈkɒfi/ Kaffee NHG 5

cold /kəʊld/ kalt NHG 5; Erkältung
NHG 7

(to) **catch a cold** *(irr)* /ˌkætʃ_ə
ˈkəʊld/ sich erkälten NHG 7

(to) **collect** /kəˈlekt/ sammeln NHG 5

collection /kəˈlekʃn/ Sammlung
NHG 6

college /ˈkɒlɪdʒ/ College *(Bildungs-
einrichtung, die zu einem eher
praxisorientierten Bachelor-
Abschluss hinführt)* p. 35, 2

colonization /ˌkɒlənaɪˈzeɪʃn/
Kolonisierung p. 14, 7

colony /ˈkɒləni/ Kolonie p. 14, 7

color *(AE)* /ˈkʌlə/ Farbe p. 165

colour /ˈkʌlə/ Farbe NHG 5

colourful /ˈkʌləfl/ bunt NHG 7

combination /ˌkɒmbɪˈneɪʃn/ Kombi-
nation; Mischung NHG 6

(to) **combine** /kəmˈbaɪn/ verbinden
p. 90, 10

(to) **come** *(irr)* /kʌm/ kommen NHG 5

(to) **come back** *(irr)* /ˌkʌm ˈbæk/
zurückkommen NHG 5

(to) **come in** *(irr)* /ˌkʌm_ˈɪn/ herein-
kommen NHG 7

(to) come to mind *(irr)* /ˌkʌm tə
ˈmaɪnd/ einfallen, in den Sinn
kommen p. 25, 7

(to) **come second** *(irr)* /ˌkʌm ˈsekənd/
Zweite/r werden p. 34, 2

(to) **come up** *(irr)* /ˈkʌm_ʌp/ auf-
kommen p. 11, 2

(to) **come up with** *(irr)* /ˌkʌm_ˈʌp
wɪð/ sich einfallen lassen p. 43, 14

comedy /ˈkɒmədi/ Komödie p. 66, 13

comfortable /ˈkʌmftəbl/ bequem
NHG 7

(to) **feel comfortable** *(irr)* /ˌfiːl
ˈkʌmftəbl/ sich wohl fühlen p. 72, 6

command /kəˈmɑːnd/ Befehl NHG 5

reported command /ˌrɪ pɔːtɪd
kəˈmɑːnd/ indirekter Befehl p. 108

(to) **commemorate** /kəˈmeməreɪt/
(einer Person oder Sache) geden-
ken p. 16, 8

comment /ˈkɒment/ Kommentar;
Bemerkung p. 61, 7

(to) **comment on** /ˈkɒment_ɒn/
kommentieren NHG 6

commercial /kəˈmɜːʃl/ kommerziell,
profitorientiert NHG 6

commercial /kəˈmɜːʃl/ Werbespot
p. 41, 10

common /ˈkɒmən/ üblich; weit
verbreitet p. 62, 8

(to) **have in common** *(irr)* /ˌhæv_ɪn
ˈkɒmən/ gemeinsam haben NHG 6

communal /ˈkɒmjənl/ Gemein-
schafts- p. 150

(to) **communicate** /kəˈmjuːnɪkeɪt/
kommunizieren, sprechen NHG 7

communication /kəˌmjuːnɪˈkeɪʃn/
Verständigung; Kommunikation
NHG 7

community /kəˈmjuːnəti/ Gemein-
schaft; Gemeinde NHG 7

community college /kəˈmjuːnəti
ˌkɒlɪdʒ/ *subventioniertes
zweijähriges College* p. 82, 2

company /ˈkʌmpni/ Firma;
Unternehmen NHG 7

comparative /kəmˈpærətɪv/ Kompa-
rativ p. 70, 3

(to) **compare** /kəmˈpeə/ vergleichen
NHG 6

compared to /kəmˈpeəd_tʊ/ im
Vergleich zu p. 68, 2

comparison /kəmˈpærɪsn/ Vergleich
NHG 6

(to) **compete** /kəmˈpiːt/ an einem
Wettkampf teilnehmen; kämpfen
NHG 7

competition /ˌkɒmpəˈtɪʃn/ Wettbewerb NHG 5

(to) **complain (to)** /kəmˈpleɪn/ sich
beklagen (bei) p. 96, 8

complete /kəmˈpliːt/ vollständig,
komplett NHG 7

(to) **complete** /kəmˈpliːt/ vervoll-
ständigen NHG 5; fertigstellen
p. 28, 13

completely /kəmˈpliːtli/ völlig,
absolut NHG 6

complex /ˈkɒmpleks/ Komplex
p. 15, 7

complicated /ˈkɒmplɪˌkeɪtɪd/ kom-
pliziert p. 48, 7

composer /kəmˈpəʊzə/ Kompo-
nist/in p. 148

compromise /ˈkɒmprəmaɪz/ Kom-
promiss NHG 6

con /kɒn/ Nachteil; Kontra NHG 6

(to) **concentrate** /ˈkɒnsn̩ˌtreɪt/ sich
konzentrieren NHG 7

concept /ˈkɒnsept/ Entwurf;
Konzept NHG 6

concert /ˈkɒnsət/ Konzert NHG 6

condition /kənˈdɪʃn/ Bedingung;
Zustand p. 15, 7

conditional (clause) /kənˈdɪʃnəl
klɔːz/ Konditional; Konditional-
satz p. 46

conflict /ˈkɒnflɪkt/ Konflikt NHG 6

confusing /kənˈfjuːzɪŋ/ verwirrend
p. 48, 7

Congratulations! /kənˌɡrætʃʊˈleɪʃnz/
Glückwunsch!; Gratuliere! p. 34, 2

congress /ˈkɒŋɡres/ Kongress p. 44, 2

(to) **connect** /kəˈnekt/ verbinden
NHG 7

(to) **be connected (to)** *(irr)* /ˌbiː
kəˈnektɪd_tə/ verbunden sein (mit),
in Verbindung stehen (mit) p. 66, 14

(to) **get connected** *(irr)* /ˌɡet
kəˈnektɪd/ sich verbinden, in
Kontakt treten p. 72, 6

connection /kəˈnekʃn/ Verbindung
p. 68, 2

constantly /ˈkɒnstəntli/ ständig;
dauernd p. 69, 2

construction /kənˈstrʌkʃn/ Bau NHG 7

construction worker /kənˈstrʌkʃn
ˌwɜːkə/ Bauarbeiter/in p. 92, 1

(to) **contact** /ˈkɒntækt/ sich in
Verbindung setzen mit NHG 6

(to) **contain** /kənˈteɪn/ enthalten
NHG 7

content /ˈkɒntent/ Inhalt NHG 7

continent /ˈkɒntɪnənt/ Kontinent
p. 14, 7

(to) **continue** /kənˈtɪnjuː/ andauern,
weitergehen p. 35, 2

conversation /ˌkɒnvəˈseɪʃn/
Gespräch; Unterhaltung NHG 7

(to) **cook** /kʊk/ kochen NHG 5;
braten, backen NHG 6

cooking /ˈkʊkɪŋ/ Kochen; Koch-
NHG 5

(to) **do the cooking** (irr) /ˌduː ðə ˈkʊkɪŋ/ kochen NHG 5

cool /kuːl/ kühl; kalt NHG 7

(to) **copy** /ˈkɒpi/ abschreiben NHG 5; kopieren NHG 7

corner /ˈkɔːnə/ Ecke NHG 6

correct /kəˈrekt/ richtig, korrekt NHG 5

(to) **correct** /kəˈrekt/ korrigieren NHG 5

(to) **cost** (irr) /kɒst/ kosten NHG 5

costume /ˈkɒstjuːm/ Kostüm NHG 6

cough /kɒf/ Husten NHG 7

could /kʊd/ könnte(st, n, t) NHG 5; Vergangenheitsform von can NHG 6

counselor (AE) = counsellor (BE) /ˈkaʊnslə/ hier: Betreuer/in p. 98, 10

(to) **count** /kaʊnt/ zählen NHG 7

country /ˈkʌntri/ Land NHG 6

country music /ˈkʌntri ˌmjuːzɪk/ Countrymusik p. 11, 2

countryside /ˈkʌntriˌsaɪd/ Land; Landschaft NHG 6

county /ˈkaʊnti/ (Verwaltungs)bezirk; Grafschaft p. 116, 1

a couple of /ə ˈkʌplˌəv/ einige, ein paar NHG 6

course /kɔːs/ Kurs NHG 6

(to) **take a course** (irr) /ˌteɪk ə ˈkɔːs/ einen Kurs machen p. 95, 7

court /kɔːt/ Platz NHG 5

cousin /ˈkʌzn/ Cousin/e NHG 5

(to) **cover** /ˈkʌvə/ bedecken NHG 6

(to) cover /ˈkʌvə/ abdecken; sich befassen mit p. 42, 13

cow /kaʊ/ Kuh NHG 6

coyote /kaɪˈəʊti/ Kojote p. 111, 7

crack /kræk/ Riss p. 65, 12

(to) **create** /kriˈeɪt/ erschaffen; erzeugen NHG 5

creative /kriˈeɪtɪv/ kreativ NHG 5

credit /ˈkredɪt/ Schein; Leistungsnachweis p. 40, 7

crime rate /ˈkraɪm reɪt/ Kriminalitätsrate p. 24, 6

crisis (pl **crises**) /ˈkraɪsɪs, ˈkraɪsiːz/ Krise p. 85, 5

crisps (pl) /krɪsps/ Chips p. 48, 7

critically /ˈkrɪtɪkli/ kritisch p. 89, 9

(to) **cross** /krɒs/ überqueren NHG 6

crowd /kraʊd/ Menschenmenge NHG 7

crowded /ˈkraʊdɪd/ überfüllt NHG 7

crown /kraʊn/ Krone p. 20, 2

(to) crown /kraʊn/ krönen p. 34, 2

(to) **cry** /kraɪ/ weinen; schreien NHG 6

cue card /ˈkjuː kɑːd/ Stichwortkarte NHG 6

culinary art /ˌkʌlɪnri ˈɑːt/ Kochkunst p. 41, 8

cultural, culturally /ˈkʌltʃərəl, ˈkʌltʃərəli/ kulturell p. 24, 6

culture /ˈkʌltʃə/ Kultur NHG 6

cup /kʌp/ Tasse NHG 5

cupboard /ˈkʌbəd/ Schrank NHG 7

curious /ˈkjʊəriəs/ neugierig p. 28, 13

current /ˈkʌrənt/ gegenwärtig; aktuell p. 98, 10

curry /ˈkʌri/ Curry(gericht) NHG 7

customer /ˈkʌstəmə/ Kunde/Kundin NHG 6

(to) **cut** (irr) /kʌt/ schneiden NHG 6

(to) cut down (irr) /ˌkʌt ˈdaʊn/ abholzen, fällen p. 93, 2

cyberbullying /ˈsaɪbəˌbʊliɪŋ/ Cybermobbing p. 69, 2

(to) **cycle** /ˈsaɪkl/ Rad fahren NHG 6

(to) **go cycling** (irr) /ˌgəʊ ˈsaɪklɪŋ/ Rad fahren gehen NHG 6

D

dad /dæd/ Papa; Vati NHG 5

daily /ˈdeɪli/ täglich NHG 5

damage /ˈdæmɪdʒ/ Schaden p. 86, 6

dance /dɑːns/ Tanz NHG 7

(to) **dance** /dɑːns/ tanzen NHG 5

dancer /ˈdɑːnsə/ Tänzer/in NHG 6

dancing /ˈdɑːnsɪŋ/ Tanzen NHG 5

danger /ˈdeɪndʒə/ Gefahr NHG 6

dangerous /ˈdeɪndʒərəs/ gefährlich NHG 6

dark /dɑːk/ Dunkelheit; dunkel NHG 6

darkness /ˈdɑːknəs/ Dunkelheit NHG 6

(to) dart /dɑːt/ flitzen, sausen p. 122, 7

date /deɪt/ Datum NHG 5

(to) **ask on a date** /ˌɑːsk ɒn ə ˈdeɪt/ um eine Verabredung bitten p. 66, 13

(to) **date back** /ˌdeɪt ˈbæk/ zurückgehen auf, stammen aus p. 120, 6

daughter /ˈdɔːtə/ Tochter NHG 5

day /deɪ/ Tag NHG 5

some day /ˈsʌmˌdeɪ/ eines Tages NHG 7

all day long /ˌɔːl deɪ ˈlɒŋ/ den ganzen Tag lang p. 21, 2

day out /ˌdeɪ ˈaʊt/ Ausflugstag NHG 6

(to) **deal with** (irr) /ˈdiːl wɪð/ sich befassen mit; umgehen mit NHG 7

dear /dɪə/ liebe/r (Anrede) NHG 5

death /deθ/ Tod p. 71, 5

debate /dɪˈbeɪt/ Debatte; Diskussion p. 44, 2

(to) **debate** /dɪˈbeɪt/ diskutieren, debattieren p. 44, 2

debating society /dɪˈbeɪtɪŋ səˌsaɪəti/ Debattiergesellschaft p. 44, 2

December /dɪˈsembə/ Dezember NHG 5

(to) **decide** /dɪˈsaɪd/ entscheiden; sich entscheiden NHG 5

(to) **declare** /dɪˈkleə/ verkünden; erklären p. 14, 7

(to) **decorate** /ˈdekəreɪt/ schmücken; dekorieren NHG 5

decoration /ˌdekəˈreɪʃn/ Dekoration; Schmuck NHG 6

(to) **decrease** /diːˈkriːs/ abnehmen, zurückgehen p. 109, 5

decrease /ˈdiːkriːs/ Rückgang p. 171

(to) dedicate /ˈdedɪkeɪt/ widmen p. 25, 7

deed /diːd/ Tat p. 71, 5

deer (pl deer) /dɪə, dɪə/ Hirsch; Reh p. 111, 7

definitely /ˈdefnətli/ eindeutig, definitiv NHG 6

(to) **delete** /dɪˈliːt/ löschen NHG 7

delicious /dɪˈlɪʃəs/ köstlich, lecker NHG 6

democracy /dɪˈmɒkrəsi/ Demokratie p. 17, 10

demonstration /ˌdemənˈstreɪʃn/ Vorführung; Demonstration p. 35, 2

dentist /ˈdentɪst/ Zahnarzt/Zahnärztin NHG 7

(to) **depend on** /dɪˈpend ɒn/ abhängen von NHG 6

depressed /dɪˈprest/ deprimiert p. 58, 2

(to) **describe** /dɪˈskraɪb/ beschreiben NHG 5

description /dɪˈskrɪpʃn/ Beschreibung NHG 6

desert /ˈdezət/ Wüste p. 8

design /dɪˈzaɪn/ Entwurf; Design NHG 6

(to) **design** /dɪˈzaɪn/ entwerfen NHG 5

desk /desk/ Schreibtisch NHG 5

desperate /ˈdesprət/ verzweifelt p. 106, 2

dessert /dɪˈzɜːt/ Nachtisch NHG 7

destination /ˌdestɪˈneɪʃn/ Ziel; Reiseziel p. 13, 6

(to) **destroy** /dɪˈstrɔɪ/ zerstören NHG 6

detail /ˈdiːteɪl/ Detail; Einzelheit NHG 5

detailed /ˈdiːteɪld/ detailliert, genau p. 149

(to) **develop** /dɪˈveləp/ erarbeiten; (sich) entwickeln p. 10, 2

development /dɪˈveləpmənt/ Entwicklung NHG 7

device /dɪˈvaɪs/ Gerät; Apparat p. 42, 12

dialogue /ˈdaɪəlɒg/ Gespräch; Dialog NHG 5

diamond cutter /ˈdaɪəmənd ˌkʌtə/ Diamantschleifer/in p. 99, 13

diary /ˈdaɪəri/ Tagebuch NHG 6

diary entry /ˈdaɪəriˌentri/ Tagebucheintrag NHG 6

dictionary /ˈdɪkʃənri/ Lexikon; Wörterbuch NHG 6

(to) **die** /daɪ/ sterben NHG 7

difference /ˈdɪfrəns/ Unterschied p. 37, 5

(to) **make a difference** (irr) /ˌmeɪk_ə ˈdɪfrəns/ einen Unterschied machen; verändern p. 85, 5

different /ˈdɪfrənt/ anders; andere(r, s); verschiedene(r, s) NHG 5

difficult /ˈdɪfɪklt/ schwierig; schwer NHG 6

dinner /ˈdɪnə/ Abendessen NHG 5

direct /daɪˈrekt/ direkt p. 85, 5

directions (pl) /daɪˈrekʃnz/ hier: Wegbeschreibungen NHG 6

(to) **give directions** (irr) /ˌgɪv daɪˈrekʃnz/ den Weg beschreiben NHG 6

director /dəˈrektə/ Regisseur/in p. 82, 2

dirty /ˈdɜːti/ dreckig; schmutzig NHG 5

disability /ˌdɪsəˈbɪləti/ Behinderung; Einschränkung p. 83, 2

disadvantage /ˌdɪsədˈvɑːntɪdʒ/ Nachteil p. 72, 6

(to) **disagree** /ˌdɪsəˈgriː/ nicht zustimmen p. 17, 10

(to) **disappear** /ˌdɪsəˈpɪə/ verschwinden NHG 6

disappointed /ˌdɪsəˈpɔɪntɪd/ enttäuscht NHG 6

disappointing /ˌdɪsəˈpɔɪntɪŋ/ enttäuschend NHG 7

discomfort /dɪsˈkʌmfət/ Unbehagen p. 65, 12

(to) **discover** /dɪˈskʌvə/ entdecken NHG 6

discovery /dɪˈskʌvri/ Entdeckung NHG 7

(to) **discuss** /dɪˈskʌs/ besprechen; diskutieren NHG 6

discussion /dɪˈskʌʃn/ Diskussion NHG 6

disease /dɪˈziːz/ Krankheit p. 14, 7

disgusting /dɪsˈgʌstɪŋ/ widerlich NHG 7

dish (pl dishes) /dɪʃ, ˈdɪʃɪz/ Gericht; Speise NHG 7

dishwasher /ˈdɪʃˌwɒʃə/ Spülmaschine NHG 5

(to) **dislike** /dɪsˈlaɪk/ nicht mögen p. 64, 11

display /dɪˈspleɪ/ Auslage; Ausstellung NHG 7

(to) **display** /dɪˈspleɪ/ aushängen; zeigen NHG 5

(to) **put on display** (irr) /ˌpʊt_ɒn dɪˈspleɪ/ ausstellen NHG 6

distance /ˈdɪstəns/ Entfernung p. 171

(to) **dive** /daɪv/ tauchen NHG 7

diverse /daɪˈvɜːs/ vielfältig, unterschiedlich p. 11, 2

diversity /daɪˈvɜːsəti/ Vielfalt p. 25, 7

diving /ˈdaɪvɪŋ/ Tauchen NHG 7

(to) **do** (irr) /duː/ tun; machen NHG 5

(to) **do athletics** (irr) /ˌduː_æθˈletɪks/ Leichtathletik machen NHG 5

(to) **do for a living** (irr) /ˌduː fər_ə ˈlɪvɪŋ/ seinen Lebensunterhalt verdienen p. 92, 2

(to) **do gymnastics** (irr) /ˌduː dʒɪmˈnæstɪks/ turnen NHG 5

(to) **do one's best** (irr) /ˌduː wʌnz ˈbest/ sein Bestes geben p. 48, 7

(to) **do research** (irr) /ˌduː rɪˈsɜːtʃ/ recherchieren NHG 5

(to) **do sports** (irr) /ˌduː ˈspɔːts/ Sport treiben NHG 6

(to) **do the cooking** (irr) /ˌduː ðə ˈkʊkɪŋ/ kochen NHG 5

(to) **do the shopping** (irr) /ˌduː ðə ˈʃɒpɪŋ/ einkaufen NHG 5

(to) do well (irr) /ˌduː ˈwel/ erfolgreich sein p. 25, 7

the docklands (pl) /ðə ˈdɒkləndz/ Hafenviertel p. 116, 1

doctor /ˈdɒktə/ Arzt/Ärztin NHG 7

(to) **see a doctor** (irr) /ˌsiː_ə ˈdɒktə/ einen Arzt/eine Ärztin aufsuchen NHG 7

at the doctor's /ˌæt_ðə ˈdɒktəz/ beim Arzt/bei der Ärztin NHG 7

document /ˈdɒkjʊmənt/ Dokument NHG 7

dog /dɒg/ Hund NHG 5

(to) take a dog for a walk (irr) /ˌteɪk_ə ˌdɒg fər_ə ˈwɔːk/ mit einem Hund Gassi gehen p. 141

dog sled /ˈdɒg sled/ Hundeschlitten p. 8

dog walking /ˈdɒg ˌwɔːkɪŋ/ Ausführen von Hunden p. 97, 9

dogsitter /ˈdɒgsɪtə/ Hundesitter/in p. 132

I'm doing OK. (informal) /ˌaɪm ˌduːɪŋ_əʊˈkeɪ/ Es läuft ganz gut. p. 40, 7

dolphin /ˈdɒlfɪn/ Delfin p. 119, 5

door /dɔː/ Tür NHG 6

dos and don'ts /ˌduːz_ən ˈdəʊnts/ was man tun und was man nicht tun sollte NHG 7

double /ˈdʌbl/ doppelt, Doppel- NHG 5

dove /dʌv/ Taube p. 82, 2

down /daʊn/ hinunter; (nach) unten NHG 6

(to) **download** /ˌdaʊnˈləʊd/ herunterladen NHG 7

downtown (AE) /ˌdaʊnˈtaʊn/ in der Innenstadt; im Zentrum p. 24, 6

Dr (= Doctor) /ˈdɒktə/ Dr. (= Doktor) NHG 6

draft /drɑːft/ Entwurf NHG 6

(to) **drag** /dræg/ ziehen, schleifen p. 93, 2

dragon /ˈdrægən/ Drache NHG 6

drama /ˈdrɑːmə/ Theater-; Schauspiel- NHG 6

dramatic /drəˈmætɪk/ dramatisch NHG 7

(to) **draw** *(irr)* /drɔː/ zeichnen NHG 5

(to) **draw attention to** *(irr)* /ˌdrɔːˈrəˈtenʃn tə/ Aufmerksamkeit lenken auf NHG 7

drawing /ˈdrɔːɪŋ/ Zeichnung NHG 6

dream /driːm/ Traum NHG 5

(to) **dream** *(irr)* /driːm/ träumen p. 36, 4

dress /dres/ Kleid; Kleidung NHG 7

(to) **dress** /dres/ sich anziehen; sich kleiden NHG 7

dress code /ˈdres kəʊd/ Bekleidungsvorschriften p. 37, 5

drink /drɪŋk/ Trinken; Getränk NHG 5

(to) **drink** *(irr)* /drɪŋk/ trinken NHG 5

(to) **drive** *(irr)* /draɪv/ fahren NHG 6

(to) drop out /ˌdrɒpˈraʊt/ abbrechen p. 45, 2

drove /drəʊv/ Herde p. 25, 7

dry /draɪ/ trocken NHG 6

due /djuː/ fällig p. 96, 8

due to /ˈdjuː tuː/ wegen p. 26, 8

during /ˈdjʊərɪŋ/ während NHG 6

E

each /iːtʃ/ jede(r, s) NHG 5; je(weils) p. 94, 6

each other /ˌiːtʃˈrʌðə/ einander NHG 5

ear /ɪə/ Ohr NHG 5

earlier /ˈɜːliə/ vorhin, früher NHG 6

early /ˈɜːli/ früh NHG 6

(to) **earn** /ɜːn/ verdienen NHG 6

earth /ɜːθ/ Erde NHG 6

easily /ˈiːzɪli/ leicht; mühelos p. 68, 2

east /iːst/ Osten p. 10, 2; östlich, Ost- p. 14, 7

Easter /ˈiːstə/ Ostern NHG 6

easy /ˈiːzi/ leicht; einfach NHG 5

(to) **eat** *(irr)* /iːt/ essen NHG 5

(to) **eat out** *(irr)* /ˌiːtˈraʊt/ auswärts essen; im Restaurant essen NHG 7

eating /ˈiːtɪŋ/ Essen p. 11, 2

eating habit /ˈiːtɪŋ ˌhæbɪt/ Essgewohnheit p. 11, 2

ecological /ˌiːkəˈlɒdʒɪkl/ ökologisch p. 93, 2

ecological footprint /ˌiːkəˌlɒdʒɪkl ˈfʊtprɪnt/ ökologischer Fußabdruck p. 85, 5

economic /ˌiːkəˈnɒmɪk/ wirtschaftlich p. 14, 7

economy /ɪˈkɒnəmi/ Wirtschaft p. 19, 13

ecosystem /ˈiːkəʊˌsɪstəm/ Ökosystem p. 11, 2

edge /edʒ/ Rand p. 13, 6

edible /ˈedɪbəl/ essbar; genießbar p. 151

(to) **edit** /ˈedɪt/ bearbeiten NHG 5

education /ˌedjʊˈkeɪʃn/ Bildung; Ausbildung; Erziehung p. 17, 10

egg /eg/ Ei NHG 5

not ... **either** /ˌnɒtˈraɪðə/ auch nicht NHG 7

either ... or ... /ˌaɪðə ˈɔː/ entweder ... oder ... NHG 6

elective /ɪˈlektɪv/ Wahlpflichtfach p. 39, 6

electric /ɪˈlektrɪk/ elektrisch; Elektro- NHG 7; elektrisierend, spannungsgeladen p. 25, 7

electrically /ɪˈlektrɪkli/ elektrisch p. 147

electrician /ɪˌlekˈtrɪʃn/ Elektriker/in p. 92, 1

electricity /ɪˌlekˈtrɪsəti/ Elektrizität; Strom NHG 7

electronic /ˌelekˈtrɒnɪk/ elektronisch p. 26, 8

elementary school *(AE)* /elɪˈmentri skuːl/ Grundschule p. 45, 2

elephant /ˈelɪfənt/ Elefant p. 65, 12

else /els/ anders; sonst NHG 5

emergency /ɪˈmɜːdʒnsi/ Notfall NHG 7

(to) **emigrate** /ˈemɪgreɪt/ auswandern NHG 7

emigration /ˌemɪˈgreɪʃn/ Auswanderung; Emigration p. 108, 4

emotion /ɪˈməʊʃn/ Gefühl; Emotion p. 71, 5

employer /ɪmˈplɔɪə/ Arbeitgeber/in p. 95, 7

empty /ˈempti/ leer p. 65, 12

(to) **empty** /ˈempti/ ausleeren; ausräumen NHG 5

(to) **encounter** /ɪnˈkaʊntə/ treffen; begegnen p. 89, 9

(to) **encourage** /ɪnˈkʌrɪdʒ/ ermutigen p. 87, 6

end /end/ Ende; Schluss NHG 5

(to) **end** /end/ (be)enden NHG 6

in the end /ˌɪn ðiˈrend/ am Ende, schließlich NHG 6

(to) **end up** /ˌendˈrʌp/ schließlich landen p. 86, 6

ending /ˈendɪŋ/ Ende; Schluss NHG 6

endless /ˈendləs/ endlos p. 13, 6

energy /ˈenədʒi/ Energie; Kraft p. 35, 2

engaged /ɪnˈgeɪdʒd/ beschäftigt; *hier:* engagiert p. 89, 9

engine /ˈendʒɪn/ Maschine; Motor NHG 7

engineer /ˌendʒɪˈnɪə/ Ingenieur/in NHG 6

English /ˈɪŋglɪʃ/ Englisch; englisch NHG 5

(to) **enjoy** /ɪnˈdʒɔɪ/ genießen NHG 5

(to) **enjoy oneself** /ɪnˈdʒɔɪ wʌnˌself/ sich amüsieren p. 48, 7

enough /ɪˈnʌf/ genug NHG 5

(to) **enter** /ˈentə/ eingeben; betreten NHG 6; eintreten in p. 15, 7

entertainment /ˌentəˈteɪnmənt/ Unterhaltung NHG 6

entrance /ˈentrəns/ Eingang; Eintritt NHG 6

entry /ˈentri/ Eintritt NHG 6; Eintrag p. 17, 10

diary entry /ˈdaɪəriˌentri/ Tagebucheintrag NHG 6

environment /ɪnˈvaɪrənmənt/ Umwelt; Umgebung NHG 6

environmentally friendly /ɪnˌvaɪrənmentli ˈfrendli/ umweltfreundlich p. 88, 7

epic *(informal)* /ˈepɪk/ super, klasse p. 123, 8

equal /ˈiːkwəl/ gleich p. 6

equality /ɪˈkwɒləti/ Gleichberechtigung; Gleichheit p. 17, 10

equipment /ɪˈkwɪpmənt/ Ausrüstung; Ausstattung NHG 5

era /ˈɪərə/ Epoche; Zeitalter p. 13, 6

eraser /ɪˈreɪzə/ Radiergummi NHG 5

(to) **escape** /ɪˈskeɪp/ fliehen; entkommen NHG 5

especially /ɪˈspeʃli/ besonders; vor allem NHG 6

essential /ɪˈsenʃl/ unbedingt erforderlich; unverzichtbar p. 27, 10

(to) **establish** /ɪˈstæblɪʃ/ gründen; einführen p. 11, 2

estimated /'estɪmeɪtəd/ geschätzt
p. 87, 6

Europe /'jʊərəp/ Europa NHG 6

European /ˌjʊərə'piːən/ Europäer/in;
europäisch p. 7

European Union /ˌjʊərəˌpiːən
'juːniən/ Europäische Union
p. 124, 11

even /'iːvn/ selbst; sogar NHG 5

evening /'iːvnɪŋ/ Abend NHG 5

evening dress /'iːvnɪŋ dres/ Abendgarderobe p. 41, 10

event /ɪ'vent/ Ereignis; Veranstal-
tung NHG 5

eventually /ɪ'ventʃuəli/ schließlich;
irgendwann p. 86, 6

ever /'evə/ jemals NHG 6

every /'evri/ jede(r, s) NHG 5

everybody /'evriˌbɒdi/ alle; jeder
NHG 5

everyday /'evriˌdeɪ/ alltäglich,
Alltags- NHG 6

everyone /'evriwʌn/ alle; jeder
NHG 5

everything /'evriθɪŋ/ alles NHG 5

everywhere /'evriweə/ überall NHG 5

exactly /ɪg'zækli/ genau NHG 6

(to) **examine** /ɪg'zæmɪn/ untersuchen NHG 7

example /ɪg'zɑːmpl/ Beispiel NHG 5

for example /fər_ɪg'zɑːmpl/ zum
Beispiel NHG 5

excellent /'eksələnt/ ausgezeichnet
NHG 5

except /ɪk'sept/ außer NHG 6

excerpt /'eksɜːpt/ Auszug; Exzerpt
p. 89, 9

exchange /ɪks'tʃeɪndʒ/ Austausch;
Austausch- p. 34, 2

exchange student /ɪks'tʃeɪndʒ
ˌstjuːdnt/ Austauschschüler/in
NHG 7

excited /ɪk'saɪtɪd/ aufgeregt NHG 6

exciting /ɪk'saɪtɪŋ/ aufregend NHG 5

exclamation point (AE) /ˌeksklə'meɪʃn
pɔɪnt/ Ausrufezeichen p. 73, 6

Excuse me! /ɪk'skjuːz ˌmi/ Entschuldigung! NHG 5

exercise /'eksəsaɪz/ Übung NHG 6

exercise book /'eksəsaɪz ˌbʊk/ Heft
NHG 5

exhausting /ɪg'zɔːstɪŋ/ anstrengend
NHG 7

exhibition /ˌeksɪ'bɪʃn/ Ausstellung
NHG 6

(to) **exist** /ɪg'zɪst/ existieren NHG 6

(to) **expect** /ɪk'spekt/ erwarten
NHG 6

expectation /ˌekspek'teɪʃn/ Erwartung p. 72, 6

(to) **expel** /ɪk'spel/ von der Schule
verweisen p. 69, 2

expensive /ɪk'spensɪv/ teuer NHG 6

experience /ɪk'spɪəriəns/ Erfahrung
NHG 5

(to) **experience** /ɪk'spɪəriəns/ erle-
ben, kennenlernen p. 13, 6

experiment /ɪk'sperɪmənt/ Experiment; Versuch NHG 5

expert /'ekspɜːt/ Experte/Expertin
NHG 6

(to) **explain** /ɪk'spleɪn/ erklären
NHG 5

(to) **explore** /ɪk'splɔː/ erforschen;
untersuchen NHG 6

(to) **express** /ɪk'spres/ ausdrücken
NHG 6

expression /ɪk'spreʃn/ Ausdruck
p. 90, 10

(to) **extend** /ɪk'stend/ sich
erstrecken p. 10, 2

extra /'ekstrə/ zusätzlich NHG 5

extract /'ekstrækt/ Auszug; Exzerpt
p. 25, 7

extremely /ɪk'striːmli/ äußerst,
höchst; außerordentlich NHG 7

eye /aɪ/ Auge NHG 5

F

face /feɪs/ Gesicht NHG 5

face-to-face /ˌfeɪs tə 'feɪs/ persönlich p. 69, 2

fact /fækt/ Tatsache; Fakt NHG 5

in fact /ɪn 'fækt/ tatsächlich; in
Wirklichkeit p. 68, 2

fact file /'fækt faɪl/ Steckbrief NHG 5

factory /'fæktri/ Fabrik p. 10, 2

falcon /'fɔːlkən/ Falke p. 122, 7

fall (AE) /fɔːl/ Herbst p. 34, 2

(to) **fall** (irr) /fɔːl/ fallen NHG 7

(to) **fall asleep** (irr) /ˌfɔːl_ə'sliːp/
einschlafen p. 36, 4

(to) **fall in love** (irr) /ˌfɔːl ɪn 'lʌv/
sich verlieben p. 65, 12

(to) **fall off** (irr) /ˌfɔːl_'ɒf/ (herunter)
fallen NHG 7

false /fɔːls/ falsch NHG 5

familiar /fə'mɪliə/ vertraut, bekannt
p. 14, 7

family /'fæmli/ Familie NHG 5

famine /'fæmɪn/ Hungersnot p. 121, 6

famous /'feɪməs/ berühmt NHG 5

fan /fæn/ Ventilator p. 65, 12

fantastic /fæn'tæstɪk/ fantastisch;
super NHG 5

far /fɑː/ weit NHG 5

(to) be far from reach (irr) /ˌbi: ˌfɑː
frəm 'riːtʃ/ außer Reichweite sein
p. 68, 2

farm /fɑːm/ Bauernhof NHG 6

farmer /'fɑːmə/ Bauer/Bäuerin
p. 106, 2

farming /'fɑːmɪŋ/ Ackerbau;
Viehzucht p. 111, 7

farmland /'fɑːmˌlænd/ Ackerland p. 8

fascinating /'fæsɪneɪtɪŋ/ faszinie-
rend p. 20, 1

fashion /'fæʃn/ Mode NHG 6

fast /fɑːst/ schnell NHG 5

fat /fæt/ dick p. 65, 12

father /'fɑːðə/ Vater NHG 5

fault /fɔːlt/ Schuld; Fehler NHG 7

favorite (AE) /'feɪvrət/ Liebling;
Lieblings- p. 28, 14

favourite /'feɪvrət/ Liebling;
Lieblings- NHG 5

February /'februəri/ Februar NHG 5

fee /fiː/ Gebühr; Geld NHG 7

(to) **feed** (irr) /fiːd/ füttern NHG 6

feedback /'fiːdbæk/ Feedback;
Rückmeldung NHG 5

(to) **feel** (irr) /fiːl/ (sich) fühlen
NHG 6

(to) **feel comfortable** (irr) /ˌfiːl
'kʌmftəbl/ sich wohl fühlen p. 72, 6

(to) **feel uncomfortable** (irr)
/ˌfiːl_ʌn'kʌmftəbl/ sich unwohl
fühlen p. 38, 6

feeling /'fiːlɪŋ/ Gefühl NHG 6

felt-tip /'felt_tɪp/ Filzstift NHG 5

ferry /'feri/ Fähre p. 20, 2

festival /'festɪvl/ Fest; Festival
NHG 6

fever /'fiːvə/ Fieber NHG 7

a few /ə 'fjuː/ einige; wenige NHG 6

fewer /'fjuːə/ weniger (bei
zählbaren Nomen) p. 45, 2

fiddle /'fɪdl/ Geige p. 117, 2

field /fiːld/ Feld NHG 5

field of work /ˌfiːld‿əv ˈwɜːk/ Arbeits-bereich p. 15, 7

fight /faɪt/ Kampf; Streit NHG 7

(to) **fight** *(irr)* /faɪt/ bekämpfen; ankämpfen gegen NHG 6; kämpfen p. 6

fighting /ˈfaɪtɪŋ/ Kämpfe; Gefechte p. 15, 7

(to) **fill** /fɪl/ füllen NHG 6

(to) **fill in** /ˌfɪl‿ˈɪn/ eintragen, ausfüllen NHG 5

(to) **film** /fɪlm/ drehen, filmen NHG 6

final /ˈfaɪnl/ letzte(r, s); endgültig NHG 5

final /ˈfaɪnl/ Endspiel; Finale p. 35, 2

finally /ˈfaɪnli/ schließlich; endlich NHG 7

finance /ˈfaɪnæns/ Finanzwirtschaft; Geldwesen p. 41, 8

finances *(pl)* /ˈfaɪnænsɪz/ Finanzen p. 41, 8

(to) **find** *(irr)* /faɪnd/ finden NHG 5

(to) **find out** *(irr)* /ˌfaɪnd‿ˈaʊt/ herausfinden NHG 5

finding /ˈfaɪndɪŋ/ Entdeckung; Ergebnis NHG 7

fine /faɪn/ in Ordnung, gut NHG 5

I'm fine. /aɪm ˈfaɪn/ Es geht mir gut. p. 40, 7

(to) **finish** /ˈfɪnɪʃ/ beenden; enden; fertigstellen NHG 6; aufessen NHG 7

fire /ˈfaɪə/ Feuer NHG 6

(to) start a fire /ˌstɑːt‿ə ˈfaɪə/ Feuer machen p. 108, 3

firefighter /ˈfaɪəˌfaɪtə/ Feuerwehr-mann/-frau NHG 6

fireworks *(pl)* /ˈfaɪəˌwɜːks/ Feuer-werk NHG 6

first /fɜːst/ erste(r, s); zuerst NHG 5

at first /ˌæt ˈfɜːst/ zuerst NHG 6

the very first /ðə ˌveri ˈfɜːst/ der/die/das allererste p. 6

first thing *(informal)* /ˌfɜːst ˈθɪŋ/ als Erstes p. 38, 6

fish *(pl* **fish** *or* **fishes)** /fɪʃ, fɪʃ, ˈfɪʃɪz/ Fisch NHG 5

fisherman *(pl* fishermen) /ˈfɪʃəmən/ Fischer; Angler p. 116, 1

(to) **fit** /fɪt/ passen NHG 5

(to) **keep fit** *(irr)* /ˌkiːp ˈfɪt/ fit bleiben, (sich) fit halten NHG 7

(to) **fix** /fɪks/ reparieren p. 111, 7

flag /flæg/ Fahne; Flagge p. 16, 9

flat /flæt/ Wohnung NHG 6

flea market /ˈfliː ˌmɑːkɪt/ Flohmarkt NHG 7

(to) **flee** *(irr)* /fliː/ fliehen p. 106, 1

flexible /ˈfleksəbl/ biegsam, gelenkig NHG 7

short-distance flight /ˌʃɔːt‿ˌdɪstəns ˈflaɪt/ Kurzstreckenflug p. 85, 5

flip /flɪp/ Salto p. 48, 7

floor /flɔː/ Fußboden NHG 5; Stockwerk p. 23, 5

(to) flow /fləʊ/ fließen; strömen p. 141

flower /ˈflaʊə/ Blume NHG 6

(to) **fly** *(irr)* /flaɪ/ fliegen NHG 6

(to) **focus on** /ˈfəʊkəs‿ɒn/ sich konzentrieren auf NHG 5

folded hands /ˌfəʊldɪd ˈhændz/ betende Hände p. 71, 5

folder /ˈfəʊldə/ Mappe; Ordner NHG 5

folks *(informal)* /fəʊks/ Leute p. 89, 9

(to) **follow** /ˈfɒləʊ/ folgen; verfolgen NHG 6; befolgen p. 98, 11

(to) follow in somebody's footsteps /ˌfɒləʊ‿ɪn ˌsʌmbədiz ˈfʊtsteps/ in jemandes Fußstapfen treten p. 121, 6

follow-up question /ˈfɒləʊ‿ʌp ˌkwestʃn/ Folgefrage p. 22, 4

following /ˈfɒləʊɪŋ/ folgende(r, s) NHG 6

food /fuːd/ Essen NHG 5

foot *(pl* **feet)** /fʊt, fiːt/ Fuß NHG 5; Fuß *(Maßeinheit, 1 Fuß = 0,3048 Meter)* p. 13, 6

(to) **set foot on** *(irr)* /ˌset ˈfʊt‿ɒn/ betreten p. 10, 2

football /ˈfʊtˌbɔːl/ Fußball NHG 5

football *(AE)* /ˈfʊtˌbɔːl/ American Football p. 34, 2

footprint /ˈfʊtˌprɪnt/ Fußabdruck; Standfläche p. 21, 2

ecological footprint /ˌiːkəˌlɒdʒɪkl ˈfʊtprɪnt/ ökologischer Fußab-druck p. 85, 5

(to) follow in somebody's footsteps /ˌfɒləʊ‿ɪn ˌsʌmbədiz ˈfʊtsteps/ in jemandes Fußstapfen treten p. 121, 6

for /fɔː/ für NHG 5

for *(+ Zeitraum)* /fɔː/ ... lang NHG 6

for a long time /fər‿ə ˈlɒŋ taɪm/ lange p. 62, 8

for example /fər‿ɪɡˈzɑːmpl/ zum Beispiel NHG 5

for free /fə ˈfriː/ gratis NHG 6

for the first time /fə ðə ˈfɜːst‿taɪm/ zum ersten Mal NHG 6

force /fɔːs/ Kraft p. 89, 9

(to) **force** /fɔːs/ (er)zwingen p. 15, 7

foreign /ˈfɒrɪn/ ausländisch; fremd NHG 7

foreign language /ˌfɒrɪn ˈlæŋgwɪdʒ/ Fremdsprache p. 95, 7

forest /ˈfɒrɪst/ Wald NHG 6

(to) **forget** *(irr)* /fəˈget/ vergessen NHG 5

(to) **forgive** *(irr)* /fəˈgɪv/ vergeben; verzeihen p. 62, 8

fork /fɔːk/ Gabel NHG 5

form /fɔːm/ Klasse NHG 5; Formular p. 98, 10

(to) **form** /fɔːm/ formen, bilden, gründen p. 149

formal /ˈfɔːml/ formell; offiziell p. 35, 2

former /ˈfɔːmə/ ehemalige(r, s); frühere(r, s) p. 21, 2

France /frɑːns/ Frankreich NHG 5

free /friː/ frei; kostenlos NHG 6

for free /fə ˈfriː/ gratis NHG 6

free time /friː ˈtaɪm/ Freizeit NHG 5

freedom /ˈfriːdəm/ Freiheit p. 14, 7

call of freedom /ˌkɔːl‿əv‿ˈfriːdəm/ Ruf der Freiheit p. 122, 7

French /frentʃ/ Französisch NHG 5

French fries *(AE, pl)* /ˌfrentʃ ˈfraɪz/ Pommes frites p. 37, 5

fresh /freʃ/ frisch; neu NHG 6

freshman *(pl* freshmen) /ˈfreʃmən, ˈfreʃmən/ *Schüler/in einer Highschool im ersten Jahr* p. 35, 2

Friday /ˈfraɪdeɪ/ Freitag NHG 5

(on) Fridays /ˈfraɪdeɪz/ freitags NHG 5

fridge /frɪdʒ/ Kühlschrank NHG 7

friend /frend/ Freund/in NHG 5

friendly /ˈfrendli/ freundlich NHG 6

(to) **make friends (with)** *(irr)* /ˌmeɪk ˈfrendz/ sich anfreunden (mit) NHG 6

friendship /ˈfrendʃɪp/ Freundschaft NHG 6

from /frɒm/ von; aus NHG 5

from abroad /frɒm‿əˈbrɔːd/ aus dem Ausland p. 132

from all over the world
/frəmˌɔːlˌəʊvə ðə ˈwɜːld/ aus der ganzen Welt NHG 5

at the front /ˌæt ðə ˈfrʌnt/ vorne NHG 5

in front of /ˌɪn ˈfrʌntˌəv/ vor NHG 5

in the front /ˌɪn ðə ˈfrʌnt/ vorne NHG 5

fruit /fruːt/ Frucht; Obst NHG 5

frustrated /frʌˈstreɪtɪd/ frustriert NHG 6

full /fʊl/ voll, vollständig NHG 6; satt NHG 7

(to) **be in full swing** *(irr)* /ˌbiˌɪnˌfʊl ˈswɪŋ/ in vollem Gang sein p. 34, 2

full-contact sport /ˌfʊl ˈkɒntækt spɔːt/ *Vollkontakt-Sportart* p. 50, 8

full-time /ˌfʊl ˈtaɪm/ Vollzeit- p. 26, 8

fun /fʌn/ Spaß NHG 5; lustig; witzig NHG 6

(to) **be (good/great) fun** *(irr)* /ˌbiːˌɡʊd/ˌɡreɪt ˈfʌn/ (viel/großen) Spaß machen NHG 5

(to) **have fun** *(irr)* /ˌhævˈfʌn/ Spaß haben NHG 6

function /ˈfʌŋkʃn/ Aufgabe; Funktion NHG 7

fundraiser /ˈfʌndˌreɪzə/ Spendensammler/in p. 35, 2

fundraising /ˈfʌndreɪzɪŋ/ Spendensammeln p. 35, 2

funny /ˈfʌni/ lustig; komisch NHG 5

furniture /ˈfɜːnɪtʃə/ Möbel(stück) NHG 5

further /ˈfɜːðə/ weiter p. 68, 2

future /ˈfjuːtʃə/ Zukunft NHG 6; zukünftig p. 44, 2

G

Gaelic football /ˌɡeɪlɪk ˈfʊtbɔːl/ *Ballsportart mit zwei Teams zu je 15 Spielern/Spielerinnen* p. 116, 1

gallery walk /ˈɡæləri wɔːk/ *Gruppendiskussion in Stationsarbeit* p. 43, 14

game /ɡeɪm/ Spiel NHG 5

board game /ˈbɔːd ɡeɪm/ Brettspiel NHG 6

gap /ɡæp/ Lücke NHG 5

garbage *(AE)* /ˈɡɑːbɪdʒ/ Abfall; Müll p. 86, 6

garden /ˈɡɑːdn/ Garten NHG 5

gardener /ˈɡɑːdnə/ Gärtner/in p. 92, 1

gardening /ˈɡɑːdnɪŋ/ Gärtnern p. 150

gate /ɡeɪt/ Tor NHG 6

general /ˈdʒenrəl/ allgemein NHG 7

genre /ˈʒɒnrə/ Genre; Gattung p. 149

geography /dʒiˈɒɡrəfi/ Erdkunde NHG 5

German /ˈdʒɜːmən/ Deutsch; deutsch NHG 5

Germany /ˈdʒɜːməni/ Deutschland NHG 5

(to) **get** *(irr)* /ɡet/ bekommen; holen; kaufen NHG 5; kommen; gelangen; werden NHG 6; bringen NHG 7

(to) **get along** *(irr)* /ˌɡetˈəˈlɒŋ/ sich verstehen NHG 6

(to) **get better** *(irr)* /ˌɡet ˈbetə/ besser werden; gesund werden NHG 7

(to) **get connected** *(irr)* /ˌɡet kəˈnektɪd/ sich verbinden, in Kontakt treten p. 72, 6

(to) **get going** *(irr)* /ˌɡet ˈɡəʊɪŋ/ in Gang bringen p. 85, 5

(to) **get involved** *(irr)* /ˌɡetˌɪnˈvɒlvd/ sich engagieren p. 85, 5

(to) **get to know** *(irr)* /ˌɡet təˈnəʊ/ kennenlernen p. 41, 8

(to) **get married** *(irr)* /ˌɡet ˈmærid/ heiraten NHG 7

(to) **get rid of** *(irr)* /ˌɡet ˈrɪdˌəv/ loswerden NHG 7

(to) **get together** *(irr)* /ˌɡetˌtəˈɡeðə/ zusammenkommen NHG 5

(to) **get up** *(irr)* /ˌɡetˈʌp/ aufstehen NHG 6

(to) **get well** *(irr)* /ˌɡet ˈwel/ gesund werden NHG 7

Get well soon! /ˌɡet ˌwel ˈsuːn/ Gute Besserung! NHG 7

ghost /ɡəʊst/ Geist; Gespenst NHG 6

girl /ɡɜːl/ Mädchen NHG 5

(to) **give** *(irr)* /ɡɪv/ geben NHG 5; angeben, mitteilen NHG 6

(to) **give a presentation** *(irr)* /ˌɡɪvˌəˌprezn̩ˈteɪʃn/ eine Präsentation halten NHG 7

(to) **give a reason** *(irr)* /ˌɡɪvˌəˈriːzn/ einen Grund nennen p. 17, 10

(to) **give a talk** *(irr)* /ˌɡɪvˌəˈtɔːk/ einen Vortrag halten p. 125, 13

(to) **give advice** *(irr)* /ˌɡɪvˌədˈvaɪs/ Rat geben NHG 7

(to) **give directions** *(irr)* /ˌɡɪv daɪˈrekʃnz/ den Weg beschreiben NHG 6

(to) **give out** *(irr)* /ˌɡɪvˈaʊt/ bekannt geben; verteilen p. 38, 6

(to) **give thanks** *(irr)* /ˌɡɪv ˈθæŋks/ Dank sagen p. 25, 7

(to) **give up** *(irr)* /ˌɡɪvˈʌp/ aufgeben p. 89, 9

glad /ɡlæd/ glücklich, froh p. 58, 2

glass /ɡlɑːs/ Glas NHG 6

glee club /ˈɡliː klʌb/ Gesangs-AG p. 44, 2

glimpse /ɡlɪmps/ flüchtiger Blick p. 14, 7

glitz /ɡlɪts/ Glanz p. 148

glove /ɡlʌv/ Handschuh p. 50, 9

glue /ɡluː/ Klebstoff NHG 5

(to) **glue** /ɡluː/ kleben p. 68, 2

(to) **go** *(irr)* /ɡəʊ/ gehen; fahren NHG 5

(to) **go abroad** *(irr)* /ˌɡəʊˌəˈbrɔːd/ ins Ausland gehen / fahren NHG 6

(to) **go away** *(irr)* /ˌɡəʊˌəˈweɪ/ weggehen; verschwinden NHG 6

(to) **go crazy** *(irr)* /ˌɡəʊ ˈkreɪzi/ verrückt werden; *hier:* ausrasten p. 49, 7

(to) **go cycling** *(irr)* /ˌɡəʊ ˈsaɪklɪŋ/ Rad fahren gehen NHG 6

(to) **go hiking** *(irr)* /ˌɡəʊ ˈhaɪkɪŋ/ wandern gehen NHG 6

(to) **go on** *(irr)* /ˌɡəʊˌˈɒn/ passieren; weitergehen, weiterreden NHG 7

(to) **go out** *(irr)* /ˌɡəʊˌˈaʊt/ (hinaus) gehen; ausgehen NHG 6

(to) **go riding** *(irr)* /ˌɡəʊ ˈraɪdɪŋ/ reiten gehen NHG 6

(to) **go shopping** *(irr)* /ˌɡəʊ ˈʃɒpɪŋ/ einkaufen gehen NHG 6

(to) **go swimming** *(irr)* /ˌɡəʊ ˈswɪmɪŋ/ schwimmen gehen NHG 6

(to) **go with** *(irr)* /ˌɡəʊ ˈwɪθ/ gehören zu; passen zu NHG 6

goal /ɡəʊl/ Tor NHG 5; Ziel p. 83, 2

goalkeeper /ˈɡəʊlˌkiːpə/ Tormann/ Torfrau p. 117, 2

God /ɡɒd/ Gott p. 38, 6

thank God /ˌθæŋk ˈɡɒd/ Gott sei Dank p. 110, 6

(to) be going to *(irr)* /ˌbiː ˈɡəʊɪŋ tʊ/ werden NHG 6

(to) get going *(irr)* /ˌget ˈɡəʊɪŋ/ in Gang bringen p. 85, 5

gold rush /ˈɡəʊld rʌʃ/ Goldrausch p. 13, 6

goldfish *(pl goldfish)* /ˈɡəʊldˌfɪʃ/ Goldfisch p. 75, 11

gone /ɡɒn/ weg NHG 6

good /ɡʊd/ gut NHG 5

(to) **be good at doing something** *(irr)* /ˌbiː ˈɡʊdˌət ˈduːɪŋ ˌsʌmθɪŋ/ gut darin sein, etwas zu tun NHG 5

(to) **be good at something** *(irr)* /ˌbiː ˈɡʊd æt ˌsʌmθɪŋ/ gut in etwas sein NHG 6

I'm good, thanks. /aɪm ˈɡʊd ˌθæŋks/ Es geht mir gut, danke. NHG 5

Good luck! /ˌɡʊd ˈlʌk/ Viel Glück! NHG 7

goodbye /ˌɡʊdˈbaɪ/ auf Wiedersehen NHG 5

(to) govern /ˈɡʌvən/ regieren p. 14, 7

government /ˈɡʌvənmənt/ Regierung NHG 7

grade /ɡreɪd/ Note p. 98, 10

grade *(AE)* /ɡreɪd/ Klasse p. 34, 2

graduate /ˈɡrædʒuət/ Absolvent/in p. 35, 2

(to) graduate *(AE)* /ˈɡrædʒueɪt/ die (Highschool-)Abschlussprüfung bestehen p. 34, 2

graduation /ˌɡrædʒuˈeɪʃn/ Schulabschluss p. 35, 2

grammar /ˈɡræmə/ Grammatik p. 12

Grand Central Station /ˌɡrænd ˌsentrəl ˈsteɪʃn/ *Bahnhof in Manhattan* p. 27, 9

grandad *(informal)* /ˈɡrænˌdæd/ Opa NHG 7

granddaughter /ˈɡrænˌdɔːtə/ Enkelin p. 107, 2

grandfather /ˈɡrænˌfɑːðə/ Großvater NHG 5

grandma *(informal)* /ˈɡrænˌmɑː/ Oma NHG 7

grandmother /ˈɡrænˌmʌðə/ Großmutter NHG 5

grandpa *(informal)* /ˈɡrænˌpɑː/ Opa NHG 7

grandparents *(pl)* /ˈɡrænˌpeərənts/ Großeltern NHG 6

grandson /ˈɡrænˌsʌn/ Enkel p. 107, 2

grape /ɡreɪp/ (Wein)traube NHG 6

graph /ɡrɑːf/ Diagramm; Graph p. 109, 5

grass /ɡrɑːs/ Gras NHG 6

grateful /ˈɡreɪtfl/ dankbar p. 83, 2

gratitude /ˈɡrætɪtjuːd/ Dankbarkeit p. 71, 5

great /ɡreɪt/ groß; großartig NHG 5

Great Britain /ˌɡreɪt ˈbrɪtn/ Großbritannien NHG 7

the Great Plains /ðə ˌɡreɪt ˈpleɪnz/ *Kurzgras-Prärien* p. 111, 7

great-great-grandparents *(pl)* /ˌɡreɪt ˌɡreɪt ˈɡrænˌpeərənts/ Urur-großeltern p. 117, 2

greatness /ˈɡreɪtnəs/ Bedeutsamkeit p. 17, 10

green /ɡriːn/ grün NHG 5; umweltfreundlich, ökologisch NHG 7

greetings *(pl)* /ˈɡriːtɪŋz/ Grüße p. 12, 3

grey /ɡreɪ/ grau NHG 5

gritty /ˈɡrɪti/ grob; mutig, tapfer p. 25, 7

ground /ɡraʊnd/ Boden NHG 6

group /ɡruːp/ Gruppe NHG 5

(to) **grow** *(irr)* /ɡrəʊ/ anbauen NHG 6; wachsen NHG 7

(to) **grow up** *(irr)* /ˌɡrəʊˈʌp/ erwachsen sein / werden NHG 6; aufwachsen NHG 7

guarantee /ˌɡærənˈtiː/ Garantie p. 71, 5

(to) **guess** /ɡes/ (er)raten NHG 5

guest /ɡest/ Gast NHG 5

guidance counsellor /ˈɡaɪdns ˌkaʊnslə/ Beratungslehrer/in p. 40, 7

tour guide /ˈtʊə ɡaɪd/ Reiseführer/in p. 26, 8

guitar /ɡɪˈtɑː/ Gitarre NHG 5

gun /ɡʌn/ Waffe p. 110, 6

(you) guys *(pl, informal)* /ɡaɪz/ Leute *(umgangssprachl.)* NHG 6

gym (= gymnasium) /dʒɪm, dʒɪmˈneɪziəm/ Turnhalle NHG 5

gym *(AE)* /dʒɪm/ Sportunterricht p. 39, 6

(to) **do gymnastics** *(irr)* /ˌduː dʒɪmˈnæstɪks/ turnen NHG 5

H

habit /ˈhæbɪt/ Gewohnheit; Angewohnheit NHG 7

hair /heə/ Haar; Haare NHG 5

hairdresser /ˈheəˌdresə/ Friseur/in NHG 6

half /hɑːf/ halb NHG 5

half *(pl halves)* /hɑːf, hɑːvz/ Hälfte NHG 6

half-time /ˌhɑːf ˈtaɪm/ Halbzeit p. 48, 7

hall /hɔːl/ Halle p. 13, 6

hallway /ˈhɔːlˌweɪ/ Korridor; Flur p. 39, 6

on the one hand, ... /ˌɒn ðə ˈwʌn hænd/ einerseits ... NHG 7

on the other hand, ... /ˌɒn ðɪ ˈʌðə hænd/ andererseits ... NHG 7

(to) **hand in** /ˌhændˈɪn/ einreichen; abgeben NHG 6

folded hands /ˌfəʊldɪd ˈhændz/ betende Hände p. 71, 5

(to) **hang out** *(informal, irr)* /ˌhæŋˈaʊt/ rumhängen; Zeit mit jemandem verbringen p. 59, 3

(to) **hang (up)** *(irr)* /ˌhæŋˈʌp/ hängen, aufhängen NHG 6

(to) **happen** /ˈhæpən/ geschehen; passieren NHG 5

(to) make happen *(irr)* /ˌmeɪk ˈhæpən/ möglich machen p. 25, 7

happy /ˈhæpi/ glücklich NHG 5; zufrieden NHG 7

Happy birthday (to you)! /ˌhæpi ˈbɜːθdeɪ tʊ juː/ Herzlichen Glückwunsch zum Geburtstag! NHG 5

(to) **harass** /ˈhærəs/ belästigen p. 69, 2

harbor *(AE)* = **harbour** *(BE)* /ˈhɑːbə/ Hafen p. 20, 2

hard /hɑːd/ hart, schwierig NHG 6; fest; kräftig NHG 7

hard skill /ˌhɑːd ˈskɪl/ *berufstypische Qualifikation* p. 95, 7

hardly /ˈhɑːdli/ kaum p. 38, 6

harm /hɑːm/ Schaden p. 86, 6

(to) **harm** /hɑːm/ schaden, Schaden zufügen p. 73, 6

harmful /ˈhɑːmfl/ schädlich p. 71, 5

harvest /ˈhɑːvɪst/ Ernte p. 106, 2

(to) **hashtag** /ˈhæʃˌtæɡ/ mit einem Hashtag versehen p. 48, 7

hat /hæt/ Hut p. 65, 12

(to) **hate** /heɪt/ hassen; nicht ausstehen können NHG 5

(to) **have** *(irr)* /hæv/ haben NHG 5; essen; trinken NHG 5 (to) **have a look at** *(irr)* /ˌhæv‿ə ˈlʊk‿ət/ sich ansehen NHG 6

(to) **have (a lot of) fun** *(irr)* /ˌhæv‿ə ˌlɒt‿əv‿ˈfʌn/ (viel) Spaß haben NHG 6

(to) **have got** *(irr)* /ˌhæv ˈɡɒt/ haben NHG 5

(to) **have in common** *(irr)* /ˌhæv‿ɪn ˈkɒmən/ gemeinsam haben NHG 6

(to) **have to** *(irr)* /ˈhæv tə/ müssen NHG 5

(to) have one's photograph taken *(irr)* /ˌhæv wʌnz ˈfəʊtəˌɡrɑːf ˌteɪkən/ sich fotografieren lassen p. 132

he /hiː/ er NHG 5

head /hed/ Kopf NHG 6

headache /ˈhedeɪk/ Kopfschmerzen NHG 7

heading /ˈhedɪŋ/ Überschrift; Titel NHG 6

headline /ˈhedlaɪn/ Überschrift; Schlagzeile p. 43, 14

health /helθ/ Gesundheit NHG 7

healthy /ˈhelθi/ gesund NHG 6

(to) **hear** *(irr)* /hɪə/ hören NHG 5

heart /hɑːt/ Herz NHG 6

by heart /ˌbaɪ ˈhɑːt/ auswendig NHG 7

(to) **heat** /hiːt/ erhitzen NHG 7

heavy /ˈhevi/ schwer NHG 5

hedgehog /ˈhedʒˌhɒɡ/ Igel NHG 6

height /haɪt/ Höhe NHG 6

hell /hel/ Hölle p. 25, 7

hello /həˈləʊ/ hallo NHG 5

helmet /ˈhelmɪt/ Helm NHG 7

help /help/ Hilfe NHG 5

(to) **help** /help/ helfen NHG 5

(to) **help out** /ˌhelp‿ˈaʊt/ aushelfen NHG 7

helpful /ˈhelpfl/ hilfreich; nützlich NHG 7

helpless /ˈhelpləs/ hilflos p. 85, 5

her /hɜː/ ihr/ihre; sie NHG 5

herb /hɜːb/ (Gewürz)kraut NHG 7

here /hɪə/ hier; hierher NHG 5

Here you are! /ˌhɪə juˈˈɑː/ Hier, bitte! NHG 5

heritage /ˈherɪtɪdʒ/ Erbe p. 27, 10

hers /hɜːz/ ihre(r, s) NHG 7

herself /həˈself/ sich; (sie) selbst NHG 7

(to) **hide** *(irr)* /haɪd/ verstecken, sich verstecken NHG 6

high /haɪ/ hoch NHG 5

high school *(AE)* /ˈhaɪ skuːl/ Highschool; weiterführende Schule p. 24, 6

highlight /ˈhaɪlaɪt/ Höhepunkt NHG 7

(to) **hijack** /ˈhaɪdʒæk/ entführen p. 15, 7

(to) **go hiking** *(irr)* /ˌɡəʊ ˈhaɪkɪŋ/ wandern gehen NHG 6

hiking trail /ˈhaɪkɪŋ treɪl/ Wanderweg p. 119, 5

hill /hɪl/ Hügel NHG 6

him /hɪm/ ihm, ihn NHG 5

himself /hɪmˈself/ selbst; sich (selbst) NHG 6

Hinduism /ˈhɪnduˌɪzm/ Hinduismus NHG 6

hip /hɪp/ hip, cool p. 120, 6

(to) **hire** /ˈhaɪə/ mieten NHG 6

his /hɪz/ sein; seine(r, s) NHG 5

Hispanic /hɪˈspænɪk/ Hispanoamerikaner/in; hispanisch p. 24, 6

historian /hɪˈstɔːriən/ Historiker/in p. 17, 10

historic /hɪˈstɒrɪk/ historisch p. 13, 6

historical /hɪˈstɒrɪkl/ geschichtlich; historisch p. 15, 7

history /ˈhɪstri/ Geschichte NHG 5

(to) **hit** *(irr)* /hɪt/ schlagen NHG 5; treffen; stoßen gegen p. 21, 2

(to) **hold** *(irr)* /həʊld/ (fest)halten NHG 5

hole /həʊl/ Loch NHG 5

holiday /ˈhɒlɪdeɪ/ Feiertag NHG 6

holiday(s) /ˈhɒlɪdeɪ(z)/ Ferien; Urlaub NHG 5

home /həʊm/ nach Hause; zu Hause; daheim NHG 5; Zuhause; Haus NHG 6

at home /ˌæt ˈhəʊm/ zu Hause NHG 5

home town /ˈhəʊm ˌtaʊn/ Heimatstadt NHG 5

home-made /ˌhəʊmˈmeɪd/ hausgemacht, selbst gemacht NHG 7

homecoming *(no pl, AE)* /ˈhəʊmˌkʌmɪŋ/ Ehemaligentreffen p. 34, 2

homeroom /ˈhəʊmruːm/ Klassenraum; Klassenlehrkraftstunde p. 38, 6

(to) be homesick *(irr)* /ˌbiː ˈhəʊmˌsɪk/ Heimweh haben NHG 7

(to) get homesick *(irr)* /ˌɡet ˈhəʊmˌsɪk/ Heimweh bekommen p. 113, 10

homework /ˈhəʊmwɜːk/ Hausaufgaben NHG 5

honest /ˈɒnɪst/ ehrlich NHG 6

(to) **honor** *(AE)* = honour *(BE)* /ˈɒnə/ ehren p. 27, 10

hope /həʊp/ Hoffnung p. 81

(to) **hope** /həʊp/ hoffen NHG 5

horizon /həˈraɪzn/ Horizont p. 105

horrible /ˈhɒrəbl/ schrecklich; gemein NHG 6

horse /hɔːs/ Pferd NHG 6

(to) **ride a horse** *(irr)* /ˌraɪd‿ə ˈhɔːs/ reiten NHG 6

hospital /ˈhɒspɪtl/ Krankenhaus NHG 6

host *(before nouns)* /həʊst/ Gast- p. 34, 2

host /həʊst/ *hier:* Podcast-Host p. 27, 10

hot /hɒt/ heiß NHG 6; scharf NHG 7

hotspot /ˈhɒtˌspɒt/ *angesagter Ort* p. 11, 2

hour /ˈaʊə/ Stunde NHG 5

house /haʊs/ Haus NHG 5

household /ˈhaʊsˌhəʊld/ Haushalt p. 41, 8

household machine /ˈhaʊsˌhəʊld məˌʃiːn/ Haushaltsgerät p. 42, 12

how /haʊ/ wie NHG 5

How about …? /ˈhaʊ‿əˌbaʊt/ Was ist mit …?, Wie wäre es mit …? NHG 7

How are you? /ˌhaʊ‿ˈɑː jɜ/ Wie geht es dir / euch / Ihnen? NHG 5

How much is it? /ˌhaʊ mʌtʃ‿ˈɪz‿ɪt/ Wie viel kostet es? NHG 5

however /haʊˈevə/ aber; wie auch immer p. 62, 8

(to) **howl** /haʊl/ brüllen; heulen p. 111, 7

huge /hjuːdʒ/ riesig NHG 6

humid /ˈhjuːmɪd/ feucht p. 110, 6

(to) **humiliate** /hjuːˈmɪlieɪt/ erniedrigen p. 69, 2

hundred /ˈhʌndrəd/ Hundert NHG 6

hungry /ˈhʌŋɡri/ hungrig NHG 5

(to) **hurry (up)** /ˌhʌriˈˈʌp/ sich beeilen NHG 5

(to) **hurt** *(irr)* /hɜːt/ wehtun; schmerzen; verletzen NHG 7

hurt /hɜːt/ verletzt; gekränkt p. 62, 8

husband /ˈhʌzbənd/ Ehemann NHG 5

I

I /aɪ/ ich NHG 5

ice /aɪs/ Eis NHG 6

ice cream /ˈaɪs ˌkriːm/ Eis NHG 5

(to) **ice-skate** /ˈaɪsˌskeɪt/ Schlitt-schuh laufen NHG 5

iced tea /ˌaɪstˈtiː/ Eistee p. 65, 12

ICT (= Information and Communication Technology) /ˌaɪˌsiːˈtiː, ˌɪnfəˈmeɪʃn ˌən kəˌmjuːnɪˈkeɪʃn tekˌnɒlədʒi/ Informatik (Schulfach) NHG 5

ID (= ID card) /ˌaɪˈdiː, ˌaɪˈdiː kɑːd/ Ausweis p. 26, 8

idea /aɪˈdɪə/ Idee; Vorstellung NHG 5

if /ɪf/ wenn; falls; ob NHG 5

(to) **ignore** /ɪgˈnɔː/ ignorieren p. 62, 8

ill /ɪl/ krank NHG 6

illness /ˈɪlnəs/ Krankheit NHG 7

illustrated /ˈɪləstreɪtɪd/ illustriert, bebildert p. 120, 6

imagination /ɪˌmædʒɪˈneɪʃn/ Fantasie; Vorstellungskraft p. 85, 5

(to) **imagine** /ɪˈmædʒɪn/ sich etwas vorstellen NHG 5

immediately /ɪˈmiːdiətli/ sofort p. 72, 6

immigrant /ˈɪmɪgrənt/ Einwande-rer/in; Immigrant/in NHG 7

immigration /ˌɪmɪˈgreɪʃn/ Einwan-derung; Immigration p. 105

impact /ˈɪmpækt/ Auswirkung; Einfluss p. 83, 2

importance /ɪmˈpɔːtns/ Bedeutung; Wichtigkeit p. 87, 6

important /ɪmˈpɔːtnt/ wichtig NHG 5

impossible /ɪmˈpɒsəbl/ unmöglich NHG 6

impression /ɪmˈpreʃn/ Eindruck p. 9

impressive /ɪmˈpresɪv/ beein-druckend NHG 7

(to) **improve** /ɪmˈpruːv/ verbessern; besser werden NHG 6

(to) **improvise** /ˈɪmprəvaɪz/ improvi-sieren p. 44, 2

in /ɪn/ in; auf NHG 5

in advance /ˌɪn ədˈvɑːns/ im Voraus p. 26, 8

in fact /ɪn ˈfækt/ tatsächlich; in Wirklichkeit p. 68, 2

in front of /ˌɪn ˈfrʌnt ˌəv/ vor NHG 5

in my opinion /ɪn ˈmaɪ əˌpɪnjən/ meiner Meinung nach NHG 6

in order to /ˌɪn ˈɔːdə tʊ/ um zu NHG 7

in person /ˌɪn ˈpɜːsn/ persönlich p. 72, 6

in the back /ˌɪn ðə ˈbæk/ hinten NHG 5

in the end /ˌɪn ðiˈend/ am Ende, schließlich NHG 6

in the front /ˌɪn ðə ˈfrʌnt/ vorne NHG 5

in the middle of /ˌɪn ðə ˈmɪdl ˌəv/ in der Mitte von; mitten in p. 21, 2

in total /ˌɪn ˈtəʊtl/ insgesamt p. 34, 2

(to) **include** /ɪnˈkluːd/ beinhalten; einbeziehen NHG 6

including /ɪnˈkluːdɪŋ/ einschließlich p. 26, 8

(to) **increase** /ɪnˈkriːs/ ansteigen p. 109, 5

increase /ˈɪŋkriːs/ Anstieg, Wachs-tum p. 171

incredible /ɪnˈkredəbl/ unglaublich p. 48, 7

independence /ˌɪndɪˈpendəns/ Unabhängigkeit p. 13, 6

Independence Day /ˌɪndɪˈpendəns deɪ/ Unabhängigkeitstag p. 6

independent /ˌɪndɪˈpendənt/ unab-hängig p. 14, 7

indigenous /ɪnˈdɪdʒənəs/ (ein)hei-misch, indigen p. 7

individual /ˌɪndɪˈvɪdʒuəl/ individuell; einzeln p. 85, 5

indivisible /ˌɪndɪˈvɪzəbl/ unteilbar p. 38, 6

indoor /ˌɪnˈdɔː/ Hallen- NHG 7

indoors /ˌɪnˈdɔːz/ drinnen, im Haus NHG 7

industrialized /ɪnˈdʌstriəlaɪzd/ industrialisiert p. 15, 7

industry /ˈɪndəstri/ Industrie NHG 7

infection /ɪnˈfekʃn/ Infektion NHG 7

influence /ˈɪnfluəns/ Einfluss NHG 7

(to) **influence** /ˈɪnfluəns/ beeinflus-sen p. 11, 2

(to) **inform** /ɪnˈfɔːm/ informieren NHG 6

information (no pl) /ˌɪnfəˈmeɪʃn/ Informationen NHG 5

information technology (= IT) /ˌɪnfəˌmeɪʃn tekˈnɒlədʒi, ˌaɪ ˈtiː/ Infor-mationstechnologie, IT p. 10, 2

informed /ɪnˈfɔːmd/ informiert p. 89, 9

ingredient /ɪnˈgriːdiənt/ Zutat p. 11, 2

(to) take the initiative (irr) /ˌteɪk ðiɪˈnɪʃətɪv/ die Initiative ergreifen p. 96, 8

injury /ˈɪndʒəri/ Verletzung NHG 7

innocence /ˈɪnəsns/ Unschuld p. 71, 5

innovation /ˌɪnəʊˈveɪʃn/ Neuerung p. 10, 2

inside /ˈɪnˌsaɪd/ innerhalb NHG 5; innen; drinnen; hinein NHG 6

inspection /ɪnˈspekʃn/ Untersu-chung p. 110, 6

(to) **inspire** /ɪnˈspaɪə/ inspirieren p. 11, 2

inspiring /ɪnˈspaɪərɪŋ/ inspirierend, anregend p. 93, 2

(to) **install** /ɪnˈstɔːl/ aufstellen, installieren p. 10, 2

instead of /ɪnˈsted ˌəv/ anstatt p. 86, 6

institution /ˌɪnstɪˈtjuːʃn/ Einrichtung; Institution p. 15, 7

instruction /ɪnˈstrʌkʃn/ Anweisung; Instruktion NHG 6

insult /ˈɪnsʌlt/ Beleidigung p. 71, 5

artificial intelligence (= AI) /ˌɑːtɪfɪʃl ɪnˈtelɪdʒns, ˌeɪ ˈaɪ/ künst-liche Intelligenz p. 10, 2

interaction /ˌɪntərˈækʃn/ Interaktion; Kommunikation p. 73, 6

interactive /ˌɪntərˈæktɪv/ interaktiv p. 135

interest /ˈɪntrəst/ Interesse; Hobby p. 72, 6

interested /ˈɪntrəstɪd/ interessiert NHG 6

(to) **be interested in** (irr) /ˌbiˈɪntrəstɪd ˌɪn/ interessiert sein an NHG 7

interesting /ˈɪntrəstɪŋ/ interessant NHG 5

(to) **interpret** /ɪnˈtɜːprɪt/ deuten, interpretieren p. 92, 2

(to) **interview** /ˈɪntəˌvjuː/ intervie-wen, befragen NHG 5

interview (= job interview) /ˈɪntəvjuː; ˈdʒɒbˌɪntəvjuː/ Bewer-bungsgespräch; Vorstellungsge-spräch p. 98, 11

into /ˈɪntuː/ in NHG 5

(to) **introduce** /ˌɪntrəˈdjuːs/ einführen; vorstellen NHG 5

introduction /ˌɪntrəˈdʌkʃn/ Einleitung NHG 5

(to) **invent** /ɪnˈvent/ erfinden NHG 6

invented /ɪnˈventɪd/ erfunden NHG 7

invention /ɪnˈvenʃn/ Erfindung NHG 6

invitation /ˌɪnvɪˈteɪʃn/ Einladung NHG 5

(to) **invite** /ɪnˈvaɪt/ einladen NHG 5

(to) **be involved in** *(irr)* /ˌbi_ɪnˈvɒlvd_ɪn/ beteiligt sein an p. 15, 7

(to) **get involved** *(irr)* /ˌget_ɪnˈvɒlvd/ sich engagieren p. 85, 5

Ireland /ˈaɪələnd/ Irland NHG 6

Irish /ˈaɪrɪʃ/ irisch p. 114, 13

the **Iron Age** /ðiˌˈaɪən_eɪdʒ/ Eisenzeit p. 132

irregular /ɪˈregjʊlə/ unregelmäßig p. 12, 3

island /ˈaɪlənd/ Insel p. 10, 2

it /ɪt/ es NHG 5

it's (= it is) /ɪts, ˈɪt_ɪz/ *hier:* es kostet NHG 5

Italian /ɪˈtæljən/ Italiener/in; italienisch p. 162

Italy /ˈɪtəli/ Italien NHG 5

item /ˈaɪtəm/ Gegenstand NHG 7

itinerary /aɪˈtɪnərəri/ Reiseroute p. 123, 9

its /ɪts/ sein(e), ihr(e) *(sächlich)* NHG 5

itself /ɪtˈself/ selbst, sich selbst NHG 7

J

jacket /ˈdʒækɪt/ Jacke NHG 6

jam /dʒæm/ Marmelade p. 51, 11

January /ˈdʒænjuəri/ Januar NHG 5

Japanese /ˌdʒæpəˈniːz/ Japaner/in; japanisch p. 71, 5

jaw /dʒɔː/ Kiefer p. 132

jewellery *(no pl)* /ˈdʒuːəlri/ Schmuck NHG 6

Jewish /ˈdʒuːɪʃ/ jüdisch NHG 6

job /dʒɒb/ Aufgabe; Beruf NHG 6; Stelle; Job p. 94, 4

job interview (= interview) /ˈdʒɒb_ˌɪntəvjuː, ˈɪntəˌvjuː/ Bewerbungsgespräch; Vorstellungsgespräch p. 98, 11

(to) **join** /dʒɔɪn/ mitmachen (bei) NHG 5; sich zu jemandem gesellen NHG 7

(to) **join in** /ˌdʒɔɪn_ˈɪn/ sich beteiligen an; mitmachen bei NHG 6

joke /dʒəʊk/ Witz p. 122, 7

journey /ˈdʒɜːni/ Reise; Fahrt NHG 6

joy /dʒɔɪ/ Freude p. 71, 5

juice /dʒuːs/ Saft NHG 5

July /dʒʊˈlaɪ/ Juli NHG 5

(to) **jump** /dʒʌmp/ springen NHG 5

jump /dʒʌmp/ Sprung p. 48, 7

June /dʒuːn/ Juni NHG 5

junior *(AE)* /ˈdʒuːniə/ Schüler/in einer Highschool im vorletzten Jahr p. 39, 6

just /dʒʌst/ nur; bloß NHG 5; einfach; wirklich; gerade NHG 6

justice /ˈdʒʌstɪs/ Gerechtigkeit p. 38, 6

K

kayak /ˈkaɪæk/ Kajak p. 7

(to) **keep** *(irr)* /kiːp/ halten; behalten; aufbewahren NHG 5

(to) **keep doing something** *(irr)* /ˌkiːp_ˈduːɪŋ_sʌmθɪŋ/ etwas weiter tun NHG 7

(to) **keep fit** *(irr)* /ˌkiːp_ˈfɪt/ fit bleiben, (sich) fit halten NHG 7

(to) **keep from doing something** *(irr)* /ˌkiːp_frəm_ˈduːɪŋ_ˌsʌmθɪŋ/ etwas unterlassen, sich etwas verkneifen p. 65, 12

(to) **keep in mind** *(irr)* /ˌkiːp_ɪn_ˈmaɪnd/ im Gedächtnis behalten p. 115, 14

(to) **keep in touch** *(irr)* /ˌkiːp_ɪn_ˈtʌtʃ/ Kontakt halten; in Verbindung bleiben NHG 7

keyword /ˈkiːˌwɜːd/ Schlüsselwort; Stichwort p. 82, 2

kg (= kilogram) /ˈkɪləˌgræm/ Kilogramm NHG 6

(to) **kick** /kɪk/ treten NHG 5

kid /kɪd/ Kind NHG 5

(to) **kill** /kɪl/ töten NHG 7

kind /kaɪnd/ Art; Sorte NHG 5; freundlich p. 51, 11

all kinds of /ˌɔːl_ˈkaɪndz_əv/ alle möglichen NHG 6

king /kɪŋ/ König NHG 6

(to) **kiss** /kɪs/ küssen p. 119, 5

kitchen /ˈkɪtʃən/ Küche NHG 5

km (= kilometre) /ˈkɪləˌmiːtə/ Kilometer NHG 7

knee /niː/ Knie NHG 6

knife *(pl knives)* /naɪf, naɪvz/ Messer NHG 5

(to) **knock** /nɒk/ klopfen NHG 6

(to) **know** *(irr)* /nəʊ/ wissen; kennen NHG 5

(to) **get to know** *(irr)* /ˌget_tə_ˈnəʊ/ kennenlernen p. 41, 8

knowledge /ˈnɒlɪdʒ/ Kenntnis; Wissen p. 95, 7

known /nəʊn/ bekannt p. 18, 12

Korean /kəˈriːən/ Koreaner/in; koreanisch p. 107, 2

L

lab /læb/ Labor p. 39, 6

label /ˈleɪbl/ Etikett NHG 7

(to) **label** /ˈleɪbl/ beschriften NHG 5

lady /ˈleɪdi/ Frau; Dame NHG 7

Lady Liberty /ˌleɪdi_ˈlɪbəti/ Freiheitsstatue in New York p. 20, 2

lake /leɪk/ See NHG 5

standing lamp /ˈstændɪŋ_læmp/ Stehlampe p. 65, 12

(to) **land** /lænd/ landen NHG 7

landfill /ˈlændˌfɪl/ Deponiegelände p. 86, 6

landmark /ˈlænˌmɑːk/ Wahrzeichen p. 25, 7

landscape /ˈlænˌskeɪp/ Landschaft p. 8

lane /leɪn/ Spur p. 150

language /ˈlæŋgwɪdʒ/ Sprache NHG 5

lantern /ˈlæntən/ Laterne NHG 6

large /lɑːdʒ/ groß NHG 6

last /lɑːst/ letzte(r, s) NHG 5

(to) **last** /lɑːst/ (an)dauern NHG 6

(to) **last** /lɑːst/ halten p. 42, 12

late /leɪt/ (zu) spät NHG 5

(to) **stay up (late)** /ˌsteɪ_ˌʌp_ˈleɪt/ lange aufbleiben NHG 7

lately /ˈleɪtli/ in letzter Zeit, kürzlich p. 59, 3

later /ˈleɪtə/ später NHG 5

latest /ˈleɪtɪst/ neueste(r, s) NHG 7

Latin /ˌlætɪn_əˈmerɪkən/ Lateinamerikaner/in; lateinamerikanisch p. 25, 7

(to) **laugh** /lɑːf/ lachen NHG 6

law /lɔ:/ Gesetz p. 83, 2

law /lɔ:/ Rechtswissenschaft p. 40, 7

business law /ˈbɪznəs lɔ:/ Wirtschaftsrecht p. 40, 7

lawn /lɔ:n/ Rasen p. 97, 9

lawyer /ˈlɔ:jə/ Rechtsanwalt /
Rechtsanwältin p. 170

lazy /ˈleɪzi/ faul NHG 6

lead /li:d/ Leine NHG 6

(to) **lead** (irr) /li:d/ führen p. 15, 7

leader /ˈli:də/ Leiter/in NHG 6;
Anführer/in p. 15, 7

leaf (pl **leaves**) /li:f, li:vz/ Blatt
NHG 6

(to) **learn** (irr) /lɜ:n/ lernen NHG 6;
erfahren p. 21, 2

least /li:st/ am wenigsten NHG 7

at least /ˌæt ˈli:st/ mindestens;
wenigstens NHG 6

(to) **leave** (irr) /li:v/ weggehen
NHG 5; verlassen, abfahren;
(übrig) lassen; zurücklassen;
hinterlassen NHG 6

Lebanon /ˈlebənən/ der Libanon
p. 24, 6

left /left/ links, nach links NHG 6;
übrig NHG 7

on the left /ˌɒn ðə ˈleft/ links, auf
der linken Seite NHG 5

leg /leg/ Bein NHG 6

legacy /ˈlegəsi/ Vermächtnis; Erbe
p. 27, 10

lemon /ˈlemən/ Zitrone NHG 5

lemonade /ˌleməˈneɪd/ Limonade
NHG 7

less /les/ weniger NHG 6

lesson /ˈlesn/ Stunde; Unterricht
NHG 5

(to) **let** (irr) /let/ lassen NHG 5

letter /ˈletə/ Buchstabe NHG 5;
Brief NHG 6

level /ˈlevl/ Stufe; Level NHG 5

liberty /ˈlɪbəti/ Freiheit p. 38, 6

library /ˈlaɪbrəri/ Bücherei NHG 5

(to) **lie** (irr) /laɪ/ liegen p. 65, 12

(to) **lie down** (irr) /ˌlaɪ ˈdaʊn/ sich
hinlegen p. 36, 4

life (pl **lives**) /laɪf, laɪvz/ Leben
NHG 5

life-saving skill /ˈlaɪfˌseɪvɪŋ skɪl/
Kenntnis im Rettungsschwimmen
p. 93, 2

lifelong /ˈlaɪfˌlɒŋ/ lebenslang p. 25, 7

lifestyle /ˈlaɪfˌstaɪl/ Lebensstil
NHG 7

(to) **lift** /lɪft/ (hoch)heben NHG 7

light /laɪt/ Licht NHG 5

(to) **light** (irr) /laɪt/ anzünden
NHG 6

light bulb /ˈlaɪt bʌlb/ Glühbirne
p. 65, 12

light technology /ˈlaɪt tekˌnɒlədʒi/
Lichttechnik p. 43, 14

lighthouse /ˈlaɪtˌhaʊs/ Leuchtturm
p. 119, 5

lightning /ˈlaɪtnɪŋ/ Blitz p. 111, 7

like /laɪk/ wie NHG 5

(to) **like** /laɪk/ mögen NHG 5

I would like … (= I'd like …)
/aɪ ˌwʊd ˈlaɪk, aɪd ˈlaɪk/ Ich würde
gern … / Ich hätte gern … NHG 5

(to) **like best** /laɪk ˈbest/ am
liebsten mögen NHG 5

(to) **like doing something** /laɪk
ˈdu:ɪŋ ˌsʌmθɪŋ/ etwas gern tun NHG 6

like that /ˌlaɪk ˈðæt/ so NHG 7

likely /ˈlaɪkli/ wahrscheinlich p. 95, 7

limit /ˈlɪmɪt/ (Höchst)grenze; Limit
p. 71, 5

line /laɪn/ Linie; Zeile NHG 5

list /lɪst/ Liste NHG 5

(to) **list** /lɪst/ auflisten NHG 5

(to) **listen (to)** /ˈlɪsn/ zuhören,
anhören NHG 5

(to) listen carefully /ˌlɪsn ˈkeəfli/
aufmerksam zuhören p. 96, 8

listening /ˈlɪsnɪŋ/ Hören p. 37, 5

literally /ˈlɪtrəli/ buchstäblich,
wirklich p. 106, 2

literature /ˈlɪtrətʃə/ Literatur p. 40, 7

little /ˈlɪtl/ klein NHG 5; wenig p. 68, 2

a little /ə ˈlɪtl/ ein bisschen NHG 6

livable (AE) = liveable (BE) /ˈlɪvəbl/
lebenswert p. 85, 5

(to) **live** /lɪv/ leben; wohnen NHG 5

lively /ˈlaɪvli/ lebhaft, lebendig
p. 20, 1

living /ˈlɪvɪŋ/ Lebensstil NHG 7

(to) **do for a living** (irr) /ˌdu: fər_ə
ˈlɪvɪŋ/ seinen Lebensunterhalt
verdienen p. 92, 2

living conditions (pl) /ˈlɪvɪŋ
kənˌdɪʃnz/ Lebensbedingungen
p. 121, 6

living room /ˈlɪvɪŋ ˌru:m/ Wohn-
zimmer NHG 5

'll (= will) /l, wɪl/ werden NHG 6

(to) **load** /ləʊd/ laden NHG 5

locally /ˈləʊkli/ am / vor Ort p. 39, 6

(to) **be located** (irr) /ˌbi: ləʊˈkeɪtɪd/
gelegen sein NHG 7

locker /ˈlɒkə/ Schließfach; Spind
p. 38, 6

log /lɒg/ Baumstamm p. 93, 2

lonely /ˈləʊnli/ einsam NHG 6

long /lɒŋ/ lang NHG 5

all day long /ˌɔ:l deɪ ˈlɒŋ/ den
ganzen Tag lang p. 21, 2

for a long time /fər_ə ˈlɒŋ taɪm/
lange p. 62, 8

look /lʊk/ Aussehen; Look NHG 7

(to) **look** /lʊk/ aussehen NHG 5

(to) **have a look at** (irr) /ˌhæv_ə
ˈlʊk_ət/ sich ansehen NHG 6

(to) take a closer look at (irr)
/ˌteɪk_ə ˌkləʊsə ˈlʊk_ət/ sich genauer
ansehen p. 148

(to) **look after** (irr) /ˌlʊk_ˈɑ:ftə/ sich
kümmern um; aufpassen auf
NHG 5

(to) **look (at)** /ˈlʊk_ət/ (an)sehen,
(an)schauen NHG 5

(to) **look away** /ˌlʊk_əˈweɪ/ weg-
sehen p. 65, 12

(to) **look for** /ˈlʊk fə/ suchen nach
NHG 5

(to) **look forward to** /ˌlʊk ˈfɔ:wəd_tʊ/
sich freuen auf NHG 6

(to) **look up** /ˌlʊk_ˈʌp/ hochschauen; nachschlagen NHG 7

(to) **lose** (irr) /lu:z/ verlieren NHG 7

a lot /ə ˈlɒt/ viel, sehr NHG 5

thanks a lot /ˌθæŋks_ə ˈlɒt/
vielen Dank NHG 5

a lot (of) /ə ˈlɒt/ viel(e), jede
Menge NHG 5

lots of /ˈlɒts_əv/ viel(e) NHG 5

loud /laʊd/ laut NHG 5

love /lʌv/ viele Grüße; alles Liebe
(in Briefen) NHG 6

(to) **love** /lʌv/ lieben, sehr mögen
NHG 5

(to) **fall in love** (irr) /ˌfɔ:l_ɪn ˈlʌv/
sich verlieben p. 65, 12

(to) **love doing something** /lʌv
ˈdu:ɪŋ ˌsʌmθɪŋ/ etwas sehr gern
tun NHG 5

I'd love to … /aɪd ˈlʌv tə/ Ich würde
sehr gern … NHG 5

love letter /ˈlʌv ˌletə/ Liebesbrief p. 25, 7

loved ones (pl) /ˈlʌvd wʌnz/ Angehörige; nahestehende Personen p. 72, 6

lovely /ˈlʌvli/ schön; herrlich p. 21, 2

lover /ˈlʌvə/ Liebhaber/in p. 13, 6

(to) lower /ˈləʊə/ senken p. 65, 12

loyal /ˈlɔɪəl/ treu; loyal p. 61, 7

(good) luck /lʌk/ Glück NHG 6

Good luck! /ˌɡʊd ˈlʌk/ Viel Glück! NHG 7

lunch /lʌntʃ/ Mittagessen NHG 5

lunchtime /ˈlʌntʃtaɪm/ Mittagszeit; Mittagspause p. 45, 2

lyrics (pl) /ˈlɪrɪks/ Liedtext p. 25, 7

M

machine /məˈʃiːn/ Maschine; Apparat NHG 6

household machine /ˈhaʊsˌhəʊld məˈʃiːn/ Haushaltsgerät p. 42, 12

made /meɪd/ hergestellt, gemacht NHG 7

magazine /ˌmæɡəˈziːn/ Zeitschrift NHG 7

magic /ˈmædʒɪk/ Magie; Zauber p. 13, 6

magnificent /mæɡˈnɪfɪsnt/ wunderbar; großartig p. 13, 6

main /meɪn/ Haupt- NHG 5

main (course) /ˈmeɪn kɔːs/ Hauptgericht NHG 7

(to) **maintain** /meɪnˈteɪn/ erhalten; pflegen p. 73, 6

maintenance /ˈmeɪntənəns/ Pflege; Wartung p. 41, 8

major /ˈmeɪdʒə/ bedeutend, wichtig p. 69, 2

majority /məˈdʒɒrəti/ Mehrheit p. 68, 2

(to) **make** (irr) /meɪk/ machen NHG 5

(to) **make** (it/something) (irr) /meɪk/ (es/etwas) schaffen p. 111, 7

(to) make (irr) /meɪk/ hier: ergeben p. 6; hier: ausmachen p. 61, 7

(to) **make a difference** (irr) /ˌmeɪk ə ˈdɪfrəns/ einen Unterschied machen; verändern p. 85, 5

(to) make camp (irr) /ˌmeɪk ˈkæmp/ das Lager aufschlagen p. 111, 7

(to) **make friends (with)** (irr) /ˌmeɪk ˈfrendz/ sich anfreunden (mit) NHG 6

(to) **make happen** (irr) /ˌmeɪk ˈhæpən/ möglich machen p. 25, 7

(to) **make money** (irr) /ˌmeɪk ˈmʌni/ Geld verdienen p. 24, 6

(to) **make notes** (irr) /ˌmeɪk ˈnəʊts/ sich Notizen machen NHG 5

(to) make one's dream come true (irr) /ˌmeɪk wʌnz ˈdriːm kʌm ˌtruː/ seinen Traum wahr werden lassen p. 149

(to) make one's mark (irr) /ˌmeɪk wʌnz ˈmɑːk/ seine Spuren hinterlassen p. 121, 6

(to) **make out** (irr) /ˌmeɪkˈaʊt/ ausmachen p. 109, 5

(to) **make sense** (irr) /ˌmeɪk ˈsens/ sinnvoll sein p. 62, 8

(to) **make somebody do something** (irr) /ˌmeɪk ˌsʌmbədi ˈduː ˌsʌmθɪŋ/ jemanden dazu bringen, etwas zu tun NHG 7

(to) **make sure** (irr) /ˌmeɪk ˈʃɔː/ darauf achten, dass … NHG 6

(to) **make up** (irr) /ˌmeɪkˈʌp/ erfinden, sich ausdenken NHG 6

man (pl **men**) /mæn, men/ Mann NHG 5; Mensch p. 10, 2

(to) **manage** /ˈmænɪdʒ/ verwalten; organisieren p. 41, 8

adverb of manner /ˌædvɜːbˌəv ˈmænə/ Adverb der Art und Weise p. 70

manners (pl) /ˈmænə/ Manieren p. 95, 7

manuscript /ˈmænjuskrɪpt/ Manuskript p. 120, 6

many /ˈmeni/ viele NHG 5

map /mæp/ Karte NHG 5

March /mɑːtʃ/ März NHG 5

marching band /ˈmɑːtʃɪŋ bænd/ Marschkapelle p. 34, 2

mark /mɑːk/ Note; Zensur NHG 6

(to) **mark** /mɑːk/ markieren, kennzeichnen NHG 7

(to) make one's mark (irr) /ˌmeɪk wʌnz ˈmɑːk/ seine Spuren hinterlassen p. 121, 6

market /ˈmɑːkɪt/ Markt NHG 5

(to) market /ˈmɑːkɪt/ vermarkten p. 41, 8

(to) **be married** (irr) /ˌbi ˈmærɪd/ verheiratet sein NHG 6

(to) **get married** (irr) /ˌɡet ˈmærɪd/ heiraten NHG 7

(to) **marry** /ˈmæri/ heiraten NHG 7

massive /ˈmæsɪv/ riesig; enorm p. 86, 6

match /mætʃ/ Spiel NHG 5

(to) **match** /mætʃ/ passen zu NHG 6

(to) **match (with/to)** /mætʃ/ zuordnen NHG 5

matching /ˈmætʃɪŋ/ passend p. 43, 14

math (AE, informal) /mæθ/ Mathe (Schulfach) p. 39, 6

mathematics /ˌmæθəˈmætɪks/ Mathematik p. 44, 2

mathletics club (informal) /mæθˈletɪks klʌb/ Mathe-AG p. 44, 2

maths (informal) /mæθ/ Mathe (Schulfach) NHG 5

matter /ˈmætə/ Angelegenheit NHG 7

What's the matter? /ˌwɒts ðə ˈmætə/ Was ist los? NHG 7

May /meɪ/ Mai NHG 5

may /meɪ/ können; dürfen NHG 6

maybe /ˈmeɪbi/ vielleicht NHG 5

me, to me /miː/ mir; mich; ich NHG 5

meal /miːl/ Mahlzeit; Essen NHG 5

mean /miːn/ gemein; bösartig p. 62, 8

(to) **mean** (irr) /miːn/ meinen; bedeuten NHG 6

meaning /ˈmiːnɪŋ/ Bedeutung NHG 7

meat /miːt/ Fleisch NHG 7

mechanic /mɪˈkænɪk/ Mechaniker/in NHG 6

medal /ˈmedl/ Medaille p. 6

the media /ðə ˈmiːdiə/ Medien p. 26, 8

social media /ˌsəʊʃl ˈmiːdiə/ soziale Medien p. 69, 2

mediation /ˌmiːdiˈeɪʃn/ Sprachmittlung; Mediation p. 16, 8

medical /ˈmedɪkl/ medizinisch p. 110, 6

medication /ˌmedɪˈkeɪʃn/ Medikamente (pl) p. 92, 2

medicine /ˈmedsn/ Medizin; Medikamente NHG 7

medieval /ˌmediˈiːvl/ mittelalterlich p. 121, 6

(to) **meet** (irr) /miːt/ treffen; sich treffen NHG 5; kennenlernen NHG 6

Nice to meet you. /ˌnaɪs tə ˈmiːt jə/ Schön, dich / euch / Sie zu treffen. NHG 5

meeting /ˈmiːtɪŋ/ Versammlung; Treffen NHG 6

member /ˈmembə/ Mitglied NHG 5

memorial /məˈmɔːriəl/ Denkmal; Ehrenmal p. 21, 2

memory /ˈmemri/ Erinnerung NHG 7

(to) mend /mend/ reparieren; in Ordnung bringen p. 25, 7

(to) **mention** /ˈmenʃn/ erwähnen NHG 7

menu /ˈmenjuː/ Speisekarte; Menü NHG 5

message /ˈmesɪdʒ/ Nachricht; Botschaft NHG 5

(to) message /ˈmesɪdʒ/ eine Nachricht schicken p. 68, 2

metal /ˈmetl/ Metall p. 86, 6

method /ˈmeθəd/ Methode NHG 7

metre /ˈmiːtə/ Meter NHG 6

Mexican /ˈmeksɪkən/ Mexikaner/in; mexikanisch p. 27, 10

mid- /mɪd/ Mitte p. 15, 7

middle /ˈmɪdl/ Mitte NHG 5

in the middle of /ˌɪn ðə ˈmɪdl_əv/ in der Mitte von; mitten in p. 21, 2

Middle-Eastern /ˌmɪdl_ˈiːstən/ Mensch aus dem Nahen Osten; Nahost-, nahöstlich p. 25, 7

might /maɪt/ könnte(st, n, t) NHG 6

mile /maɪl/ Meile NHG 6

military /ˈmɪlɪtri/ militärisch p. 15, 7

milk /mɪlk/ Milch NHG 5

(to) milk /mɪlk/ melken p. 111, 7

(to) **change one's mind** /ˌtʃeɪndʒ wʌnz ˈmaɪnd/ seine Meinung ändern NHG 6

(to) come to mind *(irr)* /ˌkʌm tə ˈmaɪnd/ einfallen, in den Sinn kommen p. 25, 7

(to) keep in mind *(irr)* /ˌkiːp_ɪn ˈmaɪnd/ im Gedächtnis behalten p. 115, 14

mine /maɪn/ meine(r, s) NHG 7

mineral water /ˈmɪnrəl ˌwɔːtə/ Mineralwasser NHG 7

(to) **miss** /mɪs/ vermissen; verpassen NHG 5

(to) miss out (on) /ˌmɪs_ˈaʊt_ˌɒn/ verpassen, sich entgehen lassen p. 163

missing /ˈmɪsɪŋ/ fehlend NHG 5

mistake /mɪˈsteɪk/ Fehler p. 115, 14

misunderstanding /ˌmɪsʌndəˈstændɪŋ/ Missverständnis p. 71, 5

(to) **mix** /mɪks/ sich (ver)mischen NHG 6

mixed /mɪkst/ gemischt p. 18, 11

mixture /ˈmɪkstʃə/ Mischung NHG 7

mobile (phone) /ˈməʊbaɪl/ Handy NHG 6

moccasin /ˈmɒkəsɪn/ Mokassin p. 7

modal verb /ˈməʊdl vɜːb/ Modalverb p. 94

model /ˈmɒdl/ Modell NHG 6

Monday /ˈmʌndeɪ/ Montag NHG 5

(on) Mondays /ˈmʌndeɪz/ montags NHG 5

money /ˈmʌni/ Geld NHG 5

(to) **make money** *(irr)* /ˌmeɪk ˈmʌni/ Geld verdienen p. 24, 6

pocket money /ˈpɒkɪt ˌmʌni/ Taschengeld NHG 7

month /mʌnθ/ Monat NHG 5

monument /ˈmɒnjʊmənt/ Denkmal p. 26, 8

mood /muːd/ Laune; Stimmung NHG 6

moon /muːn/ Mond NHG 5

more /mɔː/ mehr; weitere NHG 5

morning /ˈmɔːnɪŋ/ Morgen NHG 5

mosque /mɒsk/ Moschee NHG 6

most /məʊst/ die / am meisten NHG 7

most of the time /ˈməʊst_əv ðə ˌtaɪm/ meistens NHG 7

mostly /ˈməʊstli/ meistens, größtenteils NHG 7

mother /ˈmʌðə/ Mutter NHG 5

(to) motivate /ˈməʊtɪveɪt/ motivieren p. 82, 2

mountain /ˈmaʊntɪn/ Berg NHG 5

move /muːv/ Bewegung NHG 5

(to) **move** /muːv/ umziehen NHG 6; (sich) bewegen NHG 7

on the move /ˌɒn ðə ˈmuːv/ unterwegs p. 113, 9

(to) **move something** /ˈmuːv ˌsʌmθɪŋ/ etwas wegräumen, etwas woanders hinstellen NHG 6

movement /ˈmuːvmənt/ Bewegung p. 15, 7

movie *(AE)* /ˈmuːvi/ Film p. 41, 8

moving /ˈmuːvɪŋ/ beweglich NHG 6; bewegend; ergreifend p. 21, 2

(to) mow /məʊ/ mähen p. 97, 9

Mr /ˈmɪstə/ Herr *(Anrede)* NHG 5

Mrs /ˈmɪsɪz/ Frau *(Anrede)* NHG 5

much /mʌtʃ/ viel NHG 5; sehr NHG 7

multicultural /ˌmʌltiˈkʌltʃərəl/ multikulturell NHG 7

mum /mʌm/ Mama; Mutti NHG 5

muscle /ˈmʌsl/ Muskel NHG 7

music /ˈmjuːzɪk/ Musik NHG 5

musician /mjʊˈzɪʃn/ Musiker/in NHG 6

Muslim /ˈmʊzləm/ Muslim/in; muslimisch NHG 6

must /mʌst/ müssen NHG 6

must-see /ˌmʌst ˈsiː/ *etwas, das man unbedingt sehen muss* p. 13, 6

mustn't (= must not) /ˈmʌsnt, mʌst ˈnɒt/ nicht dürfen NHG 6

my /maɪ/ mein(e) NHG 5

myself /maɪˈself/ mir/mich/ich (selbst) NHG 7

mystical /ˈmɪstɪkl/ mystisch p. 119, 5

N

(to) **name** /neɪm/ (be)nennen NHG 5

nasty /ˈnɑːsti/ böse, gemein p. 69, 2

nation /ˈneɪʃn/ Nation; Land; Volk p. 14, 7

national park /ˌnæʃnl ˈpɑːk/ Nationalpark NHG 6

nationality /ˌnæʃəˈnæləti/ Nationalität p. 27, 10

Native American /ˌneɪtɪv_əˈmerɪkən/ *Native American (Selbstbezeichnung der ersten Bevölkerungen in den USA)* p. 14, 7

natural /ˈnætʃrəl/ natürlich p. 11, 2

nature /ˈneɪtʃə/ Natur NHG 5

Navajo /ˈnævəhəʊ/ *Sprache der Navajo* p. 82, 2

near /nɪə/ nahe, in der Nähe von NHG 5

necessary /ˈnesəsri/ notwendig, erforderlich NHG 5

(to) **need** /niːd/ brauchen NHG 5

(to) **need to** /ˈniːd_tʊ/ müssen NHG 5

negative /ˈnegətɪv/ negativ NHG 6

neighbor *(AE)* /ˈneɪbə/ Nachbar/in p. 95, 7

neighborhood *(AE)* /ˈneɪbəhʊd/ Viertel; Nachbarschaft p. 24, 6

neighbour /ˈneɪbə/ Nachbar/in NHG 7

neighbourhood /ˈneɪbəhʊd/ Viertel; Nachbarschaft NHG 5

neither /ˈnaɪðə, ˈniːðə/ auch nicht NHG 7

nervous /ˈnɜːvəs/ nervös NHG 5

net /net/ Netz NHG 5

network /'net,wɜːk/ Netzwerk NHG 7

never /'nevə/ nie, niemals NHG 5

new /njuː/ neu NHG 5

New Year /,njuː ˈjɪə/ Neujahr NHG 6

news *(no pl)* /njuːz/ Neuigkeit; Nachrichten NHG 7

newspaper /'njuːz,peɪpə/ Zeitung NHG 6

next /nekst/ nächste(r, s) NHG 5; dann, als Nächstes NHG 6

next to /'nekst_tə/ neben NHG 5

nice /naɪs/ schön; nett NHG 5

Nice to meet you. /,naɪs tə ˈmiːt jə/ Schön, dich / euch / Sie zu treffen. NHG 5

nickname /'nɪk,neɪm/ Spitzname; Kosename p. 27, 11

night /naɪt/ Nacht; Abend NHG 6

09/11 /,naɪn_ɪ,levn/ *Terrorangriffe am 11. September 2001* p. 25, 7

no /nəʊ/ kein(e); nein NHG 5

no longer /,nəʊ ˈlɒŋgə/ nicht mehr NHG 7

no one /'nəʊ wʌn/ keiner NHG 6

nobody /'nəʊbədi/ niemand; keiner NHG 7

noise /nɔɪz/ Geräusch; Lärm NHG 6

noisy /'nɔɪzi/ laut p. 20, 1

non- /nɒn/ nicht p. 117, 2

non-profit /,nɒn ˈprɒfɪt/ nicht gewinnorientiert p. 86, 6

non-stop /,nɒn ˈstɒp/ ununterbrochen p. 76, 12

north /nɔːθ/ Norden; Nord- NHG 7

North America /,nɔːθ_əˈmerɪkə/ Nordamerika p. 14, 7

northern /'nɔːðən/ nördlich, Nord- NHG 6

Northern Ireland /,nɔːðən_ˈaɪələnd/ Nordirland p. 124, 11

nose /nəʊz/ Nase NHG 5

not /nɒt/ nicht NHG 5

not ... either /,nɒt_ˈaɪðə/ auch nicht NHG 7

not any /,nɒt_ˈeni/ kein(e) NHG 5

not anymore /,nɒt_,eni ˈmɔː/ nicht mehr NHG 6

not anyone /,nɒt_ˈeniwʌn/ niemand NHG 7

not anything /,nɒt_ˈeni,θɪŋ/ nichts NHG 6

not anywhere /,nɒt_ˈeni,weə/ nirgendwo NHG 6

not at all /,nɒt_ət_ˈɔːl/ überhaupt nicht p. 48, 7

not yet /nɒt ˈjet/ noch nicht NHG 6

note /nəʊt/ Nachricht; Notiz NHG 5

(to) **note** /nəʊt/ beachten, zur Kenntnis nehmen NHG 6

notepad /'nəʊt,pæd/ Notizblock NHG 5

(to) **make notes** *(irr)* /,meɪk ˈnəʊts/ sich Notizen machen NHG 5

nothing /'nʌθɪŋ/ nichts NHG 6

(to) **notice** /'nəʊtɪs/ bemerken; wahrnehmen NHG 6

noticeboard /'nəʊtɪs,bɔːd/ Schwarzes Brett NHG 5

notorious /nəʊˈtɔːriəs/ berüchtigt p. 121, 6

noun /naʊn/ Hauptwort; Substantiv; Nomen NHG 5

November /nəʊˈvembə/ November NHG 5

now /naʊ/ jetzt NHG 5

number /'nʌmbə/ Zahl; Nummer; Anzahl NHG 5

phone number /'fəʊn ,nʌmbə/ Telefonnummer NHG 5

a number of /ə ˈnʌmbər_əv/ einige, ein paar p. 93, 2

nurse /nɜːs/ Krankenschwester; Krankenpfleger NHG 6

nursery teacher /'nɜːsəri ,tiːtʃə/ Vorschullehrer/in; Erzieher/in p. 92, 1

NYC (= New York City) /,en waɪ ˈsiː, ,njuː jɔːk ˈsɪti/ *die Stadt New York* p. 25, 7

O

o'clock /əˈklɒk/ Uhr *(bei Nennung einer Uhrzeit)* NHG 5

object /'ɒbdʒekt/ Gegenstand NHG 6

obstacle /'ɒbstəkl/ Hindernis; Hürde p. 89, 9

occasion /əˈkeɪʒn/ Gelegenheit; Anlass NHG 7

October /ɒkˈtəʊbə/ Oktober NHG 5

of /əv/ von; aus NHG 5

Of course! /əv ˈkɔːs/ Natürlich! NHG 5

off /ɒf/ von; hinunter, herunter NHG 6

(to) **offer** /'ɒfə/ anbieten NHG 6

special offer /,speʃl_ˈɒfə/ Sonderangebot p. 26, 8

offer /'ɒfə/ Angebot p. 115, 14

office /'ɒfɪs/ Büro NHG 5

office manager /'ɒfɪs ,mænɪdʒə/ Sekretär/in NHG 7

official /əˈfɪʃl/ Amtsperson p. 110, 6

official, officially /əˈfɪʃl, əˈfɪʃli/ offiziell NHG 7

often /'ɒfn/ oft; häufig NHG 5

oil /ɔɪl/ Öl NHG 7

old /əʊld/ alt NHG 5

Olympic /əˈlɪmpɪk/ olympisch p. 6

on /ɒn/ auf; an; in NHG 5

on /ɒn/ *hier:* über p. 65, 12

on board /,ɒn ˈbɔːd/ an Bord p. 121, 6

on one's own /,ɒn ,wʌnz_ˈəʊn/ allein NHG 5

on the left /,ɒn ðə ˈleft/ links, auf der linken Seite NHG 5

on the move /,ɒn ðə ˈmuːv/ unterwegs p. 113, 9

on the one hand, ... /,ɒn ðə ˈwʌn hænd/ einerseits ... NHG 7

on the other hand, ... /,ɒn ði_ˈʌðə hænd/ andererseits ... NHG 7

on the right /,ɒn ðə ˈraɪt/ rechts, auf der rechten Seite NHG 5

on the weekends *(AE)* /,ɒn ðə ˈwiːkendz/ an den Wochenenden p. 97, 9

on time /,ɒn ˈtaɪm/ pünktlich NHG 5

once /wʌns/ sobald; wenn, als p. 34, 2; einmal p. 101, 17

one /wʌn/ ein(e); eins NHG 5; eine(r, s) NHG 7

a different one /ə ˈdɪfrənt wʌn/ ein anderer/eine andere/ein anderes p. 40, 7

one day /,wʌn ˈdeɪ/ eines Tages p. 117, 2

one-minute /,wʌn ˈmɪnɪt/ einminütig p. 16, 9

the ones /ðə ˈwʌnz/ diejenigen; diese p. 38, 6

onion /'ʌnjən/ Zwiebel NHG 7

only /'əʊnli/ nur, bloß; erst; einzige(r, s) NHG 5

onto /'ɒntə/ auf, in NHG 6

open /'əʊpən/ offen; geöffnet NHG 5

(to) **open** /'əʊpən/ öffnen, aufmachen NHG 5; sich öffnen, aufgehen; eröffnen NHG 6

opening act /'əʊpənɪŋ_ækt/ Eröffnungsfeier p. 48, 7

Opening Day /ˈəʊpənɪŋ deɪ/ Eröffnungstag L&L 4

opening times *(pl)* /ˈəʊpənɪŋ taɪmz/ Öffnungszeiten NHG 6

(to) operate /ˈɒpəreɪt/ bedienen p. 93, 2

opinion /əˈpɪnjən/ Meinung; Ansicht NHG 6

in my opinion /ɪn ˈmaɪ_əˌpɪnjən/ meiner Meinung nach NHG 6

opportunity /ˌɒpəˈtjuːnəti/ Chance; Möglichkeit; Gelegenheit p. 17, 10

opposite /ˈɒpəzɪt/ Gegenteil NHG 5

optional /ˈɒpʃnəl/ optional, fakultativ p. 40, 7

or /ɔː/ oder NHG 5

orange /ˈɒrɪndʒ/ Orange; Apfelsine; orange NHG 5

order /ˈɔːdə/ Reihenfolge; Ordnung NHG 6

in order to /ɪnˈɔːdə tʊ/ um zu NHG 7

(to) **take an order** *(irr)* /ˌteɪk_ənˈɔːdə/ eine Bestellung aufnehmen NHG 7

(to) **order (in)** /ˈɔːdə, ˌɔːdərˈɪn/ bestellen NHG 7

organic /ɔːˈgænɪk/ aus biologischem Anbau, Bio- p. 39, 6

organization (= organisation) /ˌɔːgənaɪˈzeɪʃn/ Organisation; Vereinigung p. 86, 6

organizational (= organisational) /ˌɔːgənaɪˈzeɪʃnəl/ organisatorisch p. 96, 8

(to) **organize (= organise)** /ˈɔːgənaɪz/ organisieren NHG 6

origin /ˈɒrɪdʒɪn/ Ursprung; Herkunft p. 17, 10

original /əˈrɪdʒnəl/ ursprünglich NHG 7; originell, außergewöhnlich p. 93, 2

originally /əˈrɪdʒnəli/ ursprünglich NHG 7

(to) originate /əˈrɪdʒəneɪt/ entstehen, seinen Anfang nehmen p. 7

the Oscars /ðiˌ ɒskəz/ *amerikanischer Filmpreis* p. 6

other /ˈʌðə/ andere(r, s) NHG 5

our /aʊə/ unser(e) NHG 5

ours /ˈaʊəz/ unsere(r, s) NHG 7

ourselves /aʊəˈselvz/ uns; wir selbst NHG 7

out /aʊt/ heraus, hinaus; aus NHG 5; draußen NHG 6

out of /ˈaʊt_əv/ aus NHG 6; von p. 62, 8

outdoor /ˌaʊtˈdɔː/ Outdoor-, im Freien NHG 7

outdoors /ˌaʊtˈdɔːz/ draußen; im Freien NHG 7

output /ˈaʊtpʊt/ Ausstoß; Produktion p. 85, 5

outside /ˌaʊtˈsaɪd/ außen; (nach) draußen NHG 5

over /ˈəʊvə/ über, hinüber; vorbei NHG 5

all over the world /ˌɔːlˌəʊvə ðə ˈwɜːld/ auf der ganzen Welt NHG 6

over here /ˌəʊvə ˈhɪə/ hier (drüben) p. 38, 6

over there /ˌəʊvə ˈðeə/ dort (drüben) NHG 5

overboard /ˈəʊvəbɔːd/ über Bord p. 108, 3

overcrowded /ˌəʊvəˈkraʊdɪd/ überfüllt p. 106, 2

own /əʊn/ eigene(r, s) NHG 5

on one's own /ɒn ˌwʌnzˈəʊn/ allein NHG 5

owner /ˈəʊnə/ Besitzer/in NHG 7

ox *(pl* oxen) /ɒks, ˈɒksn/ Ochse p. 110, 6

P

p. (= page) /peɪdʒ/ Seite p. 10, 1

p (= penny, *pl* **pence)** /piː, ˈpeni, pens/ Penny *(brit. Währung)* NHG 5

Pacific, Pacific Ocean /pəˈsɪfɪk, pəˌsɪfɪkˈəʊʃn/ Pazifik, Pazifischer Ozean p. 119, 5

(to) **pack** /pæk/ packen NHG 5

packaging /ˈpækɪdʒɪŋ/ Verpackung NHG 7

packet /ˈpækɪt/ Packung NHG 5

page /peɪdʒ/ Seite NHG 5

painfully /ˈpeɪnfli/ schmerzlich p. 64, 9

(to) **paint** /peɪnt/ (an)malen NHG 5

painting /ˈpeɪntɪŋ/ Bild; Gemälde NHG 5

pair /peə/ Paar NHG 6

(a pair of) trousers /ə ˌpeər_əv ˈtraʊzəz/ Hose NHG 5

pajama day *(AE)* /pəˈdʒɑːmə deɪ/ *Schlafanzugtag* p. 43, 14

pajamas *(AE)* = pyjamas *(BE)* /pəˈdʒɑːməz/ Schlafanzug p. 43, 14

palace /ˈpæləs/ Palast NHG 6

Pancake Day /ˈpænkeɪk deɪ/ Pfannkuchentag p. 6

paper /ˈpeɪpə/ Papier NHG 6

piece of paper /ˌpiːs_əv ˈpeɪpə/ Blatt Papier p. 40, 7

paper boy /ˈpeɪpə bɔɪ/ Zeitungsjunge p. 97, 9

paraclimber /ˈpærəˌklaɪmə/ *Kletterer/Kletterin mit Handicap* p. 83, 2

paragraph /ˈpærəˌgrɑːf/ Absatz; Abschnitt NHG 6

Paraguayan /ˌpærəˈgwaɪən/ Paraguayaner/in; paraguayisch p. 162

Paralympic /ˌpærəˈlɪmpɪk/ paralympisch p. 83, 2

parent /ˈpeərənt/ Elternteil NHG 7

parents *(pl)* /ˈpeərənts/ Eltern NHG 5

(to) **build a park** *(irr)* /ˌbɪld_ə ˈpɑːk/ einen Park anlegen p. 21, 2

parking lot *(AE)* /ˈpɑːkɪŋ lɒt/ Parkplatz p. 47, 6

parliament /ˈpɑːləmənt/ Parlament NHG 6

part /pɑːt/ Teil NHG 5; Rolle NHG 7

particular /pəˈtɪkjʊlə/ bestimmt; besondere(r, s) p. 66, 14

(to) **pass** /pɑːs/ geben, herüberreichen NHG 5

(to) **pass** /pɑːs/ *hier:* durchgehen p. 25, 7

(to) **pass away** /ˌpɑːs_əˈweɪ/ verbringen p. 122, 7

passage /ˈpæsɪdʒ/ (Text)passage; Gang; Überfahrt p. 17, 10

passenger /ˈpæsɪndʒə/ Passagier/in NHG 7

passive /ˈpæsɪv/ Passiv p. 28, 12

password /ˈpɑːsˌwɜːd/ Passwort NHG 7

past /pɑːst/ nach; Vergangenheit NHG 5; vorbei; vorüber NHG 6

past perfect /ˌpɑːst ˈpɜːfɪkt/ Plusquamperfekt; Vorvergangenheit p. 36

past progressive /ˌpɑːst prəʊˈgresɪv/ Verlaufsform der Vergangenheit p. 114, 11

pasta /ˈpæstə/ Nudeln NHG 7

path /pɑːθ/ Weg; Pfad NHG 6
patience /ˈpeɪʃns/ Geduld p. 85, 5
patient /ˈpeɪʃnt/ geduldig p. 97, 9
pattern /ˈpætən/ Muster p. 48, 7
pay /peɪ/ Lohn p. 97, 9
(to) **pay** /peɪ/ (be)zahlen NHG 5
(to) **pay attention (to)** *(irr)*
/ˌpeɪ_əˈtenʃn tʊ/ aufpassen; achten
auf NHG 6
payment /ˈpeɪmənt/ Bezahlung
NHG 6
PE (= Physical Education) /ˌpiːˈiː,
ˌfɪzɪklˌedjʊˈkeɪʃn/ Sport *(Schulfach)*
NHG 5
peace /piːs/ Frieden p. 17, 10
(to) **peak** /piːk/ den Höhepunkt
erreichen p. 109, 5
peak /piːk/ Gipfel; Bergspitze p. 10, 2
pen /pen/ Stift NHG 5
pencil /ˈpensl/ Bleistift NHG 5
pencil case /ˈpensl ˌkeɪs/ Feder-
mäppchen NHG 5
pencil sharpener /ˈpensl ˌʃɑːpnə/
Bleistiftspitzer NHG 5
peninsula /pəˈnɪnsjələ/ Halbinsel
p. 119, 5
people /ˈpiːpl/ Leute; Menschen
NHG 5
peoples *(pl)* /ˈpiːplz/ Völker p. 25, 7
pepper /ˈpepə/ Paprika; Pfeffer NHG 7
per /pɜː/ pro NHG 5
per cent *(BE)*, **percent** *(AE)*
/pəˈsent/ Prozent p. 109, 5
perfect /ˈpɜːfɪkt/ perfekt NHG 5
(to) **perform** /pəˈfɔːm/ aufführen;
durchführen NHG 6
performance /pəˈfɔːməns/ Auffüh-
rung; Leistung NHG 6
period *(AE)* /ˈpɪəriəd/ Stunde p. 39, 6
permission /pəˈmɪʃn/ Erlaubnis;
Genehmigung NHG 6
in person /ˌɪn ˈpɜːsn/ persönlich p.72,6
personal /ˈpɜːsnəl/ persönlich NHG 5
personality /ˌpɜːsəˈnæləti/ Persön-
lichkeit p. 95, 7
pet /pet/ Haustier NHG 5
petition /pəˈtɪʃn/ Petition; Unter-
schriftenliste p. 85, 5
phone /fəʊn/ Telefon NHG 5
cell phone *(AE)* /ˈsel fəʊn/ Handy
p. 68, 2
phone call /ˈfəʊn kɔːl/ Telefonanruf
p. 72, 6

phone number /ˈfəʊn ˌnʌmbə/ Telefonnummer NHG 5
photo /ˈfəʊtəʊ/ Foto NHG 5
(to) **take a photo** *(irr)* /ˌteɪk_ə
ˈfəʊtəʊ/ ein Foto machen NHG 5
photograph /ˈfəʊtəˌɡrɑːf/ Fotografie; Foto NHG 6
photographer /fəˈtɒɡrəfə/ Foto-
graf/in NHG 6
photography /fəˈtɒɡrəfi/ Fotografie
p. 26, 8
phrase /freɪz/ Satz; Ausdruck NHG 5
physical /ˈfɪzɪkl/ körperlich NHG 7
physiotherapist /ˌfɪziəʊˈθerəpɪst/
Physiotherapeut/in p. 92, 1
piano /piˈænəʊ/ Klavier NHG 5
(to) **pick up** /ˌpɪk_ˈʌp/ aufheben;
abholen NHG 5
(to) pick up (on) /ˌpɪk_ˈʌp/ anknüp-
fen an p. 62, 8
picture /ˈpɪktʃə/ Bild NHG 5
(to) **take a picture** *(irr)* /ˌteɪk_ə
ˈpɪktʃə/ ein Foto machen NHG 5
pie /paɪ/ Pastete; Kuchen p. 37, 5
pie chart /ˈpaɪ tʃɑːt/ Tortendia-
gramm, Kuchendiagramm p. 171
piece /piːs/ Stück; Teil NHG 6
piece of advice /ˌpiːs_əv_ədˈvaɪs/
Rat(schlag) p. 74, 8
piece of paper /ˌpiːs_əv ˈpeɪpə/ Blatt
Papier p. 40, 7
pilgrim /ˈpɪlɡrɪm/ Pilger/in p. 14, 7
pillow /ˈpɪləʊ/ Kissen p. 68, 2
pitcher /ˈpɪtʃə/ Werfer/in p. 44, 2
place /pleɪs/ Ort; Platz; Haus,
Zuhause NHG 5
(to) **place** /pleɪs/ platzieren; stellen
NHG 5
(to) **take place** *(irr)* /ˌteɪk ˈpleɪs/
stattfinden NHG 6
(to) **plan** /plæn/ planen NHG 5
plane /pleɪn/ Flugzeug NHG 6
planning /ˈplænɪŋ/ Planen p. 93, 2
plant /plɑːnt/ Pflanze NHG 6
(to) **plant** /plɑːnt/ pflanzen p. 111, 7
recycling plant /riːˈsaɪklɪŋ plɑːnt/
Recyclinganlage p. 86, 6
plaster /ˈplɑːstə/ Gips; Pflaster NHG 7
plaster /ˈplɑːstə/ Verputz p. 65, 12
plastic /ˈplæstɪk/ Plastik NHG 6
plate /pleɪt/ Teller NHG 5
platform /ˈplætfɔːm/ Bahnsteig;
Plattform NHG 6

play /pleɪ/ Spiel; (Theater)stück NHG 6
(to) **play** /pleɪ/ spielen NHG 5
player /ˈpleɪə/ Spieler/in NHG 5
playground /ˈpleɪˌɡraʊnd/ Spiel-
platz NHG 5
playing /ˈpleɪɪŋ/ Spielen NHG 5
playing field /ˈpleɪɪŋ ˌfiːld/ Sport-
platz p. 48, 7
please /pliːz/ bitte NHG 5
(to) **pledge** /pledʒ/ versprechen;
schwören p. 38, 6
the Pledge of Allegiance
/ˌpledʒ_əv_əˈliːdʒns/ *Treueschwur*
p. 38, 6
plenty of /ˈplenti_əv/ reichlich;
genug p. 72, 6
plumbing /ˈplʌmɪŋ/ Klempnern
p. 40, 7
pm (= post meridiem) /ˌpiːˈem,
ˌpəʊst məˈrɪdiəm/ nachmittags;
abends *(nur hinter Uhrzeit
zwischen 12 Uhr mittags und
Mitternacht)* NHG 5
pocket /ˈpɒkɪt/ (Hosen)tasche
NHG 7
pocket money /ˈpɒkɪt ˌmʌni/
Taschengeld NHG 7
poem /ˈpəʊɪm/ Gedicht NHG 5
poet /ˈpəʊɪt/ Dichter/in NHG 7
point /pɔɪnt/ Punkt NHG 5;
Stelle p. 86, 6
(to) **point (at/to)** /pɔɪnt/ deuten
(auf); zeigen (auf) NHG 5
point of view /ˌpɔɪnt_əv_ˈvjuː/
Ansicht; Perspektive p. 59, 3
poisonous /ˈpɔɪznəs/ giftig p. 110, 6
Poland /ˈpəʊlənd/ Polen NHG 5
police officer /pəˈliːs_ˌɒfɪsə/ Polizei-
beamte/Polizeibeamtin NHG 6
Polish /ˈpəʊlɪʃ/ Polnisch; polnisch
p. 117, 2
polite /pəˈlaɪt/ höflich NHG 6
politeness /pəˈlaɪtnəs/ Höflichkeit
p. 95, 7
political /pəˈlɪtɪkl/ politisch p. 14, 7
politician /ˌpɒləˈtɪʃn/ Politiker/in
p. 11, 2
pollution /pəˈluːʃn/ Umweltver-
schmutzung p. 86, 6
poor /pɔː/ arm NHG 6
popular /ˈpɒpjʊlə/ beliebt NHG 6
population /ˌpɒpjʊˈleɪʃn/ Bevölke-
rung NHG 7

positive /'pɒzətɪv/ positiv NHG 6

possibility /ˌpɒsə'bɪləti/ Möglichkeit NHG 6

possible /'pɒsəbl/ möglich NHG 7

(to) **post** /pəʊst/ posten; bekannt geben NHG 6

postcard /'pəʊstˌkɑːd/ Postkarte; Ansichtskarte NHG 5

pot /pɒt/ Topf NHG 7

the potato famine /ðə pə'teɪtəʊ ˌfæmɪn/ Hungersnot in Irland zwischen 1845 und 1849 p. 121, 6

potato (pl **potatoes**) /pə'teɪtəʊ, pə'teɪtəʊz/ Kartoffel NHG 7

potential /pə'tenʃl/ potenziell, möglich p. 86, 6

pound (= £) /paʊnd/ Pfund (britische Währung) NHG 5

power /'paʊə/ Kraft NHG 7; Macht; Einfluss p. 81

(to) power /'paʊə/ antreiben p. 147

powerful /'paʊəfl/ mächtig; stark p. 85, 5

practical /'præktɪkl/ praktisch NHG 7

practice /'præktɪs/ Übung; Training NHG 6; Praxis NHG 7

(to) practice (AE) /'præktɪs/ üben; trainieren; praktizieren p. 35, 2

(to) **practise** /'præktɪs/ üben; trainieren NHG 5

prayer /preə/ Gebet NHG 6

(to) **prefer** /prɪ'fɜː/ vorziehen; bevorzugen NHG 7

prefix /'priːfɪks/ Vorsilbe p. 76, 13

prepaid /ˌpriː'peɪd/ im Voraus bezahlt p. 106, 2

preparation /ˌprepə'reɪʃn/ Vorbereitung; Zubereitung p. 41, 8

(to) **prepare** /prɪ'peə/ vorbereiten NHG 5; zubereiten NHG 7

(to) **prepare for** /prɪ'peə fɔː/ sich vorbereiten auf NHG 7

(to) prescribe /prɪ'skraɪb/ verschreiben p. 92, 2

presence /'prezns/ Anwesenheit; Präsenz p. 15, 7

present /'preznt/ Geschenk NHG 5; Gegenwart NHG 6

present perfect /ˌpreznt 'pɜːfɪkt/ Perfekt p. 22

present perfect progressive /ˌpreznt ˌpɜːfɪkt prəʊ'gresɪv/ Verlaufsform des Perfekt p. 118

(to) **present (to)** /prɪ'zent/ präsentieren, vorstellen NHG 5

presentation /ˌprezn'teɪʃn/ Präsentation; Vortrag NHG 5

(to) **give a presentation** (irr) /ˌgɪv ə ˌprezn'teɪʃn/ eine Präsentation halten NHG 7

(to) **preserve** /prɪ'zɜːv/ erhalten p. 11, 2

president /'prezɪdənt/ Präsident/in p. 6

pretty /'prɪti/ ziemlich NHG 5; hübsch p. 25, 7

(to) **prevent** /prɪ'vent/ verhindern, vorbeugen NHG 7

price /praɪs/ Preis (Kosten) NHG 7

primary school /'praɪməri skuːl/ Grundschule p. 45, 2

print /prɪnt/ Druck p. 26, 8

prize /praɪz/ Preis; Gewinn NHG 7

prizefighter /'praɪzˌfaɪtə/ Preisboxer/in p. 25, 7

pro /prəʊ/ Vorteil; Pro NHG 6

probably /'prɒbəbli/ wahrscheinlich NHG 6

processing /'prəʊsesɪŋ/ Bearbeiten p. 41, 8

(to) **produce** /prə'djuːs/ herstellen NHG 6; produzieren NHG 7

producer /prə'djuːsə/ Produzent/in p. 148

product /'prɒdʌkt/ Produkt p. 41, 8

production /prə'dʌkʃn/ Produktion p. 20, 2

profession /prə'feʃn/ Beruf p. 99, 13

professional /prə'feʃnəl/ professionell; beruflich p. 48, 7

profile /'prəʊfaɪl/ Profil; Porträt NHG 7

(to) **program** /'prəʊgræm/ programmieren p. 40, 7

program /'prəʊgræm/ Computerprogramm p. 170

program (AE) /'prəʊgræm/ Programm p. 34, 6

programme /'prəʊgræm/ Programm NHG 6

programming /'prəʊˌgræmɪŋ/ Programmieren p. 95, 7

project /'prɒdʒekt/ Projekt NHG 6

prom (AE) /prɒm/ Ball am Ende des Jahres (Highschool) p. 35, 2

prom king (AE) /'prɒm kɪŋ/ Ballkönig p. 35, 2

prom queen (AE) /'prɒm kwiːn/ Ballkönigin p. 35, 2

(to) **promise** /'prɒmɪs/ versprechen NHG 7

pronoun /'prəʊnaʊn/ Pronomen, Fürwort p. 52, 12

reflexive pronoun /rɪˌfleksɪv 'prəʊnaʊn/ Reflexivpronomen p. 52, 12

(to) **pronounce** /prə'naʊns/ aussprechen NHG 6

proof /pruːf/ Beweis p. 69, 2

prop /prɒp/ Requisite NHG 7

properly /'prɒpəli/ richtig NHG 7

(to) **protect** /prə'tekt/ beschützen NHG 6

(to) **protect (from)** /prə'tekt frəm/ schützen (vor) p. 74, 8

proud, proudly /praʊd, 'praʊdli/ stolz NHG 6

(to) **be proud of** (irr) /ˌbiː 'praʊd əv/ stolz sein auf p. 24, 6

(to) **prove** (irr) /pruːv/ beweisen NHG 7

(to) **provide** /prə'vaɪd/ zur Verfügung stellen p. 11, 2

psychologist /saɪ'kɒlədʒɪst/ Psychologe/Psychologin p. 62, 8

pub /pʌb/ Kneipe NHG 6

public /'pʌblɪk/ öffentlich NHG 6

the public /ðə 'pʌblɪk/ die Öffentlichkeit NHG 6

public transport /ˌpʌblɪk 'trænspɔːt/ öffentliches Verkehrsmittel p. 85, 5

(to) **publish** /'pʌblɪʃ/ veröffentlichen; herausgeben NHG 6

(to) **pull** /pʊl/ ziehen NHG 7

pumpkin /'pʌmpkɪn/ Kürbis NHG 6

(to) **punch** /pʌntʃ/ schlagen p. 123, 8

pupil /'pjuːpl/ Schüler/in NHG 7

purple /'pɜːpl/ violett; lila NHG 5

(to) **push** /pʊʃ/ schieben; stoßen NHG 6

(to) **put** (irr) /pʊt/ setzen; stellen; legen NHG 5

(to) **put in** (irr) /ˌpʊt 'ɪn/ hineintun, hinzufügen NHG 7

(to) **put on** (irr) /ˌpʊt 'ɒn/ anlegen; auftragen; anziehen (Kleidung) NHG 7

(to) **put on display** (irr) /ˌpʊt ɒn dɪ'spleɪ/ ausstellen NHG 6 (to) **put together** *(irr)* /ˌpʊt̮ təˈgeðə/ zusammenstellen; zusammensetzen NHG 6

(to) **put up** *(irr)* /ˌpʊt̮ ˈʌp/ aufhängen; aufstellen NHG 6

Q

quality /ˈkwɒləti/ Qualität NHG 7

quarter /ˈkwɔːtə/ Viertel NHG 5

queen /kwiːn/ Königin NHG 6

question /ˈkwestʃn/ Frage NHG 5

follow-up question /ˈfɒləʊ ˌʌp ˌkwestʃn/ Folgefrage p. 22, 4

(to) **question** /ˈkwestʃn/ befragen; verhören p. 110, 6

question mark /ˈkwestʃn maːk/ Fragezeichen p. 73, 6

quick /kwɪk/ schnell, kurz NHG 7

quickly /ˈkwɪkli/ schnell NHG 6

quiet /ˈkwaɪət/ leise; ruhig NHG 5

quite /kwaɪt/ ziemlich NHG 6

quota /ˈkwəʊtə/ Quote p. 109, 5

quote /kwəʊt/ Zitat p. 17, 10

R

rabbit /ˈræbɪt/ Kaninchen NHG 5

racial segregation /ˌreɪʃl segrɪˈgeɪʃn/ Rassentrennung p. 15, 7

railroad /ˈreɪlˌrəʊd/ *hier:* Eisenbahngelände p. 23, 5

rain /reɪn/ Regen NHG 6

(to) **rain** /reɪn/ regnen NHG 5

rainy /ˈreɪni/ regnerisch NHG 5

(to) **raise** /reɪz/ beschaffen; sammeln p. 35, 2

(to) **rank** /ræŋk/ einstufen; anordnen p. 17, 10

rare /reə/ selten p. 62, 8

(to) **rate** /reɪt/ einschätzen; bewerten NHG 7

rather /ˈraːðə/ eher, lieber NHG 6

rather than /ˈraːðə ðæn/ anstatt NHG 6

RE (= Religious Education) /ˌaːrˈiː, reˌlɪdʒəsˌedjʊˈkeɪʃn/ Religion *(Schulfach)* NHG 5

(to) **reach** /riːtʃ/ erreichen NHG 7

(to) be far from reach *(irr)* /ˌbiː ˌfaː frəm ˈriːtʃ/ außer Reichweite sein p. 68, 2

(to) **react (to)** /riˈækt/ reagieren (auf) NHG 6

reaction /riˈækʃn/ Reaktion NHG 6

(to) **read** *(irr)* /riːd/ lesen NHG 5

read /riːd/ Lektüre p. 34, 2

(to) **read along** *(irr)* /ˌriːd əˈlɒŋ/ mitlesen NHG 5

(to) **read out** *(irr)* /ˌriːd ˈaʊt/ (laut) vorlesen p. 67, 15

reader /ˈriːdə/ Leser/in p. 34, 2

reading /ˈriːdɪŋ/ Lesen NHG 5; Lesung NHG 7

ready /ˈredi/ fertig, bereit NHG 5

real /rɪəl/ wirklich; echt NHG 6

reality /riˈæləti/ Realität; Wirklichkeit p. 86, 6

(to) **realize (= realise)** /ˈrɪəlaɪz/ sich bewusst sein, erkennen NHG 6

really /ˈrɪəli/ wirklich NHG 5

reason /ˈriːzn/ Grund NHG 6

(to) **give a reason** *(irr)* /ˌgɪv ə ˈriːzn/ einen Grund nennen p. 25, 6

(to) **rebuild** *(irr)* /ˌriːˈbɪld/ wieder aufbauen p. 15, 7

(to) **receive** /rɪˈsiːv/ erhalten; empfangen p. 68, 2

recently /ˈriːsntli/ vor Kurzem; neulich p. 93, 2

recipe /ˈresəpi/ Rezept NHG 7

(to) **recognize (= recognise)** /ˈrekəgnaɪz/ erkennen p. 95, 7

(to) **recommend** /ˌrekəˈmend/ empfehlen NHG 6

record /ˈrekɔːd/ Rekord p. 35, 2

(to) **record** /rɪˈkɔːd/ aufnehmen NHG 5

recording /rɪˈkɔːdɪŋ/ Aufnahme NHG 5

(to) **recreate** /ˌriːkriˈeɪt/ wieder schaffen, nachschaffen p. 132

(to) **recruit** /rɪˈkruːt/ anwerben p. 87, 6

(to) **recycle** /riːˈsaɪkl/ recyceln; wiederaufbereiten p. 86, 6

recycled /riːˈsaɪkld/ wiederverwertet; Recycling- p. 93, 2

recycling plant /riːˈsaɪklɪŋ plaːnt/ Recyclinganlage p. 86, 6

red /red/ rot NHG 5

(to) **reduce** /rɪˈdjuːs/ reduzieren NHG 7

reference /ˈrefrəns/ Referenz; Zeugnis p. 98, 10

reflexive pronoun /rɪˌfleksɪv ˈprəʊnaʊn/ Reflexivpronomen p. 52, 12

regardless of /rɪˈgaːdləs əv/ trotz, ungeachtet p. 17, 10

registrar /ˌredʒɪˈstraː/ Sekretär/in p. 38, 6

registrar's office /ˌredʒɪstraːz ˈɒfɪs/ Sekretariat p. 38, 6

registration /ˌredʒɪˈstreɪʃn/ *Überprüfung der Anwesenheit* NHG 5

regular /ˈregjʊlə/ üblich, normal NHG 6

regularly /ˈregjʊləli/ regelmäßig NHG 7

(to) **reject** /rɪˈdʒekt/ ablehnen, zurückweisen p. 25, 7

(to) **relate to** /rɪˈleɪt̮ tʊ/ handeln von; zu tun haben mit p. 81

relationship /rɪˈleɪʃnʃɪp/ Beziehung p. 57

relative /ˈrelətɪv/ Verwandte/r NHG 6

(to) **relax** /rɪˈlæks/ entspannen NHG 5

relaxed /rɪˈlækst/ entspannt NHG 6

relaxing /rɪˈlæksɪŋ/ entspannend NHG 7

relevant /ˈreləvnt/ relevant; wichtig p. 98, 10

reliability /rɪˌlaɪəˈbɪlɪti/ Zuverlässigkeit p. 95, 7

reliable /rɪˈlaɪəbl/ verlässlich; zuverlässig p. 95, 7

religious /rəˈlɪdʒəs/ religiöse(r, s) NHG 6

(to) **rely on** /rɪˈlaɪ ˌɒn/ sich verlassen auf p. 61, 7

(to) **remember** /rɪˈmembə/ sich erinnern an NHG 5; bedenken, denken an p. 62, 8

(to) **remind somebody** /rɪˈmaɪnd ˌsʌmbədi/ jemanden erinnern p. 62, 8

(to) **remove** /rɪˈmuːv/ entfernen NHG 6

renewable /rɪˈnjuːəbl/ erneuerbar p. 150

renovation /ˌrenəˈveɪʃn/ Renovierung; Sanierung p. 26, 8

rent /rent/ Miete; Pacht p. 106, 2

(to) rent /rent/ mieten p. 21, 2

(to) **repair** /rɪˈpeə/ reparieren NHG 6

repair /rɪˈpeə/ Reparatur p. 41, 8

auto body repair /ˌɔːtəʊ ˌbɒdi rɪˈpeə/ Karosseriereparatur p. 40, 7

(to) **repeat** /rɪˈpiːt/ wiederholen NHG 5

(to) **reply** /rɪˈplaɪ/ antworten; erwidern NHG 6

(to) **report** /rɪˈpɔːt/ sich melden
NHG 6

report /rɪˈpɔːt/ Zeugnis p. 98, 10

(to) **report (to)** /rɪˈpɔːt/ berichten;
wiedergeben p. 60, 4

reported command /ˌrɪ ˈpɔːtɪd
kəˈmɑːnd/ indirekter Befehl p. 108

reported speech /ˌrɪ ˈpɔːtɪd ˈspiːtʃ/
indirekte Rede p. 60

(to) **represent** /ˌreprɪˈzent/ präsentieren, vertreten p. 27, 10

republic /rɪˈpʌblɪk/ Republik p. 38, 6

the Republic of Ireland /ðə
rɪˌpʌblɪk əvˈaɪələnd/ (die Republik)
Irland p. 105

research /rɪˈsɜːtʃ/ Forschung
p. 62, 8

(to) **do research** (irr) /ˌduː rɪˈsɜːtʃ/
recherchieren NHG 5

(to) **research** /rɪˈsɜːtʃ/ recherchieren NHG 7

reservation /ˌrezəˈveɪʃn/ Reservie-
rung NHG 7

resident /ˈrezɪdnt/ *hier:* heimisch
p. 147

respect /rɪˈspekt/ Respekt NHG 6

(to) **respect** /rɪˈspekt/ respektieren
NHG 6

respectfully /rɪˈspektfəli/ respekt-
voll p. 77, 15

(to) **respond** /rɪˈspɒnd/ antworten;
reagieren p. 72, 6

(to) **respond to** /rɪˈspɒndˌtə/ antworten auf, reagieren auf p. 68, 2

responsible /rɪˈspɒnsəbl/ verant-
wortungsbewusst, verantwortlich
p. 62, 8

responsibly /rɪˈspɒnsəbli/ verant-
wortungsbewusst p. 73, 6

(to) **rest** /rest/ ausruhen NHG 7

result /rɪˈzʌlt/ Ergebnis NHG 7

(to) retire /rɪˈtaɪə/ in den Ruhe-
stand treten p. 107, 2

(to) **return** /rɪˈtɜːn/ zurückgeben
NHG 6; zurückkehren, zurückkommen p. 110, 6

return ticket /rɪˌtɜːn ˈtɪkɪt/ Hin- und
Rückfahrkarte p. 130

review /rɪˈvjuː/ Kritik; Rezension
NHG 7

rhyming word /ˈraɪmɪŋ wɜːd/ Reim-
wort NHG 7

rice /raɪs/ Reis NHG 5

rich /rɪtʃ/ reich NHG 7

(to) **get rid of** (irr) /ˌget ˈrɪdˌəv/ loswerden NHG 7

ride /raɪd/ Fahrt p. 8

(to) **ride** (irr) /raɪd/ fahren; reiten
NHG 5

(to) take a ride (irr) /ˌteɪk əˈraɪd/
eine Fahrt machen p. 13, 6

(to) **ride a bike** (irr) /ˌraɪd əˈbaɪk/
Fahrrad fahren NHG 5

(to) **ride a horse** (irr) /ˌraɪd əˈhɔːs/
reiten NHG 5

(to) **go riding** (irr) /ˌgəʊ ˈraɪdɪŋ/ reiten gehen NHG 6

right /raɪt/ richtig NHG 5; rechts,
nach rechts; genau; direkt NHG 6;
Recht NHG 7

(to) **be right** (irr) /ˌbiː ˈraɪt/ recht
haben NHG 5

on the right /ˌɒn ðə ˈraɪt/ rechts,
auf der rechten Seite NHG 5

right away /ˌraɪt əˈweɪ/ sofort,
gleich p. 68, 2

right now /ˌraɪt ˈnaʊ/ jetzt; im
Moment NHG 7

ringfort /ˈrɪŋfɔːt/ Ringfestung p. 132

rise /raɪz/ Aufstieg NHG 7

rise /raɪz/ Anstieg p. 171

river /ˈrɪvə/ Fluss NHG 6

road /rəʊd/ Straße NHG 5

robot /ˈrəʊbɒt/ Roboter p. 40, 7

robotics /rəʊˈbɒtɪks/ Robotertechnik
p. 39, 6

rock /rɒk/ Stein; Fels NHG 7

role /rəʊl/ Rolle NHG 6

role play /ˈrəʊl pleɪ/ Rollenspiel
NHG 6

role-playing /ˈrəʊl ˌpleɪɪŋ/ Rollenspiel p. 44, 2

(to) **roll** /rəʊl/ rollen NHG 7

Roman /ˈrəʊmən/ Römer/in;
römisch NHG 6

romance /rəʊˈmæns/ Romanze p. 149

romantic /rəʊˈmæntɪk/ romantisch
p. 66, 13

rooftop /ˈruːfˌtɒp/ Dach p. 150

room /ruːm/ Platz; Raum; Zimmer
NHG 5

waiting room /ˈweɪtɪŋ ˌruːm/ Wartezimmer NHG 7

root /ruːt/ Wurzel NHG 7

round /raʊnd/ rund NHG 5;
(um ...) herum NHG 6

all year round /ˌɔːl ˈjɪə raʊnd/ das
ganze Jahr lang p. 10, 2

route /ruːt/ Strecke; Route p. 132

royal /ˈrɔɪəl/ königlich NHG 6

rubbish /ˈrʌbɪʃ/ Müll NHG 5

ruin /ˈruːɪn/ Ruine p. 116, 1

rule /ruːl/ Regel NHG 5

(to) **rule** /ruːl/ herrschen, regieren
NHG 6

ruler /ˈruːlə/ Lineal NHG 5

rumor (AE) = **rumour** (BE) /ˈruːmə/
Gerücht p. 69, 2

run /rʌn/ Lauf NHG 7

run /rʌn/ *Punktgewinn beim
Baseball* p. 50, 9

(to) **run** (irr) /rʌn/ laufen; rennen
NHG 6; leiten, betreiben NHG 7;
durchführen p. 87, 6

runner /ˈrʌnə/ Läufer/in NHG 6

running time /ˈrʌnɪŋ taɪm/ Laufzeit
p. 149

S

sad /sæd/ traurig NHG 6

safe /seɪf/ sicher; ungefährlich
NHG 6

safety /ˈseɪfti/ Sicherheit NHG 6

safety precaution /ˈseɪfti prɪˌkɔːʃn/
Sicherheitsvorkehrung p. 41, 8

(to) **sail** /seɪl/ segeln p. 121, 6

sailing ship /ˈseɪlɪŋ ʃɪp/ Segelschiff
p. 106, 2

salad /ˈsæləd/ Salat NHG 7

salmon /ˈsæmən/ Lachs p. 122, 7

salt /sɔːlt/ Salz NHG 5

the same /ðə ˈseɪm/ der/die/das
Gleiche; derselbe/dieselbe/
dasselbe NHG 5

at the same time /ˌæt ðə ˌseɪm
ˈtaɪm/ gleichzeitig; zur gleichen
Zeit NHG 7

Saturday /ˈsætədeɪ/ Samstag NHG 5

(on) Saturdays /ˈsætədeɪz/ sams-
tags NHG 5

sauce /sɔːs/ Soße NHG 7

(to) **save** /seɪv/ aufheben; sichern;
sparen; retten NHG 7

savoury /ˈseɪvəri/ pikant; salzig
NHG 7

(to) **say** (irr) /seɪ/ sagen NHG 5

saying /ˈseɪɪŋ/ Sprichwort p. 64, 11

(to) **scan** /skæn/ absuchen, überfliegen NHG 7

Scandinavia /ˌskændɪˈneɪviə/ Skandinavien p. 14, 7

scared /skeəd/ verängstigt, ängstlich NHG 6

(to) be scared (of) /ˌbi: ˈskeəd‿əv/ Angst haben (vor) NHG 5

scary /ˈskeəri/ Furcht erregend NHG 6

scene /siːn/ Szene NHG 5

schedule *(AE)* /ˈske‚dʒul, ˈʃedjuːl/ Stundenplan p. 38, 6

scholarship /ˈskɒləʃɪp/ Stipendium p. 113, 10

(to) win a scholarship *(irr)* /ˌwɪn‿ə ˈskɒləʃɪp/ ein Stipendium bekommen p. 82, 2

school /skuːl/ Schule NHG 5

school counsellor /ˌskuːl ˈkaʊnslə/ Beratungslehrer/in p. 131

school grounds *(pl)* /ˈskuːl ˌɡraʊndz/ Schulgelände NHG 6

schoolbag /ˈskuːl‚bæɡ/ Schultasche NHG 5

schoolchild *(pl* schoolchildren) /ˈskuːl‚tʃaɪld, ˈskuːl‚tʃɪldrən/ Schulkind p. 38, 6

science /ˈsaɪəns/ Naturwissenschaft NHG 5

scientist /ˈsaɪəntɪst/ Wissenschaftler/in NHG 7

(a pair of) scissors /ˈsɪzəz/ Schere NHG 5

(to) score /skɔː/ einen Punkt machen p. 50, 9

Scotland /ˈskɒtlənd/ Schottland NHG 5

Scottish /ˈskɒtɪʃ/ schottisch p. 162

screen /skriːn/ Bildschirm NHG 6

script /skrɪpt/ Drehbuch; Skript NHG 6

sculpture /ˈskʌlptʃə/ Bildhauerei p. 26, 8

seal /siːl/ Seehund; Robbe p. 119, 5

search /sɜːtʃ/ Suche NHG 5

(to) search /sɜːtʃ/ suchen NHG 5

search engine /ˈsɜːtʃ‚endʒɪn/ Suchmaschine NHG 7

(to) search the Internet /ˌsɜːtʃ ðɪ‿ˈɪntənet/ im Internet suchen NHG 5

seasick /ˈsiː‚sɪk/ seekrank p. 106, 2

seaside /ˈsiː‚saɪd/ (Meeres)küste; Meer NHG 6

season /ˈsiːzn/ Saison NHG 7

seat /siːt/ Sitz p. 48, 7

(to) take a seat *(irr)* /ˌteɪk‿ə ˈsiːt/ sich setzen NHG 7

second /ˈsekənd/ Sekunde; zweite(r, s) NHG 5

(to) come second *(irr)* /ˌkʌm ˈsekənd/ Zweite/r werden p. 34, 2

the Second World War /ðə ˌsekənd ˌwɜːld ˈwɔː/ Zweiter Weltkrieg p. 15, 7

second-hand /ˌsekənd ˈhænd/ gebraucht NHG 7

secretary /ˈsekrətri/ Sekretär/in p. 113, 10

section /ˈsekʃn/ Teil; Stück; Abschnitt; Abteilung NHG 7

security /sɪˈkjʊərəti/ Sicherheit p. 17, 10

(to) see *(irr)* /siː/ sehen NHG 5; empfangen, drannehmen NHG 7

(to) see a doctor *(irr)* /ˌsiː‿ə ˈdɒktə/ einen Arzt / eine Ärztin aufsuchen NHG 7

See you (soon)! /ˌsiː ju: ˈsuːn/ Bis bald! NHG 6

(to) seek advice *(irr)* /ˌsiːk‿əd'vaɪs/ Rat suchen NHG 7

(to) seem /siːm/ scheinen p. 48, 7

racial segregation /ˌreɪʃl segrɪˈɡeɪʃn/ Rassentrennung p. 15, 7

(to) sell *(irr)* /sel/ verkaufen NHG 7

seller /ˈselə/ Verkäufer/in NHG 7

(to) send *(irr)* /send/ schicken NHG 5

(to) send in *(irr)* /ˌsend‿ˈɪn/ einsenden p. 62, 8

senior /ˈsiːniə/ älterer Mensch; ältere(r, s) p. 26, 8

senior *(AE)* /ˈsiːniə/ *Schüler/in einer Highschool im letzten Jahr* p. 39, 6

(to) make sense *(irr)* /ˌmeɪk ˈsens/ sinnvoll sein p. 62, 8

sentence /ˈsentəns/ Satz NHG 5

September /sepˈtembə/ September NHG 5

series /ˈsɪəriːz/ Folge; Serie NHG 7

serious /ˈsɪəriəs/ ernst NHG 7

(to) serve /sɜːv/ servieren; reichen für NHG 7; dienen; eine Amtszeit durchlaufen p. 15, 7

session /ˈseʃn/ Stunde; Session NHG 5

set /set/ Satz; Garnitur p. 71, 5

set /set/ *hier:* Reihe p. 17, 10

(to) set foot on *(irr)* /ˌset ˈfʊt‿ɒn/ betreten p. 10, 2

(to) set the table *(irr)* /ˌset ðə ˈteɪbl/ den Tisch decken NHG 5

(to) set up *(irr)* /ˌset‿ˈʌp/ aufbauen NHG 7

(to) settle /ˈsetl/ sich niederlassen p. 14, 7

settlement /ˈsetlmənt/ Siedlung p. 14, 7

settler /ˈsetlə/ Siedler/in p. 14, 7

several /ˈsevrəl/ einige; verschiedene NHG 7

shall /ʃæl/ sollen; werden NHG 7

(to) be a shame *(irr)* /ˌbi‿ə ˈʃeɪm/ schade sein NHG 7

shape /ʃeɪp/ Form; Gestalt p. 65, 12

(to) share /ʃeə/ teilen NHG 5

sharing /ˈʃeərɪŋ/ Teilen p. 151

shark /ʃɑːk/ Hai p. 132

she /ʃiː/ sie NHG 5

sheet /ʃiːt/ Blatt; Bogen NHG 6

shelf *(pl* **shelves)** /ʃelf, ʃelvz/ Regal NHG 5

shield /ʃiːld/ Schild p. 121, 6

(to) work shifts /ˌwɜːk ˈʃɪfts/ Schichtdienst machen p. 92, 2

ship /ʃɪp/ Schiff p. 14, 7

(to) board a ship /ˌbɔːd‿ə ˈʃɪp/ ein Schiff besteigen p. 106, 2

shirt /ʃɜːt/ Hemd NHG 5

shocked /ˈʃɒkt/ schockiert, entsetzt p. 69, 2

shoe /ʃuː/ Schuh NHG 6

(to) shoot *(irr)* /ʃuːt/ schießen NHG 7

shop /ʃɒp/ Geschäft; Laden NHG 5

shop assistant /ˈʃɒp‿ə‚sɪstnt/ Verkäufer/in NHG 6

shopping /ˈʃɒpɪŋ/ Einkaufen; Einkaufs- NHG 5

(to) do the shopping *(irr)* /ˌdu: ðə ˈʃɒpɪŋ/ einkaufen NHG 5

(to) go shopping *(irr)* /ˌɡəʊ ˈʃɒpɪŋ/ einkaufen gehen NHG 5

shopping centre /ˈʃɒpɪŋ ‚sentə/ Einkaufszentrum NHG 5

shore /ʃɔː/ Küste; Ufer p. 122, 7

short /ʃɔːt/ kurz NHG 5

short-distance flight /ˈʃɔːt‚dɪstəns ˈflaɪt/ Kurzstreckenflug p. 85, 5

should /ʃʊd/ sollte(st, n, t) NHG 6

shoulder /ˈʃəʊldə/ Schulter NHG 7

(to) shout /ʃaʊt/ rufen; schreien p. 7

(to) shout at somebody /'ʃaʊt‿ət ‚sʌmbədi/ jemanden anschreien NHG 6

(to) show *(irr)* /ʃəʊ/ zeigen NHG 5

shy /ʃaɪ/ schüchtern NHG 7

sick /sɪk/ krank NHG 6

side /saɪd/ Seite NHG 6

on the side /‚ɒn ðə 'saɪd/ als Beilage NHG 7

side (dish) /'saɪd‿dɪʃ/ Beilage NHG 7

sidewalk *(AE)* /'saɪd‚wɔ:k/ Bürgersteig p. 24, 6

sight /saɪt/ Sehenswürdigkeit NHG 5

sign /saɪn/ Zeichen; Schild NHG 6

(to) sign /saɪn/ unterschreiben NHG 7

silly /'sɪli/ albern; dumm NHG 7

silver /'sɪlvə/ Silber p. 18, 12; silbern p. 122, 7

similar /'sɪmɪlə/ ähnlich NHG 6

simple /'sɪmpl/ einfach; simpel NHG 7

simple past /‚sɪmpl 'pɑ:st/ einfache Vergangenheit p. 12

simply /'sɪmpli/ einfach NHG 6

since /sɪns/ seit NHG 6; da; weil p. 68, 2

since then /sɪns 'ðen/ seitdem, seither p. 21, 2

(to) sing *(irr)* /sɪŋ/ singen NHG 5

(to) sing along *(irr)* /‚sɪŋ‿ə'lɒŋ/ mitsingen NHG 5

singer /'sɪŋə/ Sänger/in NHG 6

singing /'sɪŋɪŋ/ Singen; Gesang p. 44, 2

single /'sɪŋgl/ einzelne(r, s) NHG 6

single /'sɪŋgl/ *hier:* Einzelwettberwerb p. 35, 2

single ticket /‚sɪŋgl 'tɪkɪt/ einfache Fahrkarte, Einzelfahrkarte p. 163

sir/Sir /sɜ:/ Sir; Herr *(Anrede vor Vornamen)* NHG 7

sister /'sɪstə/ Schwester NHG 5

(to) sit *(irr)* /sɪt/ sitzen NHG 7

(to) sit down *(irr)* /‚sɪt‿'daʊn/ sich hinsetzen NHG 5

site /saɪt/ Stelle; Platz NHG 7

(to) be situated *(irr)* /‚bi: 'sɪtʃueɪtɪd/ liegen, gelegen sein p. 18, 12

size /saɪz/ Größe NHG 5

skateboarding /'skeɪtbɔ:dɪŋ/ Skateboardfahren NHG 5

skill /skɪl/ Fähigkeit; Geschick NHG 7; Fertigkeit; Kompetenz p. 41, 8

(to) skim /skɪm/ überfliegen NHG 7

skirt /skɜ:t/ Rock NHG 5

sky /skaɪ/ Himmel p. 65, 12

skyscraper /'skaɪ‚skreɪpə/ Wolkenkratzer p. 21, 2

slave /sleɪv/ Sklave/Sklavin p. 15, 7

slavery /'sleɪvəri/ Sklaverei p. 15, 7

dog sled /'dɒg sled/ Hundeschlitten p. 13, 6

sleep /sli:p/ Schlaf NHG 7

(to) sleep /sli:p/ schlafen NHG 5

sleeping bag /'sli:pɪŋ bæg/ Schlafsack p. 75, 10

(to) slice /slaɪs/ in Scheiben schneiden NHG 7

slide /slaɪd/ Folie NHG 7

slow, slowly /sləʊ, 'sləʊli/ langsam NHG 6

small /smɔ:l/ klein NHG 5

smart /smɑ:t/ schlau, clever NHG 6

(to) smell *(irr)* /smel/ riechen p. 48, 7

smile /smaɪl/ Lächeln p. 65, 12

(to) smile /smaɪl/ lächeln NHG 6

snake /sneɪk/ Schlange p. 110, 6

snow /snəʊ/ Schnee p. 10, 2

so /səʊ/ also; deshalb; daher NHG 5

so far /'səʊ fɑ:/ bisher NHG 6

so that /'səʊ ðæt/ damit NHG 6

(to) soar /sɔ:/ aufsteigen, sich erheben p. 122, 7

soccer *(AE)* /'sɒkə/ Fußball p. 165

social /'səʊʃl/ gesellschaftlich; sozial p. 17, 10

social media /‚səʊʃl 'mi:diə/ soziale Medien p. 69, 2

sociologist /‚səʊsi'ɒlədʒɪst/ Soziologe/Soziologin p. 72, 6

sock /sɒk/ Socke NHG 7

soft /sɒft/ weich NHG 7

soft skill /‚sɒft 'skɪl/ *persönliche, soziale und methodische Kompetenz* p. 95, 7

soil /sɔɪl/ Boden; Erde p. 106, 2

solution /sə'lu:ʃn/ Lösung NHG 6

(to) solve /sɒlv/ lösen NHG 6

some /sʌm/ einige, ein paar; etwas NHG 5

some day /'sʌm‚deɪ/ eines Tages NHG 7

somebody /'sʌmbədi/ jemand; irgendwer NHG 6

someone /'sʌmwʌn/ jemand; irgendwer NHG 5

something /'sʌmθɪŋ/ etwas NHG 5

sometimes /'sʌmtaɪmz/ manchmal NHG 5

somewhere /'sʌmweə/ irgendwo NHG 6

son /sʌn/ Sohn NHG 5

song /sɒŋ/ Lied NHG 5

soon /su:n/ bald NHG 7

Get well soon! /‚get ‚wel 'su:n/ Gute Besserung! NHG 7

See you (soon)! /‚si: ju: 'su:n/ Bis bald! NHG 6

sophomore *(AE)* /'sɒfə‚mɔ:/ *Schüler/in einer Highschool im zweiten Jahr* p. 39, 6

sore throat /‚sɔ: 'θrəʊt/ Halsschmerzen NHG 7

sorry /'sɒri/ Entschuldigung NHG 5

(to) be sorry *(irr)* /‚bi: 'sɒri/ bedauern; sich entschuldigen p. 62, 8

sort /sɔ:t/ Sorte; Art NHG 6

(to) sort /sɔ:t/ sortieren NHG 5

sound /saʊnd/ Geräusch; Klang NHG 6

(to) sound /saʊnd/ klingen, sich anhören NHG 5

sound technology /saʊnd‿tek‚nɒlədʒi/ Tontechnik p. 43, 14

soup /su:p/ Suppe NHG 7

source /sɔ:s/ Quelle NHG 7

south /saʊθ/ Süden; Süd- NHG 7

South Korea /‚saʊθ 'kə'rɪə/ Südkorea p. 107, 2

southern /'sʌðən/ südliche(r, s); Süd- p. 15, 7

southwest /‚saʊθ'west/ in den Südwesten, nach Südwesten p. 110, 6

space /speɪs/ Raum; Platz NHG 6; Weltall NHG 7

Spain /speɪn/ Spanien p. 14, 7

Spanish /'spænɪʃ/ Spanisch p. 7

spark /spɑ:k/ Funke; Auslöser p. 86, 6

(to) speak *(irr)* /spi:k/ sprechen; reden NHG 5

speaker /'spi:kə/ Sprecher/in p. 25, 7

This is ... speaking. /ðɪs‿ɪz ... 'spi:kɪŋ/ Hier spricht ... NHG 7

special /'speʃl/ besondere(r, s); besonders NHG 5

special offer /‚speʃl‿'ɒfə/ Sonderangebot p. 26, 8

speciality /‚speʃi'æləti/ Spezialität NHG 7

species (*pl* **species**) /'spi:ʃi:z, 'spi:ʃi:z/ Art; Spezies NHG 6

spectacular /spek'tækjʊlə/ atemberaubend; spektakulär NHG 7

speech /spi:tʃ/ Rede p. 89, 9

speech bubble /'spi:tʃ ˌbʌbl/ Sprechblase NHG 7

(to) **spell** *(irr)* /spel/ buchstabieren NHG 5

spelling /'spelɪŋ/ Buchstabieren; Rechtschreibung NHG 6

(to) **spend** *(irr)* /spend/ verbringen *(Zeit)*; ausgeben *(Geld)* NHG 6

spice /spaɪs/ Gewürz NHG 7

spicy /'spaɪsi/ würzig; scharf NHG 7

spirit /'spɪrɪt/ Geist; Stimmung p. 48, 7

splendid /'splendɪd/ großartig p. 112, 8

(to) **sponsor** /'spɒnsə/ sponsern p. 88, 8

spoon /spu:n/ Löffel NHG 5

sport /spɔ:t/ Sport; Sportart NHG 5

full-contact sport /ˌfʊl 'kɒntækt spɔ:t/ *Vollkontakt-Sportart* p. 50, 8

sportsperson /'spɔ:tsˌpɜ:sn/ Sportler/in p. 16, 9

spotlight /'spɒtˌlaɪt/ Scheinwerfer p. 10, 2

sprained /spreɪnd/ verstaucht NHG 7

(to) **spread** *(irr)* /spred/ verteilen; verbreiten p. 69, 2

spring /sprɪŋ/ Frühling NHG 6

square /'skweə/ quadratisch, Quadrat- p. 10, 2

stadium (*pl* **stadiums** *or* **stadia**) /'steɪdiəm, 'steɪdiəmz, 'steɪdiə/ Stadion p. 7

stage /steɪdʒ/ Bühne NHG 6

stair /steə/ Stufe NHG 6

stairs *(pl)* /steəz/ Treppe NHG 6

stall /stɔ:l/ Stand NHG 7

stamina /'stæmɪnə/ Durchhaltevermögen; Ausdauer p. 85, 5

(to) **stand** *(irr)* /stænd/ stehen NHG 6

(to) **stand by** *(irr)* /ˌstænd 'baɪ/ dabeistehen p. 122, 7

(to) **stand for** *(irr)* /'stænd fɔ:/ stehen für NHG 6

(to) **stand somebody** *(irr)* /'stænd ˌsʌmbədi/ jemanden leiden können p. 58, 3

(to) **stand up for** *(irr)* /ˌstænd 'ʌp fɔ:/ sich einsetzen für p. 89, 9

standing lamp /'stændɪŋ læmp/ Stehlampe p. 65, 12

star /sta:/ Stern NHG 5

(to) **star** /sta:/ die Hauptrolle spielen p. 149

(to) **stare at** /'steər ˌæt/ anstarren p. 38, 6

start /sta:t/ Anfang; Beginn NHG 5

(to) **start** /sta:t/ anfangen; beginnen NHG 5; gründen p. 93, 2

(to) **start a fire** /ˌsta:t ə 'faɪə/ Feuer machen p. 108, 3

(to) **start out** /ˌsta:t ˈaʊt/ anfangen p. 89, 9

starter /'sta:tə/ Vorspeise NHG 7

starting point /'sta:tɪŋ pɔɪnt/ Ausgangspunkt p. 87, 6

starvation /sta:'veɪʃn/ Hungertod p. 121, 6

(to) **starve** /sta:v/ verhungern p. 106, 2

state /steɪt/ Staat; Bundesstaat p. 6

statement /'steɪtmənt/ Äußerung, Aussage NHG 5

station /'steɪʃn/ U-Bahn-Station; Bahnhof NHG 5

statistics *(pl)* /stə'tɪstɪks/ Statistik p. 109, 5

the Statue of Liberty /ðə ˌstætʃu əv 'lɪbəti/ Freiheitsstatue p. 6

(to) **stay** /steɪ/ bleiben; wohnen NHG 5

(to) **stay away from** /ˌsteɪ ə'weɪ frɒm/ meiden; sich fernhalten von NHG 7

(to) **stay up (late)** /ˌsteɪ ˌʌp 'leɪt/ lange aufbleiben NHG 7

(to) **steal** *(irr)* /sti:l/ stehlen NHG 7

steam engine /'sti:m ˌendʒɪn/ Dampfmaschine NHG 7

steamboat /'sti:mbəʊt/ Dampfschiff p. 110, 6

step /step/ Stufe; Schritt NHG 5

(to) **step** /step/ treten; steigen NHG 6

(to) **take a step** *(irr)* /ˌteɪk ə 'step/ einen Schritt machen p. 87, 6

(to) **step back in time** /ˌstep ˌbæk ˌɪn 'taɪm/ sich in die Vergangenheit zurückversetzen p. 13, 6

(to) **step out** /ˌstep ˈaʊt/ heraustreten p. 13, 6

still /stɪl/ (immer) noch NHG 5; nach wie vor, trotzdem NHG 7

(to) **stir in** /ˌstɜ:r ˈɪn/ einrühren; unterrühren NHG 7

stomach /'stʌmək/ Magen; Bauch NHG 7

stomach ache /'stʌmək ˌeɪk/ Bauchschmerzen NHG 7

stone /stəʊn/ Stein NHG 7

(to) **stop** /stɒp/ stehen bleiben; anhalten NHG 5; aufhören NHG 6; stoppen NHG 7

stop /stɒp/ Halt p. 20, 2

store *(AE)* /stɔ:/ Laden p. 24, 6

storm /stɔ:m/ Sturm p. 108, 3

stormy /'stɔ:mi/ stürmisch p. 106, 2

story /'stɔ:ri/ Geschichte, Erzählung NHG 5

straight on /ˌstreɪt ˈɒn/ geradeaus NHG 6

strange /streɪndʒ/ sonderbar; merkwürdig NHG 6

stranger /'streɪndʒə/ Fremde/r p. 64, 9

strategy /'strætədʒi/ Strategie NHG 7

street /stri:t/ Straße NHG 5

strength /streŋθ/ Kraft; Stärke NHG 7

stress /stres/ Betonung NHG 6

(to) **stress** /stres/ stressen NHG 7

stressed /strest/ gestresst NHG 7

stretch /stretʃ/ *hier:* Abschnitt p. 10, 2

(to) **stretch** /stretʃ/ dehnen, spannen p. 44, 2

strict /strɪkt/ streng NHG 6

string /strɪŋ/ Schnur; Kordel NHG 6

strong /strɒŋ/ stark NHG 7

(to) **struggle** /'strʌgl/ sich abmühen; sich quälen p. 89, 9

student /'stju:dnt/ Schüler/in NHG 5; Student/in NHG 7

student council /'stju:dnt ˌkaʊnsl/ Schülervertretung p. 83, 2

studies *(pl)* /'stʌdiz/ Studium p. 113,10

study /'stʌdi/ Studie p. 68, 2

(to) **study** /'stʌdi/ studieren; lernen NHG 7

study hall /'stʌdi hɔ:l/ Lernraum; Übungsraum p. 39, 6

study period /'stʌdi ˌpɪəriəd/ Lernstunde; Übungsstunde p. 39, 6

stuff *(informal)* /stʌf/ Zeug NHG 6

stunning /'stʌnɪŋ/ toll, fantastisch p. 13, 6

stupid /ˈstjuːpɪd/ dumm, blöd NHG 6

style /staɪl/ Stil NHG 6

subject /ˈsʌbdʒɪkt/ Schulfach NHG 5; Thema; Betreff *(in Emails)* NHG 6

subway *(AE)* /ˈsʌbˌweɪ/ U-Bahn p. 25, 7

(to) **succeed** /səkˈsiːd/ erfolgreich sein p. 44, 2

success /səkˈses/ Erfolg p. 35, 2

successful /səkˈsesfl/ erfolgreich NHG 7

such /sʌtʃ/ so; solch NHG 7

such as /ˈsʌtʃˌæz/ wie p. 17, 10

suddenly /ˈsʌdnli/ plötzlich NHG 6

sugar /ˈʃʊɡə/ Zucker NHG 6

(to) **suggest** /səˈdʒest/ vorschlagen NHG 6

suggestion /səˈdʒestʃn/ Vorschlag NHG 6

suit /suːt/ Anzug p. 35, 2

suitable /ˈsuːtəbl/ geeignet; passend p. 19, 13

suitcase /ˈsuːtˌkeɪs/ Koffer p. 108, 3

(to) **sum up** /ˌsʌmˈʌp/ zusammenfassen p. 61, 7

(to) **summarize (= summarise)** /ˈsʌməraɪz/ zusammenfassen p. 95, 7

summary /ˈsʌməri/ Zusammenfassung NHG 7

summer /ˈsʌmə/ Sommer NHG 5

sun /sʌn/ Sonne NHG 5

Sunday /ˈsʌndeɪ/ Sonntag NHG 5

(on) Sundays /ˈsʌndeɪz/ sonntags NHG 5

sunny /ˈsʌni/ sonnig NHG 5

sunset /ˈsʌnˌset/ Sonnenuntergang p. 122, 7

sunshine /ˈsʌnˌʃaɪn/ Sonnenschein NHG 5

Super Bowl /ˈsuːpə bəʊl/ *Finale der US-amerikanischen American Football-Profiliga* p. 7

supermarket /ˈsuːpəˌmɑːkɪt/ Supermarkt p. 97, 9

support /səˈpɔːt/ Unterstützung; Hilfe p. 34, 2

(to) **support** /səˈpɔːt/ (unter)stützen p. 83, 2

sure /ʃɔː/ sicher NHG 5

(to) **make sure** *(irr)* /ˌmeɪk ˈʃɔː/ darauf achten, dass … NHG 6

surf instructor /ˈsɜːf ɪnˌstrʌktə/ Surflehrer/in p. 93, 2

surf school /ˈsɜːfskuːl/ Surfschule p. 94

surfing /ˈsɜːfɪŋ/ Surfen p. 8

surprised /səˈpraɪzd/ überrascht; erstaunt NHG 6

surprising /səˈpraɪzɪŋ/ überraschend NHG 6

(to) **surround** /səˈraʊnd/ umgeben p. 138

survey /ˈsɜːveɪ/ Umfrage p. 69, 2

(to) **survive** /səˈvaɪv/ überleben p. 111, 7

sustainability /səˌsteɪnəˈbɪləti/ Nachhaltigkeit p. 83, 2

sustainable /səˈsteɪnəbl/ nachhaltig p. 93, 2

(to) **swap** /swɒp/ tauschen p. 75, 10

sweater /ˈswetə/ Pullover p. 120, 6

sweet /swiːt/ süß NHG 5; Süßigkeit NHG 6

(to) **swim** *(irr)* /swɪm/ schwimmen NHG 5

swim practice /ˈswɪm ˌpræktɪs/ Schwimmtraining p. 62, 8

swimmer /ˈswɪmə/ Schwimmer/in p. 93, 2

swimming /ˈswɪmɪŋ/ Schwimmen NHG 5

(to) **go swimming** *(irr)* /ˌɡəʊ ˈswɪmɪŋ/ schwimmen gehen NHG 6

swimming pool /ˈswɪmɪŋ puːl/ Schwimmbad NHG 5

(to) **be in full swing** *(irr)* /ˌbi ɪn ˌfʊl ˈswɪŋ/ in vollem Gang sein p. 34, 2

(to) **switch off** /ˌswɪtʃˈɒf/ ausschalten NHG 7

(to) **switch on** /ˌswɪtʃˈɒn/ einschalten NHG 5

swollen /ˈswəʊlən/ geschwollen NHG 7

sword /sɔːd/ Schwert p. 121, 6

syllable /ˈsɪləbl/ Silbe NHG 7

systemic /sɪˈstiːmɪk/ systemisch p. 85, 5

T

table /ˈteɪbl/ Tisch NHG 5; Tabelle NHG 6

(to) **set the table** *(irr)* /ˌset ðə ˈteɪbl/ den Tisch decken NHG 5

table tennis /ˈteɪbl ˌtenɪs/ Tischtennis NHG 5

tailgate *(AE)* /ˈteɪlɡeɪt/ Heckklappe; *hier:* Kofferraum p. 48, 7

tailgate party *(AE)* /ˈteɪlɡeɪt ˌpɑːti/ *Picknick von der Ladefläche oder aus dem Kofferraum eines Autos während einer Sportveranstaltung oder eines Konzerts* p. 47, 6

(to) **take** *(irr)* /teɪk/ nehmen; bringen; benötigen; brauchen NHG 5; dauern NHG 6

(to) **take a break** *(irr)* /ˌteɪk ə ˈbreɪk/ eine Pause machen p. 85, 5

(to) **take a closer look at** *(irr)* /ˌteɪk ə ˌkləʊsə ˈlʊk ət/ sich genauer ansehen p. 148

(to) **take a course** *(irr)* /ˌteɪk ə ˈkɔːs/ einen Kurs machen p. 95, 7

(to) **take a dog for a walk** *(irr)* /ˌteɪk ə ˌdɒɡ fər ə ˈwɔːk/ mit einem Hund Gassi gehen p. 141

(to) **take a photo** *(irr)* /ˌteɪk ə ˈfəʊtəʊ/ ein Foto machen NHG 5

(to) **take a picture** *(irr)* /ˌteɪk ə ˈpɪktʃə/ ein Foto machen NHG 5

(to) **take a ride** *(irr)* /ˌteɪk ə ˈraɪd/ eine Fahrt machen p. 13, 6

(to) **take a seat** *(irr)* /ˌteɪk ə ˈsiːt/ sich setzen NHG 7

(to) **take a step** *(irr)* /ˌteɪk ə ˈstep/ einen Schritt machen p. 87, 6

(to) **take a tour** *(irr)* /ˌteɪk ə ˈtʊə/ eine Tour machen p. 26, 8

(to) **take action** *(irr)* /ˌteɪkˈækʃn/ handeln, Maßnahmen ergreifen p. 85, 5

(to) **take an order** *(irr)* /ˌteɪk ənˈɔːdə/ eine Bestellung aufnehmen NHG 7

(to) **take an X-ray** *(irr)* /ˌteɪk ən ˈeksreɪ/ eine Röntgenaufnahme machen NHG 7

(to) **take away** *(irr)* /ˌteɪk əˈweɪ/ wegnehmen; mitnehmen NHG 6

(to) **take care (of)** *(irr)* /ˌteɪkˈkeər əv/ sich kümmern um NHG 6

(to) **take notes (on)** *(irr)* /ˌteɪk ˈnəʊts/ sich Notizen machen (zu) NHG 5

(to) **take out** *(irr)* /ˌteɪkˈaʊt/ hinausbringen NHG 5; herausnehmen p. 48, 7 (to) **take part in** *(irr)* /ˌteɪk ˈpaːt‿ɪn/ teilnehmen an NHG 6

(to) **take place** *(irr)* /ˌteɪk ˈpleɪs/ stattfinden NHG 6

(to) take somebody's temperature *(irr)* /ˌteɪk ˌsʌmbədɪz ˈtemprɪtʃə/ Fieber bei jemandem messen p. 92, 2

(to) take the initiative *(irr)* /ˌteɪk ðiˌɪˈnɪʃətɪv/ die Initiative ergreifen p. 96, 8

(to) **take time** *(irr)* /ˌteɪk ˈtaɪm/ dauern p. 83, 2

(to) **take turns** *(irr)* /ˌteɪk ˈtɜːnz/ sich abwechseln NHG 6

takeaway /ˈteɪkəˌweɪ/ Essen zum Mitnehmen; Imbissbude NHG 7

talk /tɔːk/ Gespräch; Vortrag NHG 7

(to) **give a talk** *(irr)* /ˌɡɪv‿ə ˈtɔːk/ einen Vortrag halten p. 125, 13

(to) **talk about** /ˈtɔːk‿əˌbaʊt/ sprechen über NHG 5

(to) **talk (to)** /tɔːk/ sprechen (mit); reden (mit) NHG 5

tall /tɔːl/ groß NHG 6

target task /ˈtaːɡɪt ˌtaːsk/ Zielaufgabe p. 19, 13

task /taːsk/ Aufgabe NHG 5

Tasmanian Wolf /tæzˌmeɪniən ˈwʊlf/ Beutelwolf p. 132

taste /teɪst/ Geschmack NHG 7

(to) **taste** /teɪst/ schmecken NHG 6

tasty /ˈteɪsti/ lecker NHG 7

tax /tæks/ Steuer; Abgabe p. 14, 7

tea /tiː/ Tee NHG 5

(to) **teach** *(irr)* /tiːtʃ/ unterrichten NHG 5

teacher /ˈtiːtʃə/ Lehrer/in NHG 5

tear /tɪə/ Träne L&L 1

(to) **tease** /tiːz/ hänseln, ärgern NHG 7

teaspoon /ˈtiːˌspuːn/ Teelöffel NHG 7

technique /tekˈniːk/ Technik p. 41, 8

technology /tekˈnɒlədʒi/ Technologie; Technik NHG 6

(to) **brush one's teeth** /ˌbrʌʃ wʌnz ˈtiːθ/ sich die Zähne putzen NHG 5

telephone /ˈteliˌfəʊn/ Telefon NHG 6

television /ˈteliˌvɪʒn/ Fernseher; Fernsehen NHG 7

(to) **tell** *(irr)* /tel/ erzählen NHG 5

(to) **tell** *(irr)* /tel/ *hier:* bemerken p. 65, 12

(to) take somebody's temperature *(irr)* /ˌteɪk ˌsʌmbədiz ˈtemprɪtʃə/ Fieber bei jemandem messen p. 92, 2

tense /tens/ Zeitform p. 66, 13

term /tɜːm/ Trimester; Begriff NHG 5

terrible /ˈterəbl/ schrecklich NHG 5

territory /ˈterətri/ Gebiet; Territorium p. 110, 6

(to) **test** /test/ prüfen; testen p. 25, 7

tester /ˈtestə/ Tester/in, Prüfer/in p. 99, 13

(to) **text** /tekst/ eine Textnachricht schreiben NHG 5

text (message) /ˈtekst ˌmesɪdʒ/ Textnachricht NHG 5

than /ðæn/ als *(bei Vergleich)* NHG 6

(to) **thank** /θæŋk/ danken, sich bedanken p. 52, 13

thank God /ˌθæŋk ˈɡɒd/ Gott sei Dank p. 110, 6

thank you /ˈθæŋk ju/ danke NHG 5

thanks /θæŋks/ danke NHG 5

I'm good, thanks. /aɪm ˈɡʊd ˌθæŋks/ Es geht mir gut, danke. NHG 5

(to) **give thanks** *(irr)* /ˌɡɪv ˈθæŋks/ Dank sagen p. 25, 7

thanks a lot /ˌθæŋks‿ə ˈlɒt/ vielen Dank NHG 5

thanks to /ˈθæŋks tʊ/ dank; wegen p. 107, 2

Thanksgiving /ˈθæŋksˌɡɪvɪŋ/ Thanksgiving *(amerikanisches Erntedankfest)* p. 6

that /ðæt/ das; der/die/das (dort); dass NHG 5; so NHG 6

that way /ˈðæt weɪ/ so, auf diese Weise p. 58, 3

that's (= that is) /ðæts, ˈðæt‿ɪz/ *hier:* das kostet NHG 5

that's why /ˈðæts ˌwaɪ/ deshalb p. 93, 2

the /ðə/ der/die/das NHG 5

theater *(AE)* /ˈθɪətə/ Theater p. 20, 2

theatre /ˈθɪətə/ Theater NHG 6

their /ðeə/ ihr(e) NHG 5

theirs /ðeəz/ ihre(r, s) NHG 7

them /ðem/ sie; ihnen NHG 5

them /ðem/ ihn / sie *(zur Vermeidung von "him" oder "her")* p. 23, 5

theme /θiːm/ Thema NHG 6

themselves /ðəmˈselvz/ sich; selbst p. 18, 11

then /ðen/ dann NHG 5

then /ðen/ damals p. 107, 2

theory /ˈθɪəri/ Theorie NHG 7

there /ðeə/ dort; dahin NHG 5

there are /ˌðeəˈɹ‿ɑː/ dort sind; es gibt NHG 5

these *(pl of this)* /ðiːz/ diese; das NHG 5

they /ðeɪ/ sie NHG 5

thin /θɪn/ dünn NHG 7

thing /θɪŋ/ Ding; Gegenstand NHG 5

(to) **think** *(irr)* /θɪŋk/ denken; glauben NHG 5

(to) **think about** *(irr)* /ˈθɪŋk‿əˌbaʊt/ denken an, nachdenken über NHG 5

(to) **think of** *(irr)* /ˈθɪŋk‿əv/ denken an, sich ausdenken NHG 5

third /θɜːd/ dritte(r, s) NHG 5

this /ðɪs/ diese(r, s) NHG 5

This is ... speaking. /ˌðɪs‿ɪz ... ˈspiːkɪŋ/ Hier spricht ... NHG 7

this way /ˈðɪs weɪ/ hier entlang NHG 7

those *(pl of that)* /ðəʊz/ diese, jene NHG 5

though *(nachgestellt)* /ðəʊ/ jedoch p. 59, 3

thought /θɔːt/ Gedanke NHG 7

thought bubble /ˈθɔːt ˌbʌbl/ Gedankenblase NHG 7

thousand /ˈθaʊznd/ tausend NHG 6

threat /θret/ Bedrohung p. 69, 2

thrill /θrɪl/ Nervenkitzel; Kick p. 13, 6

sore throat /ˌsɔː ˈθrəʊt/ Halsschmerzen NHG 7

through /θruː/ durch NHG 6

(to) **throw** *(irr)* /θrəʊ/ werfen NHG 5

(to) **throw away** *(irr)* /ˌθrəʊ‿əˈweɪ/ wegwerfen NHG 6

thumb /θʌm/ Daumen NHG 7

thunder /ˈθʌndə/ Donner p. 111, 7

thunderstorm /ˈθʌndəstɔːm/ Gewitter p. 111, 7

Thursday /ˈθɜːzdeɪ/ Donnerstag NHG 5

(on) Thursdays /ˈθɜːzdeɪz/ donnerstags NHG 5

ticket office /ˈtɪkɪt‿ˌɒfɪs/ Fahrkartenschalter p. 130

tidy /ˈtaɪdi/ ordentlich; aufgeräumt NHG 5

(to) **tidy (up)** /ˈtaɪdi, ˌtaɪdiˌˈʌp/ auf-
räumen NHG 5

tie /taɪ/ Krawatte NHG 5

till /tɪl/ bis NHG 5

time /taɪm/ Zeit; Mal NHG 5

all the time /ˌɔːl ðə ˈtaɪm/ die ganze
Zeit NHG 6

at the same time /ˌæt ðə ˌseɪm
ˈtaɪm/ gleichzeitig; zur gleichen
Zeit NHG 7

for the first time /fə ðə
ˈfɜːst ˌtaɪm/ zum ersten Mal NHG 6

most of the time /ˈməʊst ˌəv ðə
ˌtaɪm/ meistens NHG 7

on time /ˌɒn ˈtaɪm/ pünktlich NHG 5

(to) **take time** *(irr)* /ˌteɪk ˈtaɪm/
dauern p. 83, 2

What time is it? /wɒtˈtaɪmˌɪzˌɪt/
Wie spät ist es? NHG 5

What's the time, please? /ˌwɒts ðə
ˈtaɪm pliːz/ Wie spät ist es, bitte?
NHG 5

at that time /ætˈðætˌtaɪm/ zu jener
Zeit p. 107, 2

for a long time /fərˌə ˈlɒŋ taɪm/
lange p. 62, 8

(to) step back in time /ˌstepˌbækˌɪn
ˈtaɪm/ sich in die Vergangenheit
zurückversetzen p. 13, 6

time-saving /ˈtaɪm seɪvɪŋ/ zeitspa-
rend p. 72, 6

timeline /ˈtaɪmlaɪm/ Zeitachse NHG 7

at all times /ætˌˌɔːl ˈtaɪmz/ jederzeit,
immer p. 72, 6

timetable /ˈtaɪmteɪbl/ Stundenplan
NHG 5; Fahrplan NHG 6

tin /tɪn/ Büchse; Dose NHG 7

tiny /ˈtaɪni/ winzig p. 106, 2

tip /tɪp/ Tipp NHG 6

tired /ˈtaɪəd/ müde NHG 6

title /ˈtaɪtl/ Titel; Überschrift NHG 6

to /tʊ/ (um) zu; in; nach; zu; an; bis;
vor NHG 5

today /təˈdeɪ/ heute NHG 5;
heutzutage NHG 6

toe /təʊ/ Zeh NHG 5

together /təˈgeðə/ zusammen NHG 5

(to) **get together** *(irr)* /ˌgetˌtəˈgeðə/
zusammenkommen NHG 5

toilet /ˈtɔɪlət/ Toilette NHG 5

Tokyo /ˈtəʊkiəʊ/ Tokio p. 115, 14

tolerance /ˈtɒlərəns/ Toleranz
p. 17, 10

tomato *(pl* **tomatoes)** /təˈmɑːtəʊ,
təˈmɑːtəʊz/ Tomate NHG 5

tomorrow /təˈmɒrəʊ/ morgen
NHG 5

tonight /təˈnaɪt/ heute Abend
p. 117, 2

too /tuː/ auch; zu NHG 5

tool /tuːl/ Werkzeug NHG 7

tooth *(pl* **teeth)** /tuːθ, tiːθ/ Zahn
NHG 7

toothache *(no pl)* /ˈtuːθeɪk/ Zahn-
schmerzen NHG 7

toothbrush /ˈtuːθbrʌʃ/ Zahnbürste
NHG 7

top /tɒp/ beste(r, s) NHG 5; oberes
Ende; Spitze NHG 6

topic /ˈtɒpɪk/ Thema NHG 5

torch /tɔːtʃ/ Taschenlampe NHG 6

in total /ˌɪn ˈtəʊtl/ insgesamt p. 34, 2

(to) **touch** /tʌtʃ/ berühren NHG 5

(to) **keep in touch** *(irr)* /ˌkiːpˌɪn ˈtʌtʃ/
Kontakt halten; in Verbindung
bleiben NHG 7

(to) **tour** /tʊə/ bereisen; erkunden
p. 20, 2

(to) take a tour /ˌteɪkˌə ˈtʊə/ eine
Tour machen p. 26, 8

tour guide /ˈtʊə gaɪd/ Reiseführer/in
p. 26, 8

tournament /ˈtʊənəmənt/ Turnier
p. 35, 2

towards /təˈwɔːdz/ in Richtung, zu;
gegenüber NHG 6

tower /ˈtaʊə/ Turm NHG 6

town /taʊn/ Stadt NHG 5

toy /tɔɪ/ Spielzeug NHG 5

tractor /ˈtræktə/ Traktor p. 93, 2

trader /ˈtreɪdə/ Händler/in p. 25, 7

traditional /trəˈdɪʃnəl/ traditionell
NHG 6

traffic /ˈtræfɪk/ Verkehr p. 150

trail /treɪl/ Weg; Pfad L&L 1

train /treɪn/ Zug NHG 5

(to) **train** /treɪn/ trainieren NHG 7;
eine Ausbildung machen p. 83, 2

(to) translate /trænsˈleɪt/ überset-
zen p. 75, 11

translator /trænsˈleɪtə/ Überset-
zer/in p. 71, 5

transport /ˈtrænspɔːt/ Transport;
Verkehrsmittel NHG 6

public transport /ˌpʌblɪk ˈtrænspɔːt/
öffentliche Verkehrsmittel p. 85, 5

trash *(AE)* /træʃ/ Müll, Abfall p. 165

travel /ˈtrævl/ Reise NHG 6

(to) **travel** /ˈtrævl/ reisen; fahren
NHG 5

travel guide /ˈtrævl gaɪd/ Reiseführer *(Buch)* p. 29, 15

travelling /ˈtrævlɪŋ/ Reisen NHG 6

(to) **treat** /triːt/ behandeln NHG 7

tree /triː/ Baum NHG 5

trick /trɪk/ Trick; Kunststück NHG 5

trip /trɪp/ Ausflug; Fahrt NHG 6;
Reise p. 13, 6

tropical /ˈtrɒpɪkl/ tropisch p. 10, 2

trouble /ˈtrʌbl/ Ärger; Schwierig-
keiten NHG 6

(a pair of) trousers /əˌpeərˌəv
ˈtraʊzəz/ Hose NHG 5

truck *(AE)* /trʌk/ Lastwagen p. 93, 2

true /truː/ wahr NHG 5

truly /ˈtruːli/ wirklich, wahrhaftig
p. 67, 15

trunk /trʌŋk/ Rüssel p. 65, 12

trunk *(AE)* /trʌŋk/ Kofferraum p. 48, 7

(to) **trust** /trʌst/ vertrauen NHG 7

(to) **try** /traɪ/ (aus)probieren;
versuchen NHG 5

(to) **try on** /ˌtraɪˈɒn/ anprobieren
NHG 7

(to) **try out** /ˌtraɪˈaʊt/ ausprobieren NHG 7

Tuesday /ˈtjuːzdeɪ/ Dienstag NHG 5

(on) Tuesdays /ˈtjuːzdeɪz/
dienstags NHG 5

tuition /tjuːˈɪʃn/ *hier:* Nachhilfe
p. 97, 9

Turkey/Türkiye /ˈtɜːki, ˈtʊəkijə/ die
Türkei p. 162

Turkish /ˈtɜːkɪʃ/ türkisch p. 162

(to) **turn** /tɜːn/ abbiegen NHG 6

(to) **turn into** /ˌtɜːnˈɪntʊ/ umwan-
deln in p. 23, 5

(to) **turn off** /ˌtɜːnˈɒf/ ausschalten
NHG 7

(to) **turn over** /ˌtɜːnˈəʊvə/ (sich)
umdrehen NHG 7

(to) **be one's turn** *(irr)* /ˌbiː wʌnz
ˈtɜːn/ an der Reihe sein NHG 5

(to) **take turns** *(irr)* /ˌteɪk ˈtɜːnz/
sich abwechseln NHG 6

tutor /ˈtjuːtə/ Nachhilfelehrer/in
p. 98, 10

(to) tutor /ˈtjuːtə/ Nachhilfe geben
p. 98, 10

tutoring /'tjuːtərɪŋ/ Nachhilfe p. 98, 10

TV (= television) /ˌtiː ˈviː, ˈtelɪˌvɪʒn/ Fernsehen; Fernseher NHG 6

(to) **watch TV** /ˌwɒtʃ tiː ˈviː/ Fernsehen gucken NHG 5

twice /twaɪs/ zweimal NHG 7

twin /twɪn/ Zwilling; Zwillings- NHG 5

Twin Towers /ˌtwɪn ˈtaʊəz/ *Zwillings-türme in New York* p. 21, 2

twisted /'twɪstɪd/ verdreht, verschlungen p. 122, 7

type /taɪp/ Art NHG 6; Typ p. 46, 4

typical /'tɪpɪkl/ typisch NHG 5

U

ugly /'ʌgli/ hässlich NHG 6

the UK /ðə ˌjuː ˈkeɪ/ Vereinigtes Königreich NHG 6

ultimate /'ʌltɪmət/ höchste(r, s); stärkste(r, s) p. 13, 6

umbrella /ʌmˈbrelə/ Regenschirm p. 65, 12

uncle /'ʌŋkl/ Onkel NHG 5

(to) **feel uncomfortable** *(irr)* /ˌfiːl ʌnˈkʌmftəbl/ sich unwohl fühlen p. 38, 6

under /'ʌndə/ unter NHG 5; darunter p. 26, 8

underground /'ʌndəˌgraʊnd/ U-Bahn NHG 6

(to) **underline** /ˌʌndəˈlaɪn/ unter-streichen p. 36, 3

(to) **understand** *(irr)* /ˌʌndəˈstænd/ verstehen NHG 5

underworld /'ʌndəwɜːld/ Unterwelt p. 141

unemployment rate /ˌʌnɪmˈplɔɪmənt reɪt/ Arbeitslosenrate p. 107, 2

unfortunately /ʌnˈfɔːtʃnətli/ unglücklicherweise NHG 6

unhappy /ʌnˈhæpi/ unglücklich p. 58, 2

unified /'juːnɪfaɪd/ vereint p. 25, 7

unit /'juːnɪt/ Kapitel NHG 7

the United Kingdom /ðə juːˌnaɪtɪd ˈkɪŋdəm/ Vereinigtes Königreich NHG 6

the United States /ðə juːˌnaɪtɪd ˈsteɪts/ Vereinigte Staaten (von Amerika) p. 6

universal /ˌjuːnɪˈvɜːsl/ allgemein; universell p. 71, 5

university /ˌjuːnɪˈvɜːsəti/ Universität NHG 7

unknown /ʌnˈnəʊn/ unbekannt p. 66, 14

unless /ənˈles/ außer wenn NHG 7

unnecessary /ʌnˈnesəsəri/ unnötig p. 111, 7

(to) **unpack** /ʌnˈpæk/ auspacken p. 48, 7

(to) unscramble /ʌnˈskræmbl/ ordnen, in die richtige Reihen-folge bringen p. 12, 4

until /ənˈtɪl/ bis NHG 6

unusual /ʌnˈjuːʒəl/ ungewöhnlich NHG 5

up /ʌp/ nach oben; hinauf; oben NHG 5

up (to) /'ʌp tuː/ bis (zu) p. 50, 8

What's up? *(informal)* /ˌwɒts ˈʌp/ Was ist los? NHG 7

(to) be up to something *(irr)* /ˌbi ˌʌp tə ˈsʌmθɪŋ/ etwas vorhaben p. 45, 2

(to) **update** /ˌʌpˈdeɪt/ auf den neuesten Stand bringen p. 97, 9

upset /ʌpˈset/ aufgebracht; aufgeregt NHG 7

urban /'ɜːrbən/ städtisch p. 150

us /ʌs/ uns NHG 5

(the) US /ðə ˌjuː ˈes/ US, Vereinigte Staaten (von Amerika); US- p. 6

US-American /ˌjuː ˌes əˈmerɪkən/ US-Amerikaner/in; US-amerika-nisch p. 6

the USA (= United States of America) /ðə ˌjuː es ˈeɪ, juːˌnaɪtɪd ˌsteɪts əv əˈmerɪkə/ USA; Vereinigte Staaten von Amerika NHG 6

use /juːs/ Verwendung; Einsatz NHG 7

(to) **use** /juːz/ benutzen NHG 5

used /juːzd/ gebraucht p. 87, 6

(to) **used to** + *infinitive* /'juːst tuː/ früher + *Vergangenheitsform* NHG 6

useful /'juːsfl/ nützlich NHG 5

usually /'juːʒuəli/ gewöhnlich; normalerweise NHG 5

V

vacation *(AE)* /vəˈkeɪʃn/ Ferien; Urlaub p. 34, 2

(to) **vacuum** /'vækjuəm/ staubsau-gen NHG 5

valuable /'væljʊbl/ wertvoll p. 86, 6

value /'vælju/ Wert p. 89, 9

variety /vəˈraɪəti/ Vielfalt; Auswahl p. 10, 2

(to) **vary** /'veəri/ variieren; verschieden sein p. 26, 8

vegan /'viːgən/ Veganer/in; vegan NHG 7

vegetable /'vedʒtəbl/ Gemüse NHG 7

vegetarian /ˌvedʒəˈteəriən/ Vegeta-rier/in; vegetarisch NHG 7

veggie *(informal)* /'vedʒi/ Gemüse NHG 7

verse /vɜːs/ Strophe; Vers NHG 6

version /'vɜːʃn/ Version, Fassung NHG 5

vertical /'vɜːtɪkl/ vertikal; senkrecht p. 150

very /'veri/ sehr NHG 5

the very first /ðə ˌveri ˈfɜːst/ der/die/das allererste p. 6

very much /ˌveri ˈmʌtʃ/ sehr NHG 6

vet /vet/ Tierarzt/-ärztin NHG 6

via /'vaɪə/ über p. 69, 2

victory /'vɪktri/ Sieg NHG 6

(to) videochat /'vɪdiəʊtʃæt/ einen Videochat machen p. 40, 7

view /vjuː/ (Aus)sicht NHG 6

point of view /ˌpɔɪnt əv ˈvjuː/ Ansicht; Perspektive p. 59, 3

Viking /'vaɪkɪŋ/ Wikinger/in; Wikinger- p. 121, 6

village /'vɪlɪdʒ/ Dorf NHG 7

violence /'vaɪələns/ Gewalt p. 14, 7

virtual /'vɜːtʃʊəl/ virtuell p. 68, 2

visa /'viːzə/ Visum p. 106, 2

vision /'vɪʒn/ Vorstellung; Vision p. 86, 6

visit /'vɪzɪt/ Besuch NHG 5

(to) **visit** /'vɪzɪt/ besuchen NHG 6

visitor /'vɪzɪtə/ Besucher/in NHG 6

voice /vɔɪs/ Stimme NHG 6

voice message /'vɔɪs ˌmesɪdʒ/ Sprachnachricht p. 68, 1

volunteer /ˌvɒlənˈtɪə/ ehrenamtlich p. 87, 6

volunteering /ˌvɒlənˈtɪərɪŋ/ Verrich-ten von Freiwilligendienst p. 95, 7

W

wagon /'wægən/ Planwagen p. 110, 6

wagon train /'wægən treɪn/ Plan-wagenzug p. 110, 6

(to) **wait** /weɪt/ (er)warten NHG 5

waiter/waitress /'weɪtə, 'weɪtrəs/ Kellner/in NHG 7

waiting room /'weɪtɪŋ ˌruːm/ Wartezimmer NHG 7

(to) **wake up** *(irr)* /ˌweɪkˈʌp/ aufwachen NHG 6

walk /wɔːk/ Spaziergang NHG 5

(to) **walk** /wɔːk/ gehen NHG 5

(to) take a dog for a walk *(irr)* /ˌteɪk_ə ˌdɒɡ fərˌə 'wɔːk/ mit einem Hund Gassi gehen p. 141

walking path /'wɔːkɪŋ pɑːθ/ Wanderpfad p. 132

walking tour /'wɔːkɪŋ tʊə/ Wanderung p. 27, 10

wall /wɔːl/ Wand NHG 6

Wall Street /'wɔːl striːt/ *Straße in New York, auf der sich viele Banken und die weltgrößte Wertpapierbörse befinden* p. 25, 7

wallpaper /'wɔːlpeɪpə/ Tapete p. 65, 12

(to) **want (to)** /wɒnt/ wollen NHG 5

war /wɔː/ Krieg NHG 7

War of Independence /ˌwɔːr_əvˌɪndɪ'pendəns/ (Amerikanischer) Unabhängigkeitskrieg p. 14, 7

ward /wɔːd/ Station p. 92, 2

(to) **warn** /wɔːn/ warnen NHG 7

warrior /'wɒriə/ Krieger/in p. 121, 6

(to) **wash** /wɒʃ/ waschen, sich waschen NHG 5

waste /weɪst/ Abfall NHG 7

waste disposal plant /ˌweɪst_dɪ'spəʊzl plɑːnt/ Abfallentsorgungsanlage p. 86, 6

watch /wɒtʃ/ (Armband)uhr NHG 6

(to) **watch** /wɒtʃ/ beobachten; ansehen NHG 5

(to) **watch TV** /ˌwɒtʃ tiːˈviː/ Fernsehen gucken NHG 5

water /'wɔːtə/ Wasser NHG 5

water tower /'wɔːtə ˌtaʊə/ Wasserturm p. 25, 7

waterfall /'wɔːtəfɔːl/ Wasserfall p. 132

wave /weɪv/ Welle p. 109, 5

way /weɪ/ Weg; Art NHG 5

way of living /ˌweɪ_əv 'lɪvɪŋ/ Lebensweise p. 14, 7

this way /'ðɪs weɪ/ hier entlang NHG 7

we /wiː/ wir NHG 5

weakness /'wiːknəs/ Schwäche p. 61, 6

(to) **wear** *(irr)* /weə/ tragen (Kleidung) NHG 5

weather /'weðə/ Wetter NHG 5

Wednesday /'wenzdeɪ/ Mittwoch NHG 5

(on) Wednesdays /'wenzdeɪz/ mittwochs NHG 5

week /wiːk/ Woche NHG 5

weekend /ˌwiːk'end/ Wochenende NHG 5

at the weekend /ˌæt_ðə 'wiːkend/ am Wochenende p. 132

on the weekends *(AE)* /ˌɒn ðə 'wiːkendz/ an den Wochenenden p. 97, 9

(to) **welcome** /'welkəm/ willkommen heißen p. 34, 2

welcome (to) /'welkəm tʊ/ willkommen (in) NHG 5

You're welcome. /jɔː 'welkəm/ Gern geschehen.; Keine Ursache. NHG 7

welding /'weldɪŋ/ Schweißen p. 43, 14

well /wel/ nun NHG 5; gut NHG 6

(to) **get well** *(irr)* /ˌget 'wel/ gesund werden NHG 7

Get well soon! /ˌget ˌwel 'suːn/ Gute Besserung! NHG 7

well done /ˌwel 'dʌn/ gut gemacht NHG 6

Welsh /welʃ/ walisisch p. 162

west /west/ Westen p. 10, 2

west /west/ westlich p. 111, 7

western /'westən/ West-, westlich p. 122, 7

wet /wet/ nass NHG 6

wetlands *(pl)* /'wetlændz/ Sumpfgebiet p. 11, 2

whale /weɪl/ Wal p. 65, 12

what /wɒt/ was; welche(r, s) NHG 5

What about …? /ˌwɒt_əˌbaʊt '…/ Was ist / Wie wäre es mit …? NHG 5

What time is it? /ˌwɒtˌ'taɪm_ɪz_ɪt/ Wie spät ist es? NHG 5

What … would you like? /ˌwɒt … wəd jə 'laɪk/ Was für ein / eine … hättest du / hättet ihr / hätten Sie gern? NHG 5

What's on? *(informal)* /ˌwɒtsˌ'ɒn/ Was ist los? NHG 6

What's the matter? /ˌwɒts_ðə 'mætə/ Was ist los? NHG 7

What's the time, please? /ˌwɒts ðə 'taɪm pliːz/ Wie spät ist es, bitte? NHG 5

What's up? *(informal)* /ˌwɒtsˌ'ʌp/ Was ist los? NHG 7

What's wrong? *(informal)* /ˌwɒtsˌ'rɒŋ/ Was ist los? NHG 7

whatever /wɒt'evə/ was (auch immer) NHG 6

wheel /wiːl/ Rad NHG 6

wheelchair /'wiːltʃeə/ Rollstuhl NHG 7

when /wen/ wann; wenn; als NHG 5

whenever /wen'evə/ wann auch immer p. 24, 6

where /weə/ wo; wohin NHG 5

whereas /weər'æz/ während; wohingegen p. 71, 5

wherever /wer'evə/ wo(her) auch immer p. 25, 7

whether /'weðə/ ob p. 42, 11

which /wɪtʃ/ welche(r, s); was NHG 5

while /waɪl/ während NHG 6; Weile NHG 7

white /waɪt/ weiß NHG 5

White /waɪt/ *Weiße/r* p. 25, 7

who /huː/ wer; der/die/das NHG 5

whoever /huː'evə/ wer auch immer p. 25, 7

whole /həʊl/ ganz, gesamt NHG 6

as a whole /əz_ə 'həʊl/ als Ganzes p. 85, 5

whose /huːz/ wessen NHG 5

why /waɪ/ warum NHG 5

wide /waɪd/ weit NHG 7; groß; breit; enorm p. 10, 2

wife *(pl* **wives)** /waɪf, waɪvz/ Ehefrau NHG 5

wildlife /'waɪldˌlaɪf/ Tier- und Pflanzenwelt; Flora und Fauna NHG 6

will /wɪl/ werden NHG 6

(to) be willing to *(irr)* /ˌbiː 'wɪlɪŋ tʊ/ bereit sein p. 89, 9

(to) **win** *(irr)* /wɪn/ gewinnen NHG 7

(to) win a scholarship *(irr)* /ˌwɪn_ə 'skɒləʃɪp/ ein Stipendium bekommen p. 82, 2

winding /'waɪndɪŋ/ gewunden, sich schlängelnd p. 147

window /'wɪndəʊ/ Fenster NHG 5

winged /wɪŋd/ mit Flügeln, geflügelt p. 122, 7

(to) **wish** /wɪʃ/ wünschen NHG 7

(to) wish for (something) /'wɪʃ fɔː/ sich (etwas) wünschen p. 90, 11

best wishes /ˌbest 'wɪʃɪz/ **viele Grüße** p. 167

with /wɪð/ mit; bei NHG 5

within /wɪð'ɪn/ innerhalb, innen p. 26, 8

without /wɪð'aʊt/ ohne NHG 5

wolf (pl wolves) /wʊlf, wʊlvz/ Wolf p. 111, 7

woman (pl **women**) /'wʊmən, 'wɪmɪn/ Frau NHG 5

women's studies /'wɪmɪnz ˌstʌdiz/ *Schulfach, das die Rolle der Frau in Geschichte, Gesellschaft und Literatur untersucht* p. 40, 7

won't /wəʊnt/ nicht werden NHG 6

(to) **wonder** /'wʌndə/ sich fragen NHG 6

wonder /'wʌndə/ Wunder p. 13, 6

wonderful /'wʌndəfl/ wunderbar, wundervoll NHG 6

wood /wʊd/ Holz NHG 6

woodland /'wʊdlənd/ Waldgebiet p. 138

woodworking /'wʊdˌwɜːkɪŋ/ Tischlern p. 41, 8

word /wɜːd/ Wort NHG 5

word web /'wɜːd web/ Wortnetz NHG 5

wordbank /'wɜːdbæŋk/ *Wortsammlung* NHG 5

work /wɜːk/ Arbeit; Werk NHG 5

(to) **work** /wɜːk/ arbeiten NHG 5; funktionieren NHG 6

(to) work on /'wɜːk ˌɒn/ arbeiten an p. 96, 8

(to) work shifts /ˌwɜːk 'ʃɪfts/ Schichtdienst machen p. 92, 2

field of work /ˌfiːld ˌəv 'wɜːk/ Arbeitsbereich p. 15, 7

workbook /'wɜːkbʊk/ Arbeitsheft p. 10, 1

worker /'wɜːkə/ Arbeiter/in p. 93, 2

working /'wɜːkɪŋ/ funktionierend NHG 7

working hours (pl) /'wɜːkɪŋˌaʊəz/ Arbeitszeiten p. 93, 3

worksheet /'wɜːkʃiːt/ Arbeitsblatt p. 29, 15

world /wɜːld/ Welt NHG 5

all over the world /ˌɔːlˌəʊvə ðə 'wɜːld/ auf der ganzen Welt NHG 6

from all over the world /frəmˌɔːlˌəʊvə ðə 'wɜːld/ aus der ganzen Welt NHG 5

World War I /ˌwɜːld ˌwɔː 'wʌn/ Erster Weltkrieg p. 15, 7

World War II /ˌwɜːld ˌwɔː 'tuː/ Zweiter Weltkrieg p. 15, 7

world-famous /ˌwɜːld 'feɪməs/ weltberühmt NHG 7

worried /'wʌrid/ beunruhigt; besorgt NHG 6

(to) **worry** /'wʌri/ sich Sorgen machen NHG 5

worse /wɜːs/ schlechter, schlimmer NHG 6

the worst /ðə 'wɜːst/ der/die/das schlechteste/schlimmste; am schlechtesten/schlimmsten NHG 6

worth /wɜːθ/ wert p. 86, 6

(to) **be worth** (irr) /ˌbi: 'wɜːθ/ (sich) lohnen; wert sein NHG 7

would /wʊd/ würde(st, n, t) NHG 5

I would like ... (= I'd like ...) /aɪ ˌwʊd 'laɪk, aɪd 'laɪk/ Ich würde gern ... / Ich hätte gern ... NHG 5

Would you like ...? /ˌwʊd ju: 'laɪk/ Hättest du / Hättet ihr / Hätten Sie gern ...? NHG 5

wound /wuːnd/ Wunde NHG 7

wound dressing /'wuːndˌdresɪŋ/ Verband p. 92, 2

wrist /rɪst/ Handgelenk NHG 7

(to) **write** (irr) /raɪt/ schreiben NHG 5

(to) **write down** (irr) /ˌraɪt 'daʊn/ aufschreiben NHG 5

writer /'raɪtə/ Schriftsteller/in p. 19, 13

writing /'raɪtɪŋ/ Schrift; Schreiben NHG 7

written /'rɪtn/ schriftlich NHG 6

wrong /rɒŋ/ falsch NHG 6

(to) **be wrong** (irr) /ˌbi: 'rɒŋ/ im Unrecht sein NHG 7

(to) **be wrong (with)** (irr) /ˌbi: 'rɒŋ wɪθ/ nicht in Ordnung sein (mit) NHG 7

What's wrong? (informal) /ˌwɒts 'rɒŋ/ Was ist los? NHG 7

X

(to) **take an X-ray** (irr) /ˌteɪk ˌən 'eksreɪ/ eine Röntgenaufnahme machen NHG 7

Y

year /jɪə/ Jahr NHG 5; Schuljahr; Klasse NHG 6

all year round /ˌɔːl jɪə raʊnd/ das ganze Jahr lang p. 10, 2

yearbook /'jɪəbʊk/ Jahrbuch p. 34, 2

yellow /'jeləʊ/ gelb NHG 5

yes /jes/ ja NHG 5

yesterday /'jestədeɪ/ gestern NHG 6

yet /jet/ schon; noch NHG 7

you /ju:/ du; dich; dir; man; ihr; euch; Sie; Ihnen NHG 5

young /jʌŋ/ jung NHG 6

your /jɔː/ dein(e); euer/eure; Ihr(e) NHG 5

yours /jɔːz/ deine(r, s); eure(r, s); Ihre(r, s) NHG 6

yours sincerely /ˌjɔːz sɪn'sɪəli/ mit freundlichen Grüßen (am Ende eines formellen Briefes) NHG 6

yourself /jɔː'self/ dir, dich; sich NHG 5

yourselves /jɔː'selvz/ euch; selbst p. 52, 12

youth club /'juːθ ˌklʌb/ Jugendklub NHG 6

youth culture /'juːθ ˌkʌltʃə/ Jugendkultur p. 11, 2

youth hostel /'juːθ ˌhɒstl/ Jugendherberge p. 75, 10

Z

zip /zɪp/ Reißverschluss NHG 7

zoological /ˌzuːə'lɒdʒɪkl/ zoologisch p. 132

First names

Aaron (m.) /ˈeərən/
Alissa (f.) /əˈlɪsə/
Amy (f.) /ˈeɪmi/
Andrea (m., f.) /ˈændriə/
Andy (m., f.) /ˈændi/
Anna (f.) /ˈænə/
Anne, Annie (f.) /æn, ˈæni/
Anthony (m.) /ˈæntəni/
Anton (m.) /ˈæntɒn/
Arda (m., f.) /ˈɑːdə/
Arnold (m.) /ˈɑːnld/
Asher (m.) /ˈæʃə/
Ashley (m., f.) /ˈæʃli/
Avery (m., f.) /ˈeɪvəri/
Barack (m.) /ˈbæræk/
Belky (f.) /ˈbelki/
Ben (m.) /ben/
Bilal (m.) /ˌbiˈlaːl/
Billy (m., f.) /ˈbɪli/
Bradey (m.) /ˈbreɪdi/
Brandon (m.) /ˈbrændən/
Brendan (m.) /ˈbrendən/
Britt (f.) /brɪt/
Bruno (m.) /ˈbruːnəʊ/
Camila (f.) /kəˈmiːlə/
Carlos (m.) /ˈkɑːlɒs/
Catherine (f.) /ˈkæθrɪn/
Chenoa (f.) /tʃeˈnəʊə/
Christopher (m.) /ˈkrɪstəfə/
Cindy (f.) /ˈsɪndi/
Clive (m.) /klaɪv/
Cody (m.) /ˈkəʊdi/
Damian (m.) /ˈdeɪmiən/
Damien (m.) /ˈdeɪmiən/
Dan (m.) /dæn/
David (m.) /ˈdeɪvɪd/
Declan (m.) /ˈdeklən/
Dharna (f.) /ˈdɑːnə/
Ed (m.) /ed/
Eleanor (f.) /ˈelənə/
Elizabeth (f.) /ɪˈlɪzəbəθ/
Ella (f.) /ˈelə/
Emily (f.) /ˈeməli/
Emma (f.) /ˈemə/
Enrico (m.) /enˈriːkəʊ/
Enrique (m.) /enˈriːkeɪ/
Eric (m.) /ˈerɪk/
Fabio (m.) /ˈfæbiəʊ/
Finn (m.) /fɪn/
Fred (m.) /fred/
Gabi (m., f.) /ˈgæbi/

Gabriel (m.) /ˈgeɪbriəl/
George (m.) /dʒɔːdʒ/
Henry (m.) /ˌɒnˈriː/
Jack (m.) /dʒæk/
Jake (m.) /dʒeɪk/
James (m.) /dʒeɪmz/
Janet (f.) /ˈdʒænɪt/
Jasmine (f.) /ˈdʒæzmɪn/
Jayden (m., f.) /ˈdʒeɪdn/
Jean (m., f.) /dʒiːn/
Jeanne (f.) /dʒiːn/
Jenna (f.) /ˈdʒenə/
Jerome (m.) /dʒəˈrəʊm/
Ji-Hoon (m.) /dʒiˈhuːn/
Jo, Joe (m., f.) /dʒəʊ/
John(ny) (m.) /dʒɒn, ˈdʒɒni/
José (m.) /həʊˈzeɪ/
Joshua (m.) /ˈdʒɒʃjuə/
Julia (f.) /ˈdʒuːliə/
June (f.) /dʒuːn/
Justin (m.) /ˈdʒʌstɪn/
Katie (f.) /ˈkeɪti/
Kelsey (m., f.) /ˈkelsi/
Kim (f.) /kɪm/
Laura (f.) /ˈlɔːrə/
Lauren (f.) /ˈlɔːrən/
Lea, Leah (f.) /ˈliːə/
Levi (m.) /ˈliːvaɪ/
Li (f.) /liː/
Liam (m.) /ˈliːəm/
Lian (m.) /ˈliːən/
Linda (f.) /ˈlɪndə/
Linh (f.) /lɪn/
Liz, Lizzie (f.) /lɪz, ˈlɪzi/
Lourdes (f.) /lʊəd/
Lucia (f.) /ˈluːsiə/
Lucy (f.) /ˈluːsi/
Luis (m.) /ˈluːɪs/
Luther (m.) /ˈluːθə/
Lyndon (m.) /ˈlɪndən/
Marcus (m.) /ˈmɑːkəs/
Marian (f.) /ˈmæriən/
Martin (m.) /ˈmɑːtɪn/
Mary (f.) /ˈmeəri/
Mason (m.) /ˈmeɪsn/
Matt (m.) /mæt/
Max (m.) /mæks/
Mia (f.) /ˈmiːə/
Michael (m.) /ˈmaɪkl/
Michelle (f.) /miˈʃel/
Mike (m.) /maɪk/
Miriam (f.) /ˈmɪriəm/

Nathan (m.) /ˈneɪθn/
Neil (m.) /niːl/
Nick (m.) /nɪk/
Nihal (m.) /nɪˈhaːl/
Noah (m.) /ˈnəʊə/
Olivia (f.) /əˈlɪviə/
Patrick (m.) /ˈpætrɪk/
Patsy (f.) /ˈpætsi/
Paul (m.) /pɔːl/
Penny (f.) /ˈpeni/
Pete (m.) /piːt/
Phil, Philip (m.) /fɪl, ˈfɪlɪp/
Rafael (m.) /ˈræfeɪəl/
Ramos (m.) /ˈrɑːmɒs/
Rebecca (f.) /rɪˈbekə/
Reese (m., f.) /riːs/
Reza (m.) /ˈriːzə/
Rhiannon (f.) /rɪˈænən/
Ro (m., f.) /rəʊ/
Robert (m.) /ˈrɒbət/
Roberto (m.) /rəˈbɜːtəʊ/
Rosa (f.) /ˈrəʊzə/
Rosanne (f.) /rəʊˈzæn/
Rosemarie (f.) /ˈrəʊzməri/
Ruby (f.) /ˈruːbi/
Ryan (m.) /ˈraɪən/
Samoset (m.) /ˈsɑːməzet/
Sandra (f.) /ˈsændrə/
Sarah (f.) /ˈseərə/
Savannah (f.) /səˈvænə/
Sebastian (m.) /səˈbæstiən/
Simon (m.) /ˈsaɪmən/
Sonia (f.) /ˈsɒniə/
Squanto (m.) /ˈskwɒntəʊ/
Sri (m.) /sriː/
Stone (f.) /stəʊn/
Sue (f.) /suː/
Suri (f.) /ˈsuri/
Suzie (f.) /ˈsuːzi/
Tamara (f.) /təˈmɑːrə/
Tami (f.) /ˈtæmi/
Taylor (m., f.) /ˈteɪlə/
Tom (m.) /tɒm/
Wan (f.) /wɒn/
Wendy (f.) /ˈwendi/

Families

Adams /ˈædəmz/
Alvarez /ælˈvaːrez/
Armstrong /ˈɑːmstrɒŋ/
Baker /ˈbeɪkə/
Baring /ˈbeərɪŋ/

Beliard /ˌbelɪˈɑːd/
Birk /bɜːk/
Blue /bluː/
Brown /braʊn/
Campbell /ˈkæmbl/
Chang /tʃæŋ/
Chazelle /tʃəˈzel/
Choi /tʃɔɪ/
Colclough /ˈkəʊlkli/
Columbus /kəˈlʌmbəs/
Cruz /kruːz/
Cunningham /ˈkʌnɪŋəm/
Curtis /ˈkɜːtɪs/
de Sousa /də ˈsuːzə/
DeWitt /də ˈwɪt/
Ferris /ˈferɪs/
Flynn /flɪn/
Ford /fɔːd/
Goldschmidt /ˈgəʊldʃmɪt/
Gosling /ˈgɒzlɪŋ/
Graham /ˈgreɪəm/
Hinawy /ˌhiˈnaːwi/
Jean /dʒiːn/
Johnson /ˈdʒɒnsn/
Jones /dʒəʊnz/
Juliana /ˌdʒuːliˈɑːnə/
Kay /keɪ/
Kennedy /ˈkenədi/
Kepler /ˈkeplə/
King /kɪŋ/
Kracinski /krəˈtʃɪnski/
Legend /ˈledʒnd/
Lighty /ˈlaɪti/
Lincoln /ˈlɪŋkən/
Mars /mɑːz/
McRae /məˈkreɪ/
Miller /ˈmɪlə/
Milligan /ˈmɪlɪgən/
Monterres /ˌmɒnˈterəz/
Moore /mʊə/
Mulvern /ˈmʌlvən/
Nazario /nəˈzɑːriəʊ/
Newman /ˈnjuːmən/
Noor /ˈnʊə/
O'Donnell /əʊ ˈdɒnl/
O'Toole /əʊ ˈtuːl/
Obama /əʊˈbɑːmə/
Olson /ˈəʊlsn/
Parekh /ˈpærek/
Parks /pɑːks/
Pearce /pɪəs/
Poppins /ˈpɒpɪnz/

Redford /ˈredfəd/
Rodriguez /rɒˈdriːgez/
Roosevelt /ˈrəʊzəvelt/
Ruth /ruːθ/
Rynhart /ˈraɪnhɑːt/
Schwarzenegger
  /ˈʃwɔːtsənegə/
Stone /stəʊn/
Strauss /straʊs/
Tammana /təˈmɑːnə/
Tiger /ˈtaɪgə/
Treuer /ˈtrɔɪə/
Trout /traʊt/
Washington /ˈwɒʃɪŋtən/
Webb /web/

Other names
the Adams /ðiːˈædəmz/
All-Ireland Senior Cham-
  pionship /ɔːlˈaɪələnd
  ˈsiːniə ˌtʃæmpiənʃɪp/
American Dream
  /əˌmerɪkən ˈdriːm/
American football
  /əˌmerɪkən ˈfʊtˌbɔːl/
b-boy /ˈbiː ˌbɔɪ/
b-boying /ˈbiː ˌbɔɪɪŋ/
b-girl /ˈbiː ˌgɜːl/
b-girling /ˈbiː ˌgɜːlɪŋ/
Babe /beɪb/
the Battery /ðə ˈbætri/
the Beastie Boys
  /ðə ˈbiːsti bɔɪz/
Bewley's /ˈbjuːliz/
Blarney Castle
  /ˌblɑːni ˈkɑːsl/
Book of Kells /ˌbʊk əv ˈkelz/
Broadway /ˈbrɔːdweɪ/
Brooklyn Bridge
  /ˌbrʊklɪn ˈbrɪdʒ/
California Institute of the
  Arts /ˌkælə.fɔːniəˌ
  ˌɪnstɪˌtjuːt əv ðiːˈɑːts/
Central Park /ˈsentrəl pɑːk/
Covid /ˈkəʊvɪd/
Dolphin Discovery
  /ˈdɒlfɪn dɪˌskʌvri/
Donkey /ˈdɒŋki/
Dublinia /dʌˈblɪniə/
Dumbo /ˈdʌmbəʊ/
Empire State Building
  /ˌempaɪə ˈsteɪt ˌbɪldɪŋ/

EPIC /ˌiː piː ˌaɪ ˈsiː, ˈepɪk/
European Union
  /ˌjʊərəˌpiːən ˈjuːniən/
FBLA /ˌef biːˌelˈeɪ/
First Nation /ˌfɜːst ˈneɪʃn/
folk /fəʊk/
Freedom Tower /ˈfriːdəm
  ˌtaʊə/
Gaelic football /ˌgeɪlɪk
  ˈfʊtbɔːl/
Golden Gate Bridge
  /ˌgəʊldən geɪt ˈbrɪdʒ/
Grafton Street /ˈgrɑːftən
  striːt/
Grand Central Station
  /ˌgrænd ˌsentrəl ˈsteɪʃn/
the High Line /ðə ˈhaɪ laɪn/
Hook Lighthouse /ˌhʊk
  ˈlaɪtˌhaʊs/
huckleberry pie /ˌhʌklbəri
  ˈpaɪ/
Immigrant Heritage Week
  /ˌɪmɪgrənt ˈherɪtɪdʒ wiːk/
Independence Day
  /ˌɪndɪˈpendəns deɪ/
Independence Hall
  /ˌɪndɪˈpendəns hɔːl/
Irish Emigration Museum
  /ˌaɪrɪʃˌemɪˈgreɪʃn
  mjuːˌziːəm/
the Irish Free State
  /ðiːˌaɪrɪʃ friː ˈsteɪt/
the Irish War of
  Independence /ðiːˌaɪrɪʃ
  ˌwɔːr əvˌɪndɪˈpendəns/
Isle of Tears /ˌaɪl əv ˈtɪəz/
Jeanie Johnston /ˌdʒiːni
  ˈdʒɒnstn/
Juneteenth /ˌdʒuːnˈtiːntθ/
Kool Herc /ˌkuːl ˈhɜːk/
Lady Liberty /ˌleɪdi ˈlɪbəti/
LaLaLand /ˈlɑːlɑːlænd/
Lemon Rock /ˌlemən ˈrɒk/
the Leonardos
  /ðə ˌliːəˈnɑːdəʊz/
Los Angeles Times
  /lɒsˌændʒəliːz ˈtaɪmz/
Marble Arch /ˌmɑːblˈɑːtʃ/
Martin Luther King Jr. Day
  /ˌmɑːtɪn ˌluːθə ˌkɪŋ ˈdʒuːniə
  deɪ/
Massasoit /ˌmæsəˈswɑː/

Mayflower /ˈmeɪˌflaʊə/
Merry-Go-Round
  /ˈmeri gəʊ ˌraʊnd/
the Met(ropolitan Opera)
  /ðə ˈmet, metrəˌpɒlɪtn ˈɒprə/
Mickey Mouse /ˌmɪki ˈmaʊs/
the MoMA, Museum of
  Modern Art /ðə ˈməʊmə,
  mjuːˌziːəm əvˌmɒdən ˈɑːt/
mood board /ˈmuːd bɔːd/
mxmtoon
  /ˌem ˌeksˌˌem ˈtuːn/
National Association for
  the Advancement of
  Colored People, NAACP
  /ˌnæʃnlˌəˌsəʊsiˌeɪʃn fə
  ðiːˌˌedˌvɑːnsmənt əvˌkʌləd
  ˈpiːpl, ˌen dʌbəlˌeɪ siː ˈpiː/
Navajo /ˈnævəhəʊ/
Nazi /ˈnɑːtsi/
NBA (= National
  Basketball Association)
  /en biːˈeɪ, ðə ˌnæʃnl
  ˈbɑːskɪtbɔːlˌəˌsəʊsiˌeɪʃn/
Nevada /nɪˈvɑːdə/
the New York Times
  /ðə ˌnjuː jɔːk ˈtaɪmz/
NFL (= National Football
  League) /enˌefˌˈel, ðə
  ˌnæʃnl ˈfʊtbɔːlˌˌliːg/
09/11 /ˌnaɪnˌɪˈlevn/
9/11 Memorial
  /ˌnaɪnˌɪˌlevn məˈmɔːriəl/
North Pool /ˈnɔːθ puːl/
North Tower /ˈnɔːθ ˌtaʊə/
Ojibwe /əʊˈdʒɪbweɪ/
One World Trade Center
  /ˌwʌn ˌwɜːldˈtreɪd ˌsentə/
Opening Day /ˈəʊpənɪŋ deɪ/
the Oscars /ðiːˈɒskəz/
Oxford Dictionary
  /ˈɒksfəd ˌdɪkʃənri/
Palacio /pəˈlɑːsɪəʊ/
Pancake Day /ˈpænkeɪk deɪ/
Panthers /ˈpænθəz/
paraclimbing
  /ˈpærəˌklaɪmɪŋ/
Parade of Flags
  /pəˌreɪdˌəvˈflægz/
Pennington /ˈpenɪŋtən/
Philly cheesesteak
  /ˌfili ˈtʃiːzˌˌsteɪk/

Pilgrim Fathers
  /ˌpɪlgrɪm ˈfɑːðəz/
Pizza Hut /ˈpiːtsə hʌt/
Powerscourt Estate
  /ˌpaʊəzkɔːtˌɪˈsteɪt/
the Ring of Kerry
  /ðə ˌrɪŋ əv ˈkeri/
Rockefeller Center
  /ˈrɒkəˌfelə ˌsentə/
Sea Adventure Waterpark
  /ˌsiː əd,ventʃə ˈwɔːtəˌpɑːk/
Sedgwick Avenue
  /ˈsedʒwɪkˌˌævənjuː/
the Shamrocks
  /ðə ˈʃæmrɒks/
Shrek /ʃrek/
Skywalk /ˈskaɪˌwɔːk/
South Pool /ˈsaʊθ puːl/
South Tower /ˈsaʊθ ˌtaʊə/
St John's Juniors
  /sənt ˌdʒɒnz ˈdʒuːniəz/
St Stephen's Green
  /sənt ˌstiːvnz ˈgriːn/
the Statue of Liberty
  /ðə ˌstætʃu əv ˈlɪbəti/
Stories from Home
  /ˌstɔːriz frəm ˈhəʊm/
Super Bowl /ˈsuːpə bəʊl/
Supreme Court
  /suˌpriːm ˈkɔːt/
Temple Bar /ˌtempl ˈbɑː/
Thanksgiving /ˈθæŋksˌgɪvɪŋ/
Top Tutoring
  /ˌtɒp ˈtjuːtərɪŋ/
Torc /tɔːk/
the Trail of Tears
  /ðə ˌtreɪl əv ˈtɪəz/
Trinity College
  /ˌtrɪnəti ˈkɒlɪdʒ/
the Troubles /ðə ˈtrʌblz/
Twin Towers /ˌtwɪn ˈtaʊəz/
the Universal Hip-Hop
  Museum /ðə ˌjuːnɪˌvɜːsl
  ˌhɪp hɒp mjuːˌziːəm/
Wall Street /ˈwɔːl striːt/
Wampanoag
  /ˌwɒmpəˈnəʊæg/
War of Independence
  /ˌwɔːr əvˌɪndɪˈpendəns/
World Trade Center
  /ˌwɜːldˈtreɪd ˌsentə/
Yankee /ˈjæŋki/

Yankees /ˈjæŋkiz/
Yellowstone /ˈjeləʊstəʊn/

Geographical Names

Africa /ˈæfrɪkə/
Alabama /ˌæləˈbæmə/
Alaska /əˈlæskə/
America /əˈmerɪkə/
Antarctica /ænˈtɑːktɪkə/
Arizona /ˌærɪˈzəʊnə/
Asia /ˈeɪʒə/
Atlantic /ətˈlæntɪk/
Atlantic Ocean
  /ətˌlæntɪkˈəʊʃn/
Australia /ɒˈstreɪliə/
Bath /bɑːθ/
Blarney /ˈblɑːni/
Boston /ˈbɒstən/
Brazil /brəˈzɪl/
Britain /ˈbrɪtn/
the Bronx /ðə ˈbrɒŋks/
Brooklyn /ˈbrʊklɪn/
Buffalo /ˈbʌfələʊ/
Caherdaniel /ˌkɑːəˌdænjəl/
Cahergal /kəˈhɜːgl/
California /ˌkæləˈfɔːniə/
Campbell County
  /ˌkæmbl ˈkaʊnti/
Canada /ˈkænədə/
the Caribbean
  /ðə ˌkærɪˈbiən/
Central America
  /ˌsentrəl_əˈmerɪkə/
Chicago /ʃɪˈkɑːgəʊ/
China /ˈtʃaɪnə/
Chinatown /ˈtʃaɪnəˌtaʊn/
Cobh /kəʊv/
Colorado /ˌkɒləˈrɑːdəʊ/
Coney Island
  /ˌkəʊniˌˈaɪlənd/
Connemara /ˌkɒnɪˈmɑːrə/
Cork /kɔːk/
Davis /ˈdeɪvɪs/
Denver /ˈdenvə/
Derrynane /ˈderineɪn/
Des Moines /də ˈmɔɪn/
Dingle /ˈdɪŋgl/
Dingle Peninsula
  /ˌdɪŋgl pəˈnɪnsjələ/
Donegal /ˌdɒnɪˈgɔːl/
Dublin /ˈdʌblɪn/
East River /ˌiːst ˈrɪvə/

Edison /ˈedɪsən/
Ellis Island /ˌelɪsˌˈaɪlənd/
England /ˈɪŋglənd/
Europe /ˈjʊərəp/
Everglades /ˈevəgleɪdz/
Fairbanks /ˈfeəbæŋks/
Florida /ˈflɒrɪdə/
France /frɑːns/
Galway /ˈgɔːlweɪ/
Germany /ˈdʒɜːməni/
Gettysburg /ˈgetɪzbɜːg/
Grand Canyon
  /ˌgrænd ˈkænjən/
Great Britain /ˌgreɪt ˈbrɪtn/
the Great Plains
  /ðə ˌgreɪt ˈpleɪnz/
Harlem /ˈhɑːləm/
Hawaii /həˈwaɪi/
Hawkeye Point
  /ˈhɔːkaɪ pɔɪnt/
Hollywood /ˈhɒliwʊd/
Honduras /hɒnˈdjʊərəs/
Honolulu /ˌhɒnəˈluːluː/
Indiana /ˌɪndiˈænə/
Iowa /ˈaɪəʊə/
Ireland /ˈaɪələnd/
Italy /ˈɪtəli/
Japan /dʒəˈpæn/
Kansas /ˈkænzəs/
Kerry /ˈkeri/
Kilkenny /kɪlˈkeni/
Korea /kəˈrɪə/
Lancaster /ˈlæŋkəstə/
Las Vegas /læs ˈveɪgəs/
Lebanon /ˈlebənən/
Liffey /ˈlɪfi/
Limerick /ˈlɪmərɪk/
London /ˈlʌndən/
Los Angeles
  /lɒsˌˈændʒəliːz/
Louisiana /luˌiːziˈænə/
Manhattan /mænˈhætn/
Massachusetts
  /ˌmæsəˈtʃuːsɪts/
Mexico /ˈmeksɪkəʊ/
Michigan /ˈmɪʃɪgən/
Mississippi /ˌmɪsɪˈsɪpi/
Missouri /mɪˈzʊəri/
Montana /mɒnˈtænə/
Montgomery
  /məntˈgʌməri/
Nashville /ˈnæʃvɪl/

Nevada /nɪˈvɑːdə/
New Haven /njuː ˈheɪvən/
New Jersey /ˌnjuː ˈdʒɜːzi/
New Orleans
  /ˌnjuː ˈɔːliənz/
New York /ˌnjuː ˈjɔːk/
New York City
  /ˌnjuː jɔːk ˈsɪti/
North America
  /ˌnɔːθ_əˈmerɪkə/
North Carolina
  /ˌnɔːθ ˌkærəˈlaɪnə/
Northern Ireland
  /ˌnɔːðənˌˈaɪələnd/
NYC (= New York City)
  /ˌen waɪ ˈsiː, ˌnjuː jɔːk ˈsɪti/
Ohio /əʊˈhaɪəʊ/
Oklahoma /ˌəʊkləˈhəʊmə/
Oregon /ˈɒrɪgən/
PA (= Philadelphia)
  /ˌpiː ˈeɪ, ˌfɪləˈdelfiə/
Pacific /pəˈsɪfɪk/
Pacific Ocean
  /pəˌsɪfɪk ˈəʊʃn/
Paraguay /ˈpærəgwaɪ/
Pennsylvania
  /ˌpentsəlˈveɪniə/
Philadelphia /ˌfɪləˈdelfiə/
Pittsburgh /ˈpɪtsbɜːg/
Poland /ˈpəʊlənd/
Portland /ˈpɔːtlənd/
Puerto Rico
  /ˌpwɜːtəʊ ˈriːkəʊ/
Queens /kwiːnz/
the Republic of Ireland
  /ðə rɪˌpʌblɪk_əv_ˈaɪələnd/
the Ring of Kerry
  /ðə ˌrɪŋ_əv ˈkeri/
Rio Grande /ˌriːəʊ ˈgrænd/
San Diego /ˌsæn diˈeɪgəʊ/
San Francisco
  /ˌsæn frənˈsɪskəʊ/
Santa Cruz /ˌsæntə ˈkruːz/
Scandinavia
  /ˌskændɪˈneɪviə/
Scotland /ˈskɒtlənd/
Shannon /ˈʃænən/
Silicon Valley /ˌsɪlɪkən ˈvæli/
Skagway /ˈskægweɪ/
Sligo /ˈslaɪgəʊ/
Sofia /ˈsəʊfiə/

South Carolina
  /ˌsaʊθ ˌkærəˈlaɪnə/
South Korea /ˌsaʊθ kəˈrɪə/
Spain /speɪn/
St. Louis /sənt ˈluɪs/
Staten /ˈstætn/
Staten Island
  /ˌstætnˌˈaɪlənd/
Tegucigalpa
  /teˌguːsɪˈgælpə/
Tennessee /ˌtenəˈsiː/
Texas /ˈteksəs/
Tokyo /ˈtəʊkiəʊ/
Topeka /təʊˈpiːkə/
Tulsa /ˈtʌlsə/
Turkey / Türkiye /ˈtɜːki,
  ˈtʊəkijə/
the UK (= United Kingdom)
  /ðə ˌjuː ˈkeɪ, juːˌnaɪtɪd
  ˈkɪŋdəm/
the US (= the United
  States) /ðə ˌjuː_ˈes, ðə
  juːˌnaɪtɪd ˈsteɪts/
the USA (= United States
  of America)
  /ðə ˌjuː_es_ˈeɪ, juːˌnaɪtɪd
  ˌsteɪts_əv_əˈmerɪkə/
Wales /weɪlz/
Washington, D.C.
  /ˌwɒʃɪŋtən diː ˈsiː/
Waterford /ˈwɔːtəfəd/
West Virginia
  /ˌwest vəˈdʒɪniə/
Wexford /ˈweksfəd/
Wisconsin /wɪˈskɒnsɪn/
Wyoming /waɪˈəʊmɪŋ/

0	oh, zero, nil	/əʊ, ˈzɪərəʊ, nɪl/
1	one	/wʌn/
2	two	/tuː/
3	three	/θriː/
4	four	/fɔː/
5	five	/faɪv/
6	six	/sɪks/
7	seven	/sevn/
8	eight	/eɪt/
9	nine	/naɪn/
10	ten	/ten/
11	eleven	/ɪˈlevn/
12	twelve	/twelv/
13	thirteen	/ˌθɜːˈtiːn/
14	fourteen	/ˌfɔːˈtiːn/
15	fifteen	/ˌfɪfˈtiːn/
16	sixteen	/ˌsɪksˈtiːn/
17	seventeen	/ˌsevnˈtiːn/
18	eighteen	/ˌeɪˈtiːn/
19	nineteen	/ˌnaɪnˈtiːn/
20	twenty	/ˈtwenti/

21	twenty-one	/ˌtwentiˈwʌn/
30	thirty	/ˈθɜːti/
33	thirty-three	/ˌθɜːtiˈθriː/
40	forty	/ˈfɔːti/
45	forty-five	/ˌfɔːtiˈfaɪv/
50	fifty	/ˈfɪfti/
56	fifty-six	/ˌfɪftiˈsɪks/
60	sixty	/ˈsɪksti/
67	sixty-seven	/ˌsɪkstiˈsevn/
70	seventy	/ˈsevnti/
78	seventy-eight	/ˌsevntiˈeɪt/
80	eighty	/ˈeɪti/
89	eighty-nine	/ˌeɪtiˈnaɪn/
90	ninety	/ˈnaɪnti/

100	a/one hundred	/ə/wʌn ˈhʌndrəd/
101	one hundred and one	/wʌn ˌhʌndrəd ən ˈwʌn/
200	two hundred	/tuː ˈhʌndrəd/

1,000	one thousand	/ə/wʌn ˈθauznd/
1,111	one thousand one hundred and eleven	
	/wʌn ˌθauznd wʌn ˌhʌndrəd ən ɪˈlevn/	
2,000	two thousand	/tuː ˈθauznd/
10,000	ten thousand	/ten ˈθauznd/
100,000	a/one hundred thousand	/ə/wʌn ˌhʌndrəd ˈθauznd/
1,000,000	a/one million	/ə/wʌn ˈmɪljən/
1,000,000,000	a/one billion	/ə/wʌn ˈbɪljən/

1st	first	/fɜːst/
2nd	second	/ˈsekənd/
3rd	third	/θɜːd/
4th	fourth	/fɔːθ/
5th	fifth	/fɪfθ/
6th	sixth	/sɪksθ/
7th	seventh	/sevnθ/
8th	eighth	/eɪtθ/
9th	ninth	/naɪnθ/
10th	tenth	/tenθ/
11th	eleventh	/ɪˈlevnθ/
12th	twelfth	/twelfθ/
13th	thirteenth	/ˌθɜːˈtiːnθ/
19th	nineteenth	/ˌnaɪnˈtiːnθ/
20th	twentieth	/ˈtwentiəθ/

21st	twenty-first	/ˌtwentiˈfɜːst/
22nd	twenty-second	/ˌtwentiˈsekənd/
23rd	twenty-third	/ˌtwentiˈθɜːd/

30th	thirtieth	/ˈθɜːtiəθ/
40th	fortieth	/ˈfɔːtiəθ/
50th	fiftieth	/ˈfɪftiəθ/
60th	sixtieth	/ˈsɪkstiəθ/
70th	seventieth	/ˈsevntiəθ/
80th	eightieth	/ˈeɪtiəθ/
90th	ninetieth	/ˈnaɪntiəθ/
100th	hundredth	/ˈhʌndrədθ/

$\frac{1}{2}$	a / one half	/ə/wʌn ˈhaːf/
$\frac{1}{3}$	a / one third	/ə/wʌn ˈθɜːd/
$\frac{1}{4}$	a / one quarter	/ə/wʌn ˈkwɔːtə/
$\frac{1}{8}$	a / one eighth	/ə/wʌn ˌˈeɪtθ/
$\frac{3}{4}$	three quarters	/θriː ˈkwɔːtəz/

Jahreszahlen sprichst du so aus:
1939 nineteen thirty-nine
1951 nineteen fifty-one
2010 two thousand and ten

Daten schreibst du im britischen Englisch so:
1 August, 2 January, 5 November

oder so:
1st / 1st August, 2nd / 2nd January,
5th / 5th November

Eine Jahreszahl schreibst du einfach dahinter:
1 August 2024 oder 01/08/24

**Im amerikanischen Englisch ist es umgekehrt!
Hier schreibt man den Monat VOR dem Tag:**
August 1, August 1st oder 08/01/2024

infinitive	simple past	past participle	German
(to) be /bi:/	was/were /wɒz/wɜː/	been /bi:n/	sein
(to) become /bɪˈkʌm/	became /bɪˈkeɪm/	become /bɪˈkʌm/	werden
(to) begin /bɪˈgɪn/	began /bɪˈgæn/	begun /bɪˈgʌn/	anfangen; beginnen
(to) bleed /bli:d/	bled /bled/	bled /bled/	bluten
(to) break /breɪk/	broke /brəʊk/	broken /ˈbrəʊkən/	(zer)brechen; kaputt machen
(to) bring /brɪŋ/	brought /brɔːt/	brought /brɔːt/	mitbringen
(to) build /bɪld/	built /bɪlt/	built /bɪlt/	bauen
(to) buy /baɪ/	bought /bɔːt/	bought /bɔːt/	kaufen
(to) catch /kætʃ/	caught /kɔːt/	caught /kɔːt/	fangen
(to) choose /tʃuːz/	chose /tʃəʊz/	chosen /ˈtʃəʊzn/	wählen; sich entscheiden
(to) come /kʌm/	came /keɪm/	come /kʌm/	kommen
(to) cost /kɒst/	cost /kɒst/	cost /kɒst/	kosten
(to) cut /kʌt/	cut /kʌt/	cut /kʌt/	schneiden
(to) deal with /ˈdiːl wɪð/	dealt with /ˈdelt wɪð/	dealt with /ˈdelt wɪð/	sich befassen mit, umgehen mit
(to) do /duː/	did /dɪd/	done /dʌn/	machen; tun
(to) draw /drɔː/	drew /druː/	drawn /drɔːn/	zeichnen
(to) dream /driːm/	dreamt/dreamed /dremt/driːmd/	dreamt/dreamed /dremt/driːmd/	träumen
(to) drink /drɪŋk/	drank /dræŋk/	drunk /drʌŋk/	trinken
(to) drive /draɪv/	drove /drəʊv/	driven /ˈdrɪvn/	fahren
(to) eat /iːt/	ate /et/eɪt/	eaten /ˈiːtn/	essen
(to) fall /fɔːl/	fell /fel/	fallen /ˈfɔːlən/	fallen
(to) feed /fiːd/	fed /fed/	fed /fed/	füttern
(to) feel /fiːl/	felt /felt/	felt /felt/	(sich) fühlen
(to) fight /faɪt/	fought /fɔːt/	fought /fɔːt/	(be)kämpfen; ankämpfen gegen
(to) find /faɪnd/	found /faʊnd/	found /faʊnd/	finden
(to) flee /fliː/	fled /fled/	fled /fled/	fliehen
(to) fly /flaɪ/	flew /fluː/	flown /fləʊn/	fliegen
(to) forget /fəˈget/	forgot /fəˈgɒt/	forgotten /fəˈgɒtən/	vergessen
(to) forgive /fəˈgɪv/	forgave /fəˈgeɪv/	forgiven /fəˈgɪvn/	vergeben; verzeihen
(to) get /get/	got /gɒt/	got /gɒt/	bekommen; holen; kaufen; kommen, gelangen; werden; bringen
(to) give /gɪv/	gave /geɪv/	given /ˈgɪvn/	geben; angeben, mitteilen
(to) go /gəʊ/	went /went/	gone /gɒn/	gehen; fahren
(to) grow /grəʊ/	grew /gruː/	grown /grəʊn/	wachsen; anbauen
(to) hang (up) /ˌhæŋˈʌp/	hung (up) /ˌhʌŋˈʌp/	hung (up) /ˌhʌŋˈʌp/	hängen, aufhängen
(to) have /hæv/	had /hæd/	had /hæd/	haben; essen; trinken
(to) hear /hɪə/	heard /hɜːd/	heard /hɜːd/	hören
(to) hide /haɪd/	hid /hɪd/	hidden /ˈhɪdn/	(sich) verstecken

infinitive	simple past	past participle	German
(to) hit /hɪt/	hit /hɪt/	hit /hɪt/	schlagen; stoßen gegen; treffen
(to) hold /həʊld/	held /held/	held /held/	(fest)halten
(to) hurt /hɜːt/	hurt /hɜːt/	hurt /hɜːt/	wehtun, schmerzen; verletzen
(to) keep /kiːp/	kept /kept/	kept /kept/	aufbewahren; (be)halten
(to) know /nəʊ/	knew /njuː/	known /nəʊn/	wissen; kennen
(to) lead /liːd/	led /led/	led /led/	führen
(to) learn /lɜːn/	learnt/learned /lɜːnt/lɜːnd/	learnt/learned /lɜːnt/lɜːnd/	lernen; erfahren
(to) leave /liːv/	left /left/	left /left/	weggehen; verlassen, abfahren; (übrig) lassen; zurücklassen; hinterlassen
(to) let /let/	let /let/	let /let/	lassen
(to) lie /laɪ/	lay /leɪ/	lain /leɪn/	liegen
(to) light /laɪt/	lit /lɪt/	lit /lɪt/	anzünden
(to) lose /luːz/	lost /lɒst/	lost /lɒst/	verlieren
(to) make /meɪk/	made /meɪd/	made /meɪd/	machen; (es/etwas) schaffen
(to) mean /miːn/	meant /ment/	meant /ment/	meinen; bedeuten
(to) meet /miːt/	met /met/	met /met/	(sich) treffen; kennenlernen
(to) pay /peɪ/	paid /peɪd/	paid /peɪd/	(be)zahlen
(to) prove /pruːv/	proved /pruːvd/	proved/proven /pruːvd/ˈpruːvn/	beweisen
(to) put /pʊt/	put /pʊt/	put /pʊt/	setzen; stellen; legen
(to) read /riːd/	read /red/	read /red/	lesen
(to) rebuild /ˌriːˈbɪld/	rebuilt /ˌriːˈbɪlt/	rebuilt /ˌriːˈbɪlt/	wieder aufbauen
(to) ride /raɪd/	rode /rəʊd/	ridden /ˈrɪdn/	fahren; reiten
(to) run /rʌn/	ran /ræn/	run /rʌn/	laufen; rennen; leiten, betreiben; durchführen
(to) say /seɪ/	said /sed/	said /sed/	sagen
(to) see /siː/	saw /sɔː/	seen /siːn/	sehen; empfangen, drannehmen
(to) sell /sel/	sold /səʊld/	sold /səʊld/	verkaufen
(to) send /send/	sent /sent/	sent /sent/	schicken
(to) shoot /ʃuːt/	shot /ʃɒt/	shot /ʃɒt/	schießen
(to) show /ʃəʊ/	showed /ʃəʊd/	shown /ʃəʊn/	zeigen
(to) sing /sɪŋ/	sang /sæŋ/	sung /sʌŋ/	singen
(to) sit /sɪt/	sat /sæt/	sat /sæt/	sitzen
(to) sit down /ˌsɪtˈdaʊn/	sat down /ˌsætˈdaʊn/	sat down /ˌsætˈdaʊn/	sich hinsetzen
(to) sleep /sliːp/	slept /slept/	slept /slept/	schlafen
(to) smell /smel/	smelt/smelled /smelt/smeld/	smelt/smelled /smelt/smeld/	riechen
(to) speak /spiːk/	spoke /spəʊk/	spoken /ˈspəʊkən/	reden; sprechen
(to) spell /spel/	spelt/spelled /spelt/speld/	spelt/spelled /spelt/speld/	buchstabieren

infinitive	simple past	past participle	German
(to) spend /spend/	spent /spent/	spent /spent/	ausgeben *(Geld)*; verbringen *(Zeit)*
(to) spread /spred/	spread /spred/	spread /spred/	verbreiten; verteilen
(to) stand /stænd/	stood /stʊd/	stood /stʊd/	stehen
(to) steal /stiːl/	stole /stəʊl/	stolen /'stəʊlən/	stehlen
(to) stick with /'stɪk wɪð/	stuck with /'stʌk wɪð/	stuck with /'stʌk wɪð/	bleiben bei, festhalten an
(to) swim /swɪm/	swam /swæm/	swum /swʌm/	schwimmen
(to) take /teɪk/	took /tʊk/	taken /'teɪkən/	nehmen; bringen; benötigen; brauchen; dauern
(to) teach /tiːtʃ/	taught /tɔːt/	taught /tɔːt/	unterrichten
(to) tell /tel/	told /təʊld/	told /təʊld/	erzählen
(to) think /θɪŋk/	thought /θɔːt/	thought /θɔːt/	denken; glauben
(to) throw /θrəʊ/	threw /θruː/	thrown /θrəʊn/	werfen
(to) understand /ˌʌndə'stænd/	understood /ˌʌndə'stʊd/	understood /ˌʌndə'stʊd/	verstehen
(to) wake up /ˌweɪk‿'ʌp/	woke up /ˌwəʊk‿'ʌp/	woken up /ˌwəʊkən‿'ʌp/	aufwachen
(to) wear /weə/	wore /wɔː/	worn /wɔːn/	tragen *(Kleidung)*
(to) win /wɪn/	won /wʌn/	won /wʌn/	gewinnen
(to) write /raɪt/	wrote /rəʊt/	written /'rɪtn/	schreiben

Tipp:

Einige Verben bilden das **simple past** und das **past participle** nach einem ähnlichen Muster. Wenn du sie dir in Gruppen sortierst, kannst du dir die Formen vielleicht besser merken. Findest du weitere Beispiele für diese Gruppen oder andere Gruppen?

bring	brought	brought	mitbringen
buy	bought	bought	kaufen
catch	c**au**ght	c**au**ght	fangen
fight	fought	fought	bekämpfen
think	thought	thought	denken; glauben
sing	sang	sung	singen
swim	swam	swum	schwimmen

draw	drew	dr**a**wn	zeichnen
fly	flew	flown	fliegen
grow	grew	grown	wachsen
know	knew	known	wissen; kennen
throw	threw	thrown	werfen
cost	cost	cost	kosten
cut	cut	cut	schneiden
hit	hit	hit	schlagen
let	let	let	lassen
put	put	put	setzen; stellen; legen

Ausführliches Inhaltsverzeichnis

Bildquellen

|akg-images GmbH, Berlin: 6.2. |Alamy Stock Photo, Abingdon/Oxfordshire: Ammentorp Photography 93.1; anton havelaar 20.3; Antonio Gravante, Antonio 9.3; Antonio Guillem Fernandez 58.1; antony baxter 116.4; B.O'Kane 21.1; Bob Daemmrich 88.1; Brennan, Clark 15.2; Bucknall, Pearl 105.2; Bujdoso, Andor 95.2; Cary T 19.1; Cavanagh, Peter 116.7; Chuck Eckert, Chuck 33.4; Costa, Denise 171.1, 171.2, 171.3, 171.4, 171.5, 171.6, 171.7; Cristino, Carmen 25.1; Cultura Creative Ltd 68.3; DCPhoto 58.2; Dee Jolie 21.2; Desert, Louis-Michel 119.6; Dieterich, Werner 120.2; Dmytro Zinkevych 167.2; Drinkwater, Ros 121.3; Drobot, Vadym 34.2; Durson, Manuela 59.3; Egorova, Olga 167.5; Filimonov, Iakov 93.3; Foy, Kevin 26.1; fStop Images GmbH 105.3; Ghiea, Vlad 9.1; Graham, Jeremy 15.3; Granger - Historical Picture Archive 112.1, 112.2; Henderson, Mark 141.2, 144.2, 147.1; imageBROKER.com GmbH & Co. KG 119.4, 120.4, 130.1, 133.1, 136.1, 139.1, 142.1, 145.1, 166.1; John A Megaw 120.3; Kinovo 167.1; Kmit, Ivan 169.2; Kneschke, Robert 124.1, 168.1; Kruse, Joana 119.1; Lubenow, Sabine 116.6; Lund, Jacob 166.3; makasana photo 119.5; Marije Pama, Marije 104.1; Maskot 24.1; McGouey, Robert 93.2; McLennan, Chris 13.2; Michael Ventura 57.4; Morandi, Tuul and Bruno 121.2; Oleksii Hrecheniuk 170.2; Oleshko, Artem 104.3; Otto, Werner 107.1; Panther Media GmbH 82.2; Parkin, Jim 12.1; passport 122.1; Pearson, Myrleen 59.4; Prostock-studio 58.3; Quality Stock 58.5; Radharc Images 116.1; Samborskyi, Roman 80.1; scenicireland.com / Christopher Hill Photographic 141.1, 144.1, 147.2; Shields, Martin 91.3; Soloman, Andy 121.1; Sparks, Jon 116.5; teddiviscious 116.2; Tetra Images 59.2; The Print Collector 112.3; thislife pictures 106.1; Thornberg, Daniel 8.8; Thornton, Bennie 13.1; tom carter 50.1; ton koene 104.2; Trovo, Paolo 132.2, 135.2, 138.2; Trujillo, Gabriel 74.1; UPI 89.1; Vallecillos, Lucas 116.3; Walker Art Library 120.1; Warren, Scott 33.2; Westend61 GmbH 59.1, 68.4; White, Liam 132.1, 135.1, 138.1; xavierlorenzo 166.2; Zap, Yury 58.4; Zhigalova, Galina 62.1; ZUMA Press, Inc. 104.4. |Alamy Stock Photo (RMB), Abingdon/Oxfordshire: Booth, Mike 128.2; BuddyMays 7.3; Cultura Creative RF 162.1; Dack, Simon 157.1; Garcia, Mariano 6.4; Granger Historical Picture Archive 17.1; grzegorz knec 7.4; Haviv, Joshua 6.3; Hurst, D. 7.2; IanDagnall Computing 31.1; Jannsen, Brian 128.1; Maridav 72.1; Pavone, Sean 20.1; Pictorial Press Ltd 30.1; RTimages 170.1; Shawshots 105.1. |Bridgeman Images, Berlin: Everett Collection 129.1. |Don Bartletti Photography, Vista, California: 127.1. |fotolia.com, New York: Ints Vikmanis 167.6; Wylezich, B. 6.1; zinkevych 92.2. |Getty Images, München: Bloomberg 103.1; Denver Post / Gehring, Karl 164.1; Don Emmert, AFP 20.2; Hill Street Studios 38.2; Hulton Archive 32.1; HUM Images/Universal Images Group 15.1; Mark Wilson 102.1; MediaNews Group / Orange County Register Archive 34.3; Mirrorpix 32.2; RRP, Team Macarie 7.1; Stock Montage 14.1; Win McNamee 103.2. |Getty Images (RF), München: clu 105.4; coldsnowstorm 83.2; fotografixx 68.2; grandriver 82.1; gremlin 91.6; Jose Luis Pelaez Inc 164.3; kali9 35.2; Marks, George 106.2; Morsa Images 95.1; onurdongel 91.8; RubberBall Productions 35.3; SDI Productions 35.4, 72.2; Stígur Már Karlsson /Heimsmyndir 91.5; wagnerokasaki 39.2. |Gilcrease Museum, Tulsa OK: 16.1. |Harper Collins Publishers Ltd, London: Electric Monkey, Harper Collins Publishers / David Levithan: Every Day / Cover Illustration: Virginia Moura 78.1. |Imago Editorial, Berlin: 54.1; Pond5 Images 119.7. |iStockphoto.com, Calgary: aeduard 92.6; anatoliy_gleb 92.3; Choreograph 16.2; coldsnowstorm 7; dbstockphoto 34.4; Dufresne, Marc 9.2; duminika 43.1; FatCamera 33.3; freerangestock 7.5; Fudio 11.2; g-stockstudio 68.1; Galan, Roberto 9.4; herkisi 117.4; Inside Creative House 73.1; JackF 57.1; JillianCain 49.1; LDProd 117.3; Le Mauff, Mathieu 11.3, 148.1; lisandrotrarbach 163.1; master1305 43.3; Monkey Business Images 164.2; monkeybusinessimages 37.1, 39.1, 57.2; Nikada 91.2; Nirian 8.3; photoguns 91.1; pixelfit 162.2; reisegraf 119.3; shapecharge 92.7; sl-f 91.4; travelview 148.3; vejaa 57.3; Voyagerix 43.1; White, Don 10.1; YinYang 11.1. |Learned, Brent, Kansas: American Indian artist Brent Learned, Cheyenne and Arapaho Graduate of the university of Kansas 14.2. |PantherMedia GmbH (panthermedia.net), München: Schmid, Christophe 156.1. |Penguin Random House LLC, New York: Enrique's Journey von Sonia Nazario, 9780812971781 / Foto: Don Bartletti 126.1. |Picture-Alliance GmbH, Frankfurt a.M.: akg-images 31.2; Deck, Uli / dpa 83.1; dpa 92.1. |Schwarz, Leonard, Braunschweig: 109.1. |Shutterstock.com, New York: Bilous, Walt 13.3; Castleski 10.2; Chagochkin, Pavel 91.7; charnsitr 165.1, 165.2; ChristianChan 51.1; Eidenweil, Thierry 8.6; fizkes 40.1, 81.1; Fotogrin 81.4; Ground Picture 34.1; Hellebaut, Oskar 81.2; Kumsri, Yongyut 8.7; LightField Studios 33.1; Medbrat_23 167.4; michaeljung 24.4; Motortion Films 166.4; MPH Photos 24.2; Nach-Noth 48.2; Olivier Le Moal 167.3; Pavone, Sean 148.2; Pierucki, Tommy 8.5; pio3 150.1; Rahman, Ryan 81.3; Rawpixel.com 92.5; sam 72 169.3; Sean Locke Photography 48.1; seto contreras 113.1; Sunny studio 169.1; trabantos 119.2; TZIDO SUN 8.2. |Shutterstock.com (RM), New York: ZUMA Press Wire / DeSlover, Daniel 56.1. |stock.adobe.com, Dublin: AlenKadr 171.8; Arid Ocean 8.4; biker3 35.1; DC Studio 61.1; DigiClack 75.3, 75.4, 75.14, 75.22, 75.28; dtiberio 24.5; fizkes 117.2; ilovemayorova 23.1; insta_photos 24.3; lucky-photo 8.1; mvp85 149.1; pololia 101.1; Production Perig 92.4; seanlockephotography 38.1; streptococcus 75.1, 75.2, 75.5, 75.6, 75.7, 75.8, 75.9, 75.10, 75.11, 75.12, 75.13, 75.15, 75.16, 75.17, 75.18, 75.19, 75.20, 75.21, 75.23, 75.24, 75.25, 75.26, 75.27; superlime 117.1; WavebreakMediaMicro 168.2. |Tammana, Sri Nihal, Monroe Township: 86.1, 86.2, 87.1. |ullstein bild, Berlin: Frankenberg 163.2. |Visuelle Lebensfreude - Bodem + Sötebier GbR, Hannover: 44.1, 44.2, 44.3, 44.4, 44.5, 44.6, 44.7, 71.1, 71.2, 71.3, 71.4, 71.5.

Textquellen

25 Liedtext „An Open Letter to NYC", Stephen J. JR Bator, Michael Louis Diamond, Adam Keefe Horovitz, John Madansky, Jeff Magnum, Eugene RichardO'Connor, David Lynn Thomas, Adam Nathaniel Yauch, Jimmy Zero. An Open Letter to NYC © Brooklyn Dust Music / Universal-Polygram International Publ. In / WB Music Corp. Neue Welt Musikverlag GmbH, Hamburg Universal Music Publ. GmbH, Berlin. 07.08.2024: https://www.lyricsmode.com/lyrics/b/beastie_boys/an_open_letter_to_nyc.html#!

54/55 „I'm not running for prom queen", Leah Johnson, in: You should see me in a crown, New York: Scholastic Children's Books 2020 © 2020 Leah Johnson.

56 Liedtext „Prom dress", mxmtoon (Maia Xiao-En Moredock-Ting), © Printrechte Hal Leonard Europe GmbH. 07.08.2024: https://www.lyrics.com/lyric-lf/1536209/mxmtoon/prom+dress

65 „On the Discomfort of Being in the Same Room as the Boy You Like", Sarah Kay, in: You Don't Have to Be Everything: Poems for Girls Becoming Themselves, New York: Workman Publishing Company, 2021.

67 „Only a true friend would be that truely honest." (Donkey, Shrek), William Steig, Ted Elliott, SHREK, Hrsg.: The Internet Movie Script Database. 23.05.2024: https://imsdb.com/scripts/Shrek.html

67 „Many people will walk in and out of your life, but only true friends will leave footprints on your heart." (Eleanor Roosevelt), Sandy Rideout, Yvonne Collins: Totally Me: The Teenage Girl's Survival Guide: New Edition (CreateSpace Independent Publishing Platform - ohne Verlagsbindung) © 2020 Yvonne Collins & Sandy Rideout.

67 „It's not enough to be friendly. You have to be a friend." (R.J. Palacio), R.J. Palacio DN: (Der Name Raquel J. Palacio ist ein Pseudonym ihres Namens Raquel Jaramillo). Wonder by Palacio. R.J. (2013) Random House Children's Publisher UK, London.

67 Liedtext „Count on Me" (Bruno Mars), Bruno Mars, Philip Martin II Lawrence, Ari Levine. © BMG Rights Management GmbH, Berlin, Neue Welt Musikverlag GmbH, Hamburg.

78/79 „Every Day" [...], David Levithan, in: Every Day, Dublin: HarperCollins Publishers, 2023.

89 „Remarks by the First Lady at the National School Counselor of the Year Event", Michelle Obama, Washington: The White House Office of the First Lady, 2017. 06.03.2024: https://obamawhitehouse.archives.gov/the-press-office/2017/01/06/remarks-first-lady-national-school-counselor-year-event

102/103 „Hope is a discipline", Dharna Noor for The Guardian, 2023. 06.03.2024: https://www.theguardian.com/us-news/2023/dec/31/alaska-youth-climate-change-activist-nathan-baring-lawsuit-fossil-fuel-government

122 Liedtext „A song for Ireland", Phil Colclough, © Leola Music / BMG Rights Management GmbH, Berlin. 07.08.2024: https://www.lyricsmode.com/lyrics/d/dubliners/song_for_ireland.html

126 „Enrique's Journey", Chapter One: The Boy Left Behind, Sonia Nazario, 2002, Los Angeles Times. 06.03.2024: https://www.latimes.com/nation/immigration/la-fg-enriques-journey-chapter-one-mainbar-story.html

127 „Enrique's Journey", Chapter Three: Defeated Seven Times, a Boy Again Faces 'the Beast', Sonia Nazario, 2002, Los Angeles Times. 06.03.2024: https://www.latimes.com/nation/immigration/la-fg-enriques-journey-chapter-three-mainbar-story.html

127 „Enrique's Journey", Chapter Six: At Journey's End, a Dark River, Perhaps a New Life, Sonia Nazario, 2002, Los Angeles Times. 06.03.2024: https://www.latimes.com/nation/immigration/la-fg-enriques-journey-chapter-six-mainbar-story.html

129 Liedtext „Isle of Hope, Isle of Tears", Brendan Joseph Graham, © Peermusic Ltd./Peermusic (Germany) GmbH, Hamburg. 07.08.2024: https://www.latimes.com/nation/immigration/la-fg-enriques-journey-chapter-six-mainbar-story.html

Teterboro
Airport
✈

N E W

J E R S E Y

Hudson River

Harlem

Central Park

Manhattan

Central Station •

East River

Ellis
Island •
Statue of
Liberty •

see detail map

Upper
New York
Bay

(K i n g s)

B r o o k l y n

Lower
New York
Bay

Coney Island

B r o n x

Long Island Sound

E a s t   R i v e r

N E W   Y O R K

La Guardia
Airport ✈

Q u e e n s

J a m a i c a   B a y

J. F. Kennedy
International
Airport ✈

Jamaica Bay
Wildlife Refuge

Staten Island
(Richmond)

Rockaway   Inlet

A t l a n t i c   O c e a n

0 mile   1¼   2½
0 km
2,5   5